The Jameson Reader

BLACKWELL READERS

In a number of disciplines, across a number of decades, and in a number of languages, writers and texts have emerged which require the attention of students and scholars around the world. United only by a concern with radical ideas, Blackwell Readers collect and introduce the works of pre-eminent theorists. Often translating works for the first time (Levinas, Irigaray, Lyotard, Blanchot, Kristeva), or presenting material previously inaccessible (C.L.R. James, Fanon, Elias), each volume in the series introduces and represents work which is now fundamental to study in the humanities and social sciences.

The Lyotard Reader
Edited by Andrew Benjamin

The Irigaray Reader
Edited by Margaret Whitford

The Kristeva Reader
Edited by Toril Moi

The Levinas Reader
Edited by Sean Hand

The C.L.R. James Reader
Edited by Anna Grimshaw

The Wittgenstein Reader (Second Edition)
Edited by Anthony Kenny

The Blanchot Reader
Edited by Michael Holland

The Lukács Reader
Edited by Arpad Kadarkay

The Cavell Reader
Edited by Stephen Mulhall

The Guattari Reader
Edited by Garry Genosko

The Bataille Reader
Edited by Fred Botting and Scott Wilson

The Eagleton Reader
Edited by Stephen Regan

The Castoriadis Reader
Edited by David Ames Curtis

The Goffman Reader
Edited by Charles Lemert and Ann Branaman

The Frege Reader
Edited by Michael Beaney

The Virilio Reader
Edited by James Der Derian

The Hegel Reader
Edited by Stephen Houlgate

The Norbert Elias Reader
Edited by Johan Goudsblom and Stephen Mennell

The Angela Y. Davis Reader
Edited by Joy James

The Stanley Fish Reader
Edited by H. Aram Veeser

The Žižek Reader
Edited by Elizabeth Wright and Edmond Wright

The Talcott Parsons Reader
Edited by Bryan S. Turner

The Certeau Reader
Edited by Graham Ward

The Adorno Reader
Edited by Brian O'Connor

The Jameson Reader
Edited by Michael Hardt and Kathi Weeks

The Bauman Reader
Edited by Peter Beilharz

The Raymond Williams Reader
Edited by John Higgins

The Kierkegaard Reader
Edited by Jane Chamberlain and Jonathan Rée

The Tocqueville Reader
Edited by Olivier Zunz and Alan S. Kahan

The Nietzsche Reader
Edited by Keith Ansell Pearson and Duncan Large

The Jameson
Reader

Edited by
Michael Hardt and Kathi Weeks

Blackwell
Publishing

BLACKWELL PUBLISHING
350 Main Street, Malden, MA 02148-5020, USA
9600 Garsington Road, Oxford OX4 2DQ, UK
550 Swanston Street, Carlton, Victoria 3053, Australia

First published 2000

4   2005

Library of Congress Cataloging-in-Publication Data

Jameson, Fredric.
The Jameson reader / edited by Michael Hardt and Kathi Weeks.
   p.   cm. – (Blackwell readers)
Collection of 22 essays and excerpts from his writings, originally published 1971–1998.
Includes bibliographical references and index.
   Contents: pt. 1. Paradigms of interpretation – pt. 2. Marxism and culture – pt. 3.
   Postmodernism – pt. 4. Exercises in cognitive mapping – pt. 5. Utopia.
ISBN 0-631-20269-2 – ISBN 0-631-20270-6 (pbk.)
1. Criticism.   2. Marxist criticism.   3. Postmodernism.   4. Cognition.   5. Utopias.
   I. Hardt, Michael.   II. Weeks, Kathi, 1958-   III. Title.   IV. Series.
PN94 . J364 2000
801'.95'09045–dc21   99–049427

ISBN-13: 978-0-631-20269-1– ISBN-13: 978-0-631-20270-7 (pbk.)

A catalogue record for this title is available from the British Library.

Set in 10.5 on 12.5pt Bembo
by Kolam Information Services Pvt Ltd, Pondicherry, India
Printed and bound in the United Kingdom
by TJ International, Padstow, Cornwall

For further information on
Blackwell Publishing, visit our website:
www.blackwellpublishing.com

Contents

Part III   Postmodernism   173

Part IV   Exercises in Cognitive Mapping   275

Part V   Utopia   359

Acknowledgments

The editors and publishers wish to thank the following for permission to use copyright material:

British Film Institute and Indiana University Press for material from Fredric Jameson, *The Geopolitical Aesthetic: Cinema and Space in the World System* (1992), pp. 9–10, 45–66;

Columbia University Press for material from Fredric Jameson, *The Seeds of Time* (1994), pp. 1–32, 52–67. Copyright © 1994 Columbia University Press;

Duke University Press for material from Fredric Jameson, "Reification and utopia in mass culture," *Social Text*, 1 (1979), pp. 130–48. Copyright © 1979; and Fredric Jameson, "Third-world literature in the era of multinational capitalism," *Social Text*, 15 (1986), pp. 65–88. Copyright © 1986.

Fredric Jameson for material from *Fables of Aggression: Wyndham Lewis, the Modernist as Fascist* by Fredric Jameson, The University of California Press (1979), pp. 87–95;

The Johns Hopkins University Press for material from "Marxism and the historicity of theory: an interview with Fredric Jameson," *New Literary History*, 29: 3 (1998), pp. 353–83. Copyright © 1998 The University of Virginia;

The Minnesota Review for Fredric Jameson, "On Jargon," *The Minnesota Review*, 9 (1977), pp. 30–1; and Fredric Jameson, "Introduction/prospectus: to reconsider the relationship of Marxism to utopian thought," *The Minnesota Review*, 6 (1976), pp. 53–8;

Midwest Modern Language Association for Fredric Jameson, "Beyond the cave: demystifying the ideology of modernism," *The Bulletin of the Midwest Modern Language Association*, 8: 1 (1975), pp. 1–20;

Monthly Review Foundation for Fredric Jameson, "Five theses on actually existing Marxism," *Monthly Review*, 47: 11 (1996), pp. 1–10;

National Council of Teachers of English for Fredric Jameson, "Class and allegory in contemporary mass culture: *Dog Day Afternoon* as a political film," *College English*, 38: 8 (1977), pp. 843–59. Copyright © 1977 by the National Council of Teachers of English;

Princeton University Press for material from Fredric Jameson, *Marxism and Form: Twentieth Century Dialectical: Theories of Literature* (1971), pp. 50–9, 403–16. Copyright © 1971 by Princeton University Press; and Fredric Jameson, *The Prison-house of Language: A Critical Account of Structuralism and Russian Formalism* (1972), pp. 144–60. Copyright © 1972 by Princeton University Press;

Routledge and Cornell University Press for material from Fredric Jameson, *The Political Unconscious: Narrative as a Socially Symbolic Act* (1981), pp. 17–21, 74–102. Copyright © 1981 by Cornell University Press;

Science Fiction Studies for Fredric Jameson, "World-reduction in Le Guin: the emergence of utopian narrative," *Science Fiction Studies*, 2: 3 (1975), pp. 221–30;

University of Illinois Press for material from Fredric Jameson, "Cognitive mapping," in Cary Nelson and Lawrence Goldberg (eds), *Marxism and the Interpretation of Culture* (1988), pp. 347–57. Copyright © 1988 by Board of Trustees of the University of Illinois;

The University of Chicago Press for Fredric Jameson, "Culture and finance capital," *Critical Inquiry*, 24: 1 (1997), pp. 246–65;

Verso for material from Fredric Jameson, *Late Marxism: Adorno, or The Persistence of the Dialectic* (1990), pp. 45–8; and Fredric Jameson, "Postmodernism, or the cultural logic of late capitalism," *New Left Review*, 146 (1984), pp. 52–92;

Yale French Studies for material from Fredric Jameson, "Imaginary and symbolic in Lacan: Marxism, psychoanalytic criticism, and the problem of the subject," *Yale French Studies*, 55: 6 (1977), pp. 338–95;

Every effort has been made to trace copyright holders and to obtain their permission for the use of copyright material. The authors and publishers will gladly receive any information enabling them to rectify any error or omission in subsequent editions.

Introduction

Fredric Jameson is a literary and cultural critic who is known most widely in two guises: as America's leading Marxist critic and as theorist supreme of postmodernism.[1] Right away we seem to be confronted with a paradoxical image since Marxism and postmodernism are presumed in contemporary polemics to be at odds. Marxism, associated often with the social sciences, is presumed to aim at a final truth and certainty, whereas postmodernism, linked closely with cultural studies, is taken to call for a thoroughgoing relativism. As with many stereotypes invoked in polemical contexts, both of these character-izations are reductive and inaccurate in important ways, but perhaps the para-dox can serve as an initial indication of how Jameson's work stands at a point of intersection that confounds any such conventional caricatures and disciplinary disputes. Indeed, we think the best way initially to approach Jameson's thought is as a translation device that moves among a wide range of intellectual positions and disciplinary frameworks.[2]

Jameson's writings encourage and even enforce inter- or cross-disciplinary thinking. One part of his audience, those involved in literary and cultural studies, may well be frustrated by all the extra-cultural discussions (of economic and social structures, for example) and, similarly, another section of his audi-ence, including social theorists, historians, and others, can easily feel uncom-fortable with the discussion of aesthetic paradigms and the continual references to novels, films, and other cultural products. But rather than a shortcoming of Jameson's project, the symmetrical uneasiness that his work often provokes is better conceived as a symptom of the limitations of the disciplines and the need to go beyond them. Jameson's work thus functions first as a kind of warning to both sides: to literary and cultural critics, it says you will not understand the texts and objects you read and interpret unless you work simultaneously to understand the larger social whole in which they are organically embedded; and, conversely, it warns humanists and social theorists that they need seriously to engage the cultural realm to understand the social and historical structures they study. We have to delve into other disciplines and other realms of social production, not merely as a hobby or a supplement to our primary work, but as an integral part of it. Perhaps we should call this a program of transdisciplinary rather than interdisciplinary study of the social field in order to highlight its integral character. Clearly, if we are to embark on such a project, we need translation devices that allow us to construct networks of mediation and communication among the different disciplines' codes and methods.

Marxism is one of the most developed modern transdisciplinary projects and still serves today as an excellent model. Introductions to Marxism have traditionally described its interdisciplinary (and international) character by situating it at the confluence of three streams: German philosophy, French politics, and British economics. But that initial characterization is too restricted. Marx and Marxism extend further into the humanities and social sciences, from anthropology and history to sociology and legal studies. Jameson emphasizes how Marxism not only stands between the disciplines, but also serves to mediate or translate among the various methodological paradigms that function within each discipline, such as structuralism, psychoanalysis, and deconstruction. In Jameson's hands in particular, Marxism is a model for an integral interdisciplinarity.

Marxism

Jameson has insisted on the importance of Marxist theory consistently throughout his career, through periods when such pronouncements may have seemed to some, especially in the United States, unfashionable, irrelevant, or even dangerous. Marxism, of course, has over the years suffered many deaths and yet continues relentlessly to spring back to life. Perhaps the deaths function as a kind of rejuvenating tonic: with each demise of Marxism there comes a re-interpretation of Marx's work, a re-evaluation of the tradition, and, most important, a replacement of doctrine by problems.[3] Death seems to open Marxism to a new life.

At the beginning of the new millennium, however, we are also witnessing a new acceptance or general confirmation of Marx's thought among non-Marxists. The realization of the world market, the commodification of culture and society, the global hegemony of capital, and other characteristically Marxist hypotheses are now often taken for granted; even the mainstream popular press can herald *The Communist Manifesto* as an accurate prediction of the global destiny of capital and a prescient reading of our future. Perhaps, with the collapse of the Soviet regime and the end of the Cold War, these Marxist ideas are no longer perceived as dangerous and their validity can thus be recognized with fewer ideological blinders.

But as much as Marxist analyses of the expansion of capital are now accepted as common sense, another aspect of Marx's thought, his *historical* interpretation of the capitalist mode of production is increasingly obscured. Marx directed one of his most violent and sustained polemics against the view of classical economists that capital and capitalist social relations are both natural and eternal – a view that seems to have blossomed again in the contemporary celebration of capitalist globalization. Marx insisted instead that capital constitutes a transient phase of world history that will eventually pass and give rise to a new phase. This historical reading is a primary lesson of Jameson's work and a central element of his Marxism. The concept of mode of production, which plays a central role in Jameson's thought, is itself historical. Every mode of production that arises, such as the ancient or the feudal, will inevitably fall and yield to another mode. The successive modes of production serve as large analytical units of human history which we can work with, something akin to the Paleozoic, Mesozoic, and Cenozoic periods in the hands of geologists. The historical reading of capital also involves a historicizing operation within the capitalist mode of production, distinguishing the passages from one phase or stage of the rule of capital to another. (The transition from the modern to the postmodern, we will see shortly, designates one such passage.) Although it has proven imprudent each time Marxists have announced the final phase of the capitalist mode of production and its imminent collapse, this recognition of movement among phases is none the less a continual reminder of the historicity of capital and its finite temporal character.

The second distinctive aspect of Jameson's Marxism is his insistence on the centrality of culture. In certain respects Jameson highlights the importance of cultural and aesthetic elements already existing in the thought of Marx and Marxists, while in other respects he transforms the tradition to reveal the ways in which culture has come to play a new and more pivotal role in contemporary capitalist society. The Marxist tradition has been haunted from the beginning by economism, that is, by the assumption that economic factors alone are sufficient for the functioning and reproduction of capitalist society and the capitalist mode of production. If Marxism considers culture irrelevant or secondary then cultural theorists can only conclude that Marxism has little relevance for their work. Jameson, however, demonstrates in a variety of ways how culture occupies a central position in the functioning and reproduction of capitalist society. One might say that culture matters not as a realm separated from economic, political, and social life, but as a domain that intersects and interacts with all the other social fields. It serves to connect the various realms of social life, providing the primary mechanisms of mediation. Culture thus functions as the ligatures of the social whole. This is one path of argumentation by which Jameson demonstrates that cultural analysis is essential for our understanding of the capitalist mode of production and, in turn, that Marxism offers powerful tools for cultural interpretation.

At the center of Jameson's various approaches to culture is a basic concern with the problematic of representation. Jameson follows Marx in emphasizing that the forms and structures that define contemporary society are not immediately available for empirical analysis. What we can grasp are what Marx calls the "appearances" of the capitalist mode of production, which are themselves not false or illusory but real symptoms of the constitutive elements and forces of society. All social theory, social analysis, and even social science is thus in this sense a matter of interpretation. In other words, we do not have access to society or the capitalist mode of production itself as an object of study, but rather only to *representations* of it. No representation offers a mimetic reproduction, but rather each necessarily calls for an act of interpretation. Our knowledge is always mediated by interpretation and representation. This does not mean we have to abandon any notion of reality and become relativists. It means rather that questions of truth and reality have to *pass first through the problematic of representation.*[4] Perhaps, in so far as the problematic of representation occupies a central position, one should say that not economics but aesthetics or epistemology is the privileged field of Marxian analysis.

This centrality of representation and interpretation is a fundamental reason why scholars throughout the humanities and social sciences should consider seriously the methods and objects of literary criticism and cultural studies. Modes of interpretation and issues of representation developed in these fields have a general relevance. Furthermore, recognizing the ineluctability of representation suddenly raises up cultural products, such as novels and films, as valid objects through which to read the structures of society and movements of history. Jameson emphasizes, however, that this does not mean that society, the capitalist mode of production, or history is itself a text, but rather that they are only available to us though representation and hence in textual or narrative form.

This should not lead us to think that we should all become literary critics or that we should elevate cultural studies to the throne of the new queen of sciences. Such hierarchies only lead to a kind of false interdisciplinarity in which scholars in one field feel authorized to treat phenomena and structures in other fields while remaining ignorant of the relevant disciplinary traditions.

Such audacity gives rise to the senseless polemics such as those we have seen around notions of postmodernism and relativism. Nor should one assume that the study of culture has some priority because of the ubiquity of cultural products and the increasing penetration of cultural forces into all realms of contemporary society. Certainly as culture has come to play a more important role in the life of capital, capital correspondingly has become ever more deeply rooted in the domain of culture. Rather than new hierarchies, what we need are new means of communication and translation among the various disciplinary orientations and methodological perspectives. This capacity for what Jameson calls "transcoding" is perhaps the character that most strongly recommends his work both for those within the literary and cultural fields and those in other disciplines.

Apprenticeships

Jameson's Marxism and his thought in general – despite the important European influences – are very firmly rooted in the United States. He grew up in southern New Jersey, attended Haverford College where he majored in French, and proceeded to earn his PhD, also in French, from Yale University in 1959. Among his teachers were two prominent figures in the field of US literary criticism: Wayne Booth at Haverford and Erich Auerbach at Yale.

Jameson's early career was really a period of apprenticeship in two schools of thought: French existentialism and German critical theory. He wrote his dissertation on the novels and philosophy of Jean-Paul Sartre (the dissertation was published in 1961 as *Sartre: The Origins of a Style*). Sartre's work provided a model for linking literary and aesthetic preoccupations to philosophical enquiry and political intervention, and his work provided too a lens that allowed Jameson to explore the rich field of cultural and theoretical production in postwar France.

It is easy to imagine how, after this initial period, Jameson could have settled in to a comfortable academic career as a specialist in French literature and civilization, but instead he enlarged his focus to include Germany. He became inspired by the authors of the Frankfurt School and worked to introduce their thought to Anglo-American audiences. Theodor Adorno, Walter Benjamin, Ernst Bloch, and, from a somewhat different tradition, Georg Lukács were the primary figures that occupied Jameson's attention during this period. Like Sartre, these authors too provided a model for bringing together aesthetic, philosophical, and political concerns. Despite these common characteristics, however, it was a remarkable feat for Jameson to bring these French and

Germanic traditions together in one synthetic perspective given the incompre-
hension and animosity that often plagues the exchanges between these national
traditions. *Marxism and Form* (published in 1971) is the book in which Jameson
first elaborates this synthesis of the French and Germanic critical traditions.[5]

This double European apprenticeship completed, Jameson was once again in
a position where he could stop and pursue a career within the confines of an
established field such as comparative European literature and theory. But
Jameson was quickly on the move again. He began to look less to Europe
and more to the rest of the world to find new inspirations. During subsequent
decades he learned numerous languages and began to discover the rich spheres
of cultural and theoretical production outside the Euro-American sphere,
particularly in Latin America and East Asia. China, in fact, became a central
reference point for the global expansion of his project. Jameson taught for a
semester at the University of Beijing in 1985 and his work is widely translated
into Chinese. As Jameson's project has broadened geographically he has also
continued to delve into other disciplines and to explore the entire spectrum of
theoretical paradigms. It is instructive to attempt a partial list of these theoretical
paradigms (including existentialism, formalism, structuralism, psychoanalysis,
deconstruction, poststructuralism, semiotics, new criticism, new historicism,
and cultural studies) and the cultural objects (such as novels, poetry, film,
architecture, painting, science fiction, video, and photography) that he engages.
Indeed, one of the most striking characteristics one notices when one begins a
conversation with him is his insatiable appetite for new discoveries. Iranian
films, Italian politics, Japanese gardens: his curiosity seems boundless. And,
consequently, one of the great pleasures of reading Jameson's work is being
introduced to so many new and unknown texts from all over the world.

Yet even as Jameson's vision moves across the globe, his arguments always
refer ultimately to the United States, to the poverty and wealth of its cultures
and consciousness. On one hand, the richness of cultural production, political
imagination, and historical consciousness in other countries serves at times to
demonstrate the poverty of the United States (despite its position at the
pinnacle of global hierarchies) and as a source of instruction for Americans.
On the other hand, Jameson constantly points toward the utopian elements in
the United States that exist throughout the various levels of cultural and social
production. The United States remains in both cases the center of gravity and
ultimate object of his project.

It is difficult to find an intellectual figure in the United States whose thought
has the same breadth and coherence as Jameson's. It is true that Noam
Chomsky moves from linguistic theory to analyses of contemporary politics,
but the two fields remain incommunicative, with different methodologies and
logics, as if he were maintaining two separate intellectual careers. The

integrating character can be found more often in the thought of European philosophers, such as Jean-Paul Sartre and Theodor Adorno, who bring together concepts and methods from various fields and analyze phenomena in an equally wide range of domains. Perhaps the best contemporary point of comparison is the French philosopher Gilles Deleuze whose work not only spans the history of European philosophy, cinema, and literature, but also integrates concepts from mathematics and the natural sciences into its broad philosophical perspective. It would be interesting to conduct an institutional analysis of academic structures to explain why such figures emerge more frequently from a philosophical training in Europe, whereas literary criticism seems to provide corresponding opportunities for transdisciplinarity in the United States.

Dialectical Sentences

Although we intend this book to appeal to a very wide public, we should recognize right away that Jameson's writing presents numerous difficulties for readers, not only because he draws on various disciplines, cites such a wide range of sources, and deals with abstract concepts, but also because his sentences themselves are so complex. A typical Jamesonian sentence may be interrupted by a long parenthetical clause that points to a parallel example in a very different context and may then conclude with a hypothesis contrary to the primary clause that puts it in question and points toward a new proposition. He is aware of the difficulty of his prose and aware too that many of the authors he admires, particularly the German philosophers, have been vilified for the impenetrability of their writing.

Jameson suggests, however, that the mandate against a complex writing style may itself be ideological, that is, that it may be used to prevent a certain kind of thinking. "What if," he asks rhetorically:

in this period of the overproduction of printed matter and the proliferation of methods of quick reading, they [the ideals of clarity and simplicity] were intended to speed the reader across a sentence in such a way that he can salute a readymade idea effortlessly in passing, without suspecting that real thought demands a descent into the materiality of language and a consent to time itself in the form of the sentence?[6]

Jameson's writing style, then, might be conceived first as a rebellion against the pressures toward simplified expression and facile analysis, but at a deeper level the difficulty of the writing only reflects the arduous work required to understand the dynamic and multifaceted relations of our culture and society.

Jameson claims that a writer cannot articulate the complexities of our social world in more simple terms and, more important, the reader cannot understand them more quickly. A complex style of writing serves to slow the reader and force her or him to grant the time necessary for critical thought.[7]

The specific difficulties of Jameson's sentences spring primarily from their dialectical nature. His sentences are dialectical in the sense that he often tries to hold together in a single sentence two seemingly contradictory ideas, which finally function together as a new synthetic proposition. Such dialectical expression within a single sentence requires numerous parenthetical clauses that articulate opposing claims and move them toward a new position.[8] The sentence acts as a bounded environment, a sort of cauldron that holds the opposing elements together and allows the alchemy of the dialectic to work. This dialectical movement beginning at the sentence level and extending up throughout his arguments is the most distinctive aspect of his style and a source of his work's many intellectual and aesthetic pleasures. If a reader takes the time to understand the movement and texture of one of Jameson's complex sentences, she or he will have made a great stride toward understanding the movement and nature of his thought as a whole.

Culture

As a cultural critic Jameson has had to work against certain streams within the Marxist tradition as well as the various stereotypes of Marxism created by its opponents. As we suggested earlier, Marxist approaches to culture have been plagued by functionalist conceptions that tend to reduce the complexity of the cultural sphere and the multiplicity of cultural phenomena to inconsequential and predictable effects of economic forces. Cultural objects, for example, can be read as simple reflections or univocal expressions of the interests of a specific socioeconomic class: a bourgeois novel, a proletarian play, and so forth. In some instances, the correspondence is established by means of homologies of form between the cultural object and the political or economic sphere. This can lead to very mechanical and formulaic systems for categorizing cultural objects and interpreting their meanings. The general model that dominates many of these functionalist approaches is the spatial metaphor of the economic base of society on which arises the cultural superstructure. The metaphor, in its most reductive usage, serves to indicate that the economic base determines the parameters of the cultural superstructure and, consequently, that the superstructure is a mere expression of the base.

Jameson too adopts the base–superstructure metaphor because it has the virtue, at least, of encouraging us to recognize that culture does not exist autonomously but always in relation to society as a whole. He finds in the metaphor, however, not a formula or a solution but rather a framework for asking the question of how culture interacts with other social spheres. In some respects, the economic base does indeed determine cultural expressions and, vice versa, culture operates a reciprocal determination on the base, but these lines of causality and determination are not really the point here. Jameson wants to treat the base–superstructure metaphor as a problematic that will force us continually to ask the question of how culture relates to other fields. It thus serves as a way to navigate between the twin dangers of viewing culture as either a realm autonomous from the rest of society or a direct product of social forces and interests.

In order to avoid viewing a cultural object as a passive reflection or univocal expression of social forces and interests, Jameson encourages us to regard the work of art or the cultural product first and foremost as a symbolic act. In other words, we should view the work as performative in the sense that it intervenes in a concrete social situation or problem and attempts to arrive at some sort of response or solution. Cultural products are full of surprises. There is nothing predictable or necessary about how they will intervene in any given situation. Texts or cultural objects are thus dynamic agents engaged in mutually constitutive relations with the societies in which they are situated.

To understand properly the relationality and social nature of cultural objects, however, we need also to investigate the other side of the equation: the social environment that cultural objects intervene in or stand in relation to. Jameson suggests that we begin by dividing the social totality into three relatively autonomous contextual horizons or hermeneutic dimensions that are distinguished by different fields and different temporalities: the first, immediately historical horizon refers us to day-to-day and year-to-year events; the second, sociopolitical horizon is the context of class formation and struggles; and the third, economic horizon involves the mode of production. As we switch from the first to the second and third analytical frames, we move into different temporal registers and levels of abstraction, into the context of progressively larger and slower moving social forces and historical dynamics. At each level the forces of determination and models of causality will be constructed differently. "Each of these three dimensions – which always coexist – has its own logic," Jameson explains, "so that in politics as in art it is advisable to sort them out for openers, it being understood that you may well want to recombine them (explosively or architectonically) later on."[9] Each also indicates its own problematics and calls for its own set of interpretive tools. The first, immediately historical dimension requires that we view the work as a symbolic act aimed at addressing a specific social situation; the second, sociopolitical dimension demands ideological analysis; and the third dimension of the mode of production opens the question of form (such as realism, modernism, or post-modernism).[10]

The combination of the various horizons and interpretive tools can lead to a rich and complex understanding of the cultural object and its relations to the larger social context. But, perhaps more important, the distinctions among these levels preserve the possibility and validity of multiple interpretations of cultural texts. Depending on which delimitation of the social and historical context is serving as the interpreter's point of reference, the cultural object will be read and reconstructed differently. The three levels thus suggest a point of departure for plural and overlapping interpretations of culture and society.

Dedifferentiation of Social Fields

At this point we can see that economic and sociopolitical systems do not determine cultural forms in any straighforward way; nor are cultural objects or cultural systems autonomous. Instead, one should say that the various social fields are mutually determining and together form one social whole. But, at least with regard to today's world, that formulation still poses the social fields as too separate and too autonomous. Jameson claims that corresponding to the processes of globalization and the passage from modernity to postmodernity there has been a progressive withering away of the boundaries between the various social realms. "I have consistently argued," Jameson writes, that the present historical conjuncture "is marked by a dedifferentiation of fields, such that economics has come to overlap with culture: that everything, including commodity production and high and speculative finance, has become cultural; and culture has equally become profoundly economic or commodity oriented."[11] The dedifferentiation of fields radically displaces the spatial or topological metaphor of base and superstructure. Now one is not standing above or below the other, but rather they mutually infuse one another.

The distinction between culture and economy or between superstructure and base none the less persists. It has simply been displaced to other levels of the system. In other words, although the molar division between superstructure and base has been blurred – because, for example, cultural production has become centrally concerned with economic factors and, similarly, economic production with cultural matters – the division reappears at the molecular level, between cultural and economic forces within the sector of financial specula-tion, for example, or within the Hollywood film industry. The problematic of base and superstructure does not become irrelevant; on the contrary, like the head of Medusa, when its general or molar instance is cut off, a multiplicity of molecular versions springs forth.

The convergence of fields that Jameson recognizes brings us back to the need for a similar convergence or dedifferentiation among the disciplines or modes of enquiry. As culture becomes increasingly economic and the economy increasingly cultural, in other words, the methods and objects of economic enquiry and cultural criticism must similarly approach and infuse one another.

History

"Always historicize!" is one of Jameson's central mandates and serves as another approach to the task of addressing how each cultural and social object is embedded in a complex web of dynamic social relations. The study of each social artifact, each novel, film, or building, must be treated as a specific lens that gives a view on history itself; and, reciprocally, the study of the grand contours and movements of history must give a fresh perspective on the individual object of study. This back and forth motion, discovering more and more complex lines of mediation in the web of social relations, is the work of historicizing.

Jameson shares this project to historicize with various historicist schools in literary theory and also with a variety of historicisms developed in philosophy, social theory, and other disciplines. Whereas many such frameworks claim that there can be no priority or hierarchy among the various contexts in which an object or phenomenon is embedded and thus give equal weight to the various realms of historical data, Jameson, as we saw earlier, gives priority to capital and the mode of production in the analysis of history. Jameson's injunction, in other words, is really always historicize with primary attention to the history of capital, its movements, and its differentiated deployments.

"Aha!," the skeptical reader might say at this point, Jameson does in fact in the final analysis give a determining role to economy over culture, politics, and other fields! This appears to be the case, however, only when one conceives of a mode of production as merely an economic system. All modes of production, and the capitalist mode of production in particular, define not only economic relationships but also cultural, political, and anthropological realms of existence. The history of capital is thus not merely an economic history but tends to incorporate all of human history. This is what Marx means when he explains that capital should not be conceived as a thing (money or property, for example) but rather as a social relation. Capital tends to become a *social* power. Perhaps we should even say that the dedifferentiation of fields that Jameson links to globalization and postmodernism is the realization of a long-standing project of capital, demonstrating its prodigious capacities of social interaction and unification. When Jameson insists that we approach history from the perspective of the mode of production, then, he is not asking us to give priority to economic laws and phenomena. Just as capital is understood as a comprehensive social (not narrowly economic) power, so too a mode of production must be conceived in terms of not only economic production but also cultural production and social production of all sorts. Production, in other words, has to be recognized in all of its many faces. On the broadest plane, a mode of production approaches a mode of life because social life is really nothing but the complete set of all the various forms and phases of production.

Jameson conceives a mode of production furthermore not as a uniform and homogeneous unit but as an internally differentiated set of structures and practices. Certainly within every mode of production there are remnants of previous modes and seeds of future ones. Economies are thus always mixed to some extent and there are always elements of "non-synchronous" consciousness that correspond to past or future modes of production. Throughout the modern era, for example, there have always existed significant realms of non-capitalist (feudal and other) cultures and economies within the capitalist mode of production. The project of capitalist modernization was precisely over the course of centuries to subsume these non-capitalist domains and elements, sometimes preserving their differences and sometimes not, but never creating a homogeneous and undifferentiated terrain. The capitalist mode of production is distinctive in the extent to which it thrives on heterogeneities, processes of differentiation, and uneven developments. The mode of production thus refers to the dominant power that rules over a heterogeneous set of forces.

If Jameson were to grant priority to one discipline or social field in the project of historicizing, it would be literature or, really, narrative. Narrative occupies a privileged position in relation to history because we only have access to history through narrative structures. In other words, we always formulate histories not merely as chronological sequences of events but rather as narratives that put the facts in relation, giving them value and meaning. Creating such narratives is indeed the task of historians and it is also the work of much of modern literature, particularly the novel. In many respects the novel, born in modern Europe and extending throughout the world, has developed in matched strides with capital. It is the literary form most closely tied to the capitalist mode of production and its various phases. The narrative practices of modern literature, and the modern novel in particular, thus provide us with one important set of tools and elements for approaching modern history.

Periodization

The first move of Jameson's project to historicize often involves locating the literary or cultural works in a specific historical period, such as realism, modernism, and later postmodernism. Projects of periodization are often maligned in literary criticism and other disciplines because they tend to make rough cuts with a blunt tool rather than drawing nuanced lines with a fine instrument. In other words, the practice tends to exaggerate the difference at the point of rupture between periods and obscure differences within each period. Moreover, the concern with periodization can draw our attention away from other relevant aspects of the works under consideration.

Jameson's practice of periodization, however, should be understood in the context of his general project to historicize cultural works and social phenomena. His mandate that we always historicize is really first another mandate: always periodize! Periodization is *an initial technique that opens the path and allows us to gain access to history and historical differences.* In other words, since the continuum of history can appear as either an undifferentiated mass or a multitude of incoherent differences, periods serve to organize history and pose a first level of difference. It is important, however, that periodization is the *first* and not the *last* move in a project to historicize. The uniform periods and radical breaks have to be made more nuanced with finer differences. This is one of Jameson's primary techniques: begin with the crude differences of periods and then proceed to make the place of a specific work and the historical field in general ever more complex and differentiated.

The practice of periodization is common in the Marxist tradition and in Marx's own work. The focus, as in Jameson's work too, is not so much on the internal uniformity of the periods but rather on the moments of change or the passages – from one mode of production to another or between phases of the capitalist mode of production itself. An historical period is never conceived in static terms, as if history only moved in sudden bursts of revolutionary change, and in the meantime things remain the same. Rather, each period must be grasped in terms of its movement, its internal dynamics, as propelled by innumerable conflicts and antagonisms, among classes, between past and future.

Realism and Modernism

Jameson inherits the period distinction between realism and modernism from a long tradition of literary criticism. Literary realism is generally understood as the collective expression of a social group or class. For example, the novels of

Honoré de Balzac, which articulate the consciousness and fortunes of the French ruling class in the early nineteenth century, are often presented as a paradigmatic example of realism. Realist literature is distinguished not by its verisimilitude or proximity to reality but rather by its expression of the consciousness of a social class, and, moreover, that class's recognition of historical movement and change, such as, for example, the aristocracy's fears and suspicions of its impending decline at the hands of the bourgeoisie. Realist literature thus has an open and explicit relation to history in the sense that realist narratives attempt to represent, at the limit, the movement of history itself.

Modernist texts, in contrast, generally express an individual perspective disjointed or alienated from the developments of the modern world. Modernism is commonly seen in literary criticism to have arisen in the late nineteenth century, with authors such as Gustave Flaubert and Charles Baudelaire, and to have reached its height in the first decades of the twentieth century. As social relations become increasingly commodified, as language is degraded by advertising, and as communal life is made impersonal and meaningless by anonymous bureaucratic structures, modernist literature both expresses the alienation of our social condition and searches for a line of flight to escape (or perhaps redeem) the modern world. Modernism's famous call to "make it new" can thus be read as an effort to break through the forces of commodification and reification to discover an authentic mode of life. Modernist texts often disrupt or displace plot and narrative and thus they often cast into the background or even deny outright processes of historical change – sometimes in a desperate effort to awaken from the nightmare that is history. In contrast to realism, then, modernism's relation to history is often covert.

In Jameson's view, the most distinctive characteristics of modernist texts are the processes of "autonomization" they set in motion. Modernists themselves consciously sought to make the aesthetic separate from other (particularly commercial and bureaucratic) domains of society. Jameson, however, recognizes processes of autonomization at all levels throughout the texts: in the separation of different perspectives and voices within a single text, in the splitting off of the different human faculties (sight, sound, and so forth), in the general parceling out of the psyche, or in the destruction of communal space and the isolation of the individual. Autonomization here should be understood as the fragmentation of an experience that was previously whole. The processes of autonomization in these texts, however, do not simply spring from the genius of modernist authors and artists, but are rather aesthetic interpretations of and responses to the processes of autonomization in modern society. Jameson can thus link modernism with social and economic forms such as Taylorism and the other industrial techniques of the specialization and division of labor that arose roughly at the same time as modernism. Just as modern society and modern industrial production break down processes that were once whole into isolated units, so too modernist texts fragment experience into so many individual parts.

Jameson inherits a Marxist debate that is bitterly divided about the political and social value of realism and modernism.[12] One side affirms realism's collective and historical perspective while condemning modernism's idiosyncrasy and irrationalism. The other side condemns realism's acceptance of and acquiescence to the terms of the present modern society and celebrates modernism's critique of and separation from its alienating forces. In a move typical of his general theoretical method, Jameson accepts and denies both of these positions, raising them up to a new synthetic position. Neither realism nor modernism is politically progressive or regressive in itself. Each corresponds rather to a specific historical moment, and its effects and possibilities have to be read in that context. Furthermore, modernism is really no less historical than realism; rather, its representations of history are merely at times more hidden and unconscious and thus require different interpretive strategies.

Jameson associates realism with the free-market phase of capital, which spanned much of the nineteenth century, and modernism with its monopoly and imperialist phase that straddled the nineteenth and twentieth centuries. The specific connection to these two economic phases, however, is not as important as the more general proposition that realism and modernism are periods not styles in the sense that their conditions of possibility are historically determined. In other words, they are sets of formal practices that are not always equally available to the choice of authors but rather can appear necessary and unavoidable or utterly inaccessible according to the dictates of the sociohistorical period.

Postmodernism

In all of Jameson's reflections about realism and modernism one can sense a certain unease because by the time he writes about them both of these periods have all but exhausted their powers and become mere residues of the past. Jameson recognized that we were living in a period of transition and that a new formal paradigm had to arise. A new realism? A renovated modernism? Something was happening, but what was not clear.

Jameson began to theorize the passage toward postmodernism in the early 1980s, adopting the notion primarily from architectural theorists. What permitted Jameson to begin thinking this passage was the recognition, which he derives primarily from the work of Ernest Mandel, that there has been a profound shift in the capitalist mode of production toward a phase of "late capitalism."[13] The passage to late capitalism is defined primarily by a completion of the processes of modernization. In other words, modernity has hitherto been characterized by a constant struggle between modern and pre-modern elements of society. Modernization was the process of transformation: the generalization of industrial production, the mechanization of the various spheres of social life, and generally the subsumption of society under capital. The completion of modernization means that there is no more "nature" in the sense that nothing remains outside the forces of modernization. All of society, and indeed the entire world, have been subsumed under the rule of capital. The two final enclaves of nature to be subsumed, according to Jameson, were the various forms of precapitalist agriculture, which were wiped out in much of the world by the so-called green revolutions, and the unconscious, which has progressively been colonized by the culture industry. Postmodernism corresponds to the phase of the capitalist mode of production when the processes of modernization are complete. This new phase is thus not in opposition to modernization or even discontinuous with it; instead, postmodernization crowns modernization as its final point of arrival.

In certain respects the completion of modernization and the real subsumption of society and nature under capital means that the world has become more homogeneous. This is the triumph of the capitalist mode of production in the effort to remake the world in its own image. The heterogeneities and differentiation we spoke of earlier remain but within the frame of a single mode of production. As our environment and ourselves are more homogeneously modernized, Jameson claims, and as capital realizes its purer form, we tend to lose our capacity for historical consciousness. Our historical faculty, he explains, used to be based on our recognition of different modes of production existing simultaneously. The remaining enclaves of the peasant or feudal world, for example, served as a constant reminder of the movement of history. In post-modernity, however, as the processes of modernization reach completion, there is no longer an "outside" of capital that points us to the difference of the past and the historicity of the present. Postmodern consciousness is thus characterized by, among other things, its failure to think historically, living instead in a series of perpetual presents.

This lack of historical consciousness is also the key to understanding some of the formal and aesthetic characteristics of postmodernism. The techniques typical of postmodern art, such as pastiche, schizophrenia, and extreme fragmentation, can be traced to a lack of depth and historicity. Jameson's most celebrated example is his comparison between Vincent Van Gogh's painting of peasant shoes and Andy Warhol's painting of Diamond Dust Shoes.[14] Jameson's reading is rich and complex, but for our purposes it is sufficient as a first approximation of the argument to point out that Van Gogh's shoes create depth by referring us to the lived experience of the peasant and, moreover, by invoking a peasant world outside capitalist modernity that is in the process of disappearing. Warhol's shoes, in contrast, are all surfaces, not only due to the shiny flatness of the image itself, although this is certainly important, but also because they seem to refuse any relation to either everyday experience and use or historical movement more generally. The surfaces of postmodern art are in this sense an instance of the lack of historicity that characterizes postmodern consciousness.

There are, of course, many distinct story-lines contained within the historical movement from realism to modernism and postmodernism. Jameson presents one of these, which highlights the changing problematic of representation, as a simple three-part tale about the advance of reification under capitalism. Reification in Jameson's usage is identified most clearly with the multiple forms of separation and compartmentalization that are concurrent with the processes of rationalization and commodification. At the first stage of the process of reification, or, as Jameson likes to say, "once upon a time," the sign emerges to replace magical language. The sign is now taken as transparent, a clear reflection of a separate referent, as opposed to the earlier confusion of the sign with what it names. This "golden age," this moment of immunity from epistemological doubt, is the moment of realism. Yet the forces of reification are constantly at work to the point where they produce a qualitative transformation: the signifier is further disjoined from its referent. The referent still exists in the object world but at a greater distance from the signifier, which, at this second stage, enjoys a kind of privileged and autonomous existence. This moment of aesthetic autonomy corresponds to modernism. All the while, however, the forces of reification continue their expansion, penetrating all the nooks and crannies of social life. They split the signifier ever further from what it signifies, rendering representation increasingly problematic. The referent tends now to disappear from view and the signifier – untethered from any particular signified – tends to drift without restrictions. Once we are left with a free play of self-referential signs we have arrived at the threshold of postmodernism.[15]

Theory

Jameson often uses the term "theory" to name the field or terrain of his transdisciplinary project. The generic and unqualified use of this term – as opposed to literary theory, political theory, or economic theory – is indicative of the breadth of the endeavor. All of the various disciplinary forms of theory, together with philosophy itself, are subsets of the general rubric. Under the category of theory the disciplines come together and lose their separation in a common critical and interpretive project. This general conception of theory has served Jameson as a tool to reorganize academic practices and structures. It cuts across various disciplinary boundaries and poses itself as a new field for teaching and scholarship. In a certain sense theory provides a kind of clearing house or foster home for scholars and students who feel exiled from the many disciplines that, especially in the United States, have marginalized theoretical approaches and become dominated instead by empiricism, positivism, quantitative methods, or rational choice frameworks.

Jameson's first formulation of this general project of theory was in the form of "metacommentary." Metacommentary asks us to step back from the interpretations of specific objects and texts, and even from different methods or modes of interpretation, to gain a more expansive view. "All thinking about interpretation," Jameson claims, "must sink itself in the strangeness, the unnaturalness, of the hermeneutic situation; or to put it another way, every individual interpretation must include an interpretation of its own existence, must show its own credentials and justify itself: every commentary must be at the same time a metacommentary as well."[16] Just as the work of interpretation is to situate the work under question in history, so too the interpretation itself and the position of the commentator have to be historicized. In other words, while we do the work of historicizing, we also have to be self-conscious of our own historical position. This metacommentary, which reflects back on the historicity of our interpretations themselves, is thus doubly historical, or, rather, it raises the project of historicizing to a second power.

Jameson's version of dialectics involves this same process of self-reflection that historicizes the interpretation and the interpreter. Dialectical criticism is in one sense another name for metacommentary because it too is doubly historical.

Dialectical thought is in its very structure self-consciousness and may be described as the attempt to think about a given object on one level, and at the same time to observe our own thought processes as we do so: or to use a more scientific figure, to reckon the position of the observer into the experiment itself.[17]

Dialectics is thus, for Jameson, not just one method of interpretation among others; it resides at a higher level. In other words, various methods and schema of interpretation, such as new criticism, formalism, or structuralism, compete in their conflicting interpretations of texts and objects. Jameson's dialectics, in contrast, competes with no methods of interpretation and repudiates none of them. From this perspective, the least interesting way to intervene in a dispute over interpretation is to declare one of them right and the other wrong.[18] Once the various theories are understood historically, the perspective of dialectics or metacommentary can reveal that each has specific contributions to offer and also blind spots that limit its capacities. They are all true and useful once situated properly with respect to history. This remove of dialectics allows Jameson to adopt an ecumenical stance and it accounts for his great generosity. When he encounters a new theoretical position or paradigm, he never says "no" to it, but always "yes and . . . ." The openness of this dialectical position makes clear how Jameson can address the field of theory as a whole. The particular varieties of theory and disciplinary specializations are all accepted and situated by dialectical reflection as so many positions within or approaches to history itself.

This description should make clear too that Jameson's dialectic is incompatible with moralistic evaluations. The dialectic, as he likes to say, is beyond good and evil.[19] Since it resides in this second, reflective level of historicizing, dialectical criticism handles moral and political questions at one remove, situating them within and against a larger historical context. This can help us understand, for example, why Jameson refuses to engage in moralizing judgments about the ultimate value of postmodernism. Both the celebration and lamentation of postmodernism are inappropriate and unproductive. From the dialectical perspective every historical development must be seen in terms of both its possibilities and its limitations, as simultaneously an opportunity and an obstacle. Think of how Marx viewed the development of capital as a triumph and promise on one hand and as an ever-deepening tragedy on the other. Absolute moralizing judgments about postmodernism ultimately distract us from the work of critical analysis, sorting through the ways in which postmodernism is at once a symptom of, support for, and challenge to the multiplicity of forces of late capitalism. The point is that postmodernism must be grasped as a cultural dominant with constitutive force, that is, a set of forces that rules and organizes the entire cultural field, one which is productive of both social reality and social subjectivities.

Transcoding

Jameson privileges Marxism over other theoretical paradigms because it is the most developed framework of dialectical thinking or metacommentary. He expresses this privilege, however, in two different forms, one organized vertically and the other horizontally, a difference perhaps due to the changing reception of Marxism in the field of theory at large. According to the vertical model, Marxism stands at the pinnacle of the set of theories, and its dialectical method allows it to subsume all other theories in its comprehensive vision. Each other theoretical perspective, although it sees clearly in certain respects, is partial and has blind spots and shortcomings. Only the synthesis of all of them at the remove of the dialectical standpoint gives a comprehensive view. Marxism is thus, according to this model, not an alternative to other theories but their completion.

The horizontal model, which tends to emerge later in Jameson's writings characterizes the privilege of Marxism not as synthetic pinnacle but as universal mediator. (It is interesting to note here that synthesis and mediation represent two faces of the dialectic and that emphasis on one or the other characterizes two different streams of the dialectical tradition.) Jameson's term for mediating among different theories is "transcoding." Transcoding is a process of translation that allows us to move from one theoretical paradigm to another, taking the best that each has to offer. For example, with the aid of transcoding we can benefit from psychoanalytic methods without being closed in the psychoanalytic framework, and combine them with the insights of formalism, structuralism, and other interpretive methods. Transcoding has indeed become ever more necessary with the explosion of poststructuralist theoretical paradigms in the 1980s and 1990s. Such movement among and combination of different methods and perspectives is not eclectic or incoherent because dialectics historicizes each theoretical position and relates one to the other while situating them all in the larger historical context. In this sense, then, Marxism stands not above but among the various theories, in the interstices, as the means of connection, communication, and translation in an open, expansive network.

At this point we can understand how Jameson's work over the course of his career has achieved that rare combination of continuity and openness to change. On the one hand, Jameson's opus is remarkably coherent and systematic. When one reads his work from the beginning one finds that the basic project does not really change much. Many of the core concepts and problematics were present early on and the process of development has not deviated from them but moved rather in a spiral, a progressive deepening of the same concepts and problematics in ever new contexts. It is sometimes shocking, in fact, to find that a concept we associate with a later stage of Jameson's work, such as cognitive mapping, was already present in embryo decades earlier.[20] It is thus understandable that a reader might get the impression at times that Jameson had thought it all out before beginning and it has only taken so many years and so many books to articulate it systematically!

On the other hand, whereas the project and concepts remain constant, Jameson is continually discovering and engaging new texts and material from all parts of the world – and this is what is truly remarkable. Systematic thinkers generally limit their field of vision to a small repertoire so as not to risk encountering anomalies that would cast doubt on the system; they tend to avoid the shock of the new or quickly to dismantle it and reduce its potency by rendering it familiar in some way. Jameson does just the opposite. He constantly seeks out new texts, new phenomena, and new theoretical paradigms – and perhaps this accounts for the fact that he was one of the first theorists to develop a theory of postmodernism and that he continues to transform it, developing the theory, for example, in response to processes associated with finance capital and globalization. This posture is dictated no doubt by history itself, or rather the dialectical view of history: we must keep up with the times, finding new and updated tools to grasp new realities. Theories too, of course, become outdated. Even Marxism, which Jameson grants such a privileged position, will one day finally be supplanted, one must assume, when its proper object, the capitalist mode of production, is no longer the dominant historical force.

Totality

We have seen that Jameson's analyses are remarkably expansive, pushing the horizon of our vision outward to include ultimately the totality of human experience. He argues that it is necessary to address the totality, first of all, because each element and phenomenon of our world is in some way related to every other. This infinite relationality is explained only at the highest level, from the perspective of the whole. The concept of totality is necessary also because of the expansive nature of capital, because the tendency of the capitalist mode of production is to make of the world a totality; an adequate analysis of capital must thus be equally total, tracing its movements both horizontally, across the various national and regional spaces, and vertically, down to the depths of the social world.

The concept of totality has frequently been met with disfavor. Critics of the concept believe that it relies on out dated ontological assumptions, suspicious methodologies, naïve epistemological claims, and even undemocratic political ideals. Such critiques are somewhat misdirected in this case, however, because Jameson's totality is not a monolithic, seamless and self-replicating web of undifferentiated and unified forces. A multiplicity of forces conflict and interact within the totality, and therefore totality must be understood as composed of differences and discontinuities, residual and emergent forces, antinomies and contradictions, and anomalies. It is important to distinguish between closed and open notions of totality. A closed totality may have internal differences and even contradictions but they are all ultimately subsumed under the order of a single, central controlling force or idea. Nothing new can arise in a closed totality and there can be no exception; instead, everything flows unerringly toward the final unity. An open totality, in contrast, is defined by the free play of differences that are not recuperable within any unity. What keeps the totality open is the creative and unpredictable efficacy of the new. New forces push in different directions such that an open totality is always moving and growing in an amorphous way, never toward any fixed or pregiven end.

The preoccupations that lead Jameson to the concept of totality are not metaphysical, but rather primarily epistemological and aesthetic. The category of totality designates not a normative ideal or a state of Being, but a methodological imperative. Totality is meant to function as a prescription to strive constantly to relate and connect, to situate and interpret each object or phenomenon in the context of those social and historical forces that shape and enable it, and ultimately with respect to the entire set of its conditions of possibilities. This is a tall task, and indeed an impossible one because no final and complete account of the entire set of forces, of all of history can ever be achieved. We can strive or aspire toward the totality but it will remain beyond our grasp, it will always exceed our knowledge. The concept of totality thus leads us back once again to the problematic of representation. Since it is an absent cause rather than something that can be grasped empirically or even analytically, "totality is not available for representation, any more than it is accessible in the form of some ultimate truth."[21] And yet we must strive to know and represent it. We are thus confronted with the paradoxical mandate to represent the unrepresentable.

Cognitive Mapping

How can we do justice to both the phenomenological richness of individual existence and the immensity and complexity of the global world system to which this life is bound? How can we conceive the connections among the most intimate local dimensions of subjective experience and the abstract and impersonal forces of a global system? One of the strategies that Jameson pursues to answer the paradoxical mandate of totality, to represent the unrepresentable, is a form of praxis he calls "cognitive mapping." This approach forms part of his intervention in the contemporary discussions of globalization. Cognitive mapping involves a series of aesthetic practices, theoretical projects, and even political activities that produce the sense of orientation that a map provides. A cognitive map is a necessarily partial and incomplete rendering of the multidimensional and constantly changing totality that serves as a kind of navigational aid.

The geographer is perhaps the archetypal personification of this activity. The metaphor of mapping, however, is somewhat misleading, as Jameson himself points out, because it makes the endeavor seem easier and more concrete than it really is and, more important, it implies that the representation can have a mimetic relation to reality. Plotting uncharted waters and unknown lands is certainly a difficult task, but the map can finally, with adequate information and proper technology, approach an exact correspondence with its real referents. The problem of representation for the geographer can be resolved. In contrast, since the referent of Jameson's cognitive mapping, the totality itself, although very real, is not fixed, concrete, or material, no stable and definitive lines of correspondence can be drawn. Representation remains constantly a problem. In other words, a cognitive mapping can never achieve a simple mimetic relation to reality, but is rather always an act of interpretation, and hence involves an aesthetic operation. A cognitive mapping can never hope actually to match the totality. The Truth is not out there, as if we could somehow grasp in an unmediated way the real conditions of our existence. It is thus useful to understand cognitive mapping as something like an ideology in the sense that Louis Althusser gives this term: an imaginary representation of our relation to our real conditions of existence.[22] The goal is not to arrive at the Truth with certainty, but rather to produce adequate, practical knowledges.

Jameson insists not only that we *ought* to engage in cognitive mapping, but also that we already do this kind of mapping all the time, often without being conscious of the fact. Cognitive mapping of some sort is a necessary and unavoidable practice that is part of being and orienting oneself in the world. It is the task of criticism to interpret these collective and unconscious mappings to make them overt and political. Consider the popularity of conspiracy theory films, one of Jameson's favorite examples.[23] A conspiracy theory offers a particularly simple understanding of the totality in the sense that it tends to trace all mysteries back to a single source or power: the shadow government, the secret brotherhood of conspirators, or the evil genius. Jameson calls conspiracy theory a poor person's cognitive mapping. Because they are so reductive and crude, conspiracy theories do not really provide the practical orientation that a cognitive mapping should, but they do negatively indicate some important points. First, by demonstrating the absurdity of tracing all phenomena to a single, identifiable source or cause – because in reality there is no man behind the curtain who pulls the levers and controls everything – conspiracy theories show that the totality is really an absent cause that is ungraspable and unrepresentable in itself. Secondly, the popularity of these films is testament to the widespread desire for a means to understand, for some sort of cognitive mapping, however imperfect, to orient us in the complexities of the contemporary world.

What remains central for Jameson through his various engagements with the concept of totality is the representational dilemma to which it gives rise. In the postmodern era, allegory, a figure that the moderns had repudiated as a relic of the ancient world, has emerged again as an important tool or strategy to address the problem of representation. Postmodern allegory does not involve a one-to-one mapping but an open and multiple representational device. In contrast to the symbol, which had a privileged position in modernism, allegory is a discontinuous form of representation that highlights its disjunction from what it represents. "In our time", Jameson explains, "the referent – the world system – is a being of such enormous complexity that it can only be mapped and modeled indirectly, by way of a simpler object that stands as its allegorical interpretant . . . ."[24] Like totality and cognitive mapping, allegory presupposes the impossibility of representation in any naïve or mimetic sense and highlights its own status as an interpretation. Just as premodern theologians approached the divine, which they recognized to be beyond their powers of comprehension, through allegorical figures, so too today in postmodernity when the totality appears increasingly beyond our grasp, allegory seems once again the appropriate figure. Allegory can become a tool to further our efforts to construct a cognitive mapping of the complexities of the contemporary world system.

Utopia

It would be easy when reading an analysis of a powerful, global system of exploitation and domination for a reader to assume that in the face of such a power we are helpless and doomed. (This is, indeed, the reaction of many readers to Michel Foucault's analyses of power.) This is precisely what many of the critics of the concept of totality fear: that any form of human agency will be rendered powerless by the sheer systematicity of the totality, that totality and resistance are mutually exclusive theoretical and political commitments. Perhaps this specter of our impotence in the face of an overpowering world is what makes Jameson feel the need to end many essays with a call to utopian thinking: to insist, despite the immensity of the system we are confronting, on our power to change the world.

Utopian thinking, however, is not confined to isolated gestures in Jameson's work but runs throughout and is implicit even in his concept of totality. Rather than annulling agency, the aspiration to totality is in fact a necessary component of transformative practice. Reviving a 1960s' slogan that he finds increasingly relevant and yet ever more difficult to realize in the contemporary world, Jameson insists that we have to "name the system" before we can change it. Anything other than piecemeal local reform presupposes some conception of the larger system to be replaced. Totality and utopia are two moments of the same process.

Utopia is not only everywhere implied in Jameson's work but is also present throughout society, particularly in the cultural sphere, equally in the realms of high and low culture. Sometimes we find explicit instances of utopian thinking, such as in some science fiction novels. In fact, Jameson has written extensively on science fiction, a literary genre that he argues is worthy of serious scholarly study. Most often, however, utopia is expressed in a hidden, unconscious form that can be revealed only through critical interpretation. For example, Jameson interprets the attachments to kinship networks in the Corleone family of *The Godfather* movies as a utopian expression of the desire for collectivity – a new collectivity, perhaps, outside the pathological structures of the Mafia family model. Once we train ourselves to look for it, we can find throughout the world of cultural objects expressions of utopian desire, just as we can find too attempts to understand the totality, however, partial, deformed, or unconscious they may be.

Jameson is particularly interested in the failures of utopian thinking. It is surprising sometimes just how limited our utopian imagination is and how closed our thinking is within the walls of the present state of things. In many respects this poverty is most pronounced in the United States, despite (or because of?) its wealth and increasing dominance over the rest of the world. Our sense of reality and its immutable solidity seems to have strangled our sense of possibility. By focusing on the inadequacies, evasions, and lacunae in the available utopian visions, Jameson demonstrates how the present system brands us and tames our political imagination. The failures of utopian thinking become yet another lesson in what we cannot represent and imagine: perhaps the failure to imagine alternative possibilities should be attributed to the poverty of our representations of the totality.

In postmodernity our incapacity for utopian thinking tends to become more pronounced. Our ability to imagine future alternatives to the present declines hand in hand with our historical consciousness because both are based on existing differences in the contemporary world. In the course of capitalist globalization, as we said earlier, some kinds of differences are preserved and others are created but all different modes of production are subsumed under capital. Most important, the end of really-existing socialism, the collapse of the Soviet and the transformation of the Chinese experiments, signaled a precipitous decline of our capacity for utopian thinking. From the perspective of the capitalist world, the socialist regimes represented a real alternative and, perhaps more important, alluded to the possibility of others.

Despite the difficulty of representing or imagining utopia in postmodernity, the desire for utopia remains. The clash between our inability and our desire leads to what Jameson calls the postmodern fear of or anxiety about utopia. Perhaps our fear of utopia serves to block our dissatisfaction with the present and quiet our yearning for a different future; perhaps it is a kind of anesthesia for the pain of being closed in a reality without alternatives, without possibility. Or perhaps we should understand the continuing anxiety about utopia, rather, as a symptom of the fact that our desire for utopia is finally ineluctable and irrepressible.

Today, when the ideology of the market and the global rule of capital seem to admit no possibility of an alternative, when it seems utterly out of the question to imagine a different world, utopian thinking is more necessary than ever. Here perhaps we should reinvent another 1960s' slogan (which in the meantime has been coopted by an Apple computer advertising campaign): *penser autrement*, "think different." Utopian thinking by itself will not change the world, but it is a good first step.

Organization

We intend this volume as an introduction to Jameson's thought that demonstrates its utility for students and scholars across a wide range of disciplines. We hope that the selections presented here will serve as a springboard and lead readers to engage seriously with his numerous books. Constructing an anthology always involves difficult choices but certain aspects of Jameson's work amplify these difficulties. The sheer quantity of his writings and breadth of their subject matter render it very difficult to put together a single volume that can adequately represent the entire body of his work. Inevitably, some areas of enquiry and types of texts will be under-represented. Thus, for example, one should note that we have included few selections that concentrate narrowly on a single text or theorist and more that deal with general theoretical problematics. The reader will thus find that a review of the bibliography at the end of the volume might provide a better sense of the whole of Jameson's opus than the table of contents.

The continuity of Jameson's project presents a different kind of challenge. Rarely does Jameson produce an essay on a single theme – one that can stand apart from his larger theoretical concerns and interpretive methods. Thus, although we have divided the selections under five different headings, there is considerable overlap between them. For example, the selections in Part I, "Paradigms of Interpretation," are all attempts to come to terms with theoretical texts and traditions, but Jameson's interests in a range of theoretical orientations are obvious in all of his writings. Similarly, Part II is reserved for "Marxism and Culture," but rarely is Jameson's Marxism or his interest in culture not made explicit in one way or another.

Finally, we should note the problems of presenting a summary account of the work of a writer who is still active. Jameson has always been a remarkably prolific writer and there was an explosion of activity in the 1990s that shows no signs of slowing down in the new millennium. In this case the reader should not mistake as complete and final what is actually a work-in-progress, an open-ended project.

Notes

1   Perry Anderson writes that in Jameson's work "the vocation of Western Marxism has reached its most complete consummation;" *The Origins of Postmodernity* (London, Verso, 1998) p. 72.

2   The vast secondary literature on Jameson now includes a number of book-length studies. Perry Anderson's *The Origins of Postmodernity* presents an excellent introduction to Jameson's thought, with special attention to his theorization of postmodernism. *Postmodernism/Jameson/Critique* (Washington, DC, Maisonneuve Press, 1989), edited by Douglas Kellner, who provides a valuable overview of Jameson's work in his introduction, also centers around the topic of postmodernism. An interesting analysis of Jameson's interpretive methods can be found in the first half of Roland Boer's *Jameson and Jeroboam* (Atlanta, Scholar's Press, 1996). Clint Burnham's *The Jamesonian Unconscious: The Aesthetics of Marxist Theory* (Durham, Duke University Press, 1995) offers a more creative appropriation of Jameson's work. William C. Dowling presents a clear and detailed reading of the theoretical chapters of *The Political Unconscious* in his book, *Jameson, Althusser, Marx: An Introduction to The Political Unconscious* (Ithaca, Cornell University Press, 1984). Christopher Wise's book, *The Marxian Hermeneutics of Fredric Jameson* (New York, Peter Lang, 1995), focuses on the hermeneutic tradition. Finally, Sean Homer offers a comprehensive examination of Jameson's work in *Fredric Jameson: Marxism, Hermeneutics, Postmodernism* (New York, Routledge, 1998).

3   Etienne Balibar cites this replacement of doctrine with problems as the key to the relevance of Marx's thought for the twenty-first century. See *The Philosophy of Marx*, trans. Chris Turner (London, Verso, 1995).

4   Along with Jameson, Louis Althusser is one of the thinkers who most clearly develops the problematic of representation in Marx's thought.

5   Perry Anderson catalogues Jameson's debts to these French and German thinkers: "From Lukács, Jameson took his commitment to periodization and fascination with narrative; from Bloch, a respect for the hopes and dreams hidden in a tarnished object-world; from Sartre, an exceptional fluency with the textures of immediate experience; from Lefebvre, the curiosity about urban space; from Marcuse, pursuit of the trail of high-tech consumption; from Althusser, a positive conception of ideology, as a necessary social imaginary; from Adorno, the ambition to represent

the totality of his object as nothing less than a 'metaphorical composition'" (*Origins of Postmodernity*, p. 71).

6   *Marxism and Form* (Princeton, Princeton University Press, 1971), p. xiii.
7   For an insightful commentary on Jameson's style, see Terry Eagleton, "Fredric Jameson: the politics of style," *Diacritics*, 12 (1982), pp. 14–22. See also Homer, *Fredric Jameson*, pp. 18–20.
8   Consider, for example, this complex embedded sentence in which Jameson challenges two traditional views on the value of mass culture and high culture. "For all these reasons, it seems to me that we must rethink the opposition high culture/ mass culture in such a way that the emphasis on evaluation to which it has traditionally given rise – and which however the binary system of value operates (mass culture is popular and thus more authentic than high culture, high culture is autonomous and, therefore, utterly incomparable to a degraded mass culture) tends to function in some timeless realm of absolute aesthetic judgment – is replaced by a genuinely historical and dialectical approach to these phenomena": "Reification and utopia in mass culture," from *Signatures of the Visible* (London, Routledge, 1992), p. 14 (see chapter 8 of the present volume).
9   *The Geopolitical Aesthetic* (Bloomington, Indiana University Press, 1992), p. 212.
10 See *The Political Unconscious*, (Ithaca, Cornell University Press, 1981), pp. 74–102 (see chapter 1 of the present volume). This schema of three horizons for interpretation has proven to be one of the aspects of Jameson's work most often adapted and applied by other critics. For an example of the use of the three levels in biblical interpretation, see Boer, *Jameson and Jeroboam*.
11 *The Cultural Turn* (London, Verso, 1998) p. 73.
12 See Jameson's "Reflections on the Brecht–Lukács debate," in *Ideologies of Theory, Volume 2* (Minneapolis, University of Minnesota Press, 1988), pp. 133–47.
13 See Ernest Mandel, *Late Capitalism*, trans. Joris De bres (London, Verso, 1978). More recently, Jameson has explored the relation of postmodernism to other periodizations of capital, most notably those of Giovanni Arrighi and Robert Brenner. For Jameson's reading of Arrighi, see "Culture and finance capital" (chapter 14 of the present volume); and for his reading of Brenner, see "Turbulence in Brenner" (forthcoming).
14 See "Postmodernism, or the cultural logic of late capitalism" (chapter 12 of the present volume).
15 See *Postmodernism, or, The Cultural Logic of Late Capitalism* (Durham, Duke University Press, 1991), pp. 95–6. For Jameson's most complete treatment of the dialectical relationship among realism, modernism, and postmodernism, with specific reference to film history, see "The existence of Italy," in *Signatures of the Visible*, pp. 155–229.
16 "Metacommentary," in *Ideologies of Theory, Volume 1*, p. 5.
17 *Marxism and Form*, p. 340.
18 See "A conversation with Fredric Jameson," *Semeia*, 59 (1992), p. 233.

19   See "The politics of theory: ideological positions in the postmodernism debate," in
     Ideologies of Theory, Volume 2, p. 111; and, more generally, the conclusion to *The
     Political Unconscious*, pp. 281–99.

20   We are thinking here specifically of Jameson's call to make a mental map of the
     world system in his 1968 essay, "On politics and literature," *Salmagundi*, 7 (spring–
     summer, 1968), pp. 17–26.

21   *The Political Unconscious* p. 55.

22   See "Postmodernism, or the cultural logic of late capitalism," *New Left Review*, 146
     (July–August, 1984), p. 90 and "Cognitive mapping," in Cary Nelson and
     Lawrence Grossberg (eds), *Marxism and the Interpretation of Culture* (Urbana, Uni-
     versity of Illinois Press, 1988), p. 353 (respectively, chapters 12 and 15 of the
     present volume).

23   See "Totality as conspiracy" (chapter 19 of the present volume).

24   *The Geopolitical Aesthetic* p. 169.

Part I

Paradigms of Interpretation

1

On Interpretation: Literature as a Socially Symbolic Act

"On Interpretation," which is the theoretical introduction to Jameson's book *The Political Unconscious* (1981), is divided into three sections. Our selection includes the opening pages of the chapter and its third section.

This book [*The Political Unconscious*] will argue the priority of the political interpretation of literary texts. It conceives of the political perspective not as some supplementary method, not as an optional auxiliary to other interpretive methods current today – the psychoanalytic or the myth-critical, the stylistic, the ethical, the structural – but rather as the absolute horizon of all reading and all interpretation.

This is evidently a much more extreme position than the modest claim, surely acceptable to everyone, that certain texts have social and historical – sometimes even political – resonance. Traditional literary history has, of course, never prohibited the investigation of such topics as the Florentine political background in Dante, Milton's relationship to the schismatics, or Irish historical allusions in Joyce. I would argue, however, that such information – even where it is not recontained, as it is in most instances, by an idealistic conception of the history of ideas – does not yield interpretation as such, but rather at best its (indispensable) preconditions.

Today this properly antiquarian relationship to the cultural past has a dialectical counterpart which is ultimately no more satisfactory; I mean the tendency of much contemporary theory to rewrite selected texts from the past in terms of its own aesthetic and, in particular, in terms of a modernist (or more properly post-modernist) conception of language. I have shown elsewhere[1] the ways in which such "ideologies of the text" construct a straw man or inessential term – variously called the "readerly" or the "realistic" or the "referential" text – over against which the essential term – the "writerly" or modernist or "open" text, écriture or textual productivity – is defined and with which it is seen as a decisive break. But Croce's great dictum that "all history is contemporary history" does not mean that all history is *our* contemporary history; and the problems begin when your epistemological break begins to displace itself in time according to your own current interests, so that Balzac may stand for unenlightened representationality when you are concerned to bring out everything that is "textual" and modern in Flaubert, but turns into something else when, with Roland Barthes in *S/Z*, you have decided to rewrite Balzac as Philippe Sollers, as sheer text and *écriture*.

This unacceptable option, or ideological double bind, between antiquarianism and modernizing "relevance" or projection demonstrates that the old dilemmas of historicism – and in particular, the question of the claims of monuments from distant and even archaic moments of the cultural past on a culturally different present[2] – do not go away just because we choose to ignore them. Our presupposition, in the analyses that follow, will be that only a genuine philosophy of history is capable of respecting the specificity and radical difference of the social and cultural past while disclosing the solidarity of its polemics and passions, its forms, structures, experiences, and struggles, with those of the present day.

But genuine philosophies of history have never been numerous, and few survive in workable, usable form in the contemporary world of consumer capitalism and the multinational system. We will have enough occasion, in the pages that follow [not included here], to emphasize the methodological interest of Christian historicism and the theological origins of the first great hermeneutic system in the Western tradition, to be permitted the additional observation that the Christian philosophy of history which emerges full blown in Augustine's *City of God* (AD 413–426) can no longer be particularly binding on us. As for the philosophy of history of a heroic bourgeoisie, its two principal variants – the vision of progress that emerges from the ideological struggles of the French Enlightenment, and that organic populism or nationalism which articulated the rather different historicity of the central and Eastern European peoples and which is generally associated with the name of Herder – are neither of them extinct, certainly, but are at the very least both discredited under their hegemonic embodiments in positivism and classical liberalism, and in nationalism respectively.

My position here is that only Marxism offers a philosophically coherent and ideologically compelling resolution to the dilemma of historicism evoked above. Only Marxism can give us an adequate account of the essential *mystery* of the cultural past, which, like Tiresias drinking the blood, is momentarily returned to life and warmth and allowed once more to speak, and to deliver its long-forgotten message in surroundings utterly alien to it. This mystery can be reenacted only if the human adventure is one; only thus – and not through the hobbies of antiquarianism or the projections of the modernists – can we glimpse the vital claims upon us of such long-dead issues as the seasonal alternation of the economy of a primitive tribe, the passionate disputes about the nature of the Trinity, the conflicting models of the *polis* or the universal Empire, or, apparently closer to us in time, the dusty parliamentary and journalistic polemics of the nineteenth-century nation states. These matters can recover their original urgency for us only if they are retold within the unity of a single great collective story; only if, in however disguised and symbolic a form, they are seen as sharing a single fundamental theme – for Marxism, the collective struggle to wrest a realm of Freedom from a realm of Necessity;[3] only if they are grasped as vital episodes in a single vast unfinished plot:

The history of all hitherto existing society is the history of class struggles: freeman and slave, patrician and plebeian, lord and serf, guild-master and journeyman – in a word, oppressor and oppressed – stood in constant opposition to one another, carried on an uninterrupted, now hidden, now open fight, a fight that each time ended, either in a revolutionary reconstitution of society at large or in the common ruin of the contending classes.[4]

It is in detecting the traces of that uninterrupted narrative, in restoring to the surface of the text the repressed and buried reality of this fundamental history, that the doctrine of a political unconscious finds its function and its necessity.

From this perspective the convenient working distinction between cultural texts that are social and political and those that are not becomes something worse than an error: namely, a symptom and a reinforcement of the reification and privatization of contemporary life. Such a distinction reconfirms that structural, experiential, and conceptual gap between the public and the private, between the social and the psychological, or the political and the poetic, between history or society and the "individual," which – the tendential law of social life under capitalism – maims our existence as individual subjects and paralyzes our thinking about time and change just as surely as it alienates us from our speech itself. To imagine that, sheltered from the omnipresence of

history and the implacable influence of the social, there already exists a realm of
freedom – whether it be that of the microscopic experience of words in a text
or the ecstasies and intensities of the various private religions – is only to
strengthen the grip of Necessity over all such blind zones in which the
individual subject seeks refuge, in pursuit of a purely individual, a
merely psychological, project of salvation. The only effective liberation from
such constraint begins with the recognition that there is nothing that is
not social and historical – indeed, that everything is "in the last analysis"
political.

The assertion of a political unconscious proposes that we undertake just such
a final analysis and explore the multiple paths that lead to the unmasking of
cultural artifacts as socially symbolic acts. It projects a rival hermeneutic to those
already enumerated; but it does so, as we shall see, not so much by repudiating
their findings as by arguing its ultimate philosophical and methodological
priority over more specialized interpretive codes whose insights are strategically
limited as much by their own situational origins as by the narrow or local ways
in which they construe or construct their objects of study.

[. . .]

III

At this point it might seem appropriate to juxtapose a Marxist method of
literary and cultural interpretation with [other methods], and to document its
claims to greater adequacy and validity. For better or for worse, however [. . .]
this obvious next step is not the strategy projected by the present book [*The
Political Unconscious*], which rather seeks to argue the perspectives of Marxism as
necessary preconditions for adequate literary comprehension. Marxist critical
insights will therefore here be defended as something like an ultimate *semantic*
precondition for the intelligibility of literary and cultural texts. Even this
argument, however, needs a certain specification: in particular we will suggest
that such semantic enrichment and enlargement of the inert givens and materials of a particular text must take place within three concentric frameworks,
which mark a widening out of the sense of the social ground of a text through
the notions, first, of political history, in the narrow sense of punctual event and
a chroniclelike sequence of happenings in time; then of society, in the now
already less diachronic and time-bound sense of a constitutive tension and
struggle between social classes; and, ultimately, of history now conceived in
its vastest sense of the sequence of modes of production and the succession and
destiny of the various human social formations, from prehistoric life to whatever far future history has in store for us.[5]

These distinct semantic horizons are, to be sure, also distinct moments of the
process of interpretation, and may in that sense be understood as dialectical
equivalents of what Frye has called the successive "phases" in our reinterpreta-

tion — our rereading and rewriting — of the literary text. What we must also note, however, is that each phase or horizon governs a distinct reconstruction of its object, and construes the very structure of what can now only in a general sense be called "the text" in a different way.

Thus, within the narrower limits of our first, narrowly political or historical, horizon, the "text," the object of study, is still more or less construed as coinciding with the individual literary work or utterance The difference between the perspective enforced and enabled by this horizon, however, and that of ordinary *explication de texte*, or individual exegesis, is that here the individual work is grasped essentially as a *symbolic act*.

When we pass into the second phase, and find that the semantic horizon within which we grasp a cultural object has widened to include the social order, we will find that the very object of our analysis has itself been thereby dialectically transformed, and that it is no longer construed as an individual "text" or work in the narrow sense, but has been reconstituted in the form of the great collective and class discourses of which a text is little more than an individual *parole* or utterance. Within this new horizon, then, our object of study will prove to be the *ideologeme*, that is, the smallest intelligible unit of the essentially antagonistic collective discourses of social classes.

When finally, even the passions and values of a particular social formation find themselves placed in a new and seemingly relativized perspective by the ultimate horizon of human history as a whole, and by their respective positions in the whole complex sequence of the modes of production, both the individual text and its ideologemes know a final transformation, and must be read in terms of what I will call the *ideology of form*, that is, the symbolic messages transmitted to us by the coexistence of various sign systems which are themselves traces or anticipations of modes of production.

[...]

We must now briefly characterize each of these semantic or interpretive horizons. We have suggested that it is only in the first narrowly political horizon — in which history is reduced to a series of punctual events and crises in time, to the diachronic agitation of the year-to-year, the chroniclelike annals of the rise and fall of political regimes and social fashions, and the passionate immediacy of struggles between historical individuals — that the "text" or object of study will tend to coincide with the individual literary work or cultural artifact. Yet to specify this individual text as a symbolic act is already fundamentally to transform the categories with which traditional *explication de texte* (whether narrative or poetic) operated and largely still operates.

The model for such an interpretive operation remains the readings of myth and aesthetic structure of Claude Lévi-Strauss as they are codified in his

fundamental essay "The Structural Study of Myth."[6] These suggestive, often
sheerly occasional, readings and speculative glosses immediately impose a basic
analytical or interpretive principle: the individual narrative, or the individual
formal structure, is to be grasped as the imaginary resolution of a real contradiction. Thus, to take only the most dramatic of Lévi-Strauss's analyses – the
"interpretation" of the unique facial decorations of the Caduveo Indians – the
starting point will be an immanent description of the formal and structural
peculiarities of this body art; yet it must be a description already pre-prepared
and oriented toward transcending the purely formalistic, a movement which is
achieved not by abandoning the formal level for something extrinsic to it – such
as some inertly social "content" – but rather immanently, by construing purely
formal patterns as a symbolic enactment of the social within the formal and the
aesthetic. Such symbolic functions are, however, rarely found by an aimless
enumeration of random formal and stylistic features; our discovery of a text's
symbolic efficacity must be oriented by a formal description which seeks to
grasp it as a determinate structure of still properly formal *contradictions*. Thus,
Lévi-Strauss orients his still purely visual analysis of Caduveo facial decorations
toward this climatic account of their contradictory dynamic: "the use of a
design which is symmetrical but yet lies across an oblique axis ... a complicated
situation based upon two contradictory forms of duality, and resulting in a
compromise brought about by a secondary opposition between the ideal axis of
the object itself [the human face] and the ideal axis of the figure which it
represents."[7] Already on the purely formal level, then, this visual text has been
grasped as a contradiction by way of the curiously provisional and asymmetrical
resolution it proposes for that contradiction.

Lévi-Strauss's "interpretation" of this formal phenomenon may now, perhaps overhastily, be specified. Caduveo are a hierarchical society, organized in
three endogamous groups or castes. In their social development, as in that of
their neighbors, this nascent hierarchy is already the place of the emergence, if
not of political power in the strict sense, then at least of relations of domination:
the inferior status of women, the subordination of youth to elders, and the
development of a hereditary aristocracy. Yet whereas this latent power structure
is, among the neighboring Guana and Bororo, masked by a division into
moieties which cuts across the three castes, and whose exogamous exchange
appears to function in a nonhierarchical, essentially egalitarian way, it is openly
present in Caduveo life, as surface inequality and conflict. The social institutions of the Guana and Bororo, on the other hand, provide a realm of
appearance, in which real hierarchy and inequality are dissimulated by the
reciprocity of the moieties, and in which, therefore, "asymmetry of class is
balanced ... by symmetry of 'moieties.'"

As for the Caduveo,

they were never lucky enough to resolve their contradictions, or to disguise them with the help of institutions artfully devised for that purpose. On the social level, the remedy was lacking... but it was never completely out of their grasp. It was within them, never objectively formulated, but present as a source of confusion and disquiet. Yet since they were unable to conceptualize or to live this solution directly, they began to dream it, to project it into the imaginary...We must therefore interpret the graphic art of Caduveo women, and explain its mysterious charm as well as its apparently gratuitous complication, as the fantasy production of a society seeking passionately to give symbolic expression to the institutions it might have had in reality, had not interest and superstition stood in the way.[8]

In this fashion, then, the visual text of Caduveo facial art constitutes a symbolic act, whereby real social contradictions, insurmountable in their own terms, find a purely formal resolution in the aesthetic realm.

This interpretive model thus allows us a first specification of the relationship between ideology and cultural texts or artifacts: a specification still conditioned by the limits of the first, narrowly historical or political horizon in which it is made. We may suggest that from this perspective, ideology is not something which informs or invests symbolic production; rather the aesthetic act is itself ideological, and the production of aesthetic or narrative form is to be seen as an ideological act in its own right, with the function of inventing imaginary or formal "solutions" to unresolvable social contradictions.

Lévi-Strauss's work also suggests a more general defense of the proposition of a political unconscious than we have hitherto been able to present, insofar as it offers the spectacle of so-called primitive peoples perplexed enough by the dynamics and contradictions of their still relatively simple forms of tribal organization to project decorative or mythic resolutions of issues that they are unable to articulate conceptually. But if this is the case for pre-capitalist and even pre-political societies, then how much more must it be true for the citizen of the modern *Gesellschaft*, faced with the great constitutional options of the revolutionary period, and with the corrosive and tradition-annihilating effects of the spread of a money and market economy, with the changing cast of collective characters which oppose the bourgeoisie, now to an embattled aristocracy, now to an urban proletariat, with the great fantasms of the various nationalisms, now themselves virtual "subjects of history" of a rather different kind, with the social homogenization and psychic constriction of the rise of the industrial city and its "masses," the sudden appearance of the great transnational forces of communism and fascism, followed by the advent of the superstates and the onset of that great ideological rivalry between capitalism and communism, which, no less passionate and obsessive than that which, at the dawn of modern times, seethed through the wars of religion, marks the final tension of our now global village? It does not, indeed, seem particularly farfetched to suggest that these texts of history, with their fantasmatic collective "actants," their narrative organization, and their immense charge of anxiety and libidinal investment, are lived by the contemporary subject as a genuine politico-historical *pensée sauvage* which necessarily informs all of our cultural artifacts, from the literary institutions of high modernism all the way to the products of mass culture. Under these circumstances, Lévi-Strauss's work suggests that the proposition whereby all cultural artifacts are to be read as symbolic resolutions of real political and social contradictions deserves serious exploration and systematic experimental verification. It will become clear in later chapters of this book [not included here] that the most readily accessible formal articulation of the operations of a political *pensée sauvage* of this kind will be found in what we will call the structure of a properly political *allegory*, as it develops from networks of topical allusion in Spenser or Milton or Swift to the symbolic narratives of class representatives or "types" in novels like those of Balzac. With political allegory, then, a sometimes repressed ur-narrative or master fantasy about the interaction of collective subjects, we have moved to the very borders of our second horizon, in which what we formerly regarded as individual texts are grasped as "utterances" in an essentially collective or class discourse.

We cannot cross those borders, however, without some final account of the critical operations involved in our first interpretive phase. We have implied that in order to be consequent, the will to read literary or cultural texts as symbolic acts must necessarily grasp them as resolutions of determinate contradictions; and it is clear that the notion of contradiction is central to any Marxist cultural analysis, just as it will remain central in our two subsequent horizons, although it will there take rather different forms. The methodological requirement to articulate a text's fundamental contradiction may then be seen as a test of the completeness of the analysis: this is why, for example, the conventional sociology of literature or culture, which modestly limits itself to the identification of class motifs or values in a given text, and feels that its work is done when it shows how a given artifact "reflects" its social background, is utterly unacceptable. Meanwhile, Kenneth Burke's play of emphases, in which a symbolic act is on the one hand affirmed as a genuine *act*, albeit on the symbolic level, while on the other it is registered as an act which is "merely" symbolic, its resolutions imaginary ones that leave the real untouched, suitably dramatizes the ambiguous status of art and culture.

Still, we need to say a little more about the status of this external reality, of which it will otherwise be thought that it is little more than the traditional notion of "context" familiar in older social or historical criticism. The type of interpretation here proposed is more satisfactorily grasped as the rewriting of the literary text in such a way that the latter may itself be seen as the rewriting or restructuration of a prior historical or ideological *subtext*, it being always understood that that "subtext" is not immediately present as such, not some common-sense external reality, nor even the conventional narratives of history manuals, but rather must itself always be (re)constructed after the fact. The literary or aesthetic act therefore always entertains some active relationship with the Real; yet in order to do so, it cannot simply allow "reality" to persevere inertly in its own being, outside the text and at distance. It must rather draw the Real into its own texture, and the ultimate paradoxes and false problems of linguistics, and most notably of semantics, are to be traced back to this process, whereby language manages to carry the Real within itself as its own intrinsic or immanent subtext. Insofar, in other words, as symbolic action — what Burke will map as "dream," "prayer," or "chart"[9] — is a way of doing something to the world, to that degree what we are calling "world" must inhere within it, as the content it has to take up into itself in order to submit it to the transformations of form. The symbolic act therefore begins by generating and producing its own context in the same moment of emergence in which it steps back from it, taking its measure with a view toward its own projects of transformation. The whole paradox of what we have here called the subtext may be summed up in this, that the literary work or cultural object, as though for the first time, brings into being that very situation to which it is also, at one and the same time, a reaction. It articulates its own situation and textualizes it, thereby encouraging and perpetuating the illusion that the situation itself did not exist before it, that there is nothing but a text, that there never was any extra- or con-textual reality before the text itself generated it in the form of a mirage. One does not have to argue the reality of history: necessity, like Dr Johnson's stone, does that for us. That history — Althusser's "absent cause," Lacan's "Real" — is *not* a text, for it is fundamentally non-narrative and nonrepresentational; what can be added, however, is the proviso that history is inaccessible to us except in textual form, or in other words, that it can be approached only by way of prior (re)textualization. Thus, to insist on either of the two inseparable yet incommensurable dimensions of the symbolic act without the other: to overemphasize the active way in which the text reorganizes its subtext (in order, presumably, to reach the triumphant conclusion that the "referent" does not exist); or on the other hand to stress the imaginary status of the symbolic act so completely as to reify its social ground, now no longer understood as a subtext but merely as some inert given that the text passively or fantasmatically "reflects" — to overstress either of these functions of the symbolic act at the expense of the other is surely to produce sheer ideology, whether it be, as in the first alternative, the ideology of structuralism, or, in the second, that of vulgar materialism.

Still, this view of the place of the "referent" will be neither complete nor methodologically usable unless we specify a supplementary distinction between several types of subtext to be (re)constructed. We have implied, indeed, that the social contradiction addressed and "resolved" by the formal prestidigitation of narrative must, however reconstructed, remain an absent cause, which cannot be directly or immediately conceptualized by the text. It seems useful, therefore, to distinguish, from this ultimate subtext which is the place of social *contradiction*, a secondary one, which is more properly the place of ideology, and which takes the form of the *aporia* or the *antinomy*: what can in the former be resolved only through the intervention of praxis here comes before the purely contemplative mind as logical scandal or double bind, the unthinkable and the conceptually paradoxical, that which cannot be unknotted by the operation of pure thought, and which must therefore generate a whole more properly narrative apparatus – the text itself – to square its circles and to dispel, through narrative movement, its intolerable closure. Such a distinction, positing a system of antinomies as the symptomatic expression and conceptual reflex of something quite different, namely a social contradiction, will now allow us to reformulate that coordination between a semiotic and a dialectical method [. . .] The operational validity of semiotic analysis, and in particular of the Greimassian semiotic rectangle,[10] derives [. . .] not from its adequacy to nature or being, nor even from its capacity to map all forms of thinking or language, but rather from its vocation specifically to model ideological closure and to articulate the workings of binary oppositions, here the privileged form of what we have called the antinomy. A dialectical reevaluation of the findings of semiotics intervenes, however, at the moment in which this entire system of ideological closure is taken as the symptomatic projection of something quite different, namely of social contradiction.

We may now leave this first textual or interpretive model behind, and pass over into the second horizon, that of the social. The latter becomes visible, and individual phenomena are revealed as social facts and institutions, only at the moment in which the organizing categories of analysis become those of social class. I have in another place described the dynamics of ideology in its constituted form as a function of social class:[11] suffice it only to recall here that for Marxism classes must always be apprehended relationally, and that the ultimate (or ideal) form of class relationship and class struggle is always dichotomous. The constitutive form of class relationships is always that between a dominant and a laboring class: and it is only in terms of this axis that class fractions (for example, the petty bourgeoisie) or ec-centric or dependent classes (such as the peasantry) are positioned. To define class in this way is sharply to differentiate the Marxian model of classes from the conventional sociological analysis of society into strata, subgroups, professional elites and the like, each of which can presumably be studied in isolation from one another in such a way that the analysis of their "values" or their "cultural space" folds back into separate and independent *Weltanschauungen*, each of which inertly reflects its particular "stratum." For Marxism, however, the very content of a class ideology is relational, in the sense that its "values" are always actively in situation with respect to the opposing class, and defined against the latter: normally, a ruling class ideology will explore various strategies of the *legitimation* of its own power position, while an oppositional culture or ideology will, often in covert and disguised strategies, seek to contest and to undermine the dominant "value system."

This is the sense in which we will say, following Mikhail Bakhtin, that within this horizon class discourse – the categories in terms of which individual texts and cultural phenomena are now rewritten – is essentially *dialogical* in its structure.[12] As Bakhtin's (and Voloshinov's) own work in this field is relatively specialized, focusing primarily on the heterogeneous and explosive pluralism of moments of carnival or festival (moments, for example, such as the immense resurfacing of the whole spectrum of the religious or political sects in the English 1640s or the Soviet 1920s) it will be necessary to add the qualification that the normal form of the dialogical is essentially an *antagonistic* one, and that the dialogue of class struggle is one in which two opposing discourses fight it out within the general unity of a shared code. Thus, for instance, the shared master code of religion becomes in the 1640s in England the place in which the dominant formulations of a hegemonic theology are reappropriated and polemically modified.[13]

Within this new horizon, then, the basic formal requirement of dialectical analysis is maintained, and its elements are still restructured in terms of *contradiction* (this is essentially, as we have said, what distinguishes the relationality of a Marxist class analysis from static analysis of the sociological type). Where the contradiction of the earlier horizon was univocal, however, and limited to the situation of the individual text, to the place of a purely individual symbolic resolution, contradiction here appears in the form of the dialogical as the irreconcilable demands and positions of antagonistic classes. Here again, then, the requirement to prolong interpretation to the point at which this ultimate contradiction begins to appear offers a criterion for the completeness or insufficiency of the analysis.

Yet to rewrite the individual text, the individual cultural artifact, in terms of the antagonistic dialogue of class voices is to perform a rather different operation from the one we have ascribed to our first horizon. Now the individual text will be refocused as a *parole*, or individual utterance, of that vaster system, or *langue*, of class discourse. The individual text retains its formal structure as a symbolic act: yet the value and character of such symbolic action are now significantly modified and enlarged. On this rewriting, the individual utterance or text is grasped as a symbolic move in an essentially polemic and strategic ideological confrontation between the classes, and to describe it in these terms (or to reveal it in this form) demands a whole set of different instruments.

For one thing, the illusion or appearance of isolation or autonomy which a printed text projects must now be systematically undermined. Indeed, since by definition the cultural monuments and masterworks that have survived tend necessarily to perpetuate only a single voice in this class dialogue, the voice of a hegemonic class, they cannot be properly assigned their relational place in a dialogical system without the restoration or artificial reconstruction of the voice to which they were initially opposed, a voice for the most part stifled and reduced to silence, marginalized, its own utterances scattered to the winds, or reappropriated in their turn by the hegemonic culture.

This is the framework in which the reconstruction of so-called popular cultures must properly take place — most notably, from the fragments of essentially peasant cultures: folk songs, fairly tales, popular festivals, occult or oppositional systems of belief such as magic and witchcraft. Such reconstruction is of a piece with the reaffirmation of the existence of marginalized or opposi- tional cultures in our own time, and the reaudition of the oppositional voices of black or ethnic cultures, women's and gay literature, "naïve" or marginalized folk art, and the like. But once again, the affirmation of such nonhegemonic cultural voices remains ineffective if it is limited to the merely "sociological" perspective of the pluralistic rediscovery of other isolated social groups: only an ultimate rewriting of these utterances in terms of their essentially polemic and subversive strategies restores them to their proper place in the dialogical system of the social classes. Thus, for instance, Bloch's reading of the fairy tale, with its magical wish-fulfillments and its Utopian fantasies of plenty and the *pays de Cocagne*,[14] restores the dialogical and antagonistic content of this "form" by exhibiting it as a systematic deconstruction and undermining of the hegemonic aristocratic form of the epic, with its somber ideology of heroism and baleful destiny; thus also the work of Eugene Genovese on black religion restores the vitality of these utterances by reading them, not as the replication of imposed beliefs, but rather as a process whereby the hegemonic Christianity of the slave-owners is appropriated, secretly emptied of its content and subverted to the transmission of quite different oppositional and coded messages.[15]

Moreover, the stress on the dialogical then allows us to reread or rewrite the hegemonic forms themselves; they also can be grasped as a process of the reappropriation and neutralization, the cooptation and class transformation, the cultural universalization, of forms which originally expressed the situation of "popular," subordinate, or dominated groups. So the slave religion of Christianity is transformed into the hegemonic ideological apparatus of the medieval system; while folk music and peasant dance find themselves transmuted into the forms of aristocratic or court festivity and into the cultural visions of the pastoral; and popular narrative from time immemorial – romance, adventure story, melodrama, and the like – is ceaselessly drawn on to restore vitality to an enfeebled and asphyxiating "high culture." Just so, in our own time, the vernacular and its still vital sources of production (as in black language) are reappropriated by the exhausted and media-standardized speech of a hegemonic middle class. In the aesthetic realm, indeed, the process of cultural "universalization" (which implies the repression of the oppositional voice, and the illusion that there is only one genuine "culture") is the specific form taken by what can be called the process of legitimation in the realm of ideology and conceptual systems.

Still, this operation of rewriting and of the restoration of an essentially dialogical or class horizon will not be complete until we specify the "units" of this larger system. The linguistic metaphor (rewriting texts in terms of the opposition of a *parole* to a *langue*) cannot, in other words, be particularly fruitful until we are able to convey something of the dynamics proper to a class *langue* itself, which is evidently, in Saussure's sense, something like an ideal construct that is never wholly visible and never fully present in any one of its individual utterances. This larger class discourse can be said to be organized around minimal "units" which we will call *ideologemes*. The advantage of this formulation lies in its capacity to mediate between conceptions of ideology as abstract opinion, class value, and the like, and the narrative materials with which we will be working here. The ideologeme is an amphibious formation, whose essential structural characteristic may be described as its possibility to manifest itself either as a pseudoidea – a conceptual or belief system, an abstract value, an opinion or prejudice – or as a protonarrative, a kind of ultimate class fantasy about the "collective characters" which are the classes in opposition. This duality means that the basic requirement for the full description of the ideologeme is already given in advance: as a construct it must be susceptible to both a conceptual description and a narrative manifestation all at once. The ideologeme can of course be elaborated in either of these directions, taking on the finished appearance of a philosophical system on the one hand, or that of a cultural text on the other; but the ideological analysis of these finished cultural products requires us to demonstrate each one as a complex work of transformation on that ultimate raw material which is the ideologeme in question. The analyst's work is thus first that of the identification of the ideologeme, and, in many cases, of its initial naming in instances where for whatever reason it had not yet been registered as such. The immense preparatory task of identifying and inventorying such ideologemes has scarcely even begun, and to it the present book [*The Political Unconscious*] will make but the most modest contribution: most notably in its isolation of that fundamental nineteenth-century ideologeme which is the "theory" of *ressentiment*, and in its "unmasking" of ethics and the ethical binary opposition of good and evil as one of the fundamental forms of ideological thought in Western culture. However, our stress here and throughout on the fundamentally narrative character of such ideologemes (even where they seem to be articulated only as abstract conceptual beliefs or values) will offer the advantage of restoring the complexity of the transactions between opinion and protonarrative or libidinal fantasy. Thus we will observe, in the case of Balzac, the generation of an overt and constituted ideological and political "value system" out of the operation of an essentially narrative and fantasy dynamic; the chapter on Gissing, on the other hand, will show how an already constituted "narrative paradigm" emits an ideological message in its own right without the mediation of authorial intervention.[16]

This focus or horizon, that of class struggle and its antagonistic discourses, is, as we have already suggested, not the ultimate form a Marxist analysis of culture can take. The example just alluded to – that of the seventeenth-century English revolution, in which the various classes and class fractions found themselves obliged to articulate their ideological struggles through the shared medium of a religious master code – can serve to dramatize the shift whereby these objects of study are reconstituted into a structurally distinct "text" specific to this final enlargement of the analytical frame. For the possibility of a displacement in emphasis is already given in this example: we have suggested that within the apparent unity of the theological code, the fundamental difference of antagonistic class positions can be made to emerge. In that case, the inverse move is also possible, and such concrete semantic differences can on the contrary be focused in such a way that what emerges is rather the all-embracing unity of a single code which they must share and which thus characterizes the larger unity of the social system. This new object – code, sign system, or system of the production of signs and codes – thus becomes an index of an entity of study which greatly transcends those earlier ones of the narrowly political (the symbolic act), and the social (class discourse and the ideologeme), and which we have proposed to term the historical in the larger sense of this word. Here the organizing unity will be what the Marxian tradition designates as a *mode of production*.

I have already observed that the "problematic" of modes of production is the most vital new area of Marxist theory in all the disciplines today; not paradoxically, it is also one of the most traditional, and we must therefore, in a brief preliminary way, sketch in the "sequence" of modes of production as classical Marxism, from Marx and Engels to Stalin, tended to enumerate them.[17] These modes, or "stages" of human society, have traditionally included the following: primitive communism or tribal society (the horde), the *gens* or hierarchical kinship societies (neolithic society), the Asiatic mode of production (so-called Oriental despotism), the *polis* or an oligarchical slaveholding society (the ancient mode of production), feudalism, capitalism, and communism (with a good deal of debate as to whether the "transitional" stage between these last – sometimes called "socialism" – is a genuine mode of production in its own right or not). What is more significant in the present context is that even this schematic or mechanical conception of historical "stages" (what the Althusserians have systematically criticized under the term "historicism") includes the notion of a cultural dominant or form of ideological coding specific to each mode of production. Following the same order these have generally been conceived as magic and mythic narrative, kinship, religion or the sacred, "politics" according to the narrower category of citizenship in the ancient city state, relations of personal domination, commodity reification, and (presumably) original and as yet nowhere fully developed forms of collective or communal association.

Before we can determine the cultural "text" or object of study specific to the horizon of modes of production, however, we must make two preliminary remarks about the methodological problems it raises. The first will bear on whether the concept of "mode of production" is a synchronic one, while the second will address the temptation to use the various modes of production for a classifying or typologizing operation, in which cultural texts are simply dropped into so many separate compartments.

Indeed, a number of theorists have been disturbed by the apparent convergence between the properly Marxian notion of an all-embracing and all-structuring mode of production (which assigns everything within itself – culture, ideological production, class articulation, technology – a specific and unique place), and non-Marxist visions of a "total system" in which the various elements or levels of social life are programmed in some increasingly constricting way. Weber's dramatic notion of the "iron cage" of an increasingly bureaucratic society,[18] Foucault's image of the gridwork of an ever more pervasive "political technology of the body,"[19] but also more traditional "synchronic" accounts of the cultural programming of a given historical "moment," such as those that have variously been proposed from Vico and Hegel to Spengler and Deleuze – all such monolithic models of the cultural unity of a given historical period have tended to confirm the suspicions of a dialectical tradition about the dangers of an emergent "synchronic" thought, in which change and development are relegated to the marginalized category of the merely "diachronic," the contingent or the rigorously nonmeaningful (and this, even where, as with Althusser, such models of cultural unity are attacked as forms of a more properly Hegelian and idealistic "expressive causality"). This theoretical foreboding about the limits of synchronic thought can perhaps be most immediately grasped in the political area, where the model of the "total system" would seem slowly and inexorably to eliminate any possibility of the *negative* as such, and to reintegrate the place of an oppositional or even merely "critical" practice and resistance back into the system as the latter's mere inversion. In particular, everything about class struggle that was anticipatory in the older dialectical framework, and seen as an emergent space for radically new social relations, would seem, in the synchronic model, to reduce itself to practices that in fact tend to reinforce the very system that foresaw and dictated their specific limits. This is the sense in which Jean Baudrillard has suggested that the "total-system" view of contemporary society reduces the options of resistance to anarchist gestures, to the sole remaining ultimate protests of the wildcat strike, terrorism, and death. Meanwhile, in the framework of the analysis of culture also, the latter's integration into a synchronic model would seem to empty cultural production of all its antisystemic capacities, and to "unmask" even the works of an overtly oppositional or political stance as instruments ultimately pro-grammed by the system itself.

It is, however, precisely the notion of a series of enlarging theoretical horizons proposed here that can assign these disturbing synchronic frameworks their appropriate analytical places and dictate their proper use. This notion projects a long view of history which is inconsistent with concrete political action and class struggle only if the specificity of the horizons is not respected; thus, even if the concept of a mode of production is to be considered a synchronic one (and we will see in a moment that things are somewhat more complicated than this), at the level of historical abstraction at which such a concept is properly to be used, the lesson of the "vision" of a total system is for the short run one of the structural limits imposed on praxis rather than the latter's impossibility.

The theoretical problem with the synchronic systems enumerated above lies elsewhere, and less in their analytical framework than in what in a Marxist perspective might be called their infrastructural regrounding. Historically, such systems have tended to fall into two general groups, which one might term respectively the hard and soft visions of the total system. The first group projects a fantasy future of a "totalitarian" type in which the mechanisms of domination – whether these are understood as part of the more general process of bureaucratization, or on the other hand derive more immediately from the deployment of physical and ideological force – are grasped as irrevocable and increasingly pervasive tendencies whose mission is to colonize the last remnants and survivals of human freedom – to occupy and organize, in other words, what still persists of Nature objectively and subjectively (very schematically, the Third World and the Unconscious).

This group of theories can perhaps hastily be associated with the central names of Weber and Foucault; the second group may then be associated with names such as those of Jean Baudrillard and the American theorists of a "post-industrial society."[20] For this second group, the characteristics of the total system of contemporary world society are less those of political domination than those of cultural programming and penetration: not the iron cage, but rather the *société de consommation* with its consumption of images and simulacra, its free-floating signifiers and its effacement of the older structures of social class and traditional ideological hegemony. For both groups, world capitalism is in evolution toward a system which is not socialist in any classical sense, on the one hand the nightmare of total control and on the other the polymorphous or schizophrenic intensities of some ultimate counterculture (which may be no less disturbing for some than the overtly threatening characteristics of the first vision). What one must add is that neither kind of analysis respects the Marxian injunction of the "ultimately determining instance" of economic organization and tendencies: for both, indeed, economics (or political economy) of that type is in the new total system of the contemporary world at an end, and the economic finds itself in both reassigned to a secondary and nondeterminant position beneath the new dominant of political power or of cultural production respectively.

There exist, however, within Marxism itself precise equivalents to these two non-Marxian visions of the contemporary total system: rewritings, if one likes, of both in specifically Marxian and "economic" terms. These are the analyses of late capitalism in terms of *capitalogic*[21] and of *disaccumulation*.[22] respectively; and while this book [*The Political Unconscious*] is clearly not the place to discuss such theories at any length, it must be observed here that both, seeing the originality of the contemporary situation in terms of systemic tendencies *within* capitalism, reassert the theoretical priority of the organizing concept of the mode of production which we have been concerned to argue.

We must therefore now turn to the second related problem about this third and ultimate horizon, and deal briefly with the objection that cultural analysis pursued within it will tend toward a purely typological or classificatory operation, in which we are called upon to "decide" such issues as whether Milton is to be read within a "precapitalist" or a nascent capitalist context, and so forth. I have insisted elsewhere on the sterility of such classificatory procedures, which may always, it seems to me, be taken as symptoms and indices of the repression of a more genuinely dialectical or historical practice of cultural analysis. This diagnosis may now be expanded to cover all three horizons at issue here, where the practice of homology, that of a merely "sociological" search for some social or class equivalent, and that, finally, of the use of some typology of social and cultural systems, respectively, may stand as examples of the misuse of these three frameworks. Furthermore, just as in our discussion of the first two we have stressed the centrality of the category of contradiction for any Marxist analysis (seen, within the first horizon, as that which the cultural and ideological artifact tries to "resolve," and in the second as the nature of the social and class conflict within which a given work is one act or gesture), so too here we can effectively validate the horizon of the mode of production by showing the form contradiction takes on this level, and the relationship of the cultural object to it.

Before we do so, we must take note of more recent objections to the very concept of the mode of production. The traditional schema of the various modes of production as so many historical "stages" has generally been felt to be unsatisfactory, not least because it encourages the kind of typologizing criticized above, in political quite as much as in cultural analysis. (The form taken in political analysis is evidently the procedure which consists in "deciding" whether a given conjuncture is to be assigned to a moment within feudalism – the result being a demand for bourgeois and parliamentary rights – or within capitalism – with the accompanying "reformist" strategy – or, on the contrary, a genuine "revolutionary" moment – in which case the appropriate revolutionary strategy is then deduced.)

On the other hand, it has become increasingly clear to a number of contemporary theorists that such classification of "empirical" materials within this or that abstract category is impermissible in large part because of the level of abstraction of the concept of a mode of production: no historical society has ever "embodied" a mode of production in any pure state (nor is *Capital* the description of a historical society, but rather the construction of the abstract concept of capitalism). This has led certain contemporary theorists, most notably Nicos Poulantzas,[23] to insist on the distinction between a "mode of production" as a purely theoretical construction and a "social formation" that would involve the description of some historical society at a certain moment of its development. This distinction seems inadequate and even misleading, to the degree that it encourages the very empirical thinking which it was concerned to denounce, in other words, subsuming a particular or an empirical "fact" under this or that corresponding "abstraction." Yet one feature of Poulantzas' discussion of the "social formation" may be retained: his suggestion that every social formation or historically existing society has in fact consisted in the overlay and structural coexistence of *several* modes of production all at once, including vestiges and survivals of older modes of production, now relegated to structurally dependent positions within the new, as well as anticipatory tendencies which are potentially inconsistent with the existing system but have not yet generated an autonomous space of their own.

But if this suggestion is valid, then the problems of the "synchronic" system and of the typological temptation are both solved at one stroke. What is synchronic is the "concept" of the mode of production; the moment of the historical coexistence of several modes of production is not synchronic in this sense, but open to history in a dialectical way. The temptation to classify texts according to the appropriate mode of production is thereby removed, since the texts emerge in a space in which we may expect them to be crisscrossed and intersected by a variety of impulses from contradictory modes of cultural production all at once.

Yet we have still not characterized the specific object of study which is constructed by this new and final horizon. It cannot, as we have shown, consist in the concept of an individual mode of production (any more than, in our second horizon, the specific object of study could consist in a particular social class in isolation from the others). We will therefore suggest that this new and ultimate object may be designated, drawing on recent historical experience, as *cultural revolution*, that moment in which the coexistence of various modes of production becomes visibly antagonistic, their contradictions moving to the very center of political, social, and historical life. The incomplete Chinese experiment with a "proletarian" cultural revolution may be invoked in support of the proposition that previous history has known a whole range of equivalents for similar processes to which the term may legitimately be extended. So the Western Enlightenment may be grasped as part of a properly bourgeois cultural revolution, in which the values and the discourse, the habits and the daily space, of the *ancien régime* were systematically dismantled so that in their place could be set the new conceptualities, habits and life forms, and value systems of a capitalist market society. This process clearly involved a vaster historical rhythm than such punctual historical events as the French Revolution or the Industrial Revolution, and includes in its *longue durée* such phenomena as those described by Weber in *The Protestant Ethic and the Spirit of Capitalism* – a work that can now in its turn be read as a contribution to the study of the bourgeois cultural revolution, just as the corpus of work on romanticism is now repositioned as the study of a significant and ambiguous moment in the resistance to this particular "great transformation," alongside the more specifically "popular" (precapitalist as well as working-class) forms of cultural resistance.

But if this is the case, then we must go further and suggest that all previous modes of production have been accompanied by cultural revolutions specific to them of which the neolithic "cultural revolution," say, the triumph of patriarchy over the older matriarchal or tribal forms, or the victory of Hellenic "justice" and the new legality of the *polis* over the vendetta system are only the most dramatic manifestations. The concept of cultural revolution, then – or more precisely, the reconstruction of the materials of cultural and literary history in the form of this new "text" or object of study which is cultural revolution – may be expected to project a whole new framework for the humanities, in which the study of culture in the widest sense could be placed on a materialist basis.

This description is, however, misleading to the degree to which it suggests that "cultural revolution" is a phenomenon limited to so-called "transitional" periods, during which social formations dominated by one mode of production undergo a radical restructuration in the course of which a different "dominant" emerges. The problem of such "transitions" is a traditional crux of the Marxian problematic of modes of production, nor can it be said that any of the solutions proposed, from Marx's own fragmentary discussions to the recent model of Etienne Balibar, are altogether satisfactory, since in all of them the inconsistency between a "synchronic" description of a given system and a "diachronic" account of the passage from one system to another seems to return with undiminished intensity. But our own discussion began with the idea that a given social formation consisted in the coexistence of various synchronic systems or modes of production, each with its own dynamic or time scheme – a kind of metasynchronicity, if one likes – while we have now shifted to a description of cultural revolution which has been couched in the more dia-chronic language of systemic transformation. I will therefore suggest that these two apparently inconsistent accounts are simply the twin perspectives which our thinking (and our presentation or *Darstellung* of that thinking) can take on this same vast historical object. Just as overt revolution is no punctual event either, but brings to the surface the innumerable daily struggles and forms of class polarization which are at work in the whole course of social life that precedes it, and which are therefore latent and implicit in "prerevolutionary" social experience, made visible as the latter's deep structure only in such "moments of truth" – so also the overtly "transitional" moments of cultural revolution are themselves but the passage to the surface of a permanent process in human societies, of a permanent struggle between the various coexisting modes of production. The triumphant moment in which a new systemic dominant gains ascendency is therefore only the diachronic manifestation of a constant struggle for the perpetuation and reproduction of its dominance, a struggle which must continue throughout its life course, accompanied at all moments by the systemic or structural antagonism of those older and newer modes of production that resist assimilation or seek deliverance from it. The task of cultural and social analysis thus construed within this final horizon will then clearly be the rewriting of its materials in such a way that this perpetual cultural revolution can be apprehended and read as the deeper and more permanent constitutive structure in which the empirical textual objects know intelligibility.

Cultural revolution thus conceived may be said to be beyond the opposition between synchrony and diachrony, and to correspond roughly to what Ernst

Bloch has called the *Ungleichzeitigkeit* (or "nonsynchronous development") of cultural and social life.[24] Such a view imposes a new use of concepts of periodization, and in particular of that older schema of the "linear" stages which is here preserved and canceled all at once. We will deal more fully with the specific problems of periodization in the next chapter [not included here]: suffice it to say at this point that such categories are produced within an initial diachronic or narrative framework, but become usable only when that initial framework has been annulled, allowing us now to coordinate or articulate categories of diachronic origin (the various distinct modes of production) in what is now a synchronic or meta-synchronic way.

We have, however, not yet specified the nature of the textual object which is constructed by this third horizon of cultural revolution, and which would be the equivalent within this dialectically new framework of the objects of our first two horizons – the symbolic act, and the ideologeme or dialogical organization of class discourse. I will suggest that within this final horizon the individual text or cultural artifact (with its appearance of autonomy which was dissolved in specific and original ways within the first two horizons as well) is here restructured as a field of force in which the dynamics of sign systems of several distinct modes of production can be registered and apprehended. These dynamics – the newly constituted "text" of our third horizon – make up what can be termed *the ideology of form*, that is, the determinate contradiction of the specific messages emitted by the varied sign systems which coexist in a given artistic process as well as in its general social formation.

What must now be stressed is that at this level "form" is apprehended as content. The study of the ideology of form is no doubt grounded on a technical and formalistic analysis in the narrower sense, even though, unlike much traditional formal analysis, it seeks to reveal the active presence within the text of a number of discontinuous and heterogeneous formal processes. But at the level of analysis in question here, a dialectical reversal has taken place in which it has become possible to grasp such formal processes as sedimented content in their own right, as carrying ideological messages of their own, distinct from the ostensible or manifest content of the works; it has become possible, in other words, to display such formal operations from the standpoint of what Louis Hjelmslev will call the "content of form" rather than the latter's "expression," which is generally the object of the various more narrowly formalizing approaches. The simplest and most accessible demonstration of this reversal may be found in the area of literary genre. Our next chapter [not included here], indeed, will model the process whereby generic specification and description can, in a given historical text, be transformed into the detection of a host of distinct generic messages – some of them objectified survivals from older modes of cultural production, some anticipatory, but all together projecting a formal conjuncture through which the "conjuncture" of coexisting modes of production at a given historical moment can be detected and allegorically articulated.

Meanwhile, that what we have called the ideology of form is something other than a retreat from social and historical questions into the more narrowly formal may be suggested by the relevance of this final perspective to more overtly political and theoretical concerns; we may take the much debated relation of Marxism to feminism as a particularly revealing illustration. The notion of overlapping modes of production outlined above has indeed the advantage of allowing us to short-circuit the false problem of the priority of the economic over the sexual, or of sexual oppression over that of social class. In our present perspective, it becomes clear that sexism and the patriarchal are to be grasped as the sedimentation and the virulent survival of forms of alienation specific to the oldest mode of production of human history, with its division of labor between men and women, and its division of power between youth and elder. The analysis of the ideology of form, properly completed, should reveal the formal persistence of such archaic structures of alienation – and the sign systems specific to them – beneath the overlay of all the more recent and historically original types of alienation – such as political domination and commodity reification – which have become the dominants of that most complex of all cultural revolutions, late capitalism, in which all the earlier modes of production in one way or another structurally coexist. The affirmation of radical feminism, therefore, that to annul the patriarchal is the most *radical* political act – insofar as it includes and subsumes more partial demands, such as the liberation from the commodity form – is thus perfectly consistent with an expanded Marxian framework, for which the transformation of our own dominant mode of production must be accompanied and completed by an equally radical restructuration of all the more archaic modes of production with which it structurally coexists.

With this final horizon, then, we emerge into a space in which History itself becomes the ultimate ground as well as the untranscendable limit of our understanding in general and our textual interpretations in particular. This is, of course, also the moment in which the whole problem of interpretive priorities returns with a vengeance, and in which the practitioners of alternate or rival interpretive codes – far from having been persuaded that History is an interpretive code that includes and transcends all the others – will again assert "History" as simply one more code among others, with no particularly privileged status. This is most succinctly achieved when the critics of Marxist interpretation, borrowing its own traditional terminology, suggest that the Marxian interpretive operation involves a thematization and a reification of "History" which is not markedly different from the process whereby the other interpretive codes produce their own forms of thematic closure and offer themselves as absolute methods.

It should by now be clear that nothing is to be gained by opposing one reified theme – History – by another – Language – in a polemic debate as to ultimate priority of one over the other. The influential forms this debate has taken in recent years – as in Jürgen Habermas' attempt to subsume the "Marxist" model of production beneath a more all-embracing model of "communication" or intersubjectivity,[25] or in Umberto Eco's assertion of the priority of the Symbolic in general over the technological and productive systems which it must organize as *signs* before they can be used as *tools*[26] – are based on the misconception that the Marxian category of a "mode of production" is a form of technological or "productionist" determinism.

It would seem therefore more useful to ask ourselves, in conclusion, how History as a ground and as an absent cause can be conceived in such a way as to resist such thematization or reification, such transformation back into one optional code among others. We may suggest such a possibility obliquely by attention to what the Aristotelians would call the generic satisfaction specific to the form of the great monuments of historiography, or what the semioticians might call the "history-effect" of such narrative texts. Whatever the raw material on which historiographic form works (and we will here only touch on that most widespread type of material which is the sheer chronology of fact as it is produced by the rote-drill of the history manual), the "emotion" of great historiographic form can then always be seen as the radical restructuration of that inert material, in this instance the powerful reorganization of otherwise inert chronological and "linear" data in the form of Necessity: why what happened (at first received as "empirical" fact) had to happen the way it did. From this perspective, then, causality is only one of the possible tropes by which this formal restructuration can be achieved, although it has obviously been a privileged and historically significant one. Meanwhile, should it be objected that Marxism is rather a "comic" or "romance" paradigm, one which sees history in the salvational perspective of some ultimate liberation, we must observe that the most powerful realizations of a Marxist historiography – from Marx's own narratives of the 1848 revolution through the rich and varied canonical studies of the dynamics of the Revolution of 1789 all the way to Charles Bettelheim's study of the Soviet revolutionary experience – remain visions of historical Necessity in the sense evoked above. But Necessity is here represented in the form of the inexorable logic involved in the determinate failure of all the revolutions that have taken place in human history: the ultimate Marxian presupposition – that socialist revolution can only be a total and worldwide process (and that this in turn presupposes the completion of the capitalist "revolution" and of the process of commodification on a global scale)

– is the perspective in which the failure or the blockage, the contradictory reversal or functional inversion, of this or that local revolutionary process is grasped as "inevitable," and as the operation of objective limits.

History is therefore the experience of Necessity, and it is this alone which can forestall its thematization or reification as a mere object of representation or as one master code among many others. Necessity is not in that sense a type of content, but rather the inexorable *form* of events; it is therefore a narrative category in the enlarged sense of some properly narrative political unconscious which has been argued here, a retextualization of History which does not propose the latter as some new representation or "vision," some new content, but as the formal effects of what Althusser, following Spinoza, calls an "absent cause." Conceived in this sense, History is what hurts, it is what refuses desire and sets inexorable limits to individual as well as collective praxis, which its "ruses" turn into grisly and ironic reversals of their overt intention. But this History can be apprehended only through its effects, and never directly as some reified force. This is indeed the ultimate sense in which History as ground and untranscendable horizon needs no particular theoretical justification: we may be sure that its alienating necessities will not forget us, however much we might prefer to ignore them.

Notes

1   See "The ideology of the text," *Salmagundi*, 31–2 (Fall, 1975/Winter, 1976), pp. 204–46.
2   This is to my mind the relevance of a theory of "modes of production" for literary and cultural criticism; see, for further reflections on this issue and a more explicit statement on the "historicist" tendencies of Marxism, my "Marxism and historicism," *New Literary History*, 11 (Autumn, 1979), pp. 41–73.
3   "The realm of freedom actually begins only where labor which is in fact determined by necessity and mundane considerations ceases; thus in the very nature of things it lies beyond the sphere of actual material production. Just as the savage must wrestle with Nature to satisfy his wants, to maintain and reproduce life, so must civilized man, and he must do so in all social formations and under all possible modes of production. With his development this realm of physical necessity expands as a result of his wants; but, at the same time, the forces of production which satisfy these wants also increase. Freedom in this field can only consist in socialized men, the associated producers, rationally regulating their interchange with Nature, bringing it under their common control, instead of being ruled by it as by the blind forces of Nature; and achieving this with the least expenditure of energy and under conditions most favorable to, and worthy of, their human nature. But it nonetheless still remains a realm of necessity. Beyond it begins that development of human energy

which is an end in itself, the true realm of freedom, which, however, can blossom forth only with this realm of necessity as its basis," Karl Marx, *Capital* (New York, International Publishers, 1977), III, p. 820.

4 Karl Marx and Friedrich Engels, "The Communist Manifesto," in K. Marx, *On Revolution*, ed. and trans. S. K. Padover (New York, McGraw-Hill, 1971), p. 81.

5 A useful discussion of the phenomenological concept of "horizon" may be found in Hans-Georg Gadamer, *Truth and Method*, trans. G. Barden and J. Cumming (New York, Seabury, 1975), pp. 216–20, 267–74. It will become clear in the course of my subsequent discussion that a Marxian conception of our relationship to the past requires a sense of our radical difference from earlier cultures which is not adequately allowed for in Gadamer's influential notion of *Horizontverschmelzung* (fusion of horizons). This is perhaps also the moment to add that from the perspective of Marxism as an "absolute historicism," the stark antithesis proposed by E. D. Hirsch, Jr, between Gadamer's historicist "relativism" and Hirsch's own conception of a more absolute interpretive validity, will no longer seem particularly irreconcilable. Hirsch's distinction between *Sinn* and *Bedeutung*, between the scientific analysis of a text's intrinsic "meaning" and what he is pleased to call our "ethical" evaluation of its "significance" for us (see, for example, *The Aims of Interpretation* [Chicago, University of Chicago Press, 1976]), corresponds to the traditional Marxist distinction between science and ideology, particularly as it has been retheorized by the Althusserians. It is surely a useful working distinction, although in the light of current revisions of the idea of science one should probably make no larger theoretical claims for it than this operative one.

6 Claude Lévi-Strauss, *Structural Anthropology*, trans. C. Jacobson and B. G. Schoepf (New York, Basic Books, 1963), pp. 206–31. The later four-volume *Mythologiques* reverse the perspective of this analysis: where the earlier essay focused on the individual mythic *parole* or utterance, the later series models the entire system or *langue* in terms of which the various individual myths are related to each other. *Mythologiques* should therefore rather be used as suggestive material on the historical difference between the narrative mode of production of primitive societies and that of our own: in this sense, the later work would find its place in the third and final horizon of interpretation.

7 Claude Lévi-Strauss, *Tristes tropiques*, trans. John Russell (New York, Atheneum, 1971), p. 176.

8 Ibid., pp. 179–80.

9 Kenneth Burke, *The Philosophy of Literary Form* (Berkeley, University of California Press, 1973), pp. 5–6; and see also my "Symbolic inference; or, Kenneth Burke and ideological analysis," *Critical Inquiry*, 4 (Spring, 1978), pp. 507–23.

10 See Fredric Jameson, *The Political Unconscious* (Ithaca, NY, Cornell University Press, 1981), ch. 3, n. 13, and pp. 46–9.

11 *Marxism and Form* (Princeton, NJ, Princeton University Press, 1971), pp. 376–82; and *The Political Unconscious*, pp. 288–91. The most authoritative contemporary Marxist statement of this view of social class is to be found in E. P. Thompson, *The Making of the English Working Class* (New York, Vintage, 1966), pp. 9–11; in *The*

Poverty of Theory (London, Merlin, 1978), Thompson has argued that his view of classes is incompatible with "structural" Marxism, for which classes are not "subjects" but rather "positions" within the social totality; see, for the Althusserian position, Nicos Poulantzas, *Political Power and Social Classes*, trans. Timothy O'Hagan (London, New Left Books, 1973).

12   Mikhail Bakhtin, *Problems of Dostoyevsky's Poetics*, trans. R. W. Rotsel (Ann Arbor, Ardis, 1973), pp. 153–69. See also Bakhtin's important book on linguistics, written under the name of V. N. Voloshinov, *Marxism and the Philosophy of Language*, trans. L. Matejka and I. R. Titunik (New York, Seminar Press, 1973), pp. 83–98; and Bakhtin's posthumous collection, *Esthétique et théorie du roman*, trans. Daria Olivier (Paris, Gallimard, 1978), esp. pp. 152–82.

13   See Christopher Hill, *The World Turned Upside Down* (London, Temple Smith, 1972).

14   Ernst Bloch, "Zerstörung, Rettung des Mythos durch Licht," in *Verfremdungen* I (Frankfurt, Suhrkamp, 1963), pp. 152–62.

15   Eugene Genovese, *Roll Jordan Roll* (New York, Vintage, 1976), pp. 161–284.

16   See *The Political Unconscious*, pp. 151–84 on Balzac, and pp. 185–205 on Gissing.

17   The "classical" texts on modes of production, besides Lewis Henry Morgan's *Ancient Society* (1877), are Karl Marx, *Pre-capitalist Economic Formations*, a section of the *Grundrisse* (1857–58) published separately by Eric Hobsbawm (New York, International, 1965), and Friedrich Engels, *The Family, Private Property, and the State* (1884). Important recent contributions to the mode of production "debate" include Etienne Balibar's contribution to Althusser's collective volume, *Reading Capital*, trans. Ben Brewster (London, New Left Books, 1970); Emmanuel Terray, *Marxism and "Primitive" Societies*, trans. M. Klopper (New York, Monthly Review, 1972); Maurice Godelier, *Horizon: trajets marxistes en anthropologie* (Paris, Maspéro, 1973); J. Chesneaux (ed.), *Sur le "mode de production asiatique"* (Paris, Editions Sociales, 1969); and Barry Hindess and Paul Hirst, *Pre-capitalist Modes of Production* (London, Routledge and Kegan Paul, 1975).

18   "The Puritan wanted to work in a calling; we are forced to do so. For when asceticism was carried out of monastic cells into everyday life, and began to dominate worldly morality, it did its part in building the tremendous cosmos of the modern economic order. This order is now bound to the technical and economic conditions of machine production which today determine the lives of all the individuals who are born into this mechanism, not only those directly concerned with economic acquisition, with irresistible force. Perhaps it will so determine them until the last ton of fossilized coal is burnt. In Baxter's view the care for external goods should only lie on the shoulders of the saint 'like a light cloak, which can be thrown aside at any moment.' But fate decreed that the cloak should become an iron cage;" *The Protestant Ethic and the Spirit of Capitalism*, trans. T. Parsons (New York, Scribners, 1958), p. 181.

19   Michel Foucault, *Surveiller et punir* (Paris, Gallimard, 1975), pp. 27–8 and passim.

20   Jean Baudrillard, *Le Système des objets* (Paris, Gallimard, 1968); *La Société de consommation* (Paris, Denöel, 1970); *Pour une économie politique du signe* (Paris,

Gallimard, 1972). The most influential statement of the American version of this "end of ideology"/consumer society position is, of course, that of Daniel Bell: see his *Coming of Post-industrial Society* (New York, Basic Books, 1973) and *The Cultural Contradictions of Capitalism* (New York, Basic Books, 1976).

21 See, for a review and critique of the basic literature, Stanley Aronowitz, "Marx, Braverman, and the logic of capital," *Insurgent Sociologist*, 8 (2/3) (Fall, 1978), pp. 126–46; and see also Hans-Georg Backhaus, "Zur Dialektik der Wertform," in A. Schmidt (ed.), *Beiträge zur marxistischen Erkenntnistheorie* (Frankfurt, Suhrkamp, 1969), pp. 128–52; and Helmut Reichelt, *Zur logischen Struktur des Kapitalbegriffs bei Karl Marx* (Frankfurt, Europäische Verlagsanstalt, 1970). For the Capitalogicians, the "materialist kernel" of Hegel is revealed by grasping the concrete or objective reality of Absolute Spirit (the Notion in-and-for-itself) as none other than capital (Reichelt, pp. 77–8). This tends, however, to force them into the post-Marxist position for which the dialectic is seen as the thought-mode proper only to capitalism (Backhaus, pp. 140–1): in that case, of course, the dialectic would become unnecessary and anachronistic in a society that had abolished the commodity form.

22 The basic texts on "disaccumulation theory" are Martin J. Sklar "On the proletarian revolution and the end of political-economic society," *Radical America*, 3 (3) (May–June, 1969), pp. 1–41; Jim O'Connor, "Productive and unproductive labor," *Politics and Society*, 5 (1975), pp. 297–336; Fred Block and Larry Hirschhorn, "New productive forces and the contradictions of contemporary capitalism," *Theory and Society*, 7 (1979), pp. 363–95; and Stanley Aronowitz, "The end of political economy", *Social Text*, 2 (1980), pp. 3–52.

23 Poulantzas, *Political Power and Social Classes*, pp. 13–16.

24 Ernst Bloch, "Nonsynchronism and dialectics," *New German Critique*, 11 (Spring, 1977), pp. 22–38; or *Erbschaft dieser Zeit* (Frankfurt, Suhrkamp, 1973). The "nonsynchronous" use of the concept of mode of production outlined above is in my opinion the only way to fulfill Marx's well-known program for dialectical knowledge "of rising from the abstract to the concrete" (1857 Introduction, *Grundrisse*, p. 101). Marx there distinguished three stages of knowledge: (1) the notation of the particular (this would correspond to something like empirical history, the collection of data and descriptive materials on the variety of human societies); (2) the conquest of abstraction, the coming into being of a properly "bourgeois" science or of what Hegel called the categories of the Understanding (this moment, that of the construction of a static and purely classificatory concept of "modes of production," is what Hindess and Hirst quite properly criticize in *Pre-capitalist Modes of Production*); (3) the transcendence of abstraction by the dialectic, the "rise to the concrete," the setting in motion of hitherto static and typologizing categories by their reinsertion in a concrete historical situation (in the present context, this is achieved by moving from a classificatory use of the categories of modes of production to a perception of their dynamic and contradictory coexistence in a given cultural moment). Althusser's own epistemology, incidentally – Generalities I, II, and III (*Pour Marx* [Paris, Maspéro, 1965], pp.

187–90) – is a gloss on this same fundamental passage of the 1857 Introduction, but one which succeeds only too well in eliminating its dialectical spirit.

25 See Jürgen Habermas, *Knowledge and Human Interests*, trans. J. Shapiro (Boston, Beacon Press, 1971), esp. part I.

26 Umberto Eco, *A Theory of Semiotics* (Bloomington, Indiana University Press 1976), pp. 21–6.

2

Towards Dialectical Criticism

"Towards Dialectical Criticism" is the concluding chapter of Jameson's book Marxism and Form (1971). This selection includes the final portion of the chapter.

[...] What we have called interpretation is therefore a misnomer: content does not need to be treated or interpreted, precisely because it is essentially and immediately meaningful in itself, meaningful as gestures in situation are meaningful, or sentences in a conversation. Content is already concrete, in that it is essentially social and historical experience, and we may say of our own interpretive or hermeneutic work what the sculptor said of his stone, that it sufficed to remove all extraneous portions for the statue to appear, already latent in the marble block. Thus the process of criticism is not so much an interpretation of content as it is a revealing of it, a laying bare, a restoration of the original message, the original experience, beneath the distortions of the various kinds of censorship that have been at work upon it; and this revelation takes the form of an explanation of why the content was so distorted and is thus inseparable from a description of the mechanisms of this censorship itself.

And since I will speak of Susan Sontag shortly, let me take as a demonstration of this process her remarkable essay on science fiction, "The Imagination of Disaster," in which she reconstructs the basic paradigm of the science fiction movie, seeing in it an expression of "the deepest anxieties about contemporary existence ... about physical disaster, the prospect of universal mutilation and even annihilation ... [but more particularly] about the condition of the individual psyche."[1] All of this is so, and her essay provides a thorough working through of the materials of science fiction *taken on its own terms*. But what if those terms were themselves but a disguise, but the "manifest content" that served to distract us from some more basic satisfaction at work in the form?

For beneath the surface diversion of these entertainments, beneath the surface preoccupation of our minds as we watch them, introspection reveals a secondary motivation quite different from the one described above. For one thing, these works, particularly during the period of their heyday after the war and in the 1950s, rather openly express the mystique of the scientist: and by that I refer not so much to external prestige or social function as rather to a kind of collective folk-dream about the life-style of the scientist himself: he doesn't do *real* work (yet power is his and social status as well), his remuneration is not monetary or at the very least money seems no object, there is something fascinating about his laboratory (the home workshop magnified to institutional dimensions, a combination of factory and clinic), about the way he works nights (he isn't bound by routine or the eight-hour day), his very intellectual operations themselves are caricatures of what the non-intellectual imagines brainwork and book-knowledge to be. There is, moreover, the suggestion of a return to older modes of work organization: to the more personal and psychologically satisfying world of the guilds, in which the older scientist is the master and the younger one the apprentice, in which the daughter of the older man becomes naturally enough the symbol of the transfer of functions. And so forth: these traits may be indefinitely enumerated and elaborated. What I want to convey is that ultimately none of this has anything to do with science itself, but is rather a distorted reflection of our own feelings and dreams about *work* alienated and nonalienated: it is a wish-fulfillment that takes as its object a vision of ideal or what Marcuse would call "libidinally gratifying" work. But it is of course a wish-fulfillment of a peculiar type, and it is this structure that it is important to analyze.

For we do not have to do here with the kind of direct and open psychic identification and wish-fulfillment that might be illustrated (for the subject matter of scientists) by the works of a C. P. Snow, for instance. Rather, this is a symbolic gratification that wishes to conceal its own presence: thus the identification with the scientist is not here the mainspring of the plot, but rather its precondition only, and it is as though, in a rather Kantian way, symbolic gratification attached itself not to the events of the story but to that framework (the universe of science, the splitting of the atom, the astronomer's gaze into outer space) without which the story could not have come into being in the first place. In this perspective all the cataclysmic violence of the science fiction narrative – the toppling buildings, the state of siege, the monsters rising out of

Tokyo bay – is nothing but a pretext, serving both to divert the mind from its deepest operations and fantasies, and to motivate those fantasies as well.

No doubt we could go on and show that alongside this fantasy about work, there is present yet another kind which deals with collective life and which uses the cosmic emergencies of science fiction as a way of reliving a kind of wartime togetherness and morale: the drawing together of the survivors of planetary catastrophe is thus itself merely a distorted dream of a more humane collectivity and social organization. In this sense, the surface violence of the work is doubly motivated, for it can now be seen as a breaking through the routine boredom of middle-class life; while in either event, the violence in the disguise may be understood as the expression of rage at the nonrealization of the unconscious fantasies thus aroused.

The inner form of such an apparently negative and anxiety-ridden type of work is therefore a positive fantasy, one which we have expressed in the language of work satisfaction. The terms in which we describe this inner form or *Erlebnis* are however less important than the movement itself, by which we reemerge into that *place of the concrete* which has been described in a previous section as the mediation between private and public, between individual and socio-economic realities, between the existential and history itself. The task of a dialectical criticism is not indeed to *relate* these two dimensions: they always are related, both in our own life experience and in any genuine work of art. Rather, such criticism is called upon to articulate the work and its content in such a way that this relationship stands revealed, and is once more visible.

For we have to do with a relationship of identity which nonetheless requires a complete translation from one set of terms into the other: the two dimensions are one, and indeed the propaedeutic value of art lies in the way in which it permits us to grasp the essentially historical and social value of what we had otherwise taken to be a question of individual experience. Yet this is done by shifting levels or points of view, by moving from the experience to its ground or concrete situation, as from a form to a content or from a content to a form. The terms in which the socio-economic dimension of experience are described are however by no means limited to those of work, as the production of value and the transformation of the world. Indeed the essential content of such experience can never be determined in advance, and varies from the most substantial kinds of grappling with the world to the smallest and most minute specialized perceptions. Such authenticity is indeed more easily described in a negative way, as being that which escapes that emptiness of routine existence, or of some dull marking time: it is therefore that which restores us to some fitful contact with genuine experience, and the form which such contact takes is at one with the historical possibilities of the socio-economic organization itself.

Yet the terminology of work satisfaction is useful because it fulfills one function for which any other description of such inner form must account in one way or another: it explains the *censorship* of the work itself, it makes us understand why such an impulse had to be disguised in order to come to artistic satisfaction in the first place. For, particularly in middle-class society, the fact of work and of production – the very key to genuine historical thinking – is also a secret as carefully concealed as anything else in our culture. This is indeed the very meaning of the commodity as a form, to obliterate the signs of work on the product in order to make it easier for us to forget the class structure which is its organizational framework. It would indeed be surprising if such an occulta-tion of work did not leave its mark upon artistic production as well, both in the form and in the content, as Adorno shows us:

Works of art owe their existence to the social division of labor, to the separation of mental and physical work. In such a situation, however, they appear under the guise of independent existence; for their medium is not that of pure and autonomous spirit, but rather that of a spirit which having become object now claims to have surmounted the opposition between the two. Such contradiction obliges the work of art to conceal the fact that it is itself a human construction: its very pretension to meaning, and indeed that of human existence in general along with it, is the more convincingly maintained the less anything in it reminds us of its character as a product, and of the fact that it owes its own existence to spirit as to something outside itself. Art which can no longer in good conscience put up with this deception – its innermost principle – has already dissolved the only element in which it can realize itself . . . And if the autonomy of art in general is unthinkable without this concealment of work, the latter nonetheless becomes problematical, itself now a program, in late capitalism, under the domination of the exchange value and the increasing contradictions of such domination.[2]

There is thus given within the very concept of work – either in the form of the division of labor in general or in the more specialized types of production characteristic of capitalism – the principle of a censorship of the work process itself, of a repression of the traces of labor on the product.

When we turn now from popular culture to the more sophisticated artifacts of official literature, we find that the fact of artistic *elaboration* adds a new complexity to the structure of the work without essentially altering the model we have given. In particular, art-literature can be said to reckon the whole value of its own creation itself into the process, so that the inner form of literary works, at least in modern times, can be said to have as their subject either production as such or *literary* production as well – both being in any case distinct from the ostensible or manifest content of the work.

Thus it is a mistake to think, for instance, that the books of Hemingway deal essentially with such things as courage, love, and death; in reality, their deepest subject is simply the writing of a certain type of sentence, the practice of a determinate style. This is indeed the most "concrete" experience in Hemingway, yet to understand its relationship to the other, more dramatic experiences we must reformulate our notion of inner form after the more complex model of a *hierarchy of motivations*, in which the various elements of the work are ordered at various levels from the surface, and serve so to speak as pretexts each for the existence of a deeper one, so that in the long run everything in the work exists in order to bring to expression that deepest level of the work which is the concrete itself; or, reversing the model after the fashion of the Prague School, to *foreground* the work's most essential content.[3]

Thus the enormous influence of Hemingway as a kind of life model would seem to derive first from a kind of ethical content, not a "philosophy of life" so much as an instinctive and intransigent refusal of what suddenly turns out to have ceased to be real living. "It isn't fun any more": such is the irrevocable boundary line between euphoria and ill humor, between real life and a kind of failure to live which exasperates and poisons the existence of the hero and everyone else around him. Such are the two poles of Hemingway's creation: those incomparable moments of plenitude in nature on the one hand, and on the other, bitching and sudden moods, sudden fits of envy or temper. Both are present indeed almost emblematically in those luminous opening pages of *Across the River and into the Trees*, where the sullen boatman comes before Colonel Cantwell as the very harbinger of death itself. It is not too much to say that this opposition corresponds to a more general one between life among things and life with other people, between nature and society; indeed, Hemingway often said so himself: "People were always the limiters of happiness except for the very few who were as good as spring itself."[4]

Yet this, which would seem to be first and foremost a life experience, is in reality merely a projection of the style itself. Hemingway's great discovery was that there was possible a kind of return to the very sources of verbal productivity if you forgot about words entirely and merely concentrated on prearranging the objects that the words were supposed to describe. So the following, which has always struck me as being the very prototype of the Hemingway sentence: "From Smith's back door Liz could see ore barges way out in the lake going toward Boyne City. When she looked at them they didn't seem to be moving at all but if she went in and dried some more dishes and then came out again they would be out of sight beyond the point."[5] Something is left out: both the actual movement itself and that full style or *parole pleine* which would have somehow "rendered" it; and Hemingway has spoken in other connections as well of the importance of omission as a literary procedure.[6] Yet in the portrayals of ill humor something is omitted also: the space between the remarks, as it were, and it is this prearrangement, now practiced on human material, which gives the Hemingway dialogue its electrical effect. Thus one is wrong to say that Hemingway began by wishing to express or convey certain basic experiences; rather, he began by wishing to write a certain type of sentence, a kind of neutral *compte rendu* of external displacements, and very quickly he found that such a sentence could do two kinds of things well: register movement in the external world, and suggest the tension and fitful resentment between people which is intermittently expressed in their spoken comment.

So we return to our initial contention that what really happens in a Hemingway novel, the most essential event, the dominant category of experience for both writer and reader alike, is the process of writing; and this is perhaps clearest in a simpler work like the *Green Hills of Africa*, where the shooting of the animal in the content is but the pretext for the *description* of the shooting in the form. The reader is not so much interested in observing the kill as he is in whether Hemingway's language will be able to rise to the occasion:

A little beyond there a flock of guineas quick-legged across the road running steady-headed with the motion of trotters. As I jumped from the car and sprinted after them they rocketed up, their legs tucked close beneath them, heavy-bodied, short wings drumming, cackling, to go over the trees ahead. I dropped two that thumped hard when they fell and as they lay, wings beating, Abdullah cut their heads off so they would be legal eating.[7]

The real "pursuit" involved is thus the pursuit of the sentence itself.

From this central point in Hemingway's creation all the rest can be deduced: the experience of sentence-production is the form taken in Hemingway's world by nonalienated work. Writing, now conceived as a *skill*, is then assimilated to the other skills of hunting and bullfighting, of fishing and warfare, which project a total image of man's active and all-absorbing technical participation in the outside world. Such an ideology of technique clearly reflects the more general American work situation, where, in the context of the open frontier and the blurring of class structure, the American male is conventionally evaluated according to the number of different jobs he has had, and skills he possesses. The Hemingway cult of *machismo* is just this attempt to come to terms with the great industrial transformation of America after World War I: it satisfies the Protestant work ethic at the same time that it glorifies leisure; it reconciles the deepest and most life-giving impulses toward wholeness with a status quo in which only sports allow you to feel alive and undamaged.

As for the human environment of Hemingway's books, expatriation is itself a kind of device or pretext for them. For the immense and complex fabric of American social reality itself is clearly inaccessible to the careful and selective type of sentence which he practices: so it is useful to have to do with a reality thinned out, the reality of foreign cultures and of foreign languages, where the individual beings come before us not in the density of a concrete social situation in which we also are involved, but rather with the cleanness of objects which can be verbally circumscribed. And when at the end of his life the world began to change, and the Cuban Revolution made a retreat back within the borders of the United States in order, it does not seem too farfetched to speculate that it was the resistance of such American reality, which as a writer he had never practiced, that brought him to stylistic impotence and ultimate suicide.

If this suggests something of the way in which a Marxist criticism would reconstruct the inner form of a literary work, as both disguise and revelation of the concrete, it remains for us to say a word about the implications of such a theory for judgment or literary evaluations as they are currently practiced. For to claim that the task of the critic is to reveal this censored dimension of the work implies precisely that, at least in art as it is practiced today, in the society in which it is practiced, the surface of the work is a kind of mystification in its structure. This is the point, in other words, at which a Marxist criticism must once again come to terms with modernism in the arts, and I have already implied that the antimodernism of a Lukács (and of the more traditional Soviet critics) is at least partly a matter of taste and of cultural conditioning.

Nonetheless it seems to me that something more must be said in the face of such articulate defenses of modernism as Susan Sontag's "new sensibility" or Ihab Hassan's *Literature of Silence*. These theories reflect a coherent culture with which we are all familiar: John Cage's music, Andy Warhol's movies, novels by Burroughs, plays by Beckett, Godard, camp, Norman O. Brown, psychedelic experiences; and no critique can have any binding force which does not begin by submitting to the fascination of all these things as stylizations of reality.

It should be pointed out, however, that this new modernism differs from the older, classical one of the turn of the century in at least one very essential way: that older modernism was in its essence profoundly antisocial, and reckoned with the instinctive hostility of the middle-class public of which it stood as a negation and a refusal. What characterizes the new modernism is however precisely that it is *popular*: maybe not in small mid-Western towns, but in the dominant world of fashion and the mass media. That can only mean, to my mind, that there has come to be something socially useful about such art from the point of view of the existing socio-economic structure; or something deeply suspect about it, if your point of view is a revolutionary one.

Yet, it will be said, such art *expresses* American reality; and there, indeed, the ambiguity lies. Insofar as we are Americans, none of us can fail to react to such things as pop art which admirably express the tangible and material realities, the specificity of that American life which is ours. It should be clear, therefore, that a critique of the new modernism cannot be an external but only an internal affair, that it is part and parcel of an increasing self-consciousness (in the heightened, dialectical sense we have given to that term), and that it involves a judgment on ourselves fully as much as a judgment on the works of art to which we react. The ambiguity, in other words, is as much in the revolutionary's own position as it is in the art object: insofar as he is himself a product of the society he condemns, his revolutionary attitude is bound to presuppose a negation of himself, an initial subjective dissociation that has to precede the objective, political one. This is why the drama of the new art involves a more complicated cast of characters than the older struggle between the philistine and the modernist: these two, in the persons of the consumer and of the art salesman and stager of happenings, have begun to merge, and to them may be added a third character, in the form of the revolutionary unhappy consciousness we have described, which in our culture finds it increasingly difficult to distinguish between real and imaginary negation, or indeed between imaginary negation and the promotion of the positive itself.

The most telling criticism of the ideology of the new sensibility or the new mysticism still remains the comment of Marx on Hegel's notion of religion in the *Economic and Philosophic Manuscripts of 1844*. For just as the spokesmen for the new modernism claim that it *expresses* our society, so Hegel showed that religion was an expression of the human spirit, its *objectification*, with all the ambiguous hesitation between embodiment and alienation which that word implies. Thus, Hegel's system

implies that self-conscious man, insofar as he has recognized and superseded the spiritual world (or the universal spiritual mode of existence of his world) then confirms it again in this alienated form and presents it as his true existence; he reestablishes it and claims to *be at home in his other being*. Thus, for example, after superseding religion, when he has recognized religion as a product of self-alienation, he then finds a confirmation of himself in *religion as religion* ... Thus reason is at home in unreason as such. Man, who has recognized that he leads an alienated life in law, politics, etc., leads his true human life in this alienated life as such.[8]

So it is that from the recognition of a work of art as a disguised expression and an alienation of reality, to making your peace with the very necessity of such disguises and such alienation, it is but a step.

In this situation the function of literary criticism grows clear. Even if ours is a critical age, it does not seem to me very becoming in critics to exalt their activity to the level of literary creation, as is loosely done in France today. It is more honest and more dialectical to point out that the scope and relevance of criticism varies with the historical and ideological moment itself. Thus, it has been said that literary criticism was a privileged instrument in the struggle against nineteenth-century despotism (particularly in Czarist Russia), because it was the only way one could smuggle ideas and covert political commentary past the censor. This is now to be understood, not in an external, but in an inner and allegorical sense. The works of culture come to us as signs in an all-but-forgotten code, as symptoms of diseases no longer even recognized as such, as fragments of a totality we have long since lost the organs to see. In the older culture, the kinds of works which a Lukács called realistic were essentially those which carried their own interpretation built into them, which were at one and the same time fact and commentary on the fact. Now the two are once again sundered from each other, and the literary fact, like the other objects that make up our social reality, cries out for commentary, for interpretation, for decipherment, for diagnosis. It appeals to the other disciplines in vain: Anglo–American philosophy has long since been shorn of its dangerous speculative capacities, and as for political science, it suffices only to think of its distance from the great political and Utopian theories of the past to realize to what degree thought asphyxiates in our culture, with its absolute inability to imagine anything other than what is. It therefore falls to literary criticism to continue to compare the inside and the outside, existence and history, to continue to pass judgment on the abstract quality of life in the present, and to keep alive the idea of a concrete future. May it prove equal to the task!

Notes

1   Susan Sontag, *Against Interpretation, and Other Essays* (New York, Farrar, Straus and Giroux, 1966), p. 220.
2   Theodor W. Adorno, *Versuch über Wagner* (Berlin, Suhrkamp Verlag, 1952), p. 88.
3   This is perhaps the moment to say that I do not regard Formalism – either Czech or Russian – as being at all irreconcilable with Marxism: indeed, I think of the analysis of Hemingway that follows as being essentially a Formalist one; but will reserve a fuller discussion of the Formalist literary model, as well as of structuralism, for another place [see *The Prison-house of Language: A Critical Account of Structuralism and Russian Formalism* (Princeton, NJ, Princeton University Press, 1972)].
4   *A Moveable Feast* (New York, 1964), p. 49.
5   "Up in Michigan," in *The First Forty-nine Stories* (London, 1962), p. 80.
6   See, for instance, *Death in the Afternoon* (New York, 1932), p. 192: "If a writer of prose knows enough about what he is writing about he may omit things that he knows and the reader, if the writer is writing truly enough, will have a feeling of

those things as strongly as though the writer had stated them." And see also *A Moveable Feast*, p. 75.

7 *The Green Hills of Africa* (New York, 1935), pp. 35–6.

8 Karl Marx, *Early Writings*, trans. and edited by T. B. Bottomore (New York, McGraw-Hill, 1964), p. 210.

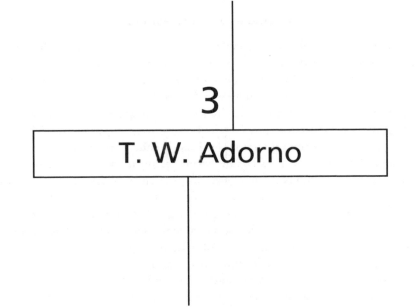

3

T. W. Adorno

The essay "T. W. Adorno," which was published in *Marxism and Form* (1971), is divided into four sections. This selection consists of the last section of the essay.

Perhaps the only way to keep faith with the Hegelian spirit of systematization in a fragmented universe is to be resolutely unsystematic. In this sense Adorno's thought is profoundly Hegelian, thinking its motifs through in a genuinely Hegelian spirit, facing thereby its principal formal problem: How to write chapters of a phenomenology when there is no longer any possibility of a whole? How to analyze the part as a part when the whole is not only no longer visible but even inconceivable? How to continue to use the terms subject and object as opposites which presuppose, in order to be meaningful, some possible synthesis, when there is no synthesis even imaginable, let alone present anywhere in concrete experience? What language to use to describe an alienated language, to what systems of reference to appeal when all systems of reference have been assimilated into the dominant system itself? How to see phenomena in the light of history, when the very movement and direction that gave history its meaning seem to have been swallowed up in sand?

Adorno himself, now in the guise of a theoretician of the essay as a form, has attributed its lack of development in Germany to the reluctance of German writers to surrender themselves to the almost frivolous and inconsequential freedom it presupposes, to make the painful apprenticeship of an intellectual life amidst the fragmentary and the ephemeral, to resist the ontological consolations of the *Hauptwerk* and the monumental and to stand in the very river of history

itself, suffering their provisory constructions to undergo those ceaseless metamorphoses which make up the life of an idea in time.

For the fundamental formal problem of the dialectical writer is precisely that
of continuity. He who has so intense a feeling for the massive continuity of
history itself is somehow paralyzed by that very awareness, as in some over-
loading of perception too physical to be any longer commensurable with
language. Where all the dimensions of history cohere in synchronic fashion,
the simple linear stories of earlier historians are no longer possible: now it is
diachrony and continuity which become problematical, mere working hypotheses. Adorno's larger form will therefore be a construct rather than a
narrative. In the work on Schoenberg [...] the formal continuity is not that
of Schoenberg's chronological development (although a loose feeling of chronology is maintained), but rather that of a series of abstract moments, of the
internal generation out of each other of the fundamental elements or parts of
Schoenberg's work seen as a total system. The individual work of art is therefore understood as a balance between inner organs, as an intersection of what
we will [...] call determinate categories of a stylistic nature, separate yet
profoundly interdependent on each other, such that a modification of one
(such as the intensity of instrumental coloration) immediately involves a shift
in the proportions of the others (temporal dimensions of the work, contra-
puntal development, and so forth). Change takes place in an artist's development as a result of such a modification in the relationships that obtain between
the fundamental categories of the work itself; the dialectical *critic*, however, will
plot this change on his graph as a series of moments which generate each other
out of their own internal contradictions.

When we turn now to the shorter pieces, and particularly to that series of
Notes on Literature which is perhaps Adorno's masterpiece, we find that as
mental operations they consist precisely in the perceptual registering and isolation, indeed in a virtual invention and naming for the first time, of those
categories or component parts of which the larger dialectical form had been an
interlocking construction. Let the subjects of some of them – the relation of
titles to works, sensitivity to punctuation, the uses of interlarded foreign words
and phrases, the physical impression books make – illustrate the working
method itself: they imply dialectical self-consciousness, a sudden distancing
which permits the most familiar elements of the reading experience to be
seen again strangely, as though for the first time, making visible the unexpected
articulation of the work into determinate categories or parts. The premise
remains that of the most thoroughgoing network of internal relationships, so
that it is precisely the apprehension of the apparently discrete and external – the
predilection in a novelist, for instance, for epigraphs to his chapters – which as a
heuristic principle leads to those deeper formal categories against which the

surface is organized. These essays are therefore the concrete working out of that formal category of Adorno's own production which we have described earlier under the sign of the *footnote*: an observation which may itself be thought of as a tribute to his method insofar as it amounts to a pastiche of it.

Such essays are thus the fragments of or footnotes to a totality which never comes into being; and what unites them, I am tempted to say, is less their thematic content than it is on the one hand their style, as a perpetual present in time of the process of dialectical thinking itself, and on the other their basic intellectual coordinates. For what as fragments they share in spite of the dispersal of their raw material is the common historical situation itself, that moment of history which marks and deforms in one way or another all the cultural phenomena which it produces and includes, and which serves as the framework within which we understand them. To this concrete situation itself the language makes fateful and monitory allusion: *the* administered world, *the* institutionalized society, *the* culture industry, *the* damaged subject – an image of our historical present which is Adorno's principal sociological contribution and which yet [. . .] is never expressed directly in the form of a *thesis*. Rather, it intervenes as a series of references to a state of things with which our familiarity is already presupposed, a reality with which we are presumed to be only too well acquainted. The mode is that characteristic German sarcasm which may be said to have been Nietzsche's contribution to the language and in which a constant play of cynical, colloquial expressions holds the disgraced real world at arm's length, while abstractions and buried conceptual rhymes compare it with the impossible ideal.

At the same time, there seems to me to be a profoundly stylistic motivation behind such indirection. We have said that for Adorno – as indeed for Hegel, as for all dialectical thinkers to the degree that they are genuinely dialectical – thinking dialectically means nothing more or less than the writing of dialectical sentences. It is a kind of stylistic obedience analogous to that which governs the work of art itself, where it is the shape of the sentences themselves, above and beyond all conscious reflection, that determines the choice of the raw material. So here also the quality of the idea is judged by the type of sentence through which it comes to expression. For insofar as dialectical thinking is thought about thought, thought to the second power, concrete thought about an object, which at the same time remains aware of its own intellectual operations in the very act of thinking, such self-consciousness must be inscribed in the very sentence itself. And insofar as dialectical thinking characteristically involves a conjunction of opposites or at least conceptually disparate phenomena, it may truly be said of the dialectical sentence what the Surrealists said about the image, namely, that its strength increases proportionately as the realities linked are distant and distinct from each other.

Thus, if the work of Adorno nowhere yields that bald statement about the administered world which would seem to be its presupposition, if he nowhere takes the trouble to express in outright sociological terms that theory of the structure of the "institutionalized society" which serves as a hidden explanation and essential cross-reference for all the phenomena under analysis, this is to be explained not only by the fact that such material belongs to a study of the infrastructure rather than of ideological materials, and that it is already implicit in classical Marxist economics, but above all by the feeling that such outright statements, such outright presentations of sheer *content*, are stylistically wrong, this stylistic failure being itself a mark and a reflection of some essential failure in the thought process itself. For in a purely sociological presentation the thinking subject eclipses himself and seems to let the social phenomenon come into view objectively, as a fact, as a thing in itself. Yet for all that the observer does not cease to have a position with respect to the thing observed, and his thoughts do not cease to be conscious operations even when he ceases to be aware of them as such. Thus the overt presentation of content in its own right, whether in sociological or in philosophical writing, stands condemned as a fall back into that positivistic and empirical illusion which dialectical thinking was designed to overcome.

Yet if what Sartre would have called the "untotalizable totality" of Adorno's system, its absent center, cannot be conceptually described as a positivistic "theory of society" in its own terms, if the placelessness of so-called objective thought is ruled out by the very commitment of the system to self-consciousness, there is nonetheless another way in which such an absent totality may be evoked. It is to this ultimate squaring of the circle that Adorno came in his two last and most systematic, most technically philosophical works, *Negative Dialectics* and *Aesthetic Theory*. Indeed, as the title of the former suggests, these works are designed to offer a theory of the untheorizable, to show why dialectical thinking is at one and the same time both indispensable and impossible, to keep the idea of system itself alive while intransigently dispelling the pretensions of any of the contingent and already realized systems to validity and even to existence.

The essential argument of *Negative Dialektik* and Adorno's ultimate philosophical position, seems to me to be an articulation on the theoretical level of that methodology which we have seen at work in a concrete, practical way in the earlier aesthetic essays and critical writings. For there we found that in the long run the content of a work of art stands judged by its form, and that it is the realized form of the work which offers the surest key to the vital possibilities of that determinate social moment from which it springs. Now the same methodological discovery proves valid in the realm of philosophical thought itself; and the practice of negative dialectics involves a constant movement away from the official content of an idea – as, for example, the "real" nature of freedom or of society as things in themselves – and toward the various determinate and contradictory forms which such ideas have taken, whose conceptual limits and inadequacies stand as immediate figures or symptoms of the limits of the concrete social situation itself.

So it is, at the very outset, with the idea of the dialectic itself, which had in Hegel "as its foundation and its result the primacy of the subject, or, in the well-known language of the introductory remarks to the *Logic*, the identity of identity and nonidentity."[1] But the very mark of the modern experience of the world itself is that precisely such identity is impossible, and that the primacy of the subject is an illusion, that subject and outside world can never find such ultimate identity or atonement under present historical circumstances. Yet if that ultimate synthesis toward which dialectical thought moves turns out to be unattainable it must not be thought that either of the terms of that synthesis, either of the conceptual opposites which are its subject and object, are any more satisfactory in their own right. The object considered in itself, the world taken as directly accessible content, results in the illusions of simple empirical positivism, or in an academic thinking which mistakes its own conceptual categories for solid parts and pieces of the real world itself. In the same way, the exclusive refuge in the subject results in what is for Adorno the subjective idealism of Heideggerian existentialism, a kind of ahistorical historicity, a mystique of anxiety, death, and individual destiny without any genuine content. Thus a negative dialectic has no choice but to affirm the notion and value of an ultimate synthesis, while negating its possibility and reality in every concrete case that comes before it.

Such thought therefore aims at maintaining contact with the concrete, painfully continuing a process of thinking about the world itself, at the same time that it rectifies its own inevitable falsifications at every moment, thus appearing to unravel everything it had been able to achieve. Yet not altogether: for the genuine content acquired remains, albeit in what Hegel would have called a canceled and transcended fashion; and negative dialectics does not result in an empty formalism, but rather in a thoroughgoing critique of forms, in a painstaking and well-nigh permanent destruction of every possible hypostasis of the various moments of thinking itself. For it is inevitable that every theory about the world, in its very moment of formation, tends to become an object for the mind and to be itself invested with all the prestige and permanency of a real thing in its own right, thus effacing the very dialectical process from which it emerged: and it is this optical illusion of the substantiality of thought itself which negative dialectics is designed to dispel.

So it is, for instance, that in a classic essay on society Adorno shows not only how every possible idea we form about society is necessarily partial and

imperfect, inadequate and contradictory, but also that those very *formal* contradictions are themselves the most precious indications as to how we stand with
respect to the concrete reality of social life itself at the present moment of time.
For society is clearly not some empirical object which we can meet and study
directly in our own experience: in this sense the neopositivistic criticism, which
considers the idea of society an inadmissible abstract construct or a mere
methodological hypothesis with no other kind of real existence, is justified.
At the same time society – precisely in the form of such an impossible,
suprapersonal abstraction – is present in the form of an ultimate constraint
upon every moment of our waking lives: absent, invisible, even untenable, it is
at the same time the most concrete of all the realities we have to face, and
"while the notion of society may not be deduced from any individual facts, nor
on the other hand be apprehended as an individual fact itself, there is nonetheless no social fact which is not determined by society as a whole."[2] Thus the
contradictions of pure thought turn out to reflect the contradictions of their
object as well, and that in the very moment when those initial conceptual
contradictions seemed to forbid us any access to the real object to which they
were supposed to correspond. Similarly, in the posthumous *Aesthetische Theorie*,
the traditional foundations of aesthetic philosophy are at once discredited and
given fresh justification by a constant shuttling back and forth between the
historical facts of the world of artistic practice and the abstract conceptual
categories through which that practice is perceived, at the same time that
they reflect it.

   We may therefore say that "the negative dialectic" represents an attempt to
save philosophy itself, and the very idea of philosophizing, from a fetishization
in time, from the optical illusion of stasis and permanency. Such antisystematic
systematization, with all the deep inner contradictions it involves, reminds me
of nothing quite so much as those equally contradictory monuments of modern
art and literature which in their attempt to say everything end up saying only
that one thing; which in their convulsive effort to present themselves, in almost
medieval fashion, as the very book of the world itself, end up being but one
book among others in a universe so disparate that no single thought can
encompass it. Thus Barthes' observation about Proust, "whose whole work
constitutes a simultaneous approach to and postponement of Literature itself,"
might also be applied to Adorno's philosophical position:

The writer thereby falls again into the power of time, for it is impossible to negate
within the temporal continuum without at the same time elaborating a positive art
which must be destroyed in its turn. Thus the greatest modern works linger as long as
possible, in a kind of miraculous suspension, on the very threshold of Literature itself, in

that waiting-room situation in which the density of life is given and protracted without yet being destroyed by the creation of an order of signs.[3]

It is therefore not to the discredit of *Negative Dialektik* to say that it is in the long run a massive failure; or, in different terms, that it stands as a kind of hyperconscious abstraction of that genuine totality of thought which Adorno's works taken as a whole embody. No doubt the emphasis on method and on the theory rather than the practice of negative dialectics risks giving an exaggerated and distorted importance to the moment of failure which is present in all modern thinking: and it is this overemphasis, more than anything else, which seems to me to account for that lack of political commitment with which radical students reproached Adorno at the end of his life. Yet his concrete studies remain incomparable models of the dialectical process, essays at once both systematic and occasional, in which pretext and consciousness meet to form the most luminous, if transitory, of figures or tropes of historical intelligibility: "like its object, knowledge remains shackled to the determinate contradiction."[4]

Notes

1   T. W. Adorno, *Negative Dialektik* (Frankfurt, Suhrkamp, 1966), p. 17.
2   T. W. Adorno, "Society," *Salmagundi*, 10–11 (Fall, 1969–Winter, 1970), p. 145.
3   Roland Barthes, *Le Degré zéro de l'écriture* (Paris, Seuil, 1953), pp. 58–9.
4   T. W. Adorno, *Philosophie der neuen Musik* (Frankfurt, Europäische Verlagsanstalt, 1958), p. 33.

4

Roland Barthes and Structuralism

This selection is taken from Jameson's book *The Prison-house of Language* (1972), which offers an interpretation and critique of both Russian form-alism and French structuralism. Our selection presents the work of Roland Barthes as representative of the structuralist movement.

(1)   The study of the dimension of the signified is what has been called (as opposed to a linguistics) a structural or semiological semantics: it is not, for all that, an any less profoundly paradoxical undertaking. The very notion of a signified as such would seem to presuppose that it had already been articulated into a system of signifiers in its own right, that is to say, dissolved *qua* signified and reorganized or assimilated into a sign–system of its own. Before the organizing and enabling act of speech itself, we cannot think of the signified as being anything more than an "undefined mass of concepts, which could be compared to a huge jelly-fish, with uncertain articulations and contours."[1] To speak of it any way at all, even to isolate the signified as such for purposes of description, would seem to imply that it had already found some determinate type of organization, or in other words that what we had taken to be a signified, what indeed had been a signified on one level and with respect to one particular type of signifier, turned out on another to be itself a signifying system with respect to some lower level of the signified, in a kind of infinite regression. We cannot at this point do any more than indicate such profound structural dissymmetry in the couple signifier/signified, the first of which seems able to

exist as a kind of free-floating autonomous organization, while the other is never visible directly to the naked eye.

(2) It is, however, an ambiguity which makes out the privileged place of Roland Barthes in the Structuralist movement; for in that peculiar distribution of roles and specialties which characterizes Structuralism, and in which Lévi-Strauss secures anthropology, and Lacan and Althusser are charged with the reinterpretations of Freud and Marx respectively, in which Derrida and Foucault assure the rewriting, the one of the history of philosophy, the other of the history of ideas, while Greimas and Todorov are at work transforming linguistics and literary criticism proper into sciences, a situation in which Merleau-Ponty, had he lived, might have assumed the central chair of philosophy itself, it would seem that the role left to devolve upon Roland Barthes is essentially that of sociologist. It is Barthes, indeed, who pursues what is basically a sociological investigation of the imaginary objects and culture-institutions of a civilization saturated with advertising and ideology: in his *Mythologies*, that marvelous picture-book of the pinups from the news of the day (boxing matches, somebody's new *Phèdre*, Billy Graham at the Vel d'hiver, the myth of the Guide bleu or of steak-frites, the strip tease, the new model cars); in his study, in *Système de la mode*, of the structure of fashion; in his reading, in *L'Empire des signes*, of that immense scroll or text which is written in characters of human flesh and formal gardens, of sliding screens and student helmets, tea ceremonies and transistorized radios, across the length and breadth of the Japanese archipelago; in his theory, finally, of the literary sign and of literature as a social institution.

Yet Barthes is of course primarily thought of as a literary critic. Our somewhat fanciful characterization of him above will be primarily useful to the degree to which it points to some deeper ambiguity in the very structure of the literary work itself, to something in the verbal construction of literature which allows it to be assimilated to, and even perhaps to serve as a paradigm for, other, more properly sociological sign-systems. This will be clearest if we isolate the type of signified with which Barthes has to deal, the privileged object of his research, or to use an older language, his obsessional themes or raw materials: for, as we have already seen, only a signified of a very distinct internal structure can be thus isolated from its signifier for experimental purposes.

What characterizes the most typical object of Barthes' perception is, it seems to me, a set of double markings in the thing signified, a structure of double functions irreducible to each other and incommensurable, operating at wholly different levels. It is as though only such an ambiguously structured signified, which seems to project two different types of signifiers and to lie at their intersection, can make itself felt as a kind of density and resistance beneath the transparency of the signs. This double structure is explicitly described in

Barthes' recent work: the object of fashion, the vestimentary article (at least insofar as it is described in the fashion magazines) signifies at one and the same time High Society and Fashion itself. Each item has two possible uses, which can be exercised simultaneously: on the one hand, it permits an imaginary identification with the rich and their way of life, and on the other it serves as a sign of fashion, momentarily embodying in itself all of what is currently fashionable.

Yet the same double structure was implicit in Barthes' earlier works as well. In the book on Michelet, for instance, Barthes postulates two simultaneous motivations for the historical text at any given point: the linear and official narrative of history itself (which Barthes leaves aside); and a kind of *combinatoire* or interplay of existential themes and motifs, an intersection of horizontal and vertical dimensions, to use a figure characteristic of Barthes in this period; while in *Sur Racine* the critic's practice generates a tension between the play as social ritual, as conventional spectacle, between classical language as an institutionalized sign of the social order, and those deeper, private zones of Freudian obsession, of symbolic fulfillment and psychic space. Barthes' most recent studies of *Sade, Fourier, Loyola*, indeed, mark a return to the description of such tensions between the sign and the body: for all three of these apparently heterogeneously juxtaposed authors attempted to create new languages or sign-systems (the mathematical combinations of Sade's orgies, Loyola's mechanical recipes for the stimulation of inner and theatrical visions, Fourier's immense classification system of the drives and their harmonious interaction), while at the same time such sign-systems are empty, and call out in all three cases for investment by wordless physiological content or *hylé*.

But it is in *S/Z*, his commentary on Balzac's *Sarrasine*, that Barthes discovers the most explicit manifestation of such a double structure, which now takes the form of a story within a story. Barthes' study is as much a meditation on a fascinating object as it is the development of a critical thesis. For Balzac's novella speaks to us at once of itself and of its subject-matter, of art and of desire, both of which are present, with reversed emphasis, in the frame and in the actual tale alike. In the frame, the narrator tells a tale in order to seduce his listener; while within the tale itself an artist is destroyed by his desire, leaving only its representation – a statue and a portrait of Zambinella – behind in the final catastrophe. This passion is narcissism and castration: the infatuated artist in reality sees his own image in the castrate with whom he falls in love, so that the gesture of symbolic castration or sexual renunciation is here given to be the very source of artistic productivity, just as it turns out elsewhere in the story to be the very source of the Lanty family's mysterious fortune (Zambinella's success as prima donna). The fable thus has something to say about the origins of classical art and the origins of capitalization and their relationship to each other; yet it does not leave the frame within which it is to d intact. Rather, it contaminates teller and listener alike, who separate at its close, in the desexualized and desexualizing atmosphere, without having consummated their desire.

With such a work, we clearly have to do with what Greimas would call the superposition of a teleological and a communicational axis: one *isotopie* or narrational level having to do with desire for an object, the other with the emission of a message. The reversal which takes place – in which the message replaces the object and becomes as it were a message about a lost object – is, as we shall see shortly, profoundly emblematic of Structuralist interpretation in general, and may fittingly be inserted here, like the *composition en abyme* of Dutch painting, into a study of it.

Once the signified has been thus isolated for study (if indeed we are able to so isolate it), by the very nature of things it turns into a sign-system in its own right. As Saussure himself warns us: "*whether we examine the signified or the signifier*, language involves neither ideas nor sounds which would preexist the linguistic system, but only conceptual or phonic differences which have resulted from that system."[2] We may conclude that insofar as we can talk about the signified at all, either it still bears traces of its organization by the signifier, or else the analyst has himself provisionally organized it into a new sign-system, in order to make it visible to us.

Thus we find again within the signified that structure of differential opposition and identity within difference that served to organize the signifier or language itself. In Barthes' study of Michelet, for instance – even though the principle is not yet formulated explicitly there – we find an organization of the essential themes by pairs of binary oppositions: grace and justice, Christianity and revolution; on the one hand, groupings of enchantment, narcosis, the sterile, "la mort sèche," and, on the other, blood, woman, the hero, energy. These combinations may at any given moment reach a high order of complexity (and it would have been interesting to watch the later Barthes rework them into semiological equations), but essentially they form what Saussure would have called a vertical level of association which is constantly in play along the syntagmatic axis of the narrative itself. Thus, for Barthes, the key episodes are heightened and intensified by these binary oppositions:

For Michelet, Blood is the cardinal substance of History. Look at the death of Robespierre for example: two types of blood there face each other: one poor, dry, so thin it needs an artificial blood supplement in the form of galvanic energy; the other, that of the women of Thermidor (solar month of history), is a superlative blood, uniting all the characteristics of superb sanguinity: the warm, the red, the unclothed, the too-well-nourished. These two types of blood stare at each other. Then the Woman-Blood devours the Priest-Cat . . . This whole meeting between the dry (electrical) and the full (feminine) in the death of Robespierre . . . is ordered in Michelet like an act of carnal humiliation, that of a chilly man, half undone in filthy linens, jaw hanging down, *looked at* by opulent women, scarlet with velvet, with nourishment and with jubilation, which is to say the very type of the sterile exposed and sold out to triumphant heat.[3]

The later evolution of Barthes makes it clear that what must at first have looked (even to Barthes himself) like a study in psychological or existential *themes*[4] was in reality the sketch of a type of discourse, that of the body itself. Michelet is indeed particularly rich in this physical dimension, in the peculiar heightened sensitivity or migraine-like nausea which he feels before the physical humors of his historical actors:

Michelet's adjective is unique; it marks a touch, an ideal palpation which has located the elementary substance of the body in question and can no longer conceive of the man under any different qualification, after the fashion of a natural epithet. Michelet says: the dessicated Louis XV, the cold Sieyès, and engages through these denominations his own judgment on the essential movements of matter itself: liquefaction, stickiness, the void, dessication, electricity.[5]

The place of this vertical dimension was for the older critical terminology the unconscious, where it is now the body: and for Barthes indeed the body is the very source of style itself as a private phenomenon, as obsession and "the decorative voice of unknown, secret flesh."[6] But in reality there is no contradiction between these two formulations if we understand both the unconscious and the body as essential forms of the signified itself.

There is a sense in which all sensory perception already constitutes a kind of organization into language. It is this more than anything else, no doubt, which explains the sympathy of Merleau-Ponty in his last years for the then emergent Structuralism. Imagine the way in which, for a trained naturalist, the disorderly undergrowth of thickets and bushes pressing in upon each other sort themselves out into order, the peculiar outlines of each type of leaf standing as a visible sign and mark of their determinate species; imagine the way in which a wholly unfamiliar landscape would offer itself to such knowledgeable perception as a kind of language the words of which were not yet known, an order already making itself felt through the clear forms of the vegetation, where for a layman there would be nothing but confused and jumbled vistas of space. This is, no doubt, what the German Romantics dimly felt when they developed their mystique of a language of organic nature; it is also the secret rationale behind Bachelardian analysis, which Barthes occasionally practices, but as to whose status he seems uncertain:[7]

Bachelard was no doubt right to see in water the opposite of wine: mythically this is so; sociologically, at least today, it is less certain; economic or historical circumstances have shifted this role to milk. Milk is now the veritable anti-wine . . . the opposite of fire by all its molecular density, by the creamy and therefore sopitive nature of its surface folds; wine is mutilating, surgical, it transmutes and brings to birth; milk is cosmetic, it unites, seals over, restores. Moreover its purity, associated with childlike innocence, is a proof of force, non-revulsive, non-congestive, one which is calm, white, lucid, on an equal footing with the real.[8]

For just as the dimension of the signified can never be completely isolated in a pure state, so also it is vain to attempt to distinguish between Nature and Culture on this level, and to separate what belongs to a genuine Bachelardian "psychoanalysis of matter" from what may stand as a cultural or ideological myth at work on the level of perception itself. As enormously influential and suggestive as Bachelard's own work was, what it lacked above all else was a theory of language: assimilating sense perception to linguistic articulation without realizing that in one way or another, all perceptual systems are already languages in their own right.

Yet it is this vertical depth of the signified, which seems grounded in the wordless and the physical itself, in complexion and organic humor, that accounts for the peculiar density of Barthes' own language as well: for his style is an attempt to lend a second voice to the signified, to articulate its organization before it finds its final and official version in the primary signifier itself, in the text. His is a style of nouns and adjectives, of neologisms, as he is well aware:

The concept is the constitutive element of myth: if I want to decipher myths, I must be able to name concepts. The dictionary furnishes some: Goodness, Charity, Health, Humanity, etc. But by definition, since it's the dictionary that supplies them, those concepts cannot be historical. What I need most frequently are ephemeral concepts, linked to limited contingencies: neologisms are at this point inevitable. China is one thing, the idea which a French petty bourgeois not so long ago had about it is something else again: there can be no other name, for this characteristic mixture of little bells, rickshaws and opium dens, than that of *sinity*.[9]

The neologism is therefore that which names the substance, just as adjectives (sopitive, dry-electrical) have as their function the attachment of a given detail to the larger structure of the signified as a whole, just as the definite articles and capital letters articulate the objects into a new relationality by their insistence and iteration ("As language, the singularity of Garbo was of a conceptual, that of Audrey Hepburn of a substantial, type of order. Garbo's face is Idea, Hepburn's is Event").[10]

Ultimately the aim of this style is the bringing into being of new and somehow synthetic entities out of the surface data of the text, as in the following evocation of the Neronian *caress* (from the discussion of *Britannicus*):

Nero is he who enwraps, because enwrapment does not know death until it has been consummated. This "gliding" has a funereal substitute in poison. Blood is a noble, theatrical matter, the sword is an instrument of rhetorical death; but Nero wishes the pure and simple effacement of Britannicus, not his spectacular undoing; like the Neronian caress, poison insinuates itself, like the caress also it only yields effects, not means; in this sense caress and poison are part of an immediate order, in which the distance from the project to the crime is absolutely diminished; Neronian poison is in any case rapid poison, its advantage lies, not in delay, but in nudity, in the refusal of bloody theater.[11]

Thus, in this sumptuous and perverse style, in which the ideas are not so much unfolded as laterally evoked by the very materiality of vocabulary itself, what comes into being are unstable conceptual entities, the very forms of the signified itself, as they darken the other side of language, constantly dissolving and reforming before our eyes. The very function of the style's artificiality is to announce itself as a metalanguage, to signal by its own impermanency the essential formlessness and ephemerality of the object itself.

Barthes had in his earlier work already evolved a theory to account for the phenomenon of double-functionality which we have described above. This theory (known as that of the "literary sign," where the term is to be understood in a far more limited way than in Saussure) is expressed in his most influential theoretical work, *Writing Degree Zero*. Literature, as a conventionalized activity – as what he will later call an "institutionalization of subjectivity" – is the very prototype of those ambiguous double-functioning substances which both have a meaning and wear a label at the same time:

I am a fifth-form student in a French lycée; I open my latin grammar and read in it the following sentence, borrowed from Aesop or Phaedrus: *quia ego nominor leo*. I stop and think: there is something ambiguous about this proposition: on the one hand, its words have a clear enough meaning: *for my name is lion*. And on the other hand the sentence is obviously there to convey something else to me: to the degree that it is addressed to me, to a fifth-form student, it tells me clearly: I am an example of grammar intended to illustrate the rule about the agreement of attributes.[12]

Thus literature, in its complexity of structure, is a construction to a higher power than the transparency of the normal object of linguistic study: in it the ordinary signifier/signified relationship is complicated by yet another type of signification which bears on the nature of the code itself. Thus each literary work, above and beyond its own determinate content, also signifies literature in general. Like the Latin sentence, above and beyond what it actually does mean, it also says: I am Literature, and in so doing, identifies itself for us as a literary product, and involves us in that particular and historical social activity which is the consumption of literature. Thus, in the nineteenth century novel, the *passé simple* and the narrative third person are both signs the function of which is to warn us that we are in the presence of official literary narration; and these peculiar markings or "signs" are somehow different in their nature from the general body of linguistic prescriptions at a given period in the history of the language (which are somehow "on this side of literature"), as well as from what we have described as style above, which is "almost beyond literature: images, an allure, a vocabulary born from the body and the past of the writer himself."[13]

Thus the history of these literary "signs" would afford the possibility of a historical mode of examining literature radically different from the history of language, on the one hand, or the evolution of styles, on the other. Rather, it would constitute a kind of history of the literary institution itself, insofar as the literary "sign" reveals the obligatory distance that obtains at any given period between the reader and the literary product and between the writer and the product as well. This is how Barthes sums up his findings, and evokes the trajectory of such a history of signs:

First an artisanal consciousness of literary manufacture, pushed to painful scruple, to the torment of the impossible (Flaubert); then the heroic will to mingle in a single written substance both literature and the thinking about literature (Mallarmé); then the hope of succeeding in eluding literary tautology by ceaselessly postponing literature until tomorrow, so to speak, by indicating at great length that you are about to write and then transforming this very declaration into literature itself (Proust); then the attack on literary good faith by the deliberate and systematic multiplication of an infinite number of meanings of the word-object without ever pausing at any univocal signified (surrealism); finally, the reverse of this process, a rarefication of meanings, to the point of hoping to obtain some *density* in literary language, a kind of whiteness of writing (but not an innocence): I am thinking of the work of Robbe-Grillet.[14]

This theory is essentially a further elaboration and working out of the basic position of Sartre in *What is Literature?* where it is by its structure that the work poses and indeed chooses its basic audience. Here it is the literary "sign" which essentially chooses the reader, and there are a whole complex of signs or indications through which a best-seller identifies itself to its clientele, through which a communist novel reveals its identity to its particular public, through which official, avant-garde literature announces at the same time its nature and the type of reading and distance it requires. But the methodological difference between Barthes and Sartre is that the former distinguishes between a selection by content (which was essentially the burden of Sartre's analysis) and the operation of these peculiar "signs" which in themselves mean nothing (thus the *passé simple* does not govern a different mode of the past from other past tenses, it merely signals the presence of "literariness"). This relational language (at its crudest often little more than a matter of recognizable in-group vocabulary) is what has often been described as "tone" in Anglo-American criticism; however, the latter, convinced of the traditional homogeneity of its public, never attempted to distinguish radically between such a sign-system and actual style itself (which for Barthes has something of the function of poetry in the Sartrean scheme in that it comes closest, in its elimination of signs, to a pure density as a language-object).

The originality of Barthes' theory was to have permitted a somewhat different outcome than that envisioned in Sartre's book. For Sartre, a genuine literature can be achieved only when its public is everyone, when through the process of social revolution the virtual and the real publics are one and the same. For Barthes also the literary "sign" is the object of a profound political and ethical disgust:[15] insofar as it marks my affiliation with a given social group, it signifies the exclusion of all the others also – in a world of classes and violence, even the most innocuous group-affiliation carries the negative value of aggression with it. Yet the objective situation is such that I cannot but belong to groups of some kind, even if they turn out to be groups which wish to abolish the existence of groups: by the very fact of my existence, I am guilty of the exclusion of others from the groups in which I am involved. Thus the use of the "sign" is a kind of historical fatality, and marks my fall into, and acceptance of, the world of classes. It is for this reason that literature, in our time, is essentially an impossible enterprise, a self-unravelling process. At the same time that it poses its own universality, the very words it uses to do so signal their complicity with that which makes universality unrealizable.

Yet in Barthes, the concept of the literary "sign" – while continuing to project that ultimate utopia of style foreseen by Sartre – offers at least the logical possibility of another, more provisional solution as well. This solution is the forcible eradication of literary "signs" from the work itself or, in other words, the practice of a kind of "white writing," the access to a kind of "zero degree" of literary language in which neither author nor public could be felt present, in which an austere neutrality and stylistic asceticism would be charged with the absolution of the guilt inherent in the practice of literature.[16] This state would be, it seems to me, the equivalent of a kind of absolute solitude in the realm of social life, in which a rigorous political logic might dictate the suppression of everything (both within and without the personality) which links us with the repressive social institutions.

The value of this concept may be measured against its speculative quality, for at the period at which Barthes wrote there did not yet exist any examples of "white writing" as such. His principal contemporary example, Camus' *Stranger*, has come to seem to us stylized and rhetorical, the very type of writing charged with signs. (In another sense, of course, this judgment only serves to confirm Barthes' intuition of the impossibility of literature: for writing cannot *stay* white, what began by being a blankness of manner little by little turns around into a mannerism, absence of sign becomes a sign itself.) Since that time, Robbe-Grillet has come to be felt as a more thoroughgoing and convincing embodiment of an elimination of signs, at least insofar as his work is based on the disappearance of the subject; but I would be tempted to prefer the more politically charged versions of such stylistic neutrality that one finds in the novels of Uwe Johnson, let us say, or in Georges Perec's *Les Choses*.

The changeover in Barthes' general positions (I hesitate to call it a *coupure épistémologique*) may be identified by a replacement (although not a repudiation) of this limited theory of the literary sign by a more complex one derived from Hjelmslev's distinction between "connotation" and "metalanguage." In both these linguistic phenomena, two distinct sign-systems are involved, stand somehow in relationship to each other. But a metalanguage takes the other language as its object, and functions as a signifier to the other language, which is thus its signified. Thus Barthean commentary is metalanguage in that it abstracts the structure of another more primary language, such as that of Michelet or that of Racine, and makes it available in a new and different form (in which, as we have shown, the neologisms function as a reminder that we have to do with a metalanguage rather than a primary, or object-language). In the phenomenon of connotation, on the other hand, in the limited and technical sense which Hjelmslev gives the word, it is the whole body of one language system which stands as a signifier for some more basic signified. The primary language system really thus has two signifieds: its regular content, which we receive consecutively as the text continues, and a second overall message sent us by the form as a whole. Thus a critique of Flaubert's style would take the form of a metalanguage; but the totality of Flaubert's own words forms a connotational system of its own, in that it signifies Literature, and tells us over and over again: I am literature of an artisanal type, I am the specialized work of the stylistic artisan.

  [. . .]

Notes

1   Roland Barthes, *Système de la mode* (Paris, Éditions du Seuil, 1967), p. 236. The image is Ferdinand de Saussure's: *Cours de linguistique générale* (Paris, Presses Universitaires de France, 1965), p. 155.

2   Quoted by Jacques Derrida in "La Différance," in Michel Foucault, Roland
    Barthes, Jacques Derrida, Jean-Louis Baudry etc., *Théorie d'ensemble* (Paris, Seuil,
    1968), p. 49 (emphasis added).
3   Roland Barthes, *Michelet par lui-même* (Paris, Seuil, 1965), pp. 105, 87.
4   Ibid., pp. 5 and 86.
5   Ibid., p. 82.
6   Roland Barthes, *Le degré zéro de l'écriture* (Paris, Seuil, 1953), pp. 14–15.
7   "Sometimes, even here in these mythologies, I have cheated: weary of constantly
    working on the evaporation of the real, I have occasionally begun to thicken it
    excessively, to find in it a surprising compacity, one which I myself found
    delectable, and have given several substantialist psychoanalyses of mythical
    objects;" Roland Barthes, *Mythologies* (Paris, Seuil, 1957), p. 267, n30.
8   Ibid., pp. 85–6.
9   Ibid., p. 228.
10 Ibid., p. 79.
11 *Sur Racine* (Paris, Seuil, 1963), pp. 91–2. This is one of the passages singled out for
    derision by Picard in *Nouvelle critique ou nouvelle imposture?*
12 Barthes, *Mythologies*, pp. 222–3.
13 Barthes, *Le degré zéro de l'écriture*, p. 14.
14 Roland Barthes, *Essais critiques* (Paris, Seuil, 1964), pp. 106–7.
15 "From an ethical point of view, what bothers one about myth is precisely that its
    form is motivated. For if there is such a thing as a 'health' of language, it is founded
    on the arbitrary quality of the sign. What disgusts in myth is the recourse to a false
    nature, the *luxury* of significative forms, as in those objects which decorate their
    usefulness with a natural appearance. The will to burden signification with all the
    justification of nature itself provokes a kind of nausea: the myth is too rich, and
    what is excessive in it is precisely its motivation. This disgust is the same as what I
    feel before arts which hesitate between *physis* and *anti-physis*, using the first as an
    ideal, and the second as a kind of reserve. Ethically, there is a kind of baseness
    involved in playing both sides against the middle" (*Mythologies*, p. 234, n7). It
    should be unnecessary to add that what Barthes calls "myths" here (the modern
    ideological objects studied in his mythologies) have nothing to do with those
    primitive myths studied by Lévi-Strauss.
16 The notion of a zero degree or negative ending (in the declension of a word) had
    already been appropriated, in a different way, by the Formalists.

5

Imaginary and Symbolic in Lacan

This chapter was originally published in *Yale French Studies* in 1977. The following selection is taken from a revised version that appears in the first volume of Jameson's collected essays, *Ideologies of Theory* (1988).

The attempt to coordinate a Marxist and a Freudian criticism confronts – but as it were explicitly, thematically articulated in the form of a problem – a dilemma that is in reality inherent in all psychoanalytic criticism as such: that of the insertion of the subject, or, in a different terminology, the difficulty of providing mediations between social phenomena and what must be called private, rather than even merely individual, facts. But what for Marxist criticism is already overtly social – in such questions as the relationship of the work to its social or historical context, or the status of its ideological content – is often merely implicitly so in that more specialized or conventional psychoanalytic criticism which imagines that it has no interest in extrinsic or social matters.

In "pure" psychoanalytic criticism, indeed, the social phenomenon with which the private materials of case history, of individual fantasy or childhood experience, must initially be confronted is simply language itself. Even prior to the establishment of the literary forms and the literary institution as official social phenomena, language – the very medium of universality and of inter-subjectivity – constitutes that primary social instance into which the preverbal, presocial facts of archaic or unconscious experience find themselves somehow inserted.[1] Anyone who has ever tried to recount a dream to someone else is in a position to measure the immense gap, the qualitative incommensurability, between the vivid memory of the dream and the dull, impoverished words that are all we can find to convey it. Yet this incommensurability, between the particular and the universal, between the *vécu* and language itself, is one in which we dwell all our lives, and it is from it that all works of literature and culture necessarily emerge.

What is so often problematical about psychoanalytic criticism is therefore not its insistence on the subterranean relationships between the literary text on the one hand and the "obsessive metaphor" or the distant and inaccessible childhood or unconscious fascination on the other. It is rather the absence of any reflection on the transformational process whereby such private materials become public – a transformation that is often, to be sure, so undramatic and inconspicuous as the very act of speech itself. Yet insofar as speech is preeminently social, in what follows we will do well to keep Durkheim's stern warning constantly before us as a standard against which to assess the various models psychoanalytic criticism has provided: "Whenever a social phenomenon is directly explained by a psychological phenomenon, we may be sure that the explanation is false."[2]

I

[...] [This analysis] suggests in turn the need for a model that is not locked into the classical opposition between the individual and the collective, but rather is able to think these discontinuities in a radically different way. Such is indeed the promise of Lacan's conception of the three orders (the Imaginary, the Symbolic, and the Real), of which it now remains for us to determine whether the hypothesis of a dialectically distinct status for each of these registers, or sectors of experience, can be maintained within the unity of a single system.

II

For the difficulties involved in an exposition of the three orders spring at least in part from their inseparability. According to Lacanian epistemology, indeed, acts of consciousness, experiences of the mature subject, necessarily imply a structural coordination between the Imaginary, the Symbolic, and the Real. "The experience of the Real presupposes the simultaneous exercise of two correlative functions, the imaginary function and the symbolic function."[3] If the notion of the Real is the most problematical of the three – since it can never be experienced immediately, but only by way of the mediation of the other two

– it is also the easiest to bracket for the purposes of this presentation. We will return to the function of this concept – neither an order nor a register, exactly – in our conclusion; suffice it to underscore here the profound heterogeneity of the Real with respect to the other two functions, between which we would then expect to discover a similar disproportion.

Yet to speak of the Imaginary independently of the Symbolic is to perpetuate the illusion that we could have a relatively pure experience of either. If, for instance, we overhastily identify the Symbolic with the dimension of language and the function of speech in general, it becomes obvious that we can hardly convey any experience of the Imaginary without presupposing the former. Meanwhile, insofar as the Imaginary is understood as the place of the insertion of my unique individuality as *Dasein* and as *corps propre*, it will become increasingly difficult to form a notion of the Symbolic Order as some pure syntactic web, which entertains no relationship to individual subjects at all.

In reality, however, the methodological danger is the obverse of this one, namely, the temptation to transform the notion of the two orders into a binary opposition, and to define each relationally in terms of the other – something it is even easier to find oneself doing when one has begun by suspending the Real itself and leaving it out of consideration. We will, however, come to learn that this process of definition by binary opposition is itself profoundly characteristic of the Imaginary, so that to allow our exposition to be influenced by it is already to slant our presentation in terms of one of its two objects of study.

Fortunately, the genetic preoccupations of psychoanalysis provide a solution to this dilemma; for Freud founded his diagnosis of psychic disorders, not only on the latter's own aetiology, but on a larger view of the process of formation of the psyche itself as a whole, and on a conception of the stages of infantile development. And we will see shortly that Lacan follows him in this, rewriting the Freudian history of the psyche in a new and unexpected way. But this means that even if they are inextricable in mature psychic life we ought to be able to distinguish Imaginary from Symbolic at the moment of emergence of each; in addition, we ought to be able to form a more reliable assessment of the role of each in the economy of the psyche by examining those moments in which their mature relationship to each other has broken down, moments that present a serious imbalance in favor of one or the other registers. Most frequently, this imbalance would seem to take the form of a degradation of the Symbolic to an Imaginary level: "The problem of the neurotic consists in a loss of the symbolic reference of the signifiers that make up the central points of the structure of his complex. Thus the neurotic may repress the signified of his symptom. This loss of the reference value of the symbol causes it to regress to the level of the imaginary, in the absence of any mediation between self and idea."[4] On the other hand, when it is appreciated to what degree, for Lacan, the

prenticeship of language is an alienation for the psyche, it will become clear
at there can also be a hypertrophy of the Symbolic at the Imaginary's expense
that is no less pathological; the recent emphasis on the critique of science and of
its alienated *sujet supposé savoir* is indeed predicated on this overdevelopment of
the Symbolic function: "The symbol is an imaginary figure in which man's
truth is alienated. The intellectual elaboration of the symbol cannot disalienate
it. Only the analysis of its imaginary elements, taken individually, reveals the
meaning and the desire that the subject had hidden within it."[5]

Even before undertaking a genetic exposition of the two registers, however,
we must observe that the very terms themselves present a preliminary difficulty,
which is none other than their respective previous histories: thus Imaginary
surely derives from the experience of the image – and of the imago – and we
are meant to retain its spatial and visual connotations. Yet as Lacan uses the
word, it has a relatively narrow and technical sense, and should not be extended
in any immediate way to the traditional conception of the imagination in
philosophical aesthetics (nor to the Sartrean doctrine of the *imaginaire*, although
the latter's material of study is doubtless Imaginary in Lacan's sense of the term).

The word "Symbolic" is even more troublesome, since much of what Lacan
will designate as Imaginary is traditionally designated by expressions like symbol
and symbolism. We will want to wrench the Lacanian term loose from its rich
history as the opposite number to allegory, particularly in Romantic thought;
nor can it maintain any of its wider suggestion to the figural as opposed to the
literal meaning (symbolism versus discursive thought, Mauss's symbolic
exchange as opposed to the market system, and so forth). Indeed, we would
be tempted to suggest that the Lacanian Symbolic Order has nothing whatsoever to do with symbols or with symbolism in the conventional sense, were it
not for the obvious problem of what then to do with the whole classical
Freudian apparatus of dream symbolism proper.

The originality of Lacan's rewriting of Freud may be judged by his radical
reorganization of this material, which had hitherto – houses, towers, cigars, and
all – been taken to constitute some storehouse of universal symbols. Most of the
latter will now be understood rather as "part-objects" in Melanie Klein's sense
of organs and parts of the body that are libidinally valorized; these part-objects
then, as we will see shortly, belong to the realm of the Imaginary rather than to
that of the Symbolic. The one exception – the notorious "phallic" symbol dear
to vulgar Freudian literary criticism – is the very instrument for the Lacanian
reinterpretation of Freud in linguistic terms. For the phallus – not, in contradistinction to the penis, an organ of the body – now comes to be considered
neither image nor symbol, but rather a signifier, indeed the fundamental
signifier of mature psychic life, and thus one of the basic organizational
categories of the Symbolic Order itself.[6]

In any case, whatever the nature of the Lacanian Symbolic, it is clear that the Imaginary – a kind of preverbal register whose logic is essentially visual – precedes it as a stage in the development of the psyche. Its moment of formation – and that existential situation in which its specificity is most strikingly dramatized – has been named the "mirror stage" by Lacan, who thereby designates that moment between six and eighteen months in which the child first demonstrably "recognizes" his or her own image in the mirror, thus tangibly making the connection between inner motricity and the specular movements stirring before him. It is important not to deduce too hastily from this very early experience some ultimate ontological possibility of an ego or an identity in the psychological sense, or even in the sense of some Hegelian self-conscious reflexivity. Whatever else the mirror stage is, indeed, for Lacan it marks a fundamental gap between the subject and its own self or imago that can never be bridged:

The important point is that this form [of the subject in the mirror stage] fixed the instance of the ego, well before any social determination, in a line of fiction that is forever irreducible for the individual himself – or rather that will rejoin the subject's evolution in asymptotic fashion only, whatever the favorable outcome of those dialectical syntheses by which as an ego he must resolve his discordance with his own reality.[7]

In our present context, we will want to retain the words "dans une ligne de fiction," which underscore the psychic function of narrative and fantasy in the attempts of the subject to reintegrate his or her alienated image.

The mirror stage, which is the precondition for primary narcissism, is also, owing to the equally irreducible gap it opens between the infant and its fellows, the very source of human aggressivity; and indeed, one of the original features of Lacan's early teaching is its insistence on the inextricable association of these two drives.[8] How could it indeed be otherwise, at a moment when, the child's investment in images of the body having been achieved, there does not yet exist the ego formation that would permit him to distinguish his own form from that of others? The result is a world of bodies and organs that in some fashion lacks a phenomenological center and a privileged point of view:

Throughout this period the emotional reactions and verbal indications of normal transitivism [Charlotte Bühler's term for the indifferentiation of subject and object] will be observed. The child who hits says he has been hit, the child who sees another child fall begins to cry. Similarly, it is by way of an identification with the other that the infant lives the entire spectrum of reactions from ostentation to generosity, whose structural ambiguity his conduct so undisguisedly reveals, slave identified with despot, actor with spectator, victim with seducer.[9]

This "structural crossroads" (Lacan) corresponds to that preindividualistic, premimetic, pre-point-of-view stage in aesthetic organization that is generally designated as "play,"[10] whose essence lies in the frequent shifts of the subject from one fixed position to another, in a kind of optional multiplicity of insertions of the subject into a relatively fixed Symbolic Order. In the realm of linguistics and psychopathology, the fundamental document on the effects of "transitivism" remains Freud's "A Child is Being Beaten," which has had considerable emblematic significance for recent theory.[11]

A description of the Imaginary will therefore on the one hand require us to come to terms with a uniquely determinate configuration of space – one that is not yet organized around the individuation of my own personal body, or differentiated hierarchically according to the perspectives of my own central point of view, but that nonetheless swarms with bodies and forms intuited in a different way, whose fundamental property is, it would seem, to be visible without their visibility being the result of the act of any particular observer, to be, as it were, always-already seen, to carry their specularity upon themselves like a color they wear or the texture of their surface. In this – the indifferentiation of their *esse* from a *percipi* that does not know a *percipiens* – these bodies of the Imaginary exemplify the very logic of mirror images; yet the existence of the normal object world of adult everyday life presupposes this prior, imaginary, experience of space:

It is normally by the possibilities of a game of imaginary transposition that the progressive valorization of objects is achieved, on what is customarily known as the affective level, by a proliferation, a fanlike disposition of all the imagination equations that allow the human being, alone in the animal realm, to have an almost infinite number of objects at his disposition, objects isolated in their form.[12]

The affective valorization of these objects ultimately derives from the primacy of the human imago in the mirror stage; and it is clear that the very investment of an object world will depend in one way or another on the possibility of symbolic association or identification of an inanimate thing with the libidinal priority of the human body. Here, then, we come upon what Melanie Klein termed "part-objects" – organs, like the breast, or objects associated with the body, like feces, whose psychic investment is then transferred to a host of other, more indifferent contents of the external world (which are then, as we will see below, valorized as good or as evil). "A trait common to such objects, Lacan insists, is that they have no specular image, which is to say that they know no alterity. 'They are the very lining, the stuff or imaginary filling of the subject itself, which identifies itself with these objects.'"[13] It is from Melanie Klein's pioneering psychoanalysis of children that the basic features of the Lacanian Imaginary are drawn: there is, as we might expect for an experience of spatiality phenomenologically so different from our own, a logic specific to Imaginary space, whose dominant category proves to be the opposition of container and contained, the fundamental relationship of inside to outside, which clearly enough originates in the infant's fantasies about the maternal body as the receptacle of part-objects (confusion between childbirth and evacuation, and so forth).[14]

This spatial syntax of the Imaginary order may then be said to be intersected by a different type of axis, whose conjunction completes it as an experience: this is the type of relationship that Lacan designates as aggressivity, and that we have seen to result from that indistinct rivalry between self and other in a period that precedes the very elaboration of a self or the construction of an ego. As with the axis of Imaginary space, we must again try to imagine something deeply sedimented in our own experience, but buried under the adult rationality of everyday life (and under the exercise of the Symbolic): a kind of situational experience of otherness as pure relationship, as struggle, violence, and antagonism, in which the child can occupy either term indifferently, or indeed, as in transitivism, both at one. A remarkable sentence of St Augustine is inscribed as a motto to the primordiality of this rivalry with the imagoes of other infants: "I have myself seen jealousy in a baby and know what it means. He was not old enough to speak, but, whenever his foster-brother was at the breast, would glare at him pale with envy [et intuebatur palidus amaro aspectu conlactaneum suum]."[15]

Provided it is understood that this moment is quite distinct from that later intervention of the Other (Lacan's capital *A* – for *Autre* – the parents, or language itself) that ratifies the assumption of the subject into the realm of language or the Symbolic Order, it will be appropriate to designate this primordial rivalry of the mirror stage as a relationship of otherness. Nowhere better can we observe the violent situational content of those judgments of good and evil that will later cool off and sediment into the various systems of ethics. Both Nietzsche and Sartre have exhaustively explored the genealogy of ethics as the latter emerges from just such an archaic valorization of space, where what is "good" is what is associated with "my" position, and the "bad" simply characterizes the affairs of my mirror rival.[16] We may further document the archaic or atavistic tendencies of ethical or moralizing thought by observing that it has no place in the Symbolic Order, or in the structure of language itself, whose shifters are positional and structurally incapable of supporting this kind of situational complicity with the subject momentarily occupying them.

The Imaginary may thus be described as a peculiar spatial configuration, whose bodies primarily entertain relationships of inside/outside with one another, which is then traversed and reorganized by that primordial rivalry

and transitivistic substitution of imagoes, that indistinction of primary narcissism and aggressivity, from which our later conceptions of good and evil derive.
This stage is already an alienation – the subject having been captivated by his or
her specular image – but in Hegelian fashion it is the kind of alienation from
which a more positive evolution is indistinguishable and without which the
latter is inconceivable. The same must be said for the next stage of psychic
development, in which the Imaginary itself is assumed into the Symbolic Order
by way of its alienation by language itself. The Hegelian model of dialectical
history – as Jean Hyppolite's interventions in Lacan's first Seminar make clear –
remains the fundamental one here:

This development [of the human anatomy and in particular the cortex] is lived as a
temporal dialectic that decisively projects the formation of the individual as history: the
mirror stage is a drama whose internal dynamic shifts from insufficiency to anticipation –
a drama that, for its subject, caught in the mirage of spatial identification, vehiculates a
whole series of fantasies which range from a fragmented image of the body to what we
will term an orthopedic form of its unity, and to that ultimate assumption of the
armature of an alienating identity, whose rigid structure will mark the subject's entire
mental development. Thus the rupture of the circle in which *Innenwelt* and *Umwelt*
are united generates that inexhaustible attempt to square it in which we reap the ego.[17]

The approach to the Symbolic is the moment to suggest the originality of
Lacan's conception of the function of language in psychoanalysis. For neo-
Freudianism, it would seem that the role of language in the analytical situation,
or the "talking cure," is understood in terms of what we may call an aesthetic of
expression and expressiveness: the patient unburdens himself or herself; his
"relief" comes from his having verbalized (or even, according to a more recent
ideology, from having "communicated"). For Lacan, on the contrary, this later
exercise of speech in the analytical situation draws its therapeutic force from
being as it were a completion and fulfillment of the first, imperfectly realized,
accession to language and to the Symbolic in early childhood.

For the emphasis of Lacan on the linguistic development of the child – an
area in which his work necessarily draws much from Piaget – has mistakenly
been criticized as a "revision" of Freud in terms of more traditional psychology,
a substitution of the psychological data of the mirror stage and of language
acquisition for the more properly psychoanalytic phenomena of infantile sexuality and the Oedipus complex. Obviously Lacan's work must be read as
presupposing the entire content of classical Freudianism, otherwise it would
be simply another philosophy or intellectual system. The linguistic materials are
not intended, it seems to me, to be substituted for the sexual ones; rather we
must understand the Lacanian notion of the Symbolic Order as an attempt to

create mediations between libidinal analysis and the linguistic categories, to provide, in other words, a transcoding scheme that allows us to speak of both within a common conceptual framework. Thus, the very cornerstone of Freud's conception of the psyche, the Oedipus complex, is transliterated by Lacan into a linguistic phenomenon, which he designates as the discovery by the subject of the Name-of-the-Father, and which consists in the transformation of an Imaginary relationship with that particular imago which is the physical parent into the new and menacing abstraction of the paternal role as the possessor of the mother and the place of the Law. [. . .]

The Symbolic Order is thus, as we have already suggested, a further alienation of the subject; and this repeated emphasis further serves to distinguish Lacan's position (what we have called his Hegelianism) from many of the more facile celebrations of the primacy of language by structuralist ideologues. Perhaps the link with Lévi-Strauss' primitivism may be made across Rousseau, for whom the social order in all its repressiveness is intimately linked with the emergence of language itself. In Lacan, however, an analogous sense of the alienating function of language is arrested in Utopian mid-course by the palpable impossibility of returning to an archaic, preverbal stage of the psyche itself (although the Deleuze–Guattari celebration of schizophrenia would appear to attempt precisely that). Far more adequately than the schizophrenic or natural man, the tragic symbol of the unavoidable alienation by language would seem to have been provided by Truffaut's film, *L'Enfant sauvage* (The Wild Child), in which language learning comes before us as a racking torture, a palpably physical kind of suffering upon which the feral child is only imperfectly willing to enter.

The clinical equivalent of this agonizing transition from the Imaginary to the Symbolic is then furnished by an analysis, by Melanie Klein, of an autistic child, which makes it clear that the "cure," the accession of the child to speech and to the Symbolic, is accompanied by an increase, rather than a lessening, of anxiety. This case history (published in 1930 under the title "The Importance of Symbol-Formation in the Development of the Ego") may also serve to correct the imbalance of our own presentation, and of the very notion of a "transition" from Imaginary to Symbolic, by demonstrating that the acquisition of the Symbolic is rather the precondition for a full mastery of the Imaginary as well. In this case, the autistic child, Dick, is not only unable to speak but unable to play as well – unable, that is, to act out fantasies and to create "symbols," a term that in this context means object substitutes. The few meager objects handled by Dick all represent in a kind of undifferentiated state "the phantasied contents [of the mother's body]. The sadistic phantasies directed against the inside of her body constitute the first and basic relation to the outside world and to reality."[18] Psychic investment in the external world – or in other words, the development of the Imaginary itself – has been arrested at its most rudimentary form, with those little trains that function as representations of Dick and of his father, and the dark space or station that represents the mother. The fear of anxiety prevents the child from developing further symbolic substitutes and expanding the narrow limits of his object world.

Melanie Klein's therapy then consists in introducing the Symbolic Order, and language, into this impoverished realm; and that, as Lacan observes, without any particular subtlety or precautions ("Elle lui fout le symbolisme avec la dernière brutalité, Melanie Klein, au petit Dick! Elle commence tout de suite par lui flanquer les interprétations majeures. Elle le flanque dans une verbalisation brutale du mythe oedipien, presque aussi révoltante pour nous que pour n'importe quel lecteur").[19] Verbalization itself heavy-handedly superposes a Symbolic relationship upon the Imaginary fantasy of the train rolling up to the station: "The station is mummy; Dick is going into mummy."[20]

It is enough: from this point on, miraculously, the child begins to develop relationships to others, jealousies, games, and much richer forms of substitution and of the exercise of language. The Symbolic now releases Imaginary investments of ever new kinds of objects, which had hitherto been blocked, and permits the development of what Melanie Klein in her paper calls "symbol formation." Such symbol or substitute formation is a fundamental precondition of psychic evolution, since it can alone lead the subject to love objects that are equivalents for the original, now forbidden or taboo, maternal presence: Lacan will then assimilate this process to the operation of the trope of metonymy in the linguistic realm,[21] and the profound effects of this new and complex "rhetorical" mechanism – unavailable in the preverbal realm of the Imaginary, where, as we have seen, only the rudimentary oppositions of inside/outside and good/bad are operative – may serve to underscore and to dramatize the extent of the transformation language brings to what without it could not yet have been called desire.

We may now attempt to give a more complete picture of Lacan's conception of language, or at least of those features of articulate speech that are the most essential in the structuration of the psyche, and which may thus be said to constitute the Symbolic Order. It will be convenient to consider these features in three groups, even though they are obviously all very closely interrelated.

The first of these groups – we have already seen it at work in the Oedipal phenomenon of the Name-of-the-Father – may be generalized as the naming function of language, something that has the most momentous consequences for the subject. For the acquisition of a name results in a thoroughgoing transformation of the position of the subject in its object world: "That a name, no matter how confused, designates a particular person – this is precisely what the passage to the human state consists in. If we must define that moment in which man [sic] becomes human, we would say that it is at that instant when, as minimally as you like, he enters into a symbolic relationship."[22] It would seem fair to observe that Lacan's attention to the components of language has centered on those kinds of words, primarily names and pronouns, on those slots that, like the shifters generally, anchor a free-floating syntax to a particular subject, those verbal joints, therefore, at which the insertion of the subject into the Symbolic is particularly detectable.

Even here, however, we must distinguish among the various possible effects of these types of words: nouns, in particular the Name-of-the-Father itself, awaken the subject to the sense of a function that is somehow objective and independent of the existence of the biological father. Such names thus provide a liberation from the here-and-now of the Imaginary; for the separation, through language, of the paternal function from the biological father is precisely what permits the child to take the father's place in his turn. The order of abstraction – the Law, as Lacan calls it – is thus also what releases the subject from the constraints of the immediate family situation and from the "bad immediacy" of the pre-Symbolic period.

Pronouns, meanwhile, are the locus for a related, yet distinct, development, which is none other than the emergence of the unconscious itself. Such is indeed for Lacan the significance of the bar that divides signifier from signified in the semiotic fraction: the pronoun, the first person, the signifier, results in division of the subject, or *Spaltung*, which drives the "real subject" as it were underground, and leaves a "representative" – the ego – in its place: "The subject is figured in symbolism by a stand-in or substitute [un tenant-lieu], whether we have to do with the personal pronoun 'I,' with the name that is given him, or with the denomination 'son of.' This stand-in is of the order of the symbol or the signifier, an order that is only perpetuated laterally, through the relationships entertained by that signifier with other signifiers. The subject mediated by language is irremediably divided because it has been excluded from the symbolic chain [the lateral relations of signifiers among themselves] at the very moment at which it became 'represented' in it."[23] Thus, the discontinuity insisted on by linguists between the *énoncé* and the subject of the enunciation (or, by Humboldt's even broader distinction between language as *ergon*, or produced object, and language as *energeia*, or force of linguistic production) corresponds to the coming into being of the unconscious itself, as that reality of the subject that has been alienated and repressed through the very process by which, in receiving a name, it is transformed into a representation of itself.

This production of the unconscious by way of a primary repression – which is none other than the acquisition of language – is then reinterpreted in terms of the communicational situation as a whole; and Lacan's redefinition of the signifier, "the signifier is what represents the subject for another signifier,"[24] now illuminates what it may be artificial to call a different form of linguistic alienation than either of the above features, but what is certainly a distinct dimension of that alienation, namely, the coming into view of the inescapable mediation of other people, and more particularly of the Other with a capital O, or A, or, in other words, the parents. Yet here the Law represented by the parents, and in particular by the father, passes over into the very nature of language itself, which the child receives from the outside and which speaks him or her just as surely as he or she learns to speak it. At this third moment of the subject's alienation by language we therefore confront a more complex version of that strategy which we have elsewhere described as the fundamental enabling device of structuralism in general, namely, the possibility – provided by the ambiguous nature of language itself – of imperceptibly shifting back and forth between a conception of speech as a linguistic structure, whose components can then be tabulated, and a conception of speech as communication, which permits a virtual dramatization of the linguistic process (sender/receiver, *destinaire/destinateur*, etc.).[25] Lacan's "Other" (capital A) is the locus of this superposition, constituting at one and the same time the dramatis personae of the Oedipal situation (but most particularly the father or his substitutes) and the very structure of articulate language itself.

So it is that this third aspect of Symbolic alienation, the alienation by the Other, passes over into the more familiar terms of the accounts of the *chaîne du signifiant* given in Lacan's mature doctrine,[26] which, embattled in a struggle against ego psychology, and emerging from a long polemic with the neo-Freudian emphasis on the analysis of resistances and the strengthening of the subject's ego, has found its fundamental principle and organizing theme in "a conception of the function of the signifier able to demonstrate the place at which the subject is subordinated to it to the point of being virtually subverted [*suborné*]."[27] The result is a determination of the subject by language – not to say a linguistic determinism – which results in a rewriting of the classical Freudian unconscious in terms of language: "the Unconscious," to quote what must be Lacan's best-known sentence, "is the discourse of the Other."[28] For those of us still accustomed to the classical image of the Freudian unconscious as a seething cauldron of archaic instincts (and inclined, also, to associate language with thinking and consciousness rather than the opposite of those things), the Lacanian redefinition must inevitably scandalize. As far as language is concerned, the references to Hegel have a strategic role to play in confronting this scandal with the philosophically more respectable idea of alienation in general, and alienation to other people in particular (the master/slave chapter is of course the basic text here). Thus, if we can bring ourselves to think of language itself as an alienating structure, particularly in those features enumerated above, we are halfway toward an appreciation of this concept.

[. . .]

We may now ask what, apart from the incidental mention of phenomena like that of animal language [. . .], can be said to be the place of the Imaginary in Lacan's later teaching; we will have occasion to see that its gradual eclipse in the later work is not foreign to a certain overestimation of the Symbolic that may be said to be properly ideological. For the moment, we may suggest that Imaginary thought patterns persist into mature psychic life in the form of what are generally thought of as ethical judgments – those implicit or explicit valorizations or repudiations in which "good" and "bad" are simply positional descriptions of the geographical relationship of the phenomenon in question to my own Imaginary conception of centrality. It is a comedy we may observe, not only in the world of action, but also in that of thought, where, in that immense proliferation of private languages which characterizes the intellectual life of consumer capitalism, the private religions that emerge around thinkers like the one presently under consideration are matched only by their anathematization by the champions of rival "codes." The Imaginary sources of passions like ethics may always be identified by the operation of the dual in them and the organization of their themes around binary oppositions; the ideological quality of such thinking must, however, be accounted for, not so much by the metaphysical nature of its categories of centrality, as Derrida and Lyotard have argued, as rather by its substitution of the categories of individual relationships for those – collective – of history and of historical, transindividual phenomena.

This view of ethics would seem to find confirmation in Lacan's essay "Kant avec Sade," in which the very prototype of an attempt to construct a rationally coherent (in other words, Symbolic) system of ethics by Kant is thoroughly discredited by a structural analogy with the delirious rationality of Sade. By attempting to universalize ethics and to establish the criteria for universally binding ethical laws that are not dependent on the logic of the individual situation, Kant merely succeeds in stripping the subject of his object (*a*) in an effort to separate pleasurability from the notion of the Good, thereby leaving the subject alone with the Law (*A*): "Cannot moral law be said to represent desire in that situation in which it is not the subject, but rather the object, that is missing?"[29] Yet this structural result turns out to be homologous with perversion, defined by Lacan as the fascination with the pleasure of the Other at the expense of the subject's own, and illustrated monotonously by the voluminous pages of Sade.

Whatever the philosophical value of this analysis, in the present context it has the merit of allowing us to conceive the possibility of transforming the topological distinction between Imaginary and Symbolic into a genuine methodology. "Kant avec Sade" would seem indeed to be the equivalent in the realm of moral philosophy of those logical paradoxes and mathematical exercises that have so disoriented the readers of Lacan in other areas. Thus, for example, we find a properly psychoanalytic reflection on the timing of the analytical situation unexpectedly punctuated by a meditation on a logical puzzle or metalogical paradox (see "Le Temps logique"), whose upshot is to force us to reintroduce the time of the individual subject back into what was supposed to be a universal or impersonal mental operation. Elsewhere the experiment is reversed, and the laws of probability are invoked to demonstrate the Symbolic regularity (in Freudian terms, the repetitive structure) of what otherwise strikes the subject as sheer individual chance. Lacan has, however, explained himself about these excursions, designed, he says, to lead

those who follow us into places where logic itself is staggered by the glaring incommensurability between Imaginary and Symbolic; and this, not out of complacency with the resultant paradoxes, nor with any so-called intellectual crisis, but rather on the contrary to restore its illicit glitter to the structural gap [*béance*] thereby revealed, a gap perpetually instructive for us, and above all to try to forge the method of a kind of calculus able to dislodge its secret by its very inappropriateness.[30]

In the same way, "Kant avec Sade" transforms the very project of a moral philosophy into an insoluble intellectual paradox by rotating it in such a way that the implicit gap in it between subject and law catches the light. It is time to ask whether a similar use of the distinction between Imaginary and Symbolic may not be possible in the realm of aesthetic theory and literary criticism, offering psychoanalytic method a more fruitful vocation than it was able to exercise in the older literary psychoanalyses.

III

We cannot do so, however, before first asking whether, alongside that Freudian criticism, of which everyone – for good or ill – has a fairly vivid idea what it ends up looking like, a properly Lacanian criticism is also conceivable. Yet it is here that the ambiguity of Lacan's relations to his original – is he rewriting him or merely restoring him? – becomes problematic. For at the point of interpretation, either the attempt at a Lacanian reading simply again generates the classic themes of all psychoanalytic literary criticism since Freud – the Oedipus complex, the double, splitting, the phallus, the lost object, and so forth – or else, trying to keep faith with the linguistic inspiration of "L'Instance de la lettre," it exercises the distinction between metaphor and metonymy to the point where the orthodox psychoanalytic preoccupations seem to have been forgotten without a trace.[31] In part, of course, this methodological fluctuation can be accounted for by what we have suggested above: namely, that on the level of interpretive codes Lacan's position is not one of substituting linguistic for classical psychoanalytic concepts, but rather of mediating between them, and this is clearly a matter of some tact that cannot be successfully realized on the occasion of every text.

But there is another, more structural, side to this problem, which raises the question of the syntagmatic organization of the work of art, rather than the issue — a more properly paradigmatic one — of the interpretive schemes into which it is to be "transcoded" or interpreted. Freud's own two greatest narrative readings, that of Jensen's *Gradiva* and that of Hoffmann's *Sandmann*, turn on delusions that either come to appeasement or culminate in the destruction of the subject. They thus recapitulate the trajectory of the cure, or of the illness, or — ultimately, and behind both — of the evolution and maturation of the psyche itself. We have here, therefore, narratives that formally require the final term of a norm (maturity, psychic health, the cure) toward which to steer their itineraries, whether catastrophic or providential; of that ultimate norm itself, however, the narrative can have nothing to say, as it is not a realm, but rather only an organizational device or term limit.

It would not be difficult to imagine a Lacanian criticism — although I do not know that there has been one[32] — in which the transition from the Imaginary to the Symbolic described above played an analogous role in organizing the syntagmatic movement of the narrative from disorder to the term limit of the Symbolic Order itself. The risk of an operation like this lies clearly in the assimilation of what is original in Lacan to the more widespread and now conventionalized structuralist paradigm of the passage from nature to culture; and this is surely the moment to ask ourselves whether the Lacanian emphasis on the Law and on the necessity of the castration anxiety in the evolution of the subject — so different in spirit from the instinctual and revolutionary Utopias of Brown's polymorphous perversity, Reich's genital sexuality, and Marcuse's maternal super-id — shares the implicit conservatism of the classical structuralist paradigm. Insofar as the Lacanian version generates a rhetoric of its own that celebrates submission to the Law, and indeed, the subordination of the subject to the Symbolic Order, conservative overtones and indeed the possibility of a conservative misappropriation of this clearly anti-Utopian scheme are unavoidable. On the other hand, if we recall that for Lacan "submission to the Law" designates, not repression, but rather something quite different, namely alienation — in the ambiguous sense in which Hegel, as opposed to Marx, conceives of this phenomenon — then the more tragic character of Lacan's thought, and the dialectical possibilities inherent in it, become evident.

Indeed, the one sustained literary exegesis that Lacan has published, the seminar on Poe's "Purloined Letter,"[33] suggests that for Lacan, in contradistinction to Freud himself, the norm *can* be the locus of a properly narrative exploration, albeit one of a uniquely didactic or "illustrative" type.[34] Poe's story is for Lacan the occasion of a magisterial demonstration of the way "a formal language determines the subject."[35] Three distinct positions are structurally available in relationship to the Letter itself, or the signifier: that of the king, that of the queen, and that of the Minister. When in the sequel to the narrative the places change, Dupin taking the place of the Minister, who then moves to that previously held by the queen, it is the positions themselves that exercise a structurating power over the subjects who momentarily occupy them. So the signifying chain becomes a vicious circle, and the story of the norm itself, of the Symbolic Order, is not that of a "happy end," but rather of a perpetual alienation. Obviously, Lacan's interpretation of the narrative is an allegorical one, in which the signified of the narrative proves to be simply language itself. Once again, the relative richness of the reading derives from the dramatic structure of the communicational process and the multiplicity of different positions available in it; but while more lively because of the musical chairs being played in it, Lacan's exegesis in this respect rejoins that now conventional structuralist conception of the autoreferentiality of the text that we have shown at work in *Tel Quel* and Derrida, as well as in Todorov's interpretations.[36] Read in this way – but as I will suggest later, it is not the only way one can read Lacan's essay – the "Seminar on 'The Purloined Letter,' " by its programmatic demonstration of the primacy of the signifier, furnishes powerful ammunition for what must properly be called, in distinction to its other achievements, the ideology of structuralism. (It may rapidly be defined here as the systematic substitution of "referent" for "signified," which allows one to pass logically from the properly linguistic assertion that the signified is an effect of the organization of signifiers to the quite different conclusion that therefore the "referent" – in other words, History – does not exist). Yet the present context suggests an explanation for this excess charge of ideology, this ideological effect, vehiculated or produced by Lacan's exposé. Indeed, its opening page, with its polemic repudiation of those "imaginary incidences [which], far from representing the essence of our experience, reveal only what remains inconsistent in it,"[37] makes a diagnosis of an overestimation of the Symbolic at the expense of the Imaginary in its presentation well-nigh inescapable.

Strengthened by this detour through Lacan's own literary criticism, we have thus returned to our hypothesis that whatever else it is, the distinction between the Imaginary and the Symbolic, and the requirement that a given analysis be able to do justice to the qualitative gap between them, may prove to be an invaluable instrument for measuring the range or the limits of a particular way of thinking. If it is always unsatisfying to speculate on what a Lacanian literary criticism ought to be in the future, if it is clear that the "Seminar on 'The Purloined Letter'" cannot possibly constitute a model for such criticism – since on the contrary the literary work is in it a mere pretext for a dazzling illustration of a nonliterary thesis – then at least we may be able to use the concept of the two orders, or registers, as a means for demonstrating the imbalance of other critical methods, and of suggesting ways in which they may be coordinated and an eclectic pluralism overcome. So, for instance, it seems abundantly clear that the whole area of image study and image hunting takes on a new appearance when we grasp the image content of a given text, not as so many clues to its ideational content (or "meaning"), but rather as the sedimentation of the imaginary material on which the text must work, as the raw materials it must transform. The relationship of the literary text to its image content is thus – in spite of the historic preponderance of the sensory in modern literature since Romanticism – not that of the production of imagery, but rather of its mastery and control in ways that range from outright repression (and the transformation of the sensory image into some more comfortable conceptual symbol) to the more complex modes of assimilation of surrealism and, more recently, of schizophrenic literature.[38] Only by grasping images – and also the surviving fragments of authentic myth and delusion – in this way, as that trace of the Imaginary, of sheer private or physiological experience, which has undergone the sea change of the Symbolic, can criticism of this kind recover a vital and hermeneutic relationship to the literary text.

[. . .]

IV

For Derrida's accusation is undoubtedly true, and what is at stake, in Lacan as well as in psychoanalysis in general, is truth; even worse, a conception of truth peculiarly affiliated to the classical existential one (that of Heidegger as a veiling/unveiling, that of Sartre as a fitful reclamation from *mauvaise foi*).[39] For that very reason, it seems arbitrary to class as logocentric and phonocentric a thought that – insofar as it is structural – proposes a decentering of the subject, and – insofar as it is "existential" – is guided by a concept of truth, not as adequation with reality (as Derrida suggests), but rather as a relationship, at best an asymptotic approach, to the Real.

This is not the place to deal with Lacan's epistemology, but it is certainly the moment to return to this term, the third of the canonical Lacanian triad, of which it must be admitted that it is at the very least astonishing that we have been able to avoid mentioning it for so long. Just as the Symbolic Order (or language itself) restructures the Imaginary by introducing a third term into the hitherto infinite regression of the duality of the latter's mirror images, so we may hope and expect that the tardy introduction of this third term, the Real, may put an end to the Imaginary opposition into which our previous discussion of Lacan's two orders has risked falling again and again. We must not, however, expect much help from Lacan himself in giving an account of a realm of which he in one place observes that it – "the Real, or what is perceived as such, – is what resists symbolization absolutely."[40]

Nonetheless, it is not terribly difficult to say what is meant by the Real in Lacan. It is simply History itself; and if for psychoanalysis the history in question here is obviously enough the history of the subject, the resonance of the word suggests that a confrontation between this particular materialism and the historical materialism of Marx can no longer be postponed. It is a confrontation whose first example has been set by Lacan himself, with his suggestion that the notion of the Symbolic as he uses it is compatible with Marxism (whose theory of language, as most Marxists would be willing to agree, remains to be worked out).[41] Meanwhile, it is certain that his entire work is permeated by dialectical tendencies, the more Hegelian ones having already been indicated above, and beyond this that the fascination of that work lies precisely in its ambiguous hesitation between dialectical formulations and those, more static, more properly structural and spatializing, of his various topologies. In Lacan, however, unlike the other varieties of structural mapping, there is always the proximity of the analytic situation to ensure the transformation of such structures back into "moments" of a more process-oriented type. Thus, in the "Seminar on 'The Purloined Letter,'" which we have hitherto taken at face value as a "structuralist" manifesto against the optical illusions of the signified, other passages on the contrary suggest that the circular trajectory of the signifier may be a little more closely related to the emergence of a dialectical self-consciousness than one might have thought, and project a second, more dialectical reading superimposed upon the structural one already outlined. In particular, the dilemma of Poe's Minister implies that it is in awareness of the Symbolic that liberation from the optical illusions of the Imaginary is to be sought:

For if it is, now as before, a question of protecting the letter from inquisitive eyes, he can do nothing but employ the same technique he himself has already foiled: leave it in the open. And we may properly doubt that he knows what he is thus doing, when we see him immediately captivated by a dual relationship in which we find all the traits of a mimetic ruse or of an animal feigning death, and, trapped in the typically imaginary situation of seeing that he is not seen, misconstrue the real situation in which he is seen not seeing.[42]

Even if the structural self-consciousness diagnostically implied by such a passage is a properly dialectical one, it would not necessarily follow that the dialectic is a Marxist one, even though psychoanalysis is unquestionably a materialism. Meanwhile the experience of a whole series of abortive Freudo-Marxisms, as well as the methodological standard of the type of radical discontinuity proposed by the model outlined in the present [chapter], suggests that no good purpose is to be served by attempting too hastly to combine them into some unified anthropology. To say that both psychoanalysis and Marxism are materialisms is simply to assert that each reveals an area in which human consciousness is not "master in its own house": only the areas decentered by each are the quite different ones of sexuality and of the class dynamics of social history. That these areas know local interrelationships – as when Reich shows how sexual repression is something like the cement that holds the authority fabric of society together – is undeniable; but none of these instinctual or ideological ion-exchanges, in which a molecular element of one system is temporarily lent to the other for purposes of stabilization, can properly furnish a model of the relationship of sexuality to class consciousness as a whole. Materialistic thinking, however, ought to have had enough practice of heterogeneity and discontinuity to entertain the possibility that human reality is fundamentally alienated in more than one way, and in ways that have little enough to do with each other.

What one can do, however, more modestly but with better hope of success, is to show what these two systems – each one essentially a hermeneutic – have to teach each other in the way of method. Marxism and psychoanalysis indeed present a number of striking analogies of structure with each other, as a checklist of their major themes can testify: the relation of theory and practice; the resistance of false consciousness and the problem as to its opposite (is it knowledge or truth? science or individual certainty?); the role and risks of the concept of a "midwife" of truth, whether analyst or vanguard party; the reappropriation of an alienated history and the function of narrative; the question of desire and value and of the nature of "false desire"; the paradox of the end of the revolutionary process, which, like analysis, must surely be considered "interminable" rather than "terminable"; and so forth. It is therefore not surprising that these two nineteenth-century "philosophies" should be the objects, at the present time and in the present intellectual atmosphere, of similar attacks, which focus on their "naïve semanticism."

It is at least clear that the nineteenth century is to be blamed for the absence until very recently, in both Marxism and psychoanalysis, of a concept of language that would permit the proper answer to this objection. Lacan is therefore in this perspective an exemplary figure, provided we understand his life's work, not as the transformation of Freud into linguistics, but as the disengagement of a linguistic theory that was implicit in Freud's practice but for which he did not yet have the appropriate conceptual instruments; and clearly enough, it is Lacan's third term, his addition of the Real to a relatively harmless conceptual opposition between Imaginary and Symbolic, that sticks in the craw and causes all the trouble. For what is scandalous for contemporary philosophy in both of these "materialisms" – to emphasize the fundamental distance between each of these "unities-of-theory-and-practice" and conventional philosophy as such – is the stubborn retention by both of something the sophisticated philosopher was long since supposed to have put between parentheses, namely a conception of the referent. For model-building and language-oriented philosophies, indeed (and in our time they span an immense range of tendencies and styles from Nietzsche to common language philosophy and from pragmatism to existentialism and structuralism) – for an intellectual climate dominated, in other words, by the conviction that the realities we confront or experience come before us preformed and preordered, not so much by the human "mind" (that is the older form of classical idealism), as rather by the various modes in which human language can work – it is clear that there must be something unacceptable about this affirmation of the persistence, behind our representations, of that indestructible nucleus of what Lacan calls the Real, of which we have already said above that it was simply History itself. If we can have an idea of it, it is objected, then it has already become part of our representations; if not, it is just another Kantian *Ding-an-sich* (a formulation that will probably no longer satisfy anyone). Yet the objection presupposes an epistemology for which knowledge is in one way or another an identity with the things, a presupposition peculiarly without force over the Lacanian conception of the decentered subject, which can know union neither with language nor with the Real and which is structurally at a distance from both in its very being. The Lacanian notion of an "asymptotic" approach to the Real, moreover, maps a situation in which the action of this "absent cause" can be understood as a term limit, both indistinguishable from the Symbolic (or the Imaginary) and also independent of it.

The other version of this objection – that history is a text, and that in that case, as one text is worth another, it can no longer be appealed to as the "ground" of truth – raises the issue of narrative fundamental both for psychoanalysis and for historical materialism, and requires us to lay at least the groundwork for a materialist philosophy of language. For both psychoanalysis and Marxism depend very fundamentally on history in its other sense, as story and storytelling: if the Marxian narrative of the irreversible dynamism of human society as it develops into capitalism be disallowed, little or nothing remains of Marxism as a system and the meaning of the acts of all those who have associated their praxis with it bleeds away. Meanwhile, it is clear that the analytic situation is nothing if not a systematic reconstruction or rewriting of the subject's past,[43] as indeed the very status of the Freudian corpus as an immense body of narrative analyses testifies. We cannot here fully argue the distinction between this narrative orientation of both Marxism and Freudianism and the nonreferential philosophies alluded to above. Suffice it to observe this: that history is not so much a text, as rather a text-to-be-(re-)constructed. Better still, it is an obligation to do so, whose means and techniques are themselves historically irreversible, so that we are not at liberty to construct any historical narrative at all (we are not free, for instance, to return to theodicies or providential narratives, or even to the older nationalistic ones), and the refusal of the Marxist paradigm can generally be demonstrated to be at one with the refusal of historical narration itself, or at least, with its systematic strategic delimitation.

In terms of language, we must distinguish between our own narrative of history – whether psychoanalytic or political – and the Real itself, which our narratives can only approximate in asymptotic fashion and which "resists symbolization absolutely." Nor can the historical paradigm furnished us by psychoanalysis or by Marxism – that of the Oedipus complex or of the class struggle – be considered as anything more Real than a master text, an abstract one, hardly even a protonarrative, in terms of which we construct the text of our own lives with our own concrete praxis. This is the point at which the intervention of Lacan's fundamental distinction between truth and knowledge (or science) must be decisive: the abstract schemata of psychoanalysis or of the Marxian philosophy of history constitute a body of knowledge, indeed, of what many of us would be willing to call scientific knowledge, but they do not embody the "truth" of the subject, nor are the texts in which they are elaborated to be thought of as a *parole pleine*. A materialistic philosophy of language reserves a status for scientific language of this kind, which designates the Real without claiming to coincide with it, which offers the very theory of its own incapacity to signify fully as its credentials for transcending both Imaginary and Symbolic alike. "Il y a des formules qu'on n'imagine pas," Lacan observes of Newton's laws: "Au moins pour un temps, elles font assemblée avec le réel".[44]

The chief defect of all hitherto existing materialism is that it has been conceived as a series of propositions about matter – and in particular the relationship of matter to consciousness, which is to say of the natural sciences to the so-called human sciences[45] – rather than as a set of propositions about language. A materialistic philosophy of language is not a semanticism, naïve or otherwise, because its fundamental tenet is a rigorous distinction between the signified – the realm of semantics proper, of interpretation, of the study of the text's ostensible meaning – and the referent. The study of the referent, however, is the study, not of the meaning of the text, but of the limits of its meanings and of their historical preconditions, and of what is and must remain incommensurable with individual expression. In our present terms, this means that a relationship to objective knowledge (in other words, to what is of such a different order of magnitude and organization from the individual subject that it can never be adequately "represented" within the latter's lived experience save as a term limit) is conceivable only for a thought able to do justice to radical discontinuities, not only between the Lacanian "orders," but within language itself, between its various types of propositions as they entertain wholly different structural relations with the subject. [. . .]

Notes

1 See G. W. F. Hegel, *Phenomenology of Mind* (New York, Humanities Press, 1964), ch. 1 ("Certainty at the Level of Sense Experience"), for the classic description of the way in which the unique experience of the individual subject (sense-perception, the feeling of the here-and-now, the consciousness of some incomparable individuality) turns around into its opposite, into what is most empty and abstract, as it emerges into the universal medium of language. And see, for a demonstration of the social nature of the object of linguistic study, V. N. Voloshinov, *Marxism and the Philosophy of Language* (New York, 1973).

2 Emile Durkheim, *Les Règles de méthode sociologique* (Paris, 1901), p. 128.

3 Serge Leclaire, "A la recherche des principes d'une psychothérapie des psychoses," *La Solution psychiatrique* (1958), p. 383.

4 Rifflet–Lemaire, *Jacques Lacan*, p. 364.

5 A. Vergote, quoted in ibid., p. 138.

6 The fundamental text here is Ernest Jones, "The theory of symbolism," in *Papers on Psychoanalysis* (Boston, 1961); to juxtapose this essay, one of the most painfully orthodox in the Freudian canon, with the Lacanian doctrine of the signifier, which appeals to it for authority, is to have a vivid and paradoxical sense of the meaning of Lacan's "return to the original Freud." This is also the place to observe that American feminist attacks on Lacan, and on the Lacanian doctrine of the signifier, which seem largely inspired by A. G. Wilden, "The critique of phallocentrism," in *System and Structure* (London, 1972), tend to be vitiated by their confusion of the penis as an organ of the body with the phallus as a signifier.

7 "Le Stade du miroir," *Ecrits*, p. 94.

8 Insofar as this insistence becomes the basis for an anthropology or a psychology proper – that is, for a theory of human nature on which a political or a social theory may then be built – it is ideological in the strict sense of the term; we are thus entitled to find Lacan's stress on the "prepolitical" nature of the phenomenon of aggressivity (see Jacques Lacan, *Le Séminaire*, ed. Jacques–Alain Miller [Paris, Seuil, 1973], vol. I, p. 202) somewhat defensive.

9   "L'Aggressivité en psychanalyse," *Ecrits*, p. 113.

10 Hans-Georg Gadamer, "Der Begriff des Spiels," in *Wahrheit und Methode* (Tübingen, 1965), pp. 97–105.

11 Sigmund Freud, *Standard Edition* (London, Hogarth Press, 1955), vol. 17, pp. 179–204; and compare Jean-Louis Baudry's discussion of the 1911 essay, "On the mechanism of paranoia," in his "Ecriture, fiction, idéologie" in *Théorie d'ensemble* (Paris, Seuil, 1968), pp. 145–6.

12 *Le Séminaire*, I, p. 98.

13 Rifflet-Lemaire, *Jacques Lacan*, p. 219; and for an analysis of schizophrenic language in terms of part-objects, see Gilles Deleuze, "Préface" to Louis Wolfson, *Le Schizo et les langues* (Paris, 1970).

14 The archetypal realization of these fantasies must surely be Philip Jose Farmer's classic story "Mother," in *Strange Relations* (London, 1966), which has the additional interest of being a historic document of the psychological or vulgar Freudian *weltanschauung* of the 1950s, and in particular of the ideology of "momism" elaborated by writers like Philip Wylie.

15 St Augustine, *Confessions*, Book I, part 7, quoted in *Ecrits*, p. 114.

16 See in particular *The Genealogy of Morals* and *Saint Genêt*. Neither fully realizes his intent to transcend the categories of "good and evil": Sartre for reasons more fully developed below, Nietzsche insofar as his philosophy of history aims at reviving the more archaic forms of rivalry rather than dissolving them.

17 "Le Stade du miroir," *Ecrits*, p. 97.

18 Melanie Klein, *Contributions to Psychoanalysis, 1921–1945* (London, 1950), p. 238.

19 *Le Séminaire*, I, p. 81.

20 Klein, *Contributions to Psychoanalysis*, p. 242.

21 See "L'Instance de la lettre dans l'inconscient," *Ecrits*, p. 515; or, in translation, "The insistence of the letter in the unconscious," *Yale French Studies*, 36/37 (1966), p. 133. But for a powerful critique of the Lacanian figural mechanism, see Tzvetan Todorov, *Théories du symbole* (Paris, 1977), ch. 8, esp. pp. 302–5; and for a more general analysis of Lacan's linguistic philosophy, Henri Meschonnic, *Le Signe et le poème* (Paris, 1975), pp. 314–22.

22 *Le Séminaire*, I, p. 178.

23 Rifflet-Lemaire, *Jacques Lacan*, p. 129.

24 "Subversion du sujet et dialectique du désir dans l'inconscient freudien," *Ecrits*, p. 819.

25 Fredric Jameson, *The Prison-house of Language* (Princeton, NJ, 1972), p. 205. This is the place to add that, while I would maintain my position on the other thinkers there discussed, I no longer consider the accounts of Lacan and of Althusser given in that book to be adequate: let this chapter and the next [chapters 3 and 4 of Fredric Jameson, *The Ideology of Theory, volume I* (Minneapolis, University of Minnesota Press, 1988)] serve as their replacements.

26 Its fundamental texts are now available in English: "The function of language in psychoanalysis" or so-called "Discours de Rome" (translated in Wilden, *The Language of the Self*); "The insistence of the letter" (see n. 21 above) and

the "Seminar on 'The Purloined Letter,'" *Yale French Studies*, 48 (1972), pp. 39–72.

27 "La Direction de la cure et les principes de son pouvoir," *Ecrits*, p. 593.

28 As, e.g., in "Subversion du sujet et dialectique du désir," *Ecrits*, p. 814.

29 "Kant avec Sade," *Ecrits*, p. 780.

30 "Subversion du sujet et dialectique du désir," *Ecrits*, p. 820.

31 The aesthetic chapters of Guy Rosolato, *Essais sur le symbolique* (Paris, 1969), may serve to document this proposition: they also suggest that our frequent discomfort with psychoanalytic criticism may spring just as much from those ahistorical and systematizing categories of an older philosophical aesthetics in which it remains locked, as from its Freudian interpretative scheme itself. It will indeed have become clear that in the perspective of the present [chapter] all of that more conventional Freudian criticism—a criticism that, above and beyond some "vision" of human nature, offers the critic a privileged interpretative code and the onto-logical security of some ultimate content – must for this very reason be understood as profoundly ideological. What now becomes clearer is that the structural oscillation here referred to in Lacanian conceptuality itself – the strategic alternation between linguistic and "orthodox Freudian" codes – often determines a slippage in the literary or cultural analyses of its practitioners whereby the properly Lacanian tension (or "heterogeneity") tends to relax into more conventional Freudian interpretations.

32 But see the chapter on Michel Leiris in Jeffrey Mehlman, *A Structural Study of Autobiography* (Ithaca, NY, 1974), as well as ch. 3 of Fredric Jameson, *The Political Unconscious* (Ithaca, NY, 1981), pp. 151–84; and see also Christian Metz, "The imaginary signifier," *Screen*, 16 (2) (Summer, 1975), pp. 14–76. With respect to this last, not strictly speaking an analysis of an individual work, it may be observed that the structural discontinuity, in film, between the visual plenitude of the filmic image and its "diegetic" use in the narrative of a given film makes it a privileged object for the exercise of the Lacanian dual registers.

33 *Ecrits*, pp. 11–41 (for English translation, see n. 26).

34 See Jacques Derrida, "The purveyor of truth," *Yale French Studies*, 52 (1975), esp. pp. 45–7. But it might be argued against Derrida that it was Poe himself who first opened up this gap between the abstract concept and its narrative illustration in the lengthy reflections on detection and ratiocination with which the tale is inter-larded.

35 "Présentation de la suite," *Ecrits*, p. 42.

36 See Jameson, *The Prison-house of Language*, pp. 182–3, 197–201.

37 "Seminar on 'The Purloined Letter,'" p. 39 (or *Ecrits*, p. 11). Derrida's reading (see n. 34), which emphasizes the moment of "dissemination" in the Poe story (in particular, the generation of doubles ad infinitum: the narrator as the double of Dupin, Dupin as the double of the Minister, the story itself as the double of the two other Dupin stories, etc.), thus in opposition to the Lacanian seminar fore-grounds what we have learned to identify as the Imaginary, rather than the Symbolic, elements of Poe's text. Whatever the merits of the polemic here

engaged with Lacan, as far as the tale itself is concerned, there emerges a sense of the tension between these two kinds of elements which suggests that it is not so much Lacan as rather Poe's text itself that tends toward a suppression of the traces of just this Imaginary "drift" of which Derrida here reminds us; and that is precisely the "work" of the text itself to transform these Imaginary elements into the closed Symbolic circuit that is Lacan's own object of commentary. This is why it does not seem quite right to conclude, from such a reemphasis on the Imaginary and "disseminatory," that "the opposition of the imaginary and symbolic, and above all its implicit hierarchy, seem to be of very limited relevance" (Derrida, pp. 108–9). On the contrary, it is precisely from this opposition that the exegetical polemic here launched by Derrida draws its interest.

38 Reread from this perspective, Walter Benjamin's seminal essay on *Elective Affinities*, "Goethe's *Wahlverwandtschaften*," in *Schriften*, vol. 1 (Frankfurt, 1955, pp. 55–140), takes on a suggestively Lacanian ring.

39 Derrida, "The purveyor of truth," pp. 81–94.

40 *Le Séminaire*, I, p. 80.

41 "La Science et la vérité," *Ecrits*, p. 876; and see also the remarks on historiography in the "Discours de Rome" (Wilden, *The Language of the Self*, pp. 22ff, p. 50; or *Ecrits*, pp. 260ff, p. 287). The problem of the function of a genetic or evolutionary set of stages within a more genuinely dialectical conception of historical time is common to both psychoanalysis and Marxism. Lacan's insistence on the purely schematic or operational nature of the Freudian stages (oral, anal, genital) may be compared with Etienne Balibar's reflections on the proper uses of the Marxian evolutionary schema (savage, barbarian, civilized) in *Lire le capital*, vol. 2 (Paris, 1968), pp. 79–226.

42 "Seminar on 'The Purloined Letter,'" p. 61, or *Ecrits*, pp. 30–1.

43 The reproach that patients in analysis do not so much rediscover as rather "rewrite" their pasts is a familiar one, argued, however, most rigorously by Jürgen Habermas, in *Knowledge and Human Interests* (Boston, 1971), pp. 246–73.

44 Jacques Lacan, "Radiophonie," *Scilicet*, (1970), p. 75: "Some formulations are not just made up. At least for a time, they fellow-travel with the Real."

45 For the most powerful of recent attempts to reinvent this older kind of materialism, see Sebastiano Timpanaro, "Considerations on materialism," *New Left Review*, 85 (May–June 1974), pp. 3–22. The reckoning on Timpanaro's attempt to replace human history within the "history" of nature comes due, not in his politics, nor even in his epistemology, but rather in his aesthetics, which, proposing that Marxism now "do justice" to the natural elements of the human condition – to death, sickness, old age, and the like – turns out to be nothing more than a replay of existentialism. It is a significant paradox that at the other end of the Marxist spectrum – that of the Frankfurt School – an analogous development may be observed in Herbert Marcuse's late aesthetics.

Part II

Marxism and Culture

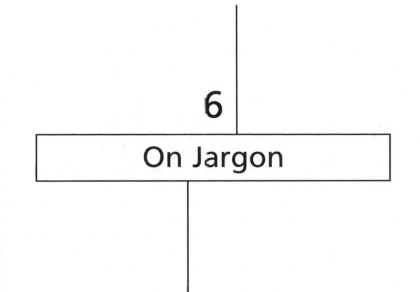

6

On Jargon

This brief piece was written in response to a questionnaire about Marxism and the arts circulated by *The Minnesota Review* (1977).

A number of things have to be touched on in order to explain why theoretical writing today is difficult. For one thing, from a Marxist viewpoint, the truth about social relations and about the place of culture in them does not lie on the surface of everyday life; it is structurally concealed by that phenomenon called reification, a phenomenon generated by the presence of commodities all around us. (See Lukács' difficult but important study of this process in *History and Class Consciousness*.) And, clearly enough, if commodities are the source of this opacity or obfuscation of daily life, it will get worse rather than better as consumer society develops and becomes world-wide. Indeed, it is a kind of axiom of Marxism that Marx's own discovery of the fundamental laws of social life under capitalism (the labor theory of value) was a unique historical possibility, available only after the dissolution of feudal society and the emergence of industrial capitalism, but then in the late-nineteenth and twentieth centuries increasingly covered over again by reification. This means not only that any true account of the mechanisms at work behind daily life and lived experience is going to look "unnatural" and untrue to "common sense" (how can we analyze reification without inventing an ugly word for it?); but also that one of the features of such an account will have to be the destruction of our own habits of reified perception, and the explanation of why we cannot directly or immediately perceive the truth in the first place. A Marxian description of social and cultural life is therefore going to have to be reflexive and self-conscious, as well as hermeneutic, because part of the point to be made by such writing is precisely our own conscious or unconscious resistance to it. Here it should be added that the call for a "plain style," for clarity and simplicity in writing, is an ideology in its own right, and one which has its own history in the Anglo-American tradition. One of its basic functions is precisely to discredit dialectical writing and to secure the ground for one or the other versions of British empiricism or common-sense philosophy.   *wow!*

Now when you block out the situation of dialectical writing in this way, some interesting parallels come to mind. The first is a little too easy, and asks why in a time when all the other sciences are becoming increasingly specialized and impossible of access to the layman, the study of a complex society like the capitalist one should be any easier. Everyone breathes, but that does not give everyone the right to propose biological hypotheses; everyone talks, but talkers are not automatically linguists; it would be surprising if some such difficulty did not hold for the study of social life.

But the parallel which interests me more in the present context is that with poetry itself. Surely one of the unique features of the situation of poetry today — what we call modernist and Romantic poetry, as opposed to the fixed forms and genres of the verse or chant of precapitalist societies — is its mission to overcome the reification of everyday language. Modern poetry emerges from the inarticulacy of people in contemporary capitalist society. Over against their sense of the "seriality" of daily life and daily speech, that is, the feeling that the center is always elsewhere, that this language belongs not to us who use it, but to someone else, in distant centers of production of the media, publishing, and the like, over against this sense of the draining away to some absent center of the very power to speak, modern poetry reasserts its production of language and reinvents a center. The very difficulty of modern poetry is in direct proportion to the degree of reification of everyday speech; and the simplicity of much of poetry today, in the tradition of William Carlos Williams, is itself a second-degree phenomenon which builds on the complexity of the first wave of poetic modernism.

But if this is the case, then what is striking is not the vast gap between theoretical jargon and poetic speech, but rather the similarity of the situations they face and the dilemmas they have to overcome. The poets and the theoreticians are both at work desperately in an increasingly constricted network of reifying processes, and both violently have recourse to invented speech and private languages in order to reopen a space in which to breathe. That they should not recognize their mutual interests in each other, that they should, as in the mirror, take each other's image for that of the Other or the enemy, is itself only one of the more advanced ruses of reification, the way capitalism works to separate its subjects from each other and imprison them in the specialized compartments of their own apparently isolated activities.

Is he being negative or sarcastic?

7

Base and Superstructure

This selection is extracted from Jameson's book-length reading of the work of Theodor Adorno, *Late Marxism* (1990).

[...] The dilemma of the cultural has in fact very significant consequences – as Adorno demonstrates in one of the most brilliant "fragments" of *Minima Moralia*, entitled "Baby with the Bath Water" (47–50/43–5)[1] – for what has often been thought of as one of the essential working principles of the Marxist tradition: the distinction between base and superstructure: it being understood that very serious qualms and reservations about this, ranging all the way to the most drastic proposals for its total removal, are also a recurrent part of the Marxist tradition, virtually from Engels himself onward. Raymond Williams's extensive and influential critique of the doctrine is thus only one of the most recent of many suggestions that we give it, as Perry Anderson once put it about another staple of the Marxist tradition, a decent burial; the post-Marxists did not bother to wait for the family's permission. It is one thing, however, to drop the matter altogether; but quite another to find a better and more satisfactory substitute for it, as Williams tries to do by proposing the Gramscian notion of hegemony. What happens is that in so far as the new idea proves to be an adequate substitute, and performs the functions of the old one in a suitable way, all of the arguments against the old concept return in force against the new one; whereas if it turns out to be relatively unassailable, what gradually dawns on us is that it is not a substitute at all, but a wholly new and different idea. (Much the same can be observed about proposals to substitute for the old and shopworn concept of ideology any number of new terms and ideas, such as discourse,

practice, episteme, and the like.) My own position has always been that everything changes when you grasp base-and-superstructure not as a full-fledged
theory in its own right, but rather as the name for a problem, whose solution is
always a unique, and hoc invention.

But we must initially separate the figuration of the terms base and superstructure – only the initial shape of the problem – from the type of efficacity or
causal law it is supposed to imply. *Überbau* and *Basis*, for example, which so
often suggest to people a house and its foundations, seem in fact to have been
railroad terminology and to have designated the rolling stock and the rails
respectively, something which suddenly jolts us into a rather different picture
of ideology and its effects. Engels's notion of "reciprocal interaction," meanwhile, sounds like the positivistic science textbooks of his day; while Gramsci's
military and strategic conceptions of "hegemony" seem far enough removed
from the placid landscape of those older Second International dwellings and
foundations. Benjamin suggested, in the *Passagenwerk*, that the superstructure
might be thought to *express* the base – thus giving us a kind of linguistic model
(albeit a prestructuralist one). It would not be doing violence to Sartre's
thought, meanwhile, to suggest that for him the *situation* (in the multi-dimen-
sional class and psychoanalytic senses he gave to that term) stood as the
infrastructure to which the act of "free" choice brought a superstructural
response and solution. But if we stress the limiting force of the situation and
minimize the creative features of the freedom inventing itself within it, we then
have something closer to Marx's own remarks on the relationship between
ideologues and class-fractions in *The Eighteenth Brumaire*, from which the
elaborate Lukácsean system of ideological epistemology in *History and Class
Consciousness* subsequently derives.

Meanwhile, we have here essentially been concerned to argue that Adorno's
stereoscopic conception of the coexistence of the universal and the particular
constitutes his particular version of the base/superstructure opposition, since
the universal (concept, system, totality, exchange system itself) is the immediately unknowable infrastructure, while the particular stands as the act or event
of consciousness or culture that seems to be our only individual reality, at the
same time that equivalence controls it like a force field.

But none of these figures (and others are surely conceivable) fatally suggests
the operation of any inevitable causal or deterministic law. What is distinctive
about the Marxist problematic lies in the centrality of this problem and this
question, conceived to be the most urgent and fundamental one – namely, the
relationship to be established between "culture" (or consciousness, or
"existence") and its socioeconomic context, or "base." Once the problem is
acknowledged, the local solutions may range from the most lawful of all – the
most vulgar and demystifying registration of ideological reflex and collective

bad faith – to the local hypothesis of a mysterious autonomy of the cultural under certain circumstances, not excluding situations where culture runs on ahead and seems itself for a brief time "determinant." It is when one has decided in advance that the relationship to be thus established is no longer an interesting or an important question that we may speak, using Adorno's formula, of throwing the baby out with the bath water.

To be sure, Adorno also means it the other way round, in the spirit of his analysis of Veblen: to see culture as a "superstructure" is also already to have thrown the baby out with the bath water, for it implies that culture must always be grasped as something like a functional lie, creating "the illusion of a society worthy of man which does not exist," so that it would be preferable, on such a view, to do away with those illusions and to "demand that relationships be entirely reduced to their material origin, ruthlessly and openly formed according to the interests of the participants." Thus a (perfectly proper) denunciation of illusion turns into a new kind of illusion in its own right: ' this notion, like all expostulation about lies, has a suspicious tendency to become itself ideology." A Marxian materialism, then, tends under its own momentum towards an anti-aesthetic anti-culturalism in which it oddly meets the *ressentiment* of its fascist opponents: "Emphasis on the material element, as against the spirit as a lie, gives rise to a kind of dubious affinity with that political economy which is subjected to an immanent criticism, comparable with the complicity between police and underworld" (*Minima Moralia*, 49/44). As can be imagined, this is very precisely the kind of paradigmatic situation and contradictory dilemma for which "negative dialectics" has been devised in the first place:

If material reality is called the world of exchange value, and any culture whatever refuses to accept the domination of that world, then it is true that such refusal is illusory as long as the existent exists... [yet] in the face of the lie of the commodity world, even the lie that denounces it becomes a corrective. That culture so far has failed is no justification for furthering its failure. (*Minima Moralia*, 49/44)

The methodological conclusion, then – a conclusion which holds not merely for *Kulturkritik* but for thinking on all its other levels – is that we must denounce culture (as an idea but also as a phenomenon) all the time we continue to perpetuate it, and perpetuate it while continuing tirelessly to denounce it. It is with culture as with philosophy, which famously "lived on because the moment to realize it was missed" (*Negative Dialektik*, 15/3);[2] there is, as we shall see, a utopian power in keeping alive the impossible idea of philosophizing (as of producing culture) even while ruthlessly exposing the necessary failure to go on doing it today. (In the same way, according to my own proposal, the stigmatizing term of superstructure needs to be retained in order to remind us of a gap that has to be overcome in some more adequate way than forgetting about it.) For like philosophy, culture is itself marked by the original sin of the division between manual and mental labor:

Cultural criticism is, however, only able to reproach culture so penetratingly for prostituting itself, for violating in its decline the pure autonomy of the mind, because culture originates in the radical separation of mental and physical work. It is from this separation, the original sin as it were, that culture draws it strength. When culture simply denies the separation and feigns harmonious union, it falls back behind its own notion.[3]

[...]

Notes

1   T. W. Adorno, *Minima Moralia* (Frankfurt, Suhrkamp, 1986); trans. E. F. N. Jephcott, *Minima Moralia* (London, Verso, 1974).
2   T. W. Adorno, *Negative Dialektik* (Frankfurt, Suhrkamp, 1975); trans. E. B. Ashton, *Negative Dialectics* (New York, Continuum, 1973).
3   T. W. Adorno, *Prismen* (Frankfurt, Suhrkamp, 1955); trans. S. and S. Weber, *Prisms* (London, Spearman, 1967), pp. 50/49.

8

Reification and Utopia in Mass Culture

This chapter was originally published in *Social Text* in 1979. The following version was published in Jameson's *Signatures of the Visible* (1992).

The theory of mass culture – or mass audience culture, commercial culture, "popular" culture, the culture industry, as it is variously known – has always tended to define its object against so-called high culture without reflecting on the objective status of this opposition. As so often, positions in this field reduce themselves to two mirror images, which are essentially staged in terms of value. Thus the familiar motif of *elitism* argues for the priority of mass culture on the grounds of the sheer numbers of people exposed to it; the pursuit of high or hermetic culture is then stigmatized as a status hobby of small groups of intellectuals. As its anti-intellectual thrust suggests, this essentially negative position has little theoretical content but clearly responds to a deeply rooted conviction in American populism and articulates a widely based sense that high culture is an establishment phenomenon, irredeemably tainted by its association with institutions, in particular with the university. The value invoked is therefore a social one: it would be preferable to deal with TV programs, *The Godfather*, or *Jaws*, rather than with Wallace Stevens or Henry James, because the former clearly speak a cultural language meaningful to far wider strata of the population than what is socially represented by intellectuals. Populist radicals are however also intellectuals, so that this position has suspicious overtones of the guilt trip; meanwhile it overlooks the anti-social and critical, negative (although generally not revolutionary) stance of much of the most important forms of modern art; finally, it offers no method for reading even those cultural objects it valorizes and has had little of interest to say about their content.

This position is then reversed in the theory of culture worked out by the Frankfurt School; as is appropriate for this exact antithesis of the populist position, the work of Adorno, Horkheimer, Marcuse, and others is an intensely theoretical one and provides a working methodology for the close analysis of precisely those products of the culture industry which it stigmatizes and which the radical view exalted. Briefly, this view can be characterized as the extension and application of Marxist theories of commodity reification to the works of mass culture. The theory of reification (here strongly overlaid with Max Weber's analysis of rationalization) describes the way in which, under capitalism, the older traditional forms of human activity are instrumentally reorganized and "taylorized," analytically fragmented and reconstructed according to various rational models of efficiency, and essentially restructured along the lines of a differentiation between means and ends. This is a paradoxical idea: it cannot be properly appreciated until it is understood to what degree the means/ends split effectively brackets or suspends ends themselves, hence the strategic value of the Frankfurt School's term "instrumentalization" which usefully foregrounds the organization of the means themselves over against any particular end or value which is assigned to their practice.[1] In traditional activity, in other words, the value of the activity is immanent to it, and qualitatively distinct from other ends or values articulated in other forms of human work or play. Socially, this meant that various kinds of work in such communities were properly incomparable; in ancient Greece, for instance, the familiar Aristotelian schema of the fourfold causes at work in handicraft or poeisis (material, formal, efficient, and final) were applicable only to artisanal labor, and not to agriculture or war which had a quite different "natural" – which is to say supernatural or divine – basis.[2] It is only with the universal commodification of labor power, which Marx's Capital designates as the fundamental precondition of capitalism, that all forms of human labor can be separated out from their unique qualitative differentiation as distinct types of activity (mining as opposed to farming, opera composition as distinct from textile manufacture), and all universally ranged under the common denominator of the quantitative, that is, under the universal exchange value of money.[3] At this point, then, the quality of the various forms of human activity, their unique and distinct "ends" or values, has effectively been bracketed or suspended by the market system, leaving all these activities free to be ruthlessly reorganized in efficiency terms, as sheer means or instrumentality.

The force of the application of this notion to works of art can be measured against the definition of art by traditional aesthetic philosophy (in particular by

Kant) as a "finality without an end," that is, as a goal-oriented activity which nonetheless has no practical purpose or end in the "real world" of business or politics or concrete human praxis generally. This traditional definition surely holds for all art that works as such: not for stories that fall flat or home movies or inept poetic scribblings, but rather for the successful works of mass and high culture alike. We suspend our real lives and our immediate practical preoccupations just as completely when we watch *The Godfather* as when we read *The Wings of the Dove* or hear a Beethoven sonata.

At this point, however, the concept of the commodity introduces the possibility of structural and historical differentiation into what was conceived as the universal description of the aesthetic experience as such and in whatever form. The concept of the commodity cuts across the phenomenon of reification — described above in terms of activity or production — from a different angle, that of consumption. In a world in which everything, including labor power, has become a commodity, ends remain no less undifferentiated than in the production schema — they are all rigorously quantified, and have become abstractly comparable through the medium of money, their respective price or wage — yet we can now formulate their instrumentalization, their reorganization along the means/ends split, in a new way by saying that, by its transformation into a commodity, a thing of whatever type has been reduced to a means for its own consumption. It no longer has any qualitative value in itself, but only insofar as it can be "used": the various forms of activity lose their immanent intrinsic satisfactions as activity and become means to an end.

The objects of the commodity world of capitalism also shed their independent "being" and intrinsic qualities and come to be so many instruments of commodity satisfaction: the familiar example is that of tourism — the American tourist no longer lets the landscape "be in its being" as Heidegger would have said, but takes a snapshot of it, thereby graphically transforming space into its own material image. The concrete activity of looking at a landscape — including, no doubt, the disquieting bewilderment with the activity itself, the anxiety that must arise when human beings, confronting the non-human, wonder what they are doing there and what the point or purpose of such a confrontation might be in the first place[4] — is thus comfortably replaced by the act of taking possession of it and converting it into a form of personal property. This is the meaning of the great scene in Godard's *Les Carabiniers* (1962–3) when the new world conquerors exhibit their spoils: unlike Alexander, "Michel-Ange" and "Ulysse" merely own images of everything, and triumphantly display their postcards of the Coliseum, the pyramids, Wall Street, Angkor Wat, like so many dirty pictures. This is also the sense of Guy Debord's assertion, in an important book, *The Society of the Spectacle*, that the ultimate form of commodity reification in contemporary consumer society is precisely the image itself.[5]

With this universal commodification of our object world, the familiar accounts
of the other-directedness of contemporary conspicuous consumption and of the
sexualization of our objects and activities are also given: the new model car is
essentially an image for other people to have of us, and we consume, less the
thing itself, than its abstract idea, open to all the libidinal investments ingeni-
ously arrayed for us by advertising.

   It is clear that such an account of commodification has immediate relevance
to aesthetics, if only because it implies that everything in consumer society has
taken on an aesthetic dimension. The force of the Adorno–Horkheimer analysis of the culture industry, however, lies in its demonstration of the unexpected and imperceptible introduction of commodity structure into the very
form and content of the work of art itself. Yet this is something like the ultimate
squaring of the circle, the triumph of instrumentalization over that "finality
without an end" which is art itself, the steady conquest and colonization of the
ultimate realm of non-practicality, of sheer play and anti-use, by the logic of the
world of means and ends. But how can the sheer materiality of a poetic
sentence be "used" in that sense? And while it is clear how we can buy the
idea of an automobile or smoke for the sheer libidinal image of actors, writers,
and models with cigarettes in their hands, it is much less clear how a narrative
could be "consumed" for the benefit of its own idea.

   In its simplest form, this view of instrumentalized culture – and it is implicit
in the aesthetics of the *Tel Quel* group as well as in that of the Frankfurt School
– suggests that the reading process is itself restructured along a means/ends
differentiation. It is instructive here to juxtapose Auerbach's discussion of the
Odyssey in *Mimesis,* and his description of the way in which at every point the
poem is as it were vertical to itself, self-contained, each verse paragraph and
tableau somehow timeless and immanent, bereft of any necessary or indispensable links with what precedes it and what follows; in this light it becomes
possible to appreciate the strangeness, the historical un-naturality (in a Brechtian
sense) of contemporary books which, like detective stories, you read "for the
end" – the bulk of the pages becoming sheer devalued means to an end – in this
case, the "solution" which is itself utterly insignificant insofar as we are not
thereby in the real world and by the latter's practical standards the identity of an
imaginary murderer is supremely trivial.

   The detective story is to be sure an extremely specialized form: still, the
essential commodification of which it may serve as an emblem can be detected
everywhere in the sub-genres of contemporary commercial art, in the way in
which the materialization of this or that sector or zone of such forms comes to
constitute an end and a consumption-satisfaction around which the rest of the
work is then "degraded" to the status of sheer means. Thus, in the older
adventure tale, not only does the *dénouement* (victory of hero or villains,

discovery of the treasure, rescue of the heroine or the imprisoned comrades, foiling of a monstrous plot, or arrival in time to reveal an urgent message or a secret) stand as the reified end in view of which the rest of the narrative is consumed – this reifying structure also reaches down into the very page-by-page detail of the book's composition. Each chapter recapitulates a smaller consumption process in its own right, ending with the frozen image of a new and catastrophic reversal of the situation, constructing the smaller gratifications of a flat character who actualizes his single potentiality (the "choleric" Ned Land finally exploding in anger), organizing its sentences into paragraphs each of which is a sub-plot in its own right, or around the object-like stasis of the "fateful" sentence or the "dramatic" tableau, the whole tempo of such reading meanwhile overprogrammed by its intermittent illustrations which, either before or after the fact, reconfirm our readerly business, which is to transform the transparent flow of language as much as possible into material images and objects we can consume.[6]

Yet this is still a relatively primitive stage in the commodification of narrative. More subtle and more interesting is the way in which, since naturalism, the best-seller has tended to produce a quasi-material "feeling tone" which floats about the narrative but is only intermittently realized by it: the sense of destiny in family novels, for instance or the "epic" rhythms of the earth or of great movements of "history" in the various sagas can be seen as so many commod-ities towards whose consumption the narratives are little more than means, their essential materiality then being confirmed and embodied in the movie music that accompanies their screen versions.[7] This structural differentiation of narra-tive and consumable feeling tone is a broader and historically and formally more significant manifestation of the kind of "fetishism of hearing" which Adorno denounced when he spoke about the way the contemporary listener restructures a classical symphony so that the sonata form itself becomes an instrumental means toward the consumption of the isolatable tune or melody.

It will be clear, then, that I consider the Frankfurt School's analysis of the commodity structure of mass culture of the greatest interest: if, below, I propose a somewhat different way of looking at the same phenomena, it is not because I feel that their approach has been exhausted. On the contrary, we have scarcely begun to work out all the consequences of such descriptions, let alone to make an exhaustive inventory of variant models and of other features besides com-modity reification in terms of which such artifacts might be analyzed.

What is unsatisfactory about the Frankfurt School's position is not its nega-tive and critical apparatus, but rather the positive value on which the latter depends, namely the valorization of traditional modernist high art as the locus of some genuinely critical and subversive, "autonomous" aesthetic production. Here Adorno's later work (as well as Marcuse's *The Aesthetic Dimension*) mark a retreat over the former's dialectically ambivalent assessment, in *The Philosophy of Modern Music*, of Arnold Schoenberg's achievement: what has been omitted from the later judgments is precisely Adorno's fundamental discovery of the historicity, and in particular, the irreversible aging process, of the greatest modernist forms. But if this is so, then the great work of modern high culture – whether it be Schoenberg, Beckett, or even Brecht himself – cannot serve as a fixed point or eternal standard against which to measure the "degraded" status of mass culture: indeed, fragmentary and as yet undeveloped tendencies[8] in recent art production – hyper-or photo-realism in visual art; "new music" of the type of LaMonte Young, Terry Riley, or Philip Glass; postmodernist literary texts like those of Pynchon – suggest an increasing interpenetration of high and mass cultures.

For all these reasons, it seems to me that we must rethink the opposition high culture/mass culture in such a way that the emphasis on evaluation to which it has traditionally given rise – and which however the binary system of value operates (mass culture is popular and thus more authentic than high culture, high culture is autonomous and, therefore, utterly incomparable to a degraded mass culture) tends to function in some timeless realm of absolute aesthetic judgment – is replaced by a genuinely historical and dialectical approach to these phenomena. Such an approach demands that we read high and mass culture as objectively related and dialectically interdependent phenomena, as twin and inseparable forms of the fission of aesthetic production under capitalism. In this, capitalism's third or multinational stage, however, the dilemma of the double standard of high and mass culture remains, but it has become – not the subjective problem of our own standards of judgment – but rather an objective contradiction which has its own social grounding.

Indeed, this view of the emergence of mass culture obliges us historically to respecify the nature of the "high culture" to which it has conventionally been opposed: the older culture critics indeed tended loosely to raise comparative issues about the "popular culture" of the past. Thus, if you see Greek tragedy, Shakespeare, *Don Quijote*, still widely read romantic lyrics of the type of Hugo, and best-selling realistic novels like those of Balzac or Dickens, as uniting a wide "popular" audience with high aesthetic quality, then you are fatally locked into such false problems as the relative value – weighed against Shakespeare or even Dickens – of such popular contemporary auteurs of high quality as Chaplin, John Ford, Hitchcock, or even Robert Frost, Andrew Wyeth, Simenon, or John O'Hara. The utter senselessness of this interesting subject of conversation becomes clear when it is understood that from a historical point of view the only form of "high culture" which can be said to constitute the dialectical opposite of mass culture is that high culture production contemporaneous with the latter, which is to say that artistic production generally designated as *modernism*. The other term would then be Wallace Stevens, or Joyce, or Schoenberg, or Jackson Pollock, but surely not cultural artifacts such as the novels of Balzac or the plays of Molière which essentially antedate the historical separation between high and mass culture.

But such specification clearly obliges us to rethink our definitions of mass culture as well: the commercial products of the latter can surely not without intellectual dishonesty be assimilated to so-called popular, let alone folk, art of the past, which reflected and were dependent for their production on quite different social realities, and were in fact the "organic" expression of so many distinct social communities or castes, such as the peasant village, the court, the medieval town, the polis, and even the classical bourgeoisie when it was still a unified social group with its own cultural specificity. The historically unique tendential effect of late capitalism on all such groups has been to dissolve and to fragment or atomize them into agglomerations (*Gesellschaften*) of isolated and equivalent private individuals, by way of the corrosive action of universal commodification and the market system. Thus, the "popular" as such no longer exists, except under very specific and marginalized conditions (internal and external pockets of so-called underdevelopment within the capitalist world system); the commodity production of contemporary or industrial mass culture has nothing whatsoever to do, and nothing in common, with older forms of popular or folk art.

Thus understood, the dialectical opposition and profound structural inter-relatedness of modernism and contemporary mass culture opens up a whole new field for cultural study, which promises to be more intelligible historically and socially than research or disciplines which have strategically conceived their missions as a specialization in this or that branch (e.g., in the university, English departments *v.* Popular Culture programs). Now the emphasis must lie squarely on the social and aesthetic situation – the dilemma of form and of a public – shared and faced by both modernism and mass culture, but "solved" in antithetical ways. Modernism also can only be adequately understood in terms of that commodity production whose all-informing structural influence on mass culture I have described above: only for modernism, the commodity form signals the vocation *not* to be a commodity, to devise an aesthetic language incapable of offering commodity satisfaction, and resistant to instrumentalization. The difference between this position and the valorization of modernism by the Frankfurt School (or, later, by *Tel Quel*) lies in my designation of modernism as reactive, that is, as a symptom and as a result of cultural crises, rather than a new "solution" in its own right: not only is the commodity the prior form in terms of which alone modernism can be structurally grasped, but the very terms of its solution – the conception of the modernist text as the production and the protest of an isolated individual, and the logic of its sign systems as so many private languages ("styles") and private religions – are contradictory and made the social or collective realization of its aesthetic project (Mallarmé's ideal of *Le Livre* can be taken as the latter's fundamental formulation)[9] an impossible one (a judgment which, it ought not to be necessary to add, is not a judgment of value about the "greatness" of the modernist texts).

Yet there are other aspects of the situation of art under monopoly and late capitalism which have remained unexplored and offer equally rich perspectives in which to examine modernism and mass culture and their structural dependency. Another such issue, for example, is that of *materialization* in contemporary art – a phenomenon woefully misunderstood by much contemporary Marxist theory (for obvious reasons, it is not an issue that has attracted academic formalism). Here the misunderstanding is dramatized by the pejorative emphasis of the Hegelian tradition (Lukács as well as the Frankfurt School) on phenomena of aesthetic reification – which furnishes the term of a negative value judgment – in juxtaposition to the celebration of the "material signifier" and the "materiality of the text" or of "textual production" by the French tradition which appeals for its authority to Althusser and Lacan. If you are willing to entertain the possibility that "reification" and the emergence of increasingly materialized signifiers are one and the same phenomenon – both historically and culturally – then this ideological great debate turns out to be based on a fundamental misunderstanding. Once again, the confusion stems from the introduction of the false problem of value (which fatally programs every binary opposition into its good and bad, positive and negative, essential and inessential terms) into a more properly ambivalent dialectical and historical situation in which reification or materialization is a key structural feature of both modernism and mass culture.

The task of defining this new area of study would then initially involve making an inventory of other such problematic themes or phenomena in terms of which the interrelationship of mass culture and modernism can usefully be explored, something it is too early to do here. At this point, I will merely note one further such theme, which has seemed to me to be of the greatest significance in specifying the antithetical formal reactions of modernism and mass culture to their common social situation, and that is the notion of *repetition*. This concept, which in its modern form we owe to Kierkegaard, has known rich and interesting new elaborations in recent post-structuralism: for Jean Baudrillard, for example, the repetitive structure of what he calls the simulacrum (that is, the reproduction of "copies" which have no original) characterizes the commodity production of consumer capitalism and marks our object world with an unreality and a free-floating absence of "the referent" (e.g., the place hitherto taken by nature, by raw materials and primary production, or by the "originals" of artisanal production or handicraft) utterly unlike anything experienced in any earlier social formation.

If this is the case, then we would expect repetition to constitute yet another feature of the contradictory situation of contemporary aesthetic production to which both modernism and mass culture in one way or another cannot but react. This is in fact the case, and one need only invoke the traditional ideological stance of all modernizing theory and practice from the romantics to the *Tel Quel* group, and passing through the hegemonic formulations of classical Anglo-American modernism, to observe the strategic emphasis on innovation and novelty, the obligatory break with previous styles, the pressure – geometrically increasing with the ever swifter temporality of consumer society, with its yearly or quarterly style and fashion changes – to "make it new," to produce something which resists and breaks through the force of gravity of repetition as a universal feature of commodity equivalence. Such aesthetic ideologies have, to be sure, no critical or theoretical value – for one thing, they are purely formal, and by abstracting some empty concept of innovation from the concrete content of stylistic change in any given period end up flattening out even the history of forms, let alone social history, and projecting a kind of cyclical view of change – yet they are useful symptoms for detecting the ways in which the various modernisms have been forced, in spite of themselves, and in the very flesh and bone of their form, to respond to the objective reality of repetition itself. In our own time, the postmodernist conception of a "text" and the ideal of schizophrenic writing openly demonstrate this vocation of the modernist aesthetic to produce sentences which are radically discontinuous, and which defy repetition not merely on the level of the break with older forms or older formal models but now within the microcosm of the text itself. Meanwhile, the kinds of repetition which, from Gertrude Stein to Robbe-Grillet, the modernist project has appropriated and made its own, can be seen as a kind of homeopathic strategy whereby the scandalous and intolerable external irritant is drawn into the aesthetic process itself and thereby systematically worked over, "acted out," and symbolically neutralized.

But it is clear that the influence of repetition on mass culture has been no less decisive. Indeed, it has frequently been observed that the older generic discourses – stigmatized by the various modernist revolutions, which have successively repudiated the older fixed forms of lyric, tragedy, and comedy, and at length even "the novel" itself, now replaced by the unclassifiable "livre" or "text" – retain a powerful afterlife in the realm of mass culture. Paperback drugstore or airport displays reinforce all of the now sub-generic distinctions between gothic, best-seller, mysteries, science fiction, biography, or pornography, as do the conventional classification of weekly TV series, and the production and marketing of Hollywood films (to be sure, the generic system at work in contemporary commercial film is utterly distinct from the traditional pattern of the 1930s and 1940s production, and has had to respond to television competition by devising new meta-generic or omnibus forms, which, however, at once become new "genres" in their own right, and fold back into the usual generic stereotyping and reproduction – as, recently, with disaster film or occult film).

But we must specify this development historically: the older pre-capitalist genres were signs of something like an aesthetic "contract" between a cultural producer and a certain homogeneous class or group public; they drew their vitality from the social and collective status (which to be sure, varied widely according to the mode of production in question) of the situation of aesthetic production and consumption – that is to say, from the fact that the relationship between artist and public was still in one way or another a social institution and a concrete social and interpersonal relationship with its own validation and specificity. With the coming of the market, this institutional status of artistic consumption and production vanishes: art becomes one more branch of commodity production, the artist loses all social status and faces the options of becoming a *poète maudit* or a journalist, the relationship to the public is problematized, and the latter becomes a virtual "public introuvable" (the appeals to posterity, Stendhal's dedication "To the Happy Few," or Gertrude Stein's remark, "I write for myself and for strangers," are revealing testimony to this intolerable new state of affairs).

The survival of genre in emergent mass culture can thus in no way be taken as a return to the stability of the publics of pre-capitalist societies: on the contrary, the generic forms and signals of mass culture are very specifically to be understood as the historical reappropriation and displacement of older structures in the service of the qualitatively very different situation of repetition. The atomized or serial "public" of mass culture wants to see the same thing over and over again, hence the urgency of the generic structure and the generic signal: if you doubt this, think of your own consternation at finding that the paperback you selected from the mystery shelf turns out to be a romance or a science fiction novel; think of the exasperation of people in the row next to you who bought their tickets imagining that they were about to see a thriller or a political mystery instead of the horror or occult film actually underway. Think also of the much misunderstood "aesthetic bankruptcy" of television: the structural reason for the inability of the various television series to produce episodes which are either socially "realistic" or have an aesthetic and formal autonomy that transcends mere variation has little enough to do with the talent of the people involved (although it is certainly exacerbated by the increasing "exhaustion" of material and the ever-increasing tempo of the production of new episodes), but lies precisely in our "set" towards repetition. Even if you are a reader of Kafka or Dostoyevsky, when you watch a cop show or a detective series, you do so in expectation of the stereotyped format and would be annoyed to find the video narrative making "high cultural" demands on you. Much the same situation obtains for film, where it has however been institutionalized as the distinction between American (now multinational) film – determining the expection of generic repetition – and foreign films, which determine a shifting of gears of the "horizon of expectations" to the reception of high cultural discourse or so-called art films.

This situation has important consequences for the analysis of mass culture which have not yet been fully appreciated. The philosophical paradox of repetition – formulated by Kierkegaard, Freud, and others – can be grasped in this, that it can as it were only take place "a second time." The first-time event is by definition not a repetition of anything; it is then reconverted into repetition the second time round, by the peculiar action of what Freud called "retroactivity" (*Nachträglichkeit*). But this means that, as with the simulacrum, there is no "first time" of repetition, no "original" of which succeeding repetitions are mere copies; and here too, modernism furnishes a curious echo in its production of books which, like Hegel's *Phenomenology* or Proust or *Finnegans Wake*, you can only *reread*. Still, in modernism, the hermetic text remains, not only as an Everest to assault, but also as a book to whose stable reality you can return over and over again. In mass culture, repetition effectively volatilizes the original object – the "text," the "work of art" – so that the student of mass culture has no primary object of study.

The most striking demonstration of this process can be witnessed in our reception of contemporary pop music of whatever type – the various kinds of rock, blues, country western, or disco. I will argue that we never hear any of the singles produced in these genres "for the first time"; instead, we live a constant exposure to them in all kinds of different situations, from the steady beat of the car radio through the sounds at lunch, or in the work place, or in shopping centers, all the way to those apparently full-dress performances of the "work" in a nightclub or stadium concert or on the records you buy and take home to hear. This is a very different situation from the first bewildered audition of a complicated classical piece, which you hear again in the concert hall or listen to at home. The passionate attachment one can form to this or that pop single, the rich personal investment of all kinds of private associations and existential symbolism which is the feature of such attachment, are fully as much a function of our own familiarity as of the work itself: the pop single, by means of repetition, insensibly becomes part of the existential fabric of our own lives, so that what we listen to is ourselves, our own previous auditions.[10]

Under these circumstances, it would make no sense to try to recover a feeling for the "original" musical text, as it really was, or as it might have been heard "for the first time." Whatever the results of such a scholarly or analytical project, its object of study would be quite distinct, quite differently constituted, from the same "musical text" grasped as mass culture, or in other works, as sheer repetition. The dilemma of the student of mass culture therefore lies in the structural absence, or repetitive volatilization, of the "primary texts"; nor is anything to be gained by reconstituting a "corpus" of texts after the fashion of, say, the medievalists who work with pre-capitalist generic and repetitive structures only superficially similar to those of contemporary mass or commercial culture. Nor, to my mind, is anything explained by recourse to the currently fashionable term of "intertextuality," which seems to me at best to designate a problem rather than a solution. Mass culture presents us with a methodological dilemma which the conventional habit of positing a stable object of commentary or exegesis in the form of a primary text or work is disturbingly unable to focus, let alone to resolve; in this sense, also, a dialectical conception of this field of study in which modernism and mass culture are grasped as a single historical and aesthetic phenomenon has the advantage of positing the survival of the primary text at one of its poles, and thus providing a guide-rail for the bewildering exploration of the aesthetic universe which lies at the other, a message or semiotic bombardment from which the textual referent has disappeared.

The above reflections by no means raise, let alone address, all the most urgent issues which confront an approach to mass culture today. In particular, we have neglected a somewhat different judgment on mass culture, which also loosely derives from the Frankfurt School position on the subject, but whose adherents number "radicals" as well as "elitists" on the Left today. This is the conception of mass culture as sheer manipulation, sheer commercial brainwashing and empty distraction by the multinational corporations who obviously control every feature of the production and distribution of mass culture today. If this were the case, then it is clear that the study of mass culture would at best be assimilated to the anatomy of the techniques of ideological marketing and be subsumed under the analysis of advertising texts and materials. Roland Barthes's seminal investigation of the latter, however, in his *Mythologies*, opened them up to the whole realm of the operations and functions of culture in everyday life; but since the sociologists of manipulation (with the exception, of course, of the Frankfurt School itself) have, almost by definition, no interest in the hermetic or "high" art production whose dialectical interdependency with mass culture we have argued above, the general effect of their position is to suppress considerations of culture altogether, save as a kind of sandbox affair on the most epiphenomenal level of the superstructure.

The implication is thus to suggest that real social life – the only features of social life worth addressing or taking into consideration when political theory and strategy is at stake – are what the Marxian tradition designates as the political, the ideological, and the juridical levels of superstructural reality. Not only is this repression of the cultural moment determined by the university structure and by the ideologies of the various disciplines – thus, political science and sociology at best consign cultural issues to that ghettoizing rubric and marginalized field of specialization called the "sociology of culture" – it is also and in a more general way the unwitting perpetuation of the most fundamental ideological stance of American business society itself, for which "culture" – reduced to plays and poems and high-brow concerts – is *par excellence* the most trivial and non-serious activity in the "real life" of the rat race of daily existence.

Yet even the vocation of the esthete (last sighted in the US during the pre-political heyday of the 1950s) and of his successor, the university literature professor acknowledging uniquely high cultural "values," had a socially symbolic content and expressed (generally unconsciously) the anxiety aroused by market competition and the repudiation of the primacy of business pursuits and business values: these are then, to be sure, as thoroughly repressed from academic formalism as culture is from the work of the sociologists of manipulation, a repression which goes a long way towards accounting for the resistance and defensiveness of contemporary literary study towards anything which smacks of the painful reintroduction of just that "real life" – the socio-economic, the historical context – which it was the function of aesthetic vocation to deny or to mask out in the first place.

What we must ask the sociologists of manipulation, however, is whether culture, far from being an occasional matter of the reading of a monthly good book or a trip to the drive-in, is not the very element of consumer society itself. No society, indeed, has ever been saturated with signs and messages like this one. If we follow Debord's argument about the omnipresence and the omnipotence of the image in consumer capitalism today, then if anything the priorities of the real become reversed, and everything is mediated by culture, to the point where even the political and the ideological "levels" have initially to be disentangled from their primary mode of representation which is cultural. Howard Jarvis, Jimmy Carter, even Castro, the Red Brigades, B J. Vorster, the Communist "penetration" of Africa, the war in Vietnam, strikes, inflation itself – all are images, all come before us with the immediacy of cultural representations about which one can be fairly certain that they are by a long shot not historical reality itself. If we want to go on believing in categories like social class, then we are going to have to dig for them in them in the insubstantial bottomless realm of cultural and collective fantasy. Even ideology has in our society lost its clarity as prejudice, false consciousness, readily identifiable opinion: our racism gets all mixed up with clean-cut black actors on TV and in commercials, our sexism has to make a detour through new stereotypes of the "women's libber" on the network series. After that, if one wants to stress the primacy of the political, so be it: until the omnipresence of culture in this society is even dimly sensed, realistic conceptions of the nature and function of political praxis today can scarcely be framed.

It is true that manipulation theory sometimes finds a special place in its scheme for those rare cultural objects which can be said to have overt political and social content: sixties protest songs, *The Salt of the Earth* (Biberman, 1954), Clancy Sigal's novels or Sol Yurick's, Chicano murals, the San Francisco Mime Troop. This is not the place to raise the complicated problem of political art today, except to say that our business as culture critics requires us to raise it, and to rethink what are still essentially thirties categories in some new and more satisfactory contemporary way. But the problem of political art – and we have nothing worth saying about it if we do not realize that it is a problem, rather than a choice or a ready-made option – suggests an important qualification to the scheme outlined in the first part of [this chapter]. The implied presupposition of those earlier remarks was that authentic cultural creation is dependent for its existence on authentic collective life, on the vitality of the "organic" social group in whatever form (and such groups can range from the classical polis to the peasant village, from the commonality of the ghetto to the shared values of an embattled pre-revolutionary bourgeoisie). Capitalism systematically dissolves the fabric of all cohesive social groups without exception, including its own ruling class, and thereby problematizes aesthetic production and linguistic invention which have their source in group life. The result, discussed above, is the dialectical fission of older aesthetic expression into two modes, modernism and mass culture, equally dissociated from group praxis. Both of these modes have attained an admirable level of technical virtuosity; but it is a daydream to expect that either of these semiotic structures could be retransformed, by fiat, miracle, or sheer talent, into what could be called, in its strong form, political art, or in a more general way, that living and authentic culture of which we have virtually lost the memory, so rare an experience it has become. This is to say that of the two most influential recent Left aesthetics – the Brecht–Benjamin position, which hoped for the transformation of the nascent mass-cultural techniques and channels of communication of the 1930s into an openly political art, and the *Tel Quel* position which reaffirms the "subversive" and revolutionary efficacy of language revolution and modernist and post-modernist formal innovation – we must reluctantly conclude that neither addresses the specific conditions of our own time.

The only authentic cultural production today has seemed to be that which can draw on the collective experience of marginal pockets of the social life of the world system: black literature and blues, British working-class rock, women's literature, gay literature, the *roman québécois*, the literature of the Third World; and this production is possible only to the degree to which these forms of collective life or collective solidarity have not yet been fully penetrated by the market and by the commodity system. This is not necessarily a negative prognosis, unless you believe in an increasingly windless and all-embracing total system; what shatters such a system – it has unquestionably been falling into place all around us since the development of industrial capitalism – is however very precisely collective praxis or, to pronounce its traditional unmentionable name, class struggle. Yet the relationship between class struggle and cultural production is not an immediate one; you do not reinvent an access onto political art and authentic cultural production by studding your individual artistic discourse with class and political signals. Rather, class struggle, and the slow and intermittent development of genuine class consciousness, are them-selves the process whereby a new and organic group constitutes itself, whereby the collective breaks through the reified atomization (Sartre calls it the seriality) of capitalist social life. At that point, to say that the group exists and that it generates its own specific cultural life and expression, are one and the same. That is, if you like, the third term missing from my initial picture of the fate of the aesthetic and the cultural under capitalism; yet no useful purpose is served by speculation on the forms such a third and authentic type of cultural language might take in situations which do not yet exist. As for the artists, for them too "the owl of Minerva takes its flight at dusk," for them too, as with Lenin in April, the test of historical inevitability is always after the fact, and they cannot be told any more than the rest of us what is historically possible until after it has been tried.

This said, we can now return to the question of mass culture and manipula-tion. Brecht taught us that under the right circumstances you could remake anybody over into anything you liked (*Mann ist Mann*), only he insisted on the situation and the raw materials fully as much or more than on the techniques stressed by manipulation theory. Perhaps the key problem about the concept, or pseudo-concept, of manipulation can be dramatized by juxtaposing it to the Freudian notion of repression. The Freudian mechanism indeed, comes into play only after its object – trauma, charged memory, guilty or threatening desire, anxiety – has in some way been aroused, and risks emerging into the subject's consciousness. Freudian repression is therefore determinate, it has specific content, and may even be said to be something like a "recognition" of that content which expresses itself in the form of denial, forgetfulness, slip, *mauvaise foi*, displacement or substitution.

But of course the classical Freudian model of the work of art (as of the dream or the joke) was that of the symbolic fulfillment of the repressed wish, of a complex structure of indirection whereby desire could elude the repressive censor and achieve some measure of a, to be sure, purely symbolic satisfaction. A more recent "revision" of the Freudian model, however – Norman Holland's *The Dynamics of Literary Response* – proposes a scheme more useful for our present problem, which is to conceive how (commercial) works of art can possibly be said to "manipulate" their publics. For Holland, the psychic function of the work of art must be described in such a way that these two inconsistent and even incompatible features of aesthetic gratification – on the one hand, its wish-fulfilling function, but on the other the necessity that its symbolic structure protect the psyche against the frightening and potentially damaging eruption of powerful archaic desires and wish-material – be somehow harmonized and assigned their place as twin drives of a single structure. Hence Holland's suggestive conception of the vocation of the work of art to *manage* this raw material of the drives and the archaic wish or fantasy material. To rewrite the concept of a management of desire in social terms now allows us to think repression and wish-fulfillment together within the unity of a single mechanism, which gives and takes alike in a kind of psychic compromise or horse-trading; which strategically arouses fantasy content within careful symbolic containment structures which defuse it, gratifying intolerable, unrealizable, properly imperishable desires only to the degree to which they can be momentarily stilled.

This model seems to me to permit a far more adequate account of the mechanisms of manipulation, diversion, and degradation, which are undeniably at work in mass culture and in the media. In particular it allows us to grasp mass culture not as empty distraction or "mere" false consciousness, but rather as a transformational work on social and political anxieties and fantasies which must then have some effective presence in the mass cultural text in order subsequently to be "managed" or repressed. Indeed, the initial reflections of the present [chapter] suggest that such a thesis ought to be extended to modernism as well, even though I will not here be able to develop this part of the argument further.[11] I will therefore argue that both mass culture and modernism have as much content, in the loose sense of the word, as the older social realisms; but that this content is processed in all three in very different ways. Both modernism and mass culture entertain relations of repression with the fundamental social anxieties and concerns, hopes and blind spots, ideological antinomies and fantasies of disaster, which are their raw material; only where modernism tends to handle this material by producing compensatory structures of various kinds, mass culture represses them by the narrative construction of imaginary resolutions and by the projection of an optical illusion of social harmony.

I will now demonstrate this proposition by a reading of three extremely successful recent commercial films: Steven Spielberg's *Jaws* (1975) and the two parts of Francis Ford Coppola's *The Godfather*, (1972, 1974). The readings I will propose are at least consistent with my earlier remarks about the volatilization of the primary text in mass culture by repetition, to the degree of which they are differential, "intertextually" comparative decodings of each of these filmic messages.

In the case of *Jaws*, however, the version or variant against which the film will be read is not the shoddy and disappointing sequels, but rather the best-selling novel by Peter Benchley from which the film – one of the most successful box office attractions in movie history – was adapted. As we will see, the adaptation involved significant changes from the original narrative; my attention to these strategic alterations may indeed arouse some initial suspicion of the official or "manifest" content preserved in both these texts, and on which most of the discussion of *Jaws* has tended to focus. Thus critics from Gore Vidal and *Pravda* all the way to Stephen Heath[12] have tended to emphasize the problem of the shark itself and what it "represents:" such speculation ranges from the psychoanalytic to historic anxieties about the Other that menace American society – whether it be the Communist conspiracy or the Third World – and even to internal fears about the unreality of daily life in America today, and in particular the haunting and unmentionable persistence of the organic – of birth, copulation, and death – which the cellophane society of consumer capitalism desperately recontains in hospitals and old age homes, and sanitizes by means of a whole strategy of linguistic euphemisms which enlarge the older, purely sexual ones: on this view, the Nantucket beaches "represent" consumer society itself, with its glossy and commodified images of gratification, and its scandalous and fragile, ever suppressed, sense of its own possible mortality.

Now none of these readings can be said to be wrong or aberrant, but their very multiplicity suggests that the vocation of the symbol – the killer shark – lies less in any single message or meaning than in its very capacity to absorb and organize all of these quite distinct anxieties together. As a symbolic vehicle, then, the shark must be understood in terms of its essentially polysemous function rather than any particular content attributable to it by this or that spectator. Yet it is precisely this polysemousness which is profoundly ideo-logical, insofar as it allows essentially social and historical anxieties to be folded back into apparently "natural" ones, both to express and to be recontained in what looks like a conflict with other forms of biological existence.

Interpretive emphasis on the shark, indeed, tends to drive all these quite varied readings in the direction of myth criticism, where the shark is naturally enough taken to be the most recent embodiment of Leviathan, so that the struggle with it effortlessly folds back into one of the fundamental paradigms or archetypes of Northrop Frye's storehouse of myth. To rewrite the film in terms of myth is thus to emphasize what I will shortly call its Utopian dimension, that is, its ritual celebration of the renewal of the social order and its salvation, not merely from divine wrath, but also from unworthy leadership.

But to put it this way is also to begin to shift our attention from the shark itself to the emergence of the hero – or heroes – whose mythic task it is to rid the civilized world of the archetypal monster. That is, however, precisely the issue – the nature and the specification of the "mythic" hero – about which the discrepancies between the film and the novel have something instructive to tell us. For the novel involves an undisguised expression of class conflict in the tension between the island cop, Brody (Roy Scheider), and the high-society oceanographer, Hooper (Richard Dreyfuss), who used to summer in East-hampton and ends up sleeping with Brody's wife: Hooper is indeed a much more important figure in the novel than in the film, while by the same token the novel assigns the shark-hunter, Quint (Robert Shaw), a very minor role in comparison to his crucial presence in the film. Yet the most dramatic surprise the novel holds in store for viewers of the film will evidently be the discovery that in the book Hooper dies, a virtual suicide and a sacrifice to his somber and romantic fascination with death in the person of the shark. Now while it is unclear to me how the American reading public can have responded to the rather alien and exotic resonance of this element of the fantasy – the aristocratic obsession with death would seem to be a more European motif – the social overtones of the novel's resolution – the triumph of the islander and the yankee over the decadent playboy challenger – are surely unmistakable, as is the systematic elimination and suppression of all such class overtones from the film itself.

The latter therefore provides us with a striking illustration of a whole work of displacement by which the written narrative of an essentially class fantasy has been transformed, in the Hollywood product, into something quite different, which it now remains to characterize. Gone is the whole decadent and aristo-cratic brooding over death, along with the erotic rivalry in which class antag-onisms were dramatized; the Hooper of the film is nothing but a technocratic whiz-kid, no tragic hero but instead a good-natured creature of grants and foundations and scientific know-how. But Brody has also undergone an important modification: he is no longer the small-town island boy married to a girl from a socially prominent summer family; rather, he has been transformed into a retired cop from New York City, relocating on Nantucket in an effort to flee the hassle of urban crime, race war, and ghettoization. The figure of Brody now therefore introduces overtones and connotations of law-and-order, rather than a yankee shrewdness, and functions as a TV police-show hero transposed into this apparently more sheltered but in reality equally contradictory milieu which is the great American summer vacation.

I will therefore suggest that in the film the socially resonant conflict between these two characters has, for some reason that remains to be formulated, been transformed into a vision of their ultimate partnership, and joint triumph over Leviathan. This is then clearly the moment to turn to Quint, whose enlarged role in the film thereby becomes strategic. The myth-critical option for reading this figure must at once be noted: it is indeed tempting to see Quint as the end term of the threefold figure of the ages of man into which the team of shark-hunters is so obviously articulated, Hooper and Brody then standing as youth and maturity over against Quint's authority as an elder. But such a reading leaves the basic interpretive problem intact: what can be the allegorical meaning of a ritual in which the older figure follows the intertextual paradigm of Melville's Ahab to destruction while the other two paddle back in triumph on the wreckage of his vessel? Or, to formulate it in a different way, why is the Ishmael survivor-figure split into the two survivors of the film (and credited with the triumphant destruction of the monster in the bargain)?

Quint's determinations in the film seem to be of two kinds: first, unlike the bureaucracies of law enforcement and science-and-technology (Brody and Hooper), but also in distinction to the corrupt island Major with his tourist investments and big business interests, Quint is defined as the locus of old-fashioned private enterprise, of the individual entrepreneurship not merely of small business, but also of local business – hence the insistence on his salty Down-East typicality. Meanwhile – but this feature is also a new addition to the very schematic treatment of the figure of Quint in the novel – he also strongly associates himself with a now distant American past by way of his otherwise gratuitous reminiscences about World War II and the campaign in the Pacific. We are thus authorized to read the death of Quint in the film as the twofold symbolic destruction of an older America – the America of small business and individual private enterprise of a now outmoded kind, but also the America of the New Deal and the crusade against Nazism, the older America of the depression and the war and of the heyday of classical liberalism.

Now the content of the partnership between Hooper and Brody projected by the film may be specified socially and politically, as the allegory of an alliance between the forces of law-and-order and the new technocracy of the multi-national corporations: an alliance which must be cemented, not merely by its fantasized triumph over the ill-defined menace of the shark itself, but above all by the indispensable precondition of the effacement of that more traditional image of an older America which must be eliminated from historical conscious-ness and social memory before the new power system takes its place. This operation may continue to be read in terms of mythic archetypes, if one likes, but then in that case it is a Utopian and ritual vision which is also a whole – very alarming – political and social program. It touches on present-day social contradictions and anxieties only to use them for its new task of ideological resolution, symbolically urging us to bury the older populisms and to respond to an image of political partnership which projects a whole new strategy of legitimation; and it effectively displaces the class antagonisms between rich and poor which persist in consumer society (and in the novel from which the film was adapted) by substituting for them a new and spurious kind of fraternity in which the viewer rejoices without understanding that he or she is excluded from it.

Exclusion?

ideological manipulation

    Jaws is therefore an excellent example, not merely of ideological manipulation, but also of the way in which genuine social and historical content must be first tapped and given some initial expression if it is subsequently to be the object of successful manipulation and containment. In my second reading, I want to give this new model of manipulation an even more decisive and paradoxical turn: I will now indeed argue that we cannot fully do justice to the ideological function of works like these unless we are willing to concede the presence within them of a more positive function as well: of what I will call, following the Frankfurt School, their Utopian or transcendent potential – that dimension of even the most degraded type of mass culture which remains implicitly, and no matter how faintly, negative and critical of the social order from which, as a product and a commodity, it springs. At this point in the argument, then, the hypothesis is that the works of mass culture cannot be ideological without at one and the same time being implicitly or explicitly Utopian as well: they cannot manipulate unless they offer some genuine shred of content as a fantasy bribe to the public about to be so manipulated. [Even the "false consciousness" of so monstrous a phenomenon [as] Nazism was nourished by collective fantasies of a Utopian type, in "socialist" as well as in nationalist guises.] Our proposition about the drawing power of the works of mass culture has implied that such works cannot manage anxieties about the social order unless they have first revived them and given them some rudimentary expression; we will now suggest that anxiety and hope are two faces of the same collective consciousness, so that the works of mass culture, even if their function lies in the legitimation of the existing order – or some worse one – cannot do their job without deflecting in the latter's service the deepest and most fundamental hopes and fantasies of the collectivity, to which they can therefore, no matter in how distorted a fashion, be found to have given voice.

    We therefore need a method capable of doing justice to both the ideological and the Utopian or transcendent functions of mass culture simultaneously. Nothing less will do, as the suppression of either of these terms may testify: we have already commented on the sterility of the older kind of ideological analysis, which, ignoring the Utopian components of mass culture, ends up with the empty denunciation of the latter's manipulatory function and degraded status. But it is equally obvious that the complementary extreme – a method that would celebrate Utopian impulses in the absence of any conception or mention of the ideological vocation of mass culture – simply reproduces the litanies of myth criticism at its most academic and aestheticizing and impoverishes these texts of their semantic content at the same time that it abstracts them from their concrete social and historical situation.

The two parts of the *The Godfather* have seemed to me to offer a virtual textbook illustration of these propositions; for one thing, recapitulating the whole generic tradition of the gangster film, it reinvents a certain "myth" of the Mafia in such a way as to allow us to see that ideology is not necessarily a matter of false consciousness, or of the incorrect or distorted representation of historical "fact," but can rather be quite consistent with a "realistic" faithfulness to the latter. To be sure, historical inaccuracy (as, e.g., when the fifties are telescoped into the sixties and seventies in the narrative of Jimmy Hoffa's career in the 1978 movie, *F.I.S.T.*) can often provide a suggestive lead towards ideological function: not because there is any scientific virtue in the facts themselves, but rather as a symptom of a resistance of the "logic of the content," of the substance of historicity in question, to the narrative and ideological paradigm into which it has been thereby forcibly assimilated.[13]

The Godfather, however, obviously works in and is a permutation of a generic convention; one could write a history of the changing social and ideological functions of this convention, showing how analogous motifs are called upon in distinct historical situations to emit strategically distinct yet symbolically intelligible messages. Thus the gangsters of the classical thirties films (Robinson, Cagney, etc.) were dramatized as psychopaths, sick loners striking out against a society essentially made up of wholesome people (the archetypal democratic "common man" of New Deal populism). The post-war gangsters of the Bogart era remain loners in this sense but have unexpectedly become invested with tragic pathos in such a way as to express the confusion of veterans returning from World War II, struggling with the unsympathetic rigidity of institutions, and ultimately crushed by a petty and vindictive social order.

The Mafia material was drawn on and alluded to in these earlier versions of the gangster paradigm, but did not emerge as such until the late fifties and the early sixties. This very distinctive narrative content – a kind of saga or family material analogous to that of the medieval *chansons de geste*, with its recurrent episodes and legendary figures returning again and again in different perspectives and contexts – can at once be structurally differentiated from the older paradigms by its collective nature: in this, reflecting an evolution towards organizational themes and team narratives which studies like Will Wright's book on the western, *Sixguns* and *Society*, have shown to be significant developments in the other sub-genres of mass culture (the western, the caper film, etc.) during the 1960s.[14]

Such an evolution, however, suggests a global transformation of post-war American social life and a global transformation of the potential logic of its narrative content without yet specifying the ideological function of the Mafia paradigm itself. Yet this is surely not very difficult to identify. When indeed we reflect on an organized conspiracy against the public, one which reaches into every corner of our daily lives and our political structures to exercise a wanton ecocidal and genocidal violence at the behest of distant decision-makers and in the name of an abstract conception of profit – surely it is not about the Mafia, but rather about American business itself that we are thinking, American capitalism in its most systematized and computerized, dehumanized, "multinational" and corporate form. What kind of crime, said Brecht, is the robbing of a bank, compared to the founding of a bank? Yet until recent years, American business has enjoyed a singular freedom from popular criticism and articulated collective resentment; since the depolitization of the New Deal, the McCarthy era and the beginning of the Cold War and of media or consumer society, it has known an inexplicable holiday from the kinds of populist antagonisms which have only recently (white collar crime, hostility to utility companies or to the medical profession) shown signs of reemerging. Such freedom from blame is all the more remarkable when we observe the increasing squalor that daily life in the US owes to big business and to its unenviable position as the purest form of commodity and market capitalism functioning anywhere in the world today.

This is the context in which the ideological function of the myth of the Mafia can be understood, as the substitution of crime for big business, as the strategic displacement of all the rage generated by the American system onto this mirror image of big business provided by the movie screen and the various TV series, it being understood that the fascination with the Mafia remains ideological even if in reality organized crime has exactly the importance and influence in American life which such representations attribute to it. The function of the Mafia narrative is indeed to encourage the conviction that the deterioration of the daily life in the United States today is an ethical rather than economic matter, connected, not with profit, but rather "merely" with dishonesty, and with some omnipresent moral corruption whose ultimate mythic source lies in the pure Evil of the Mafiosi themselves. For genuinely political insights into the economic realities of late capitalism, the myth of the Mafia strategically substitutes the vision of what is seen to be a criminal aberration from the norm, rather than the norm itself; indeed, the displacement of political and historical analysis by ethical judgments and considerations is generally the sign of an ideological maneuver and of the intent to mystify. Mafia movies thus project a "solution" to social contradictions – incorruptibility, honesty, crime fighting, and finally law-and-order itself – which is evidently a very different proposition from that diagnosis of the American misery whose prescription would be social revolution.

But if this is the ideological function of Mafia narratives like *The Godfather*, what can be said to be their transcendent or Utopian function? The latter is to be sought, it seems to me, in the fantasy message projected by the title of this film, that is, in the family itself, seen as a figure of collectivity and as the object of a Utopian longing, if not a Utopian envy. A narrative synthesis like *The Godfather* is possible only at the conjuncture in which ethnic content – the reference to an alien collectivity – comes to fill the older gangster schemas and to inflect them powerfully in the direction of the social; the superposition on conspiracy of fantasy material related to ethnic groups then triggers the Utopian function of this transformed narrative paradigm. In the United States, indeed, ethnic groups are not only the object of prejudice, they are also the object of envy; and these two impulses are deeply intermingled and reinforce each other mutually. The dominant white middle-class groups – already given over to *anomie* and social fragmentation and atomization – find in the ethnic and racial groups which are the object of their social repression and status contempt at one and the same time the image of some older collective ghetto or ethnic neighborhood solidarity; they feel the envy and *ressentiment* of the *Gesellschaft* for the older *Gemeinschaft* which it is simultaneously exploiting and liquidating.

Thus, at a time when the disintegration of the dominant communities is persistently "explained" in the (profoundly ideological) terms of a deterioration of the family, the growth of permissiveness, and the loss of authority of the father, the ethnic group can seem to project an image of social reintegration by way of the patriarchal and authoritarian family of the past. Thus the tightly knit bonds of the Mafia family (in both senses), the protective security of the (god-) father with his omnipresent authority, offers a contemporary pretext for a Utopian fantasy which can no longer express itself through such outmoded paradigms and stereotypes as the image of the now extinct American small town.

The drawing power of a mass cultural artifact like *The Godfather* may thus be measured by its twin capacity to perform an urgent ideological function at the same time that it provides the vehicle for the investment of a desperate Utopian fantasy. Yet the film is doubly interesting from our present point of view in the way in which its sequel – released from the restrictions of Mario Puzo's bestselling novel on which Part I was based – tangibly betrays the momentum and the operation of an ideological and Utopian logic in something like a free or unbound State. *Godfather II*, indeed, offers a striking illustration of Pierre Macherey's thesis, in *Towards a Theory of Literary Production*, that the work of art does not so much *express* ideology as, by endowing the latter with aesthetic representation and figuration, it ends up enacting the latter's own virtual unmasking and self-criticism.

It is as though the unconscious ideological and Utopian impulses at work in *Godfather I* could in the sequel be observed to work themselves towards the light and towards thematic or reflexive foregrounding in their own right. The first film held the two dimensions of ideology and Utopia together within a single generic structure, whose conventions remained intact. With the second film, however, this structure falls as it were into history itself, which submits it to a patient deconstruction that will in the end leave its ideological content undisguised and its displacements visible to the naked eye. Thus the Mafia material, which in the first film served as a substitute for business, now slowly transforms itself into the overt thematics of business itself, just as "in reality" the need for the cover of legitimate investments ends up turning the Mafiosi into real businessmen. The climactic end moment of the historical development is then reached (in the film, but also in real history) when American business, and with it American imperialism, meet that supreme ultimate obstacle to their internal dynamism and structurally necessary expansion which is the Cuban Revolution.

Meanwhile, the Utopian strand of this filmic text, the material of the older patriarchal family, now slowly disengages itself from this first or ideological one, and, working its way back in time to its own historical origins, betrays its roots in the pre-capitalist social formation of a backward and feudal Sicily. Thus these two narrative impulses as it were reverse each other: the ideological myth of the Mafia ends up generating the authentically Utopian vision of revolutionary liberation; while the degraded Utopian content of the family paradigm ulti-mately unmasks itself as the survival of more archaic forms of repression and sexism and violence. Meanwhile, both of these narrative strands, freed to pursue their own inner logic to its limits, are thereby driven to the other reaches and historical boundaries of capitalism itself, the one as it touches the pre-capitalist societies of the past, the other at the beginnings of the future and the dawn of socialism.

These two parts of *The Godfather* – the second so much more demonstrably political than the first – may serve to dramatize our second basic proposition in the present [chapter], namely the thesis that all contemporary works of art – whether those of high culture and modernism or of mass culture and commer-cial culture – have as their underlying impulse – albeit in what is often distorted and repressed unconscious form – our deepest fantasies about the nature of social life, both as we live it now, and as we feel in our bones it ought rather to be lived. To reawaken, in the midst of a privatized and psychologizing society, obsessed with commodities and bombarded by the ideological slogans of big business, some sense of the ineradicable drive towards collectivity that can be detected, no matter how faintly and feebly, in the most degraded works of mass culture just as surely as in the classics of modernism – is surely an indispensable precondition for any meaningful Marxist intervention in contemporary culture.

Notes

1 See for the theoretical sources of this opposition my essay on Max Weber, "The vanishing mediator," in *The Ideologies of Theory*, vol. II (Minnesota, University of Minnesota Press, 1988), pp. 3–34.

2 The classical study remains that of J-P. Vernant; see his "Travail et nature dans la Grece ancienne" and "Aspects psychologiques du travail," in *Mythe et pensée chez les grecs* (Paris, Maspéro, 1965).

3 Besides Marx, see Georg Simmel, *Philosophy of Money* (London, Routledge, 1978) and also his classic "Metropolis and mental life," translated in Simmel, *On Individuality and Social Forms* (Chicago, University of Chicago Press, 1971), pp. 324–39.

4 "[Bourgeois city-dwellers] wander through the woods as through the moist tender soil of the child they once were; they stare at the poplars and plane trees planted along the road, they have nothing to say about them because they are doing nothing with them, and they marvel at the wondrous quality of this silence," etc. J-P. Sartre, *Saint Genêt* (Paris, Gallimard, 1952), pp. 249–50.

5 Guy Debord, *The Society of the Spectacle* (Detroit, Black and Red Press, 1973).

6 Reification by way of the *tableau* was already an eighteenth-century theatrical device (reproduced in Buñuel's *Viridiana*), but the significance of the book illustration was anticipated by Sartre's description of "perfect moments" and "privileged situations" in *Nausea* (the illustrations in Annie's childhood edition of Michelet's *History of France*).

7 In my opinion, this "feeling tone" (or secondary libidinal investment) is essentially an invention of Zola and part of the new technology of the naturalist novel (one of the most successful French exports of its period).

8 Written in 1976. A passage like this one cannot be properly evaluated unless it is understood that it was written before the elaboration of a theory of what we now call the postmodern [. . .].

9 See Jacques Schérer, *Le "Livre" de Mallarmé* (Paris, Gallimard, 1957).

10 My own fieldwork has thus been seriously impeded by the demise some years ago of both car radios: so much the greater is my amazement when rental cars today (which are probably not time machines) fill up with exactly the same hit songs I used to listen to in the early seventies, repeated over and over again!

11 Written before a preliminary attempt to do so in *The Political Unconscious* (Ithaca, Cornell University Press, 1981); see in particular ch. 3: "Realism and desire."

12 Up to but not including: see Stephen Heath, "*Jaws*: ideology and film theory," *Framework*, 4 (1976), pp. 25–7. Still, Heath's plea to study the filmic effect rather

than the content does leave the "shark-effect" itself open to interpretation. It is meanwhile also worth mentioning the interpretation attributed to Fidel, in which the beleaguered island stands for Cuba and the shark for North American imperialism: an interpretation that will be less astonishing for US readers who know this Latin American political iconography. This image of the US probably predates the classic "Fable of the Shark and the Sardines," published by the former Guatemalan President Juan Jose Arévalo in 1956, after the American intervention, and is still current, as witness Ruben Bladés's recent ballad.

13   See Adorno's thoughts on the "resistance" of chronology in a letter to Thomas Mann, quoted in *Marxism and Form* (Princeton, Princeton University Press, 1971), pp. 234–350.

14   See my review of Wright, in *Theory and Society*, 4 (1977), pp. 543–59.

9

Marxism and the Historicity of Theory: An Interview by Xudong Zhang

This interview was conducted in 1995 and published in *New Literary History* (1998).

The Historicity of Theory

Xudong Zhang: My first question concerns the overall outlook of your theoretical language and the constitution of your methodology. It is a common view that you combined Marxism and structuralism – not structuralism *per se* but the general emphasis on language and textuality since the so-called linguistic turn – to make these things indispensable to one another in your critical practice. Is this picture misleading? Could you explain the way in which these dimensions become interwined in the development of theory in general and in your own interventions in particular?

Fredric Jameson: Several things have to be said. First of all, what we have called structuralism or theory in the largest sense, ranging from psychoanalysis to linguistics and everything else, not as a precise term but as a general historical term, emerged within the Marxist problematic. If we limit ourselves to France, the dominant French thought right after the Second World War was, of course, existentialism. But it very quickly became existential Marxism. And that was the point at which structuralism as a problematic began to emerge. I do not mean the structuralist position – particularly that language is the ultimate determining instance, but the question as to the relationship of language to other social levels emerges from the Marxist framework, which did not yet have an answer for it. I would say in general that you could probably show where all the specific themes of poststructuralism emerged from this Marxist problematic, which was at that point attempting to arrive at a more refined notion of culture and ideology.

I also want to add something else: the other important influence I have been interested in lately is that of Brecht, because Brecht's appearance at the Théâtre des nations in Paris in 1954 was really a very decisive event. Brecht was not normally thought of as a philosopher or theoretician. But his dialectic also set an agenda that would turn out to be poststructuralism – something in particular to be called anti-humanism. In Brecht you have the simultaneous attack on the bourgeois classical tradition that Lukács, for example, defended, as well as on the socialist humanist tradition of which Lukács was obviously also a proponent. Then this antihumanism was further developed by people like Althusser – Althusser wrote something on Brecht incidentally, so there was a direct connection. So the point I want to make is that you can certainly read various poststructuralist texts outside their history for their immediate truth value, but if you want to put them in context to see how the problematic was developed, then you have to look at the larger Marxist framework. In a country like France after the war, an overwhelming percent of the intellectuals thought they were Marxist. At any rate at least they found the Marxist problematic – class struggle, modes of production, how to connect base and superstructure, what the nature of ideology is, what representation is – essential to their programs.

Another thing to be said about this first point is that it also explains why, surprisingly for some, we get this intervention of Derrida, in his book *Specters of Marx*. It is because, I think, now that France has de-Marxified, and many fewer intellectuals consider them-selves Marxist, the great theoreticians – this is true for Deleuze, too, although, unfortu-nately, he did not have time to write his Marx book, but it is also true for others – understand more acutely how their own framework built on the Marxist problematic (again I do not want to say Marxism). And I think what Derrida was trying to rescue there is a multiple thing: he is making commentaries on certain texts of Marx, he is making a political intervention in a situation in which there seem to be no radical alternatives back to the moment. But I think he is also trying historically to save that base of Marxism from which he himself in an idiosyncratic way emerged.

As to the problem of what the relationship is in specific cases, I believe this has to do with the nature of theory itself. Theory emerging after the end of great philosophical systems, in a kind of market environment, has tended to become a whole set of different name brands. If that seems too frivolous to say, then we can say that theory exists as named theories, as specific idiolects or private languages. The whole point of the philosophical system is to take a mass of ideas in the air of all kinds and give them a single coherent language, conceptuality, and set of terms. In that sense, the end of philosophy means that no one thinks that coherence is possible any more. This means that we have to speak all these theoretical languages all at the same time. There really is no way to synthesize them into a master language, nor is there even a desire to do so. I think this situation then creates some of the appearances you are alluding to; it looks for one minute that we are talking about Marxist language, but suddenly you begin to sound like a Jakobsonian structuralist, or Lévi-Straussian, or Lacanian, or something like that. I am often accused of eclecticism in this respect, but I think we have to think about it in terms of language. It is as though we could say certain things sharply only in French, but what you can say sharply in German is less clear in French; you can say certain things in Chinese, but that does not work in French, and vice versa and so on and so forth. So the ideal would be switching languages depending on the problems you are addressing, but obviously that is also next to impossible. That is why I believe there are far closer connections between the various Marxist problems and some of those poststructural theories with which on first glance you do not see any relationship.

I guess it is very difficult to pursue these discussions without some reconstruction of the historical development. I would like to hope that when I explain some of these complex things for myself, that can also serve as an introduction to some of the more primary theoretical philosophical questions. But I have to keep the names there. If I just speak of these without the names, it would look as though I am claiming the ideas for myself. That is not the case. It can often evidently be bewildering when you get all these philosophical references without knowing the original texts.

XZ: The common perception is that you are both "French" and "German": The French side being "poststructuralist," and the "German" side dialectical – the Frankfurt School, and so on. Now you are saying that the "French" aspect is not purely linguistic or "theoretical" but also part of the Marxist problematic.

FJ: That is right. It is an accident of my own background that I am fluent in both French and German, and that I had contact with both national traditions as a student. I always found it as understandable as it is strange and deplorable when people take sides for the French against the German or the German against the French. On the other hand, as I said before, I do not think syntheses are desirable. I also think that to borrow back and forth is not very successful. I am thinking in particular of the moment in the 1970s when Adorno became better known in France. Then the so-called "anti-identity" side of Adorno – a German theme, so to speak – became enlisted in French poststructuralism's attack on Marxism. I think that does violence to Adorno's thought. But how you dialogue between positions is very complicated. You recall the attempts of Habermas to talk to Foucault, or Foucault to talk to Chomsky, or vice versa. Except on basic political and cultural matters, a simple dialogue between these languages is not possible. I believe myself that I am Eurocentric to the degree that I believe that the French and the German are the two great philosophical-theoretical traditions I happen to have been formed in that atmosphere in which Anglo-American thought – empiricism and common language philosophy and Wittgenstein and logical positivism – was really in some sense an obstacle for me. All those things seemed to me to be a "resistance to theory," as Paul de Man puts it. Therefore it is often objected that I am not sufficiently hospitable to these things, even though they have included interesting thoughts, beginning with Peirce in the Anglo-American tradition. But my basic frames of reference remain French and German.

[. . .]

XZ: You understand by asking this question I am curious not so much about the structural relationship between Marxism and liberalism but about the habit for many to see things in terms of a position-taking between radicalism, liberalism, and conservatism

FJ: I understand that. I think it is a matter of existential politics, which we all do. But I think it would be best to begin with the philosophical questions themselves and only later to decide if these are liberal positions, radical positions, or conservative positions. Because all these poststructuralist themes and problems can be inflected in a number of directions. While it is essential that at the end of the line political judgments be made, I think the problem initially should be analyzed and discussed in terms of their inherent, immanent conceptuality. The same would be true for works of art. I have always stood for political, social, and historical readings of works of art, but I certainly do not think that you start that way. You start with aesthetics, purely aesthetic problems, and then, at the term of these analyses, you end up in the political. People have said about Brecht that, for example, whenever in Brecht you started with aesthetics, by the time you came to the end, you came to politics; and whenever you started with politics, at the end you came to aesthetics. I think that is a much more desirable rhythm for these analyses. But that of course makes my positions sometimes very ambiguous for people, because they want a political message right away, whereas I am interested in going through the problems or the aesthetic form in order eventually to get to a political judgment.

[. . .]

XZ: Recently there seems to be some interest in figuring out your career or intellectual development, which for many remains miraculous in some senses. For instance, in the preface to your Geopolitical Aesthetics, Colin MacCabe describes your career in a very interesting way. He says that you spent more than two decades working out your theoretical premises "patiently"; and, once that was achieved, it was replaced by a "riot of cultural analyses." He describes it in a way in which yours seems to be a very deliberate self-design and personal strategy.

FJ: I was very gratified by Colin's essay, which I think is one of the few that has really given an overall picture of my work. I do suspect that Colin wishes to downplay the more specifically Marxist side of things and the political elements and so forth. I wouldn't necessarily tell the story that way myself, although I can see that the story he tells has a certain persuasiveness. I would not myself start like that. I would say that between methodological questions there are always tensions which open onto larger philosophical problems. Ultimately, this goes to the base and superstructure problem if you like, that is to say, how do you link culture and consciousness to the context or to the situation? It is the tension between those terms that set the terms for interrogations in any reading of any individual text. So when one talks about the "riot of cultural analyses," the same thing can be said about my literary work. That is, there is a tension between a whole methodological-philosophical side of things, and the reading of the individual, literary text, just as much as between that and the reading of any specific mass-cultural text. I don't think that the problem is one of passing from a general canonical or literary set of preoccupations into some more mass-cultural, Cultural Studies environment. I seem to have written more on films and mass-cultural things in the last few years. But actually I have several very long literary analyses that have not been published. I think the two demand very different approaches, which I would not necessarily want to combine. But the real problem, the real alternation here is between, let's say, the general and the particular, between specific readings and the more general theoretical approach. I am not sure that I would say that first I took care of my theoretical problems and then I moved on to those specific analyses. In this new global capitalism, in this age of postmodernity, the older theories that one involved for the earlier world of modernity must now also be rethought. I consider that the theoretical task. The speculative task is not finished and done with, allowing one simply to do readings. Rather, it is also an ongoing one, which surely demands further theoretical works.

XZ: What is implied here, other than a career design, might be something like this: conceptually, you can still, for a moment, concentrate on your theoretical-philosophical infrastructure, so to speak. Then that infrastructure can serve as a sort of inner drive and mode of thinking, which motivate and navigate your journey through a fragmented terrain.

FJ: The notion in *The Political Unconscious* of the three levels of context the three frameworks − historical, political, economic − in which one can focus a concrete context implies that you could work on an immediate social-historical level (then you might be talking about the whole roll-back of the welfare state). You could also talk in the larger context, the class dynamics, which are slower, and include the history of classes, their memory of their struggles and their defeats. Then, finally, you can talk on this largest level of the mode of production. So, already, in that notion of the three levels, was implicit the sense that the context was not only the here-and-now politically, but could be approached in somewhat longer time frames. I use there, maybe without saying so, Braudel's idea of multiple temporalities and longer or shorter durées. I do not often write in terms of specific political struggles, partly because works of art take somewhat longer to write and to put together anyway. It is only in mass culture that you get a more immediate kind of response. But there is a time lag involved even in those most ephemeral cultural statements. I certainly admire the people whose task is immediate cultural and political commentary. I am not sure I am best qualified to do that kind of work, particularly because my formation is not in American Studies but in other languages and national cultures.

I also want to add a rather different kind of remark about what Lukács has meant to me. One of the things that Lukács taught, and one of the most valuable, I think, is that the form of work of art – and I would include the form of mass cultural product – is a place in which one can observe social conditioning and thus the social situation. And sometimes form is a place where one can observe that concrete social context more adequately than in the flow of daily events and immediate historical happenings. I guess I would resist the idea that I start with aesthetics, then I look around for some historical context, and then put them together, even though Marxist analysis has often been understood in those terms. And there is a truth in this, because we are attempting to look at the aesthetic and extra-or nonaesthetic simultaneously. That often makes for a slippage between these two realms. I think the clumsier Marxist analyses do tend to take this form of a break in the essay in which, first, you put all the social facts, and then, you turn to the work and talk about form and ideology. That in principle ought to make writing Marxist analyses interesting, because there is a fundamental formal problem in writing such essays that demands to be solved; there are no ready-made solutions in advance. But I think what Lukács meant to me is that ideally, one should somehow get to the content through the forms.

To that I would add something else. The difference between Lukács and this humanism that Brecht attributed to him in a critical, negative sense is that Lukács always talked about achieved form, successful form. It seems to me rather that we have to look at failures of form, the impossibility of certain kinds of representation in a certain context, the flaws, limits, obstacles, which become the clue to the social truth or social meaning, and not so much canonical success in that old Lukácsian sense.

XZ: When you say that, do you have in mind the mass cultural products or the avant-garde "work of art"?

FJ: What makes the matter of determinate representational failure interesting is that it happens to both. I think the most interesting way to look at mass cultural debates is precisely through just these failures as formal failures and formal impossibilities. Of course, we can also talk about failures, formal flaws and constraints in so-called high literature. That would be the point, I think, in which what is to me a more adequate kind of cultural studies would not feel obliged to choose between literature and canon on the one hand, and television and pop music on the other. It seems to me that these are dialectically part of a united field. The most interesting comments on both sides are made by those who are, like people hesitating between France and Germany, committed to both rather than to taking sides for one or the other: the one being elitist, the other being populist. I understand why that is done. Sometimes I feel that way myself. But I do not think that is ultimately a very productive attitude.

XZ: I think your readers would understand very well that both the social-political and the aesthetic-theoretical are constant in your critical intervention. And that is one of the most persuasive aspects of your work. But I am wondering if the "theoretical moment" in your career can be seen as a moment of intensification, a process of encoding in which you acquired not only a style or philosophical form, but also power, subjectivity, some kind of organizing principle, which now enables you to engage the field at a different level. Given that your position is perceived as a privileged one, meaning that when everybody gets stuck in a schizophrenic world, you still maintain a certain kind of coherence, continuity, and energy, the politics of which is not determined only by your immediate social-cultural location. Does that have to do with the "decades" of theoretical mortification, so to speak?

FJ: There, too, we have to make an historical remark. The theoretical books [*Marxism and Form* and *The Prison-house of Language*] which precede the later analyses (in MacCabe's view) were written at a time when neither of these two traditions [the French and the German critical traditions] were very well-known in the Anglo-American world. So my task was partly to introduce and popularize these things. But then with translation, with wide dissemination and the greater theoretical sophistication that the American intellectuals began to acquire in the 1970s and 1980s, that particular kind of project was no longer necessary. Or if it is the case of newer theory – I guess this is the question about whether newer theories are being produced – then other people are better qualified than I was. That is the one note I want to make.

The second is that for me the practical readings have only been interesting insofar as they contain a theoretical point. That is why this connection between theory and interpretation has always been very close. It is an odd fact, a strange paradox, that just because you are excited about an object does not mean that you are qualified to write well about it. One would think that one would always have something to say if you are interested. There are great cultural journalists whom I very much admire and whose gift is to respond immediately to all their situations and objects. But for me, the works that I have felt empowered to write about are always ones that allowed me to focus on a specific theoretical problem. I think the reverse is also true. That is, even though sometimes it does not seem that way, the theoretical problems that interested me are the ones that ultimately had a connection to interpretations of specific texts. There is a whole range of philosophical problems that do not interest me at all, because they do not bear on this. That may also have something to do with this connection you are talking about.

As for the motive for the speculations on postmodernism and postmodernity, I would say that before the 1980s, historical contexts seemed more clear and stable than they began to be in the 1980s and 1990s. When I began to think about these things, at least what I described as postmodern suddenly seemed to be connected up with some very basic structural changes in infrastructure, in the economic, in globalization, and so forth. That then again gave me a coherent framework to look at all these things as manifestations of the larger cultural logic or experience of the period.

Marxism and Late Capitalism

XZ: But this framework of periodization is basically a Marxist one.

FJ: Yes, of course. I consider this essentially a Marxist periodization. I have colleagues and comrades who feel that this is giving in to the most frivolous tastes generated by capitalism. But I think of the notion of periodization in terms of realism, the relatively limited national framework of capitalism, imperialism, this larger global – not yet global in our sense, but larger worldwide – expansion of capitalism, and finally the whole dynamic of this new globalized capitalism. I think these are stages in the evolution of capital, and their conception is profoundly Marxist. That is why I am often pleased when people try to avoid terms like late capitalism, because that shows that they understand that some terms are at base political ones and imply political positions. There is the accusation that I do not think enough in terms of class. That may be so for certain kinds of things. But I believe in class, class dynamics, and class struggles. These are always present. Only today they take very complicated forms. There is no clear-cut working class ideology. There is no clear-cut ruling class ideology either. It is a more complicated game. I would not want to say that Marx was an economic determinist, but for me the important historical, original, unsurpassable thing about Marx and Marxism is that it requires you somehow to include the economic. It requires you to work back in such a way that you finally touch economic structures. If you limit yourself only to class, that can very rapidly turn into political considerations of power; then it begins to lose its connections to the economic structure. That is why I often felt hesitation about the emphasis on power coming out of Foucault and others today, which I think sometimes is a little too easy. For me, the theory of the postmodern stage is an economic theory. If you do it right, you have to end up talking about capitalism. Therefore, the coherence of my work comes from the stage we are in. The Marxist component comes from this ultimately economic dynamic of the stage.

XZ: In that particular sense, Marxism becomes a philosophy, or does it?

FJ: No. This is the value of Derrida's latest work, which reminds us insistently that Marxism is not an ontology, and should be neither an ontology nor a philosophy. I agree with that. What is very peculiar about both Marx and Freud is that they are this thing which in the Marxist tradition is called a unity of theory and practice. That means that there is not a philosophical system of Marxism that you can write down, rather, there are some very important philosophical implications and speculations, which offer the construction of something like the presuppositions of a Marxist philosophy, that is, Lukács's *History and Class Consciousness*. I have even perversely suggested that Heidegger's *Sein und Zeit* could be that. But there are many others. I think that the deplorable mistake of the so-called eastern, orthodox, or Soviet Marxism was the idea that you could have a full picture of the world called dialectic materialism, that could be written down the way the old philosophical treaties were written down. You start with matter and move on to this or that. I am very resistant to that notion. I can see why in loose terms one can still talk about various Marxist philosophies. But I would not want to think Marxism is a philosophy in that sense.

Now the other thing people sometimes do with this word is to say, not that Marxism is a philosophical system, but, even worse, that it is that rather different thing: a philosophy of history. I think that objection demands a different approach. There is certainly an ambition to think history in Marxism, and I am very interested in the so-called philosophy of history – it seems to me that those are some of the most exciting texts we have, which range from bourgeois philosophies of history, to Ibn Khaldun or St Augustine or Thucydides. I must feel generally that it is not quite right to call Marxism a philosophy of history in that sense either. But that is a different matter from Marxism being a philosophical system.

XY: You invented a now widely circulated term – metacommentary – to indicate a certain mode of cultural–intellectual production and intervention. The ground cleared by this notion is, in your case, and probably in the way this notion functions, reserved for Marxism. In that respect Marxism does not seem to be just another brand name in the market, at least not for those who write along that line. For others in the field, it seems that you can always draw from a historical and theoretical source, from which they would rather disengage, but which allows you somehow to place yourself beyond the field.

FJ: You could say that in several ways. You could say that in terms of these theoretical discourses and, finally, despite everything I have said about the various theoretical discourses, there is a Marxist theoretical position that is more privileged than others. But today there are a number of different Marxist theoretical discourses, so one cannot really say that exactly. Is it, then, the survival of the older philosophical foundation, which for old antifoundationalists is suspicious? That would be so, if Marxism altogether were a philosophy in their sense. I do not consider that accusation to be entirely accurate either. I would also want to say that there are probably people who do metacommentary who do not know what they are doing is Marxism. I do not think that one has to be conscious of this intellectual commitment to have a Marxist view of the world. After all, Marxism has really suffused into all the disciplines to the point where it is present and active without any longer being a separate field or specialization.

As for the idea that I have some secret truth that nobody else has, well, the whole point of the public sphere is that you make your own interpretation and then people take it or leave it; they find it plausible or not plausible. The real problem, I think, is that a lot of the interpretations made today do not push things far enough, and are thus not really in the running. Or else they are not aware of themselves as ideologies. I do think that there are Marxist ideologies, that we are all ideological in our specific situations, national, personal, psychoanalytical, and so forth, which determine generally very deep ideological and classical commitments that we are not always aware of, and this is true of Marxism as well. All the great Marxist thinkers, including Marx, came out of specific personal, class, and national situations. What they have produced, alongside what Marxism calls "science," are a number of Marxist ideologies. I try to be interested in a range of those [ideologies] and move back and forth. I am not sure how to describe my own personal view of Marxism, and am perhaps not particularly interested in turning it into another brand name ideology.

XY: Does the view that Marxism has a certain power over other theoretical discourses have to do with its internal unity, its interest in "grand narratives" and "totality"?

FJ: Let me try to answer that question by going back to the notion of theory being an idiolect or private language. My feeling is that if you are going to address a range of people formed in different disciplines, you have to be able to translate these things and speak their language up to a certain point, even if you seek to undermine or criticize it. What I would like to propose is that this sort of belief or philosophy that people think they see unifying my work is, rather, a translation mechanism. I would like to defend the idea that Marxism is a far more subtle and supple mode of translating between these languages than most of the other systems. It is true that the great universal systems – Catholicism, for instance – had that once; maybe Catholicism still does. There was great power in the way in which certain kinds of Catholic theologians, the Jesuits, for example, were able to pass from one philosophical language to another. Marxism is the only secular version of this capacity I know today. I do not think structural linguistics or semiotics has that ambition, nor was it successful; and there remains to be analyzed from a historical point of view the connection of the various semiotics with existentialism and with Marxism. It is a very interesting historical story. But I think Marxism remains the only one of these translation techniques or machines that can encompass all these things.

If you want to say that this is a privileged thought-mode, then it is because of that, not because you insist on knowing the truth. It is because you mediate between these various theoretical codes far more comprehensibly than anything these codes themselves allow. Žižek now wants to tell us that Lacanism is just such a translating code, or better, one that includes the dialectic and Marxism. I have always been fascinated with Lacan, and I am certainly willing to toy with that idea, which Žižek does a good deal better than I do. The notion of mediation between these codes is the crucial one, not the truth-power of one code or philosophy – like Marxism – over the other. Reality takes care of truth; the codes are our business.

[...]

XY: Besides the ideal form of intellectual life and cultural activity, people, especially people in the non-Western societies, I suppose, are looking for an ideal form of representation or narrative, a mode of thinking as a way to organize your private and collective experiences, which might otherwise be utterly fragile and fragmented. Marxism seems also to promise some possibilities in these areas.

FJ: Absolutely. I think that is the whole point of the narrative of postmodernity, and its relationship to late capitalism. Whatever is going on in the other parts of the world, in the Pacific Rim, for example, it seems to me that everyone in one way or another is caught in this force field of late capitalism (automation, structural unemployment, finance capital, globalization, and so on). That then, it seems to me, is the organizing dynamic. One does not necessarily solve this fragmented reality in existential terms.

One does not map that out or represent it by turning it from fragments into something unified. One theorizes the fragmentary.

It seems to me that this framework that I have developed – for me an historical framework – is the one in which one best does that and best provides a coherent narrative even if it is a narrative that explains incoherence. This is what I think we have to do today. Then we come back to some of the things we have talked about, formal failure, for example. I think it is a mistake to imagine that, because there have been great and successful representational moments in the past, we have to struggle to make a new one now. It can often be the emphasis on the impossibility of representation that gives the clue and organizes things. I think my global narrative does both these things better than the other ones I know of, the narrative of liberalism, of the market, or the various political narratives, of freedom and democracy, or of law and order, and so forth.

[…]

Dialectical Thinking

XY: So far, it seems to me, you have been focusing on the objective side of Marxism defined by its relationship to the situation. How about the active, to avoid the term "subjective," side of this powerful mechanism for mapping something out, for narrative presentations? I guess this points to the question of the dialectic.

FJ: The question of the dialectic is very complicated. There have been Marxisms – Althusser's, for example – that thought we should get rid of this idea all together, partly because it was too idealistic, or perhaps too complicated to explain. I think that, first, there are number of forms that the dialectic can take. It seems abusive, except in a philosophy seminar, to speak of the dialectic.

Also, I think the dialectic has never been fully realized. That is, there is this massive corpus of Hegelian writings, and also Marx's equally massive but much more fragmentary writings. I would prefer to see the dialectic in utopian ways as a thought-mode of the future, rather than as something that once existed in the 1820s in Berlin or the 1870s in London. I think there would be simpler and more usable ways of talking about the dialectic. I see maybe three of those that interest me right now. One would be an emphasis on the logic of the situation, rather than the logic of the individual consciousness or reified substances like society. The emphasis on the logic of the situation, the constant changeability of the situation, its primacy and the way in which it allows certain things to be possible and others not. That would lead to a kind of thinking that I would call dialectical.

Then, there is the matter of the so-called philosophy or dialectic of history. There, too, the dialectic is a kind of constant, undermining or demystifying various historical narratives already in place, including some of the Marxist ones, like the inevitability of socialism. It would not be an elimination of causality, because I think that narrative and causality go together, and that narrative logic is causal logic. But the dialectic would be an undermining of the received forms of narrative and historical causality. Because if you look at Marx's *Eighteenth Brumaire of Louis Bonaparte*, you do not see syntheses in any simple form. Instead, you see a bewildering number of new and more complex social and historical causalities correct those simpler ways in which people tell themselves about history.

The third thing is an emphasis on contradiction. If one insists on that, then one is always dialectical whether one knows it or not, whether one has a philosophical approach or not. It seems to me that we all have an existential stake in not seeing contradictions. We would like things to be stable, we would like to think that time was this habit of presence that has played its role in contemporary theory. We would like to think that we are unified subjects, and that the problems we face are representational and thus relatively easy to think through. If at every moment in which we represent something to ourselves in a unified way, we try to undo that and see the contradictions and multiplicities behind that particular experience, then we are thinking dialectically.

And there are obviously many more pragmatic ways of describing how the dialectic operates in terms of the way we think of the concrete situation, in terms of the way we think of history, and in terms of the way we think of reality.

XY: The way you describe the operation of the dialectic, especially the entanglement between things that themselves become the form of thinking, reminds me of Benjamin's allegorical mapping of the Parisian space (which is itself reminiscent of Marx's *Eighteenth Brumaire*). What is the relationship between the dialectic and allegory? For Adorno, the Benjaminian mode was "undialectical."

FJ: I guess one should make some proposals. First of all, a lot of people have described the dialectic by asserting that the dialectic is a method rather than a system. In one sense I agree and have sometimes said so myself. But it is also very misleading. Because when you say method, you think that all you have to do is learn some recipe: you could learn it, and then do things, and keep on doing it and being in the truth. The dialectic is not a method in that sense yet, even though there is something of the spirit of a method in it.

Now, as to allegory, I think that is something else: a mode of representation. The reason why allegory is important is that even though we talk about holding to the situation in its historical changeability, trying to break through old narratives of change and seeing fresh ones and perceiving contradictions, none of these targets were really objects to begin with. Therefore, there is the second problem of how you would describe those phenomena, how you model your consciousness of them, if they are not really things. That is where allegory comes in. Because it reminds us that even if we believe in the situation, the situation is not a realistic thing for us to make a simple representation of even if we believe in narrative, that also is not so easy. Saying that the world has a narrative structure does not mean that you can tell a simple story about it, or that there are representational techniques existing for doing that. Insisting on contradictions does not mean that anybody ever saw one, or it would be easy to paint a picture of whatever it is. So the insistence on allegory is an insistence on the difficulty, or even impossibility, of representation of these deeper realities. I hesitate to say impossibility, not because it is not so – I do think that it is impossible to represent these things – but because the minute you say that, then you feed into some other ideologies about silence, ultimate unknowability, the chaos of the world, unrepresentability, indeterminacy, and so forth. I do not think that it is desirable. Allegory happens when you know you cannot represent something, but you also cannot not do it.

[...]

XY: In your view, dialectical thinking cannot be a purely "intellectual" or speculative operation, it is a constant struggle, which involves economics, politics, personal history...

FJ: And your own ideologies. No, I agree. The mark of some successful dialectic is shock, surprise, an undermining of pre-conceived notions, and so forth. You can glimpse the truth or the Real, but then your own ideologies seep back – your own illusions of the world, your own wish-fulfillments – and then you are out of it again. There psychoanalysis offers a good analogy, teaching that the moment of truth is this fitful, fleeting, and painful thing; that you necessarily lose all the time and only fitfully regain.

That is another reason why it is wrong to think of the dialectic as a philosophy. Because presumably in a philosophy you can write down your truth once you have found it. Hegel thought he was doing that (or at least pretended to think so). Capitalism is a much more complicated thing than ontology. Marx knows that you cannot see Capital as such. His book then was a very interesting – as he says – literary experiment, a *Darstellung*: how you put this together some way to have a glimpse of the real; for if the dialectic is as I have described it, it cannot be a systematic philosophy of a representational kind.

Cultural Studies and Locality

[...]

XY: Yesterday, as you know, you were mentioned by someone at the conference as a "red Kant." Reading the first pages of the concluding chapter of your postmodernism book, interestingly, one notices something you have said which is kind of Kantian. You say that there are three levels of things which we may have an interest in separating: the level of taste, or judgment (at which you admit you like many things about postmodernism – food, music, video, and so on), the level of analysis, and finally the level of evaluation.

FJ: Did I say that? Interesting. No, I think that it ties in with things we were talking about earlier, namely, the ways of getting rid of the Self so that one could experience cultural, social, and other realities more aesthetically or directly. That is to say, it seems to me that the level of taste is the one at which we surprise, within ourselves, our attractions to certain kinds of cultural phenomena. Suddenly, cyberpunk appears, and we understand something new and important is going on here. Generally we also like these new things; I suppose the experience could also be negative, but I do not think one often does good work on things one dislikes. So the moment of taste is this moment of surprising new perceptions and of realizing new needs within yourself. Then the moment of analysis is one in which one looks at the way it functions, what is it that is new that has emerged, why it emerged, what the conditions of possibility are of this new thing, why cyberpunk comes into American cultural life at this particular time, for example. That would be the level that I would call analysis. That is trying to determine the shape of the novel, its relationship both to ourselves and to our situations and contexts. Then the level of evaluation is the one in which a historical perspective is going to evolve. That may not be possible for immediate things, but may be possible later on to decide if cyberpunk is an expression of late capitalism or a resistance to it or whatever.

I guess one could artificially divide up this process of perception or thinking in that way. But I am not at all wedded to formulations like that. I tend to think that you are probably right that it could be sucked back into more traditional and even Kantian modes of aesthetics, into something that obviously ought to be resisted.

XY: But wouldn't it also be interesting to see that as a juxtaposition of a kind of Kantian differentiation with the contemporary multiplicity of one's positions?

FJ: If it were Kantian, then the difference would lie in the Western and postmodern emphasis on history. In other words, I would never want to do an evaluation on some eternal or timeless thing, but only in terms of historical change. Maybe that makes a Kantian system impossible.

XY: Geopolitically, the shift from philosophy to theory, and then maybe from theory to critical analysis of contemporary culture, is paralleled with the shift of power or productivity from Europe to North America. How would you describe this process and also your own role in that?

FJ: That is the kind of self-knowledge one is probably least comfortable with. I think that, as you know, we Americans have been, in terms of theory, a kind of transmission belt. For example, French theory first came through England to the United States; it was transmitted by Verso, by Ben Brewster's translation of Althusser, and so forth. So England then served as a kind of transmission, at least for us. I think that we may be serving some of that function for China. So that the excitement we had in the 1970s in discovering all those things, now you get in a more concentrated form, because it is delivered all at once.

I know there are positions that hold that there is a new division of theory and practice. The Third World does the practice and produces the text, and the First World delivers the theory and thinks about it. But we increasingly have a lot of very specific forms of theory that come from the other parts of the world, India being the most notable one where that is happening right now. I also think there is a kind of situational, vested interest in the United States of not knowing what it is doing, and therefore of not becoming the center of theoretical production as you would think of the center of industrial production moving from England to the United States or something like that.

But on the other hand, I am sure that this must also be considered in economic terms. After all it *is* American culture that is now the principal export of late capitalism all over the world. Therefore the theory of that culture would necessarily go along with it. One can always distinguish between this imperial export of culture and these theories themselves. For good or ill, this has to reflect a world in which the production of the United States, namely entertainment and culture, is dominant. I am against guilt-trips and self-denunciations, so I feel temperamentally that we should not always be beating our chest and lamenting the fact that we should not be exporting our own theories and that we are sorry to be cultural imperialists. I think there are things to analyze in the United States that we have a privileged viewpoint on. If we think about our work as political and cultural intellectuals, we have certain kinds of important tasks to fulfill.

If, on the other hand as in the tendency in the market society like this, we think of ourselves just as producing new kinds of products that we then want to have diffused, then that is naturally a less attractive view of our intellectual roles. I suppose one of the things is that, unlike the period of imperialism, this new system of globalization really is a system in which intellectuals from different national situations can talk much more directly to each other. They can answer back, and they do answer back.

There is the sense that in large parts of the world the political as such has become hopeless; that the market is there, we can do nothing about it; that the strikes in France or the Zapatista rebellion seem going nowhere, because they do not have an overall political agenda, and so forth. I feel that, too. I think we should think about it as citizens. But I do not think that we are especially in a position to develop new ideas of praxis. But if someone tries to, then we should look at those. I think that part of this is, again, my peculiar position in connection with American realities. Because I work here, I certainly try to have a pedagogy that addresses the United States. The notion of postmodernity emerges from my experience as an American, and I am an American. But on the other hand, part of my intellectual formation is elsewhere. If I had a different formation I would probably talk more specifically about American cultural problems than I often intend to do.

I think that in the United States, we are also relatively limited by this very successful institutional form which is federalism, constitution, and the states and so forth. Politics here, when it is effective in terms of power, the people, the distribution, and so forth, feeds immediately and exclusively back into local politics. [. . .]

10

Five Theses on Actually Existing Marxism

This chapter was published in *Monthly Review* in 1996. The text is a revised and reduced version of Jameson's essay, "Actually Existing Marxism" (1993). It is dedicated to the memory of William Pomerance.

First Thesis

"Post-Marxisms" regularly emerge at those moments in which capitalism itself undergoes a structural metamorphosis.

Marxism is the science of capitalism, or better still, in order to give depth at once to both terms, it is the science of the inherent contradictions of capitalism. This means on the one hand that it is incoherent to celebrate the "death of Marxism" in the same breath with which one announces the definitive triumph of capitalism and the market. The latter would rather seem to augur a secure future for the former, leaving aside the matter of how "definitive" its triumph could possibly be.[1] On the other hand, the "contradictions" of capitalism are not some formless internal dissolution, but relatively lawful and regular, and subject at least to theorization after the fact. For example, for any given moment of capitalism, the space it controls will eventually become over-saturated with the commodities it is technically capable of producing. This crisis is then systemic.

Capitalism is however not merely a system or mode of production, it is the most elastic and adaptable mode of production that has appeared thus far in human history, and has previously overcome such cyclic crises. It has achieved this by means of two basic strategies: the expansion of the system, and the production of radically new types of commodities.

The expansion of the system. Capitalism has always had a center, recently the hegemony of the United States and previously that of England.[2] Each new center is spatially larger and more inclusive than preceding centers, and thus opens up a wider territory for commodification in general, and for new markets and new products alike. According to a somewhat different version of the historical narrative, we can speak of a national moment of capitalism that emerged from the eighteenth century industrial revolution. This first moment is that which Marx himself experienced and theorized, albeit prophetically. It was followed at the end of the nineteenth century by the moment of imperialism, in which the limits of the national markets were burst and a kind of world-wide colonial system established. Finally, after the Second World War and in our own time, the older imperial system was dismantled and a new "world system" set in its place, dominated by the so-called multinational corporations. This current moment of a "multinational" capitalism is uneasily balanced (after the disappearance of the Soviet Union) between the three centers of Europe, the United States, and Japan, each with its immense hinterland of satellite states. This third moment, whose convulsive stages of emergence were not really complete until the end of the Cold War (if then), is clearly far more "global" than the preceding age of imperialism. With the "deregulation" (so to speak) of the immense areas of India, Brazil, and Eastern Europe, there is a scope for the penetration of capital and the market qualitatively greater than in earlier stages of capitalism. Is this then to be considered the definitive achievement of what Marx prophesied as the world market, and thereby the final stage of capitalism – including, among other things, "the universal commodification of labor power"? It is to be doubted. The inner class dynamics of the new moment have scarcely had time to work themselves out, in particular the emergence of new forms of labor organization and political struggle appropriate to the scale at which "globalization" has transformed the world of business.

The production of radically new types of commodities. There is a second requirement for overcoming systemic crises: that is, the recourse to innovations and even "revolutions" in technology. Ernest Mandel makes these changes coincident with the stages just described: steam technology for the moment of national capitalism; electricity and the combustion engine for the moment of imperialism; atomic energy and the cybernetic for our own moment of multinational capitalism and globalization, which has come to be labeled by some as postmodernity. These technologies are both productive of new types of commodities and instrumental in opening up new world spaces, thus "shrinking" the globe and reorganizing capitalism according to a new scale. This is the sense in which characterizations of late capitalism in terms of information or cybernetics are appropriate (and very revealing culturally), but need to be recoupled with the economic dynamics from which they tend rather easily to be severed, rhetorically, intellectually, and ideologically.

If the overall lines of this periodization of capital are accepted, it becomes at once clear that the various "post-Marxisms" of, in particular, Bernstein at the turn of the last century or of poststructuralism in the 1980s, along with their posited "crisis" or "death" of Marxism, have been simultaneous with precisely those moments in which capitalism is restructured and prodigiously enlarged. And these in turn have been followed by various theoretical projects of a more modern – or indeed in our time postmodern – Marxism attempting to theorize the new and unexpected dimensions taken on by its traditional object of study, capitalism as such.

Second Thesis

Socialism as a vision of freedom – freedom from unwanted and avoidable economic and material constraints, freedom for collective praxis – is in our time threatened on two ideological levels at once: that of "discursive struggle" (in the words of Stuart Hall) in an argument with world-wide Thatcherism about the market system;[3] and that which plays on even deeper anti-Utopian anxieties and fears of change. The two levels clearly imply one another, insofar as the market argument presupposes a set of views about human nature which the anti-Utopian vision then rehearses in more apocalyptic and libidinal ways.

Discursive struggle (as opposed to outright ideological conflict) succeeds by way of discrediting its alternatives and rendering unmentionable a whole series of thematic topics. It appeals to trivialization, naïveté, material interest, "experience," political fear, and historical lessons, as the "grounds" for decisively delegitimizing such formerly serious possibilities as nationalization, regulation, deficit spending, Keynesianism, planning, protection of national industries, the security net, and ultimately the welfare state itself. Identifying this last with socialism then allows market rhetoric to win a double victory, over liberals (in the US usage, as in "New Deal liberals") as well as the Left. The Left is thus today placed in the position of having to defend big government and the welfare state, something its elaborate and sophisticated traditions of the critique of social democracy make it embarrasing to do without a more dialectical understanding of history than much of that Left possesses. In particular, it is desirable to regain some sense of the way historical situations change, and the appropriate political and strategic responses along with them. But this also demands an engagement with the so-called end of history, that is, the fundamental ahistoricality of the postmodern in general.

Meanwhile, the anxieties associated with Utopia, which spring from the fear that everything that makes up our current identity and our current habits and forms of libidinal gratification would disappear under some new social dispensation, some radical change in the societal order, are now far more easily mobilizable than at other moments in the recent past. Evidently, at least in the richer half of the world and not only in the dominant strata, the hope for change of destitute people in the modern period has been replaced by the terror of loss. These anti-Utopian anxieties need to be addressed head on, in a kind of cultural diagnosis and therapy, and not evaded by way of consent to this or that feature of the general market argument and rhetoric. All arguments about human nature – that it is basically good and cooperative, or that it is evil and aggressive and requires the taming of the market, if not Leviathan – are "humanistic" and ideological (as Althusser taught us), and should be replaced by the perspective of radical change and the collective project. In the meantime, the Left needs aggressively to defend big government and the welfare state, and to continuously attack market rhetoric on the basis of the historical record of the destructiveness of the free market (as Polenyi theorized it and Eastern Europe demonstrates).

Third Thesis

But such arguments in their turn presuppose the taking of a position on what is surely the central concept in any Marxian "unity-of-theory-and-practice," namely Revolution itself. This is the case because it is the untenability of that concept that is the principal exhibit in the post- or anti-Marxian arsenal. The defense of this concept, however, requires a number of preliminary preparations: in particular, we need to abandon to iconology everything that suggests that revolution is a punctual moment rather than an elaborate and complex process. For example, many of our most cherished iconic images of the various historical revolutions, such as the taking of the Winter Palace and the Tennis Court Oath, need to be set aside.

Social revolution is not a moment in time, but it can be affirmed in terms of the necessity of change in what is a synchronic system, in which everything holds together and is interrelated with everything else. Such a system then demands a kind of absolute systemic change, rather than piecemeal "reform," which turns out to be what is in the pejorative sense "Utopian," that is, illusory, not feasible. That is to say that the system demands the ideological vision of a radical social alternative to the existing social order, something which can no longer be taken for granted or inherited, under the state of current discursive struggle, but which demands reinvention. Religious fundamentalism (whether Islamic, Christian, or Hindu), that claims to offer a radical alternative to consumerism and "the American way of life," only comes into significant being when the traditional Left alternatives, and in particular the great revolutionary traditions of Marxism and communism, have suddenly seemed unavailable.

We must imagine revolution – as something which is both a process and the undoing of a synchronic system – as a set of demands which can be triggered by a punctual or political event such as a Left victory in an electoral struggle or the dismantling of colonial authority, but which then take the form of wider and wider popular diffusion and radicalization. These waves of new popular demands, which emerge from ever deeper layers of the hitherto silenced and deprived population, then radicalize even an ostensibly Left government and force ever more decisive transformations on the state. The nation (but in our time the world, as well) is then polarized in the classical dichotomous fashion in which everyone, however reluctantly, must take sides. The question of violence is then necessarily posed: if the process is not really a social revolution it does not necessarily have to be accompanied by violence. But if it is, then the previously dominant side of the dichotomy will of necessity have recourse to violent resistance, and in that sense alone, then, violence (however undesirable) is the outward sign or visible symptom that a genuinely social revolutionary process is in course.

The more basic issue raised here is thus not whether the concept of revolution is still viable, but rather that of national autonomy. We must ask whether, in the world system today, it is possible for any segment of integrated sections to uncouple and delink (to use Samir Amin's term) and then to pursue a different kind of social development and a radically different type of collective project.

Fourth Thesis

The collapse of the Soviet Union was not due to the failure of communism but rather to the success of communism, provided one understands this last, as the West generally does, as a mere strategy of modernization. For it is by way of rapid modernization that the Soviet Union was thought, even fifteen years ago, virtually to have caught up with the West (an officially anxiety-provoking perspective we can scarcely remember any longer).

Three further propositions need to be affirmed in connection with the collapse of the Soviet Union. The first is that internal social and political disintegration is part of a larger world-wide pattern in the 1980s which has enveloped in a structural corruption both the West (Reaganism and Thatcherism, other parallel forms in Italy and France) and the Arab countries (what Hisham Sharabi calls "neopatriarchy"). It would be misleading to explain causally this structural corruption in moral terms as it springs from the quite material social process of the accumulation of wealth unproductively in the very top layers of these societies. It has become clear that this stagnation is intimately related to what has been known as finance capital as it distances itself and diverges from its origin in production. Giovanni Arrighi has shown that the various moments of capital all seem to know a final stage in which production passes over into speculation, in which value parts from its origin in production and is exchanged more abstractly (something not without its cultural consequences as well).

It must also be stressed that categories like those of efficiency, productivity, and fiscal solvency are comparative ones, that is to say, their consequences come into play only in a field in which several unequal phenomena are competing. More efficient and productive technique drives out older machinery and older plant only when the latter enters its force field and thereby offers or is challenged to compete.

This leads us to the third point, namely that the Soviet Union "became" inefficient and collapsed when it attempted to integrate itself into a world system that was passing from its modernizing to its postmodern stage, a system that by its new rules of operation was therefore running at an incomparably higher rate of "productivity" than anything inside the Soviet sphere. Driven by cultural motives (consumerism, the newer information technologies, etc.), drawn in by calculated military-technological competition, by the bait of the debt, and intensifying forms of commercial coexistence, Soviet society entered an element in which it could not survive. It may be claimed that the Soviet Union and its satellites, hitherto isolated in their own specific pressure area as under some ideological and socioeconomic geodesic dome, now began imprudently to open the airlocks without spacesuits prepared and thus to allow themselves and their institutions to be subjected to the infinitely more intense pressures characteristic of the world outside. The result can be imagined as comparable to what the sheer blast pressures did to the flimsy structures in the immediate vicinity of the first atomic bomb; or to the grotesque and deforming weight of water pressure at the bottom of the sea on unprotected organisms evolved for the upper air. Indeed, this result confirms Wallerstein's prescient warning that the Soviet bloc, despite its importance, did not constitute an alternative system to that of capitalism, but merely an antisystemic space or zone within it, one now evidently blown away, with only a few surviving pockets in which various socialist experiments are still able to continue.

Fifth Thesis

The Marxisms (the political movements as well as the forms of intellectual and theoretical resistance) that emerge from the present system of late capitalism, from postmodernity, from Mandel's third stage of informational or multinational capitalism, will necessarily be distinct from those that developed during the modern period, the second stage, the age of imperialism. They will have a radically different relationship to globalization and will also, by contrast to earlier Marxisms, appear to be more cultural in character, turning fundamentally on those phenomena hitherto known as commodity reification and consumerism.

The increasing significance of culture for both the political and the economic is not a consequence of the tendential separation or differentiation of these realms, but rather of the more universal saturation and penetration of commodification itself, which has now been able to colonize large zones of that cultural area hitherto sheltered from it and indeed for the most part hostile to and inconsistent with its logic. The fact that culture has today largely become business has as a consequence that most of what used to be considered specifically economic and commercial has also become cultural, a characterization under which the various diagnoses of so-called image society or consumerism need to be subsumed.

And in a more general way Marxism enjoys a theoretical advantage in such analysis, namely that its conception of commodification is a structural and a non-moralizing one. Moral passion generates political action, but only of the most ephemeral kind, quickly reabsorbed and recontained and little inclined to share its specific issues and topics with other movements. But it is only by way of such amalgamation and construction that political movements can develop and grow more extensive. Indeed, I am tempted to make the point the other way around, that a moralizing politics tends to develop where a structural cognition and mapping of society is blocked. The influence of the religious and the ethnic today is to be grasped as a rage at the perception of the failure of socialism, and a desperate blind attempt to fill that vacuum with new motivations.

As for consumerism, it may well be hoped that it will turn out to have been as historically significant as it was necessary for human society to pass through the experience of consumerism as a way of life, if only in order more consciously to choose something radically different in its place. But for most of the world the addictions of consumerism will not be objectively available; it then seems possible that the prescient diagnosis of the radical theory of the 1960s – that capitalism was itself a revolutionary force in the way in which it produced new needs and desires that the system could not satisfy – will now find its realization on the global scale of the new world system.

On a theoretical level, it may be suggested that the currently urgent issues of permanent structural unemployment, of financial speculation and ungovernable capital movements, of the image society, are all profoundly interrelated on the level of what might be called their lack of content, their abstraction (as opposed to what another age might have termed their "alienation"). The more paradoxical level of the dialectic is met when we rejoin issues of globalization and informatization. There is a seemingly intransigent dilemma when the political and ideological possibilities of the new world networks (on the Left as well as in business or on the Right) are then coupled with the loss of autonomy in the world system today and the impossibility for any national or regional area to achieve its own autonomy and subsistence or to delink or uncouple itself from the world market. Intellectuals cannot find a way through this passage by the mere taking of a thought. It is the ripening of structural contradictions in reality that produce the dawning anticipation of new possibilities: yet we can at least keep this very dilemma alive by "cleaving to the negative" as Hegel might have said, by keeping alive that place from which the new can be expected, unexpectedly, to emerge.

Notes

1   The "critique of political economy" never wished to be a science in the sense in which "political economy" was itself conceived, let alone academic forms of "economics." That is, as "critique" it isolates the basis of the error it identifies, rejecting a radical discontinuity between theory and practice, facts and values.
2   Following Giovanni Arrighi, *The Long Twentieth Century* (London, New York, Verso, 1994) in sequence the Spanish–Genoese moment, the Dutch supersession, the English empire, the US hegemony, and beyond that the possibility of the prospect of the Japanese supremacy.
3   "Discursive struggle" in this usage is struggle for control of the terms and rules of the discourse.

Part III

Postmodernism

11

Beyond the Cave: Demystifying the Ideology of Modernism

In order to understand Jameson's theory of postmodernism, it is necessary first to situate it as an extension of his theorization of the preceding periods of realism and modernism. This chapter, which first appeared in 1975, explores these issues of periodization before postmodernism.

[...] I have suggested elsewhere that our habit of studying individual writers one by one, in a kind of respectful stylistic isolation, was a very useful strategy in preventing genuinely social and historical problems from intruding into literary study.[1] The position I want to defend here is not unlike this one, but for whole periods rather than individual writers. I suggest that the ghettoization of primitive storytelling is an excellent example of this, but the ambiguity of the word "myth," as loosely brandished in our discipline today, makes primitive storytelling a fairly complicated example to use. Our own myth school – or rather, what it might be clearer to call archetypal criticism – obviously has in mind a very different object of study, and a very different kind of textual satisfaction, than that afforded by the primitive storytellers of, say, the Bororo Encyclopedia. Indeed, whatever the ultimate usefulness of the intellectual brilliance invested in Claude Lévi-Strauss' *Mythologiques*, those four volumes will at least have had the effect of giving us a feeling for those genuinely episodic, molecular strings of events in which the Jungian hero, wearing all his archetypal masks, must inevitably find himself structurally ill at ease.

So we set aside the problem of myth for one much closer to home, which indeed involves that literature most explicitly repudiated by the practice and the values of the ideology of modernism: I refer to realism itself. And perhaps my point about boredom [not included here] may now make a little more sense to you, when you think, on the one hand, of the inevitable tediousness for us today, programmed by the rapid gearshifts of television, of the old endless three-decker novels; and when, on the other hand, you heave a sigh at the thought of yet another rehearsal of the tiresome polemics waged in the name of realism, to accept the terms of which is perhaps already to find yourself compromised in advance.

Now obviously I share that feeling too to some degree, and am not interested here in making some puritanical attack on modernism in the name of the older realistic values; I simply want to underscore the limits of the ideology of modernism in accounting for the great realistic works, and to suggest that to prove Dickens was really a symbolist, Flaubert the first modernist, Balzac a myth-maker, and George Eliot some Victorian version of Henry James if not even of Dostoevsky, is an intellectually dishonest operation that skirts all the real issues.

Modern literary theory has in fact given us what are essentially two irreconcilable accounts of realism. On the one hand, there are the classical apologias for this narrative mode, most dramatically associated with the position of Georg Lukács, but of which Erich Auerbach provides a less controversial and perhaps more patient documentation. For this position, the realistic mode – like the sonata form in music, or the conquest of perspective in painting – is one of the most complex and vital realizations of Western culture, to which it is indeed, like those other two artistic phenomena I mentioned, well-nigh unique. Any reader of Auerbach's *Mimesis* will have retained a vivid picture of the way in which realism slowly takes shape over many centuries by a progressive enlargement and refinement of literary techniques – from the unlimbering of epic sentence structure and the development of narrative perspective to the great plots of the nineteenth-century novels – an expansion of the literary and linguistic recording apparatus in such a way as to make ever larger areas of social and individual reality accessible to us. Here realism is shown to have epistemological truth, as a privileged mode of knowing the world we live in and the lives we lead in it; and for a position of this kind, of course, the modern dissatisfaction or boredom with realism cannot be expected to be taken very seriously.

Yet when we turn to that dissatisfaction itself and to the repudiation of realism in the name of modernism and in the interests of the latter's own developing apologia, we may well find that this other position is by no means dismissed as easily as all that. For the ideologues of modernism[2] do not indeed seek to refute the Lukács–Auerbach defense of the realistic mode in its own terms, which are primarily aesthetic and cognitive; rather they sense its weak link to be preaesthetic, part and parcel of its basic philosophical presuppositions. Thus, the target of their attack becomes the very concept of reality itself which is implied by the realistic aesthetic as Lukács or Auerbach outline it, the new position suggesting that what is intolerable for us today, aesthetically, about the so-called old-fashioned realism is to be accounted for by the inadmissible philosophical and metaphysical view of the world which underlies it and which it in its turn reinforces. The objection is thus, clearly, a critique of something like an *ideology of realism*, and charges that realism, by suggesting that representation is possible, and by encouraging an aesthetic of mimesis or imitation, tends to perpetuate a preconceived notion of some external reality to be imitated, and indeed, to foster a belief in the existence of some such common-sense everyday ordinary shared secular reality in the first place. Yet the great discoveries of modern science – relativity and the uncertainty principle – the movement in modern philosophy toward theories of models and various linguistic dimensions of reality, present-day French investigations of the category of representation itself – above all, however, the sheer accumulated weight and habit of the great modern works of art from the cubists and Joyce all the way to Beckett and Andy Warhol – all these things tend to confirm the idea that there is something quite naïve, in a sense quite profoundly *unrealistic*, and in the full sense of the word ideological, about the notion that reality is out there simply, quite objective and independent of us, and that knowing it involves the relatively unproblematical process of getting an adequate picture of it into our own heads.

Now I have to confess that I find both these positions – the defense of realism just as much as the denunciation of it – equally convincing, equally persuasive, equally true; so that, even though they would appear to be logically incompatible, I cannot persuade myself that they are as final as they look. But before I suggest a resolution that has seemed satisfactory to me, I want to remind you again of the reason we brought the subject up in the first place. The quarrel we have evoked is more fundamental, it seems to me, than a mere difference in aesthetic theories and positions (or else, if you prefer, such mere differences are perhaps themselves more fundamental than we have been accustomed to think): to be sure, in one sense, they simply correspond to differences in taste – it is clear that Lukács and Auerbach, for whatever reasons of background and upbringing and the like, deep down really don't like modern art. But again: perhaps what we call taste is not so simple either. I want to suggest that these two conflicting aesthetic positions correspond in the long run to two quite

different cultures: there was a culture of realism, that of the nineteenth century
– and a few of its inhabitants still survive here and there, native informants who
provide us with very useful reports and testimony about its nature and values –
and there is today a different culture altogether, that of modernism. Alongside
these two, as we suggested earlier, there is yet a third kind, namely what we
called in the most general way primitive or at least precapitalist, and whose
products – incomprehensible to both modernist and realist aesthetics alike – we
call myths or oral tales. So the limits of our own personal tastes have brought us
to the point where we can see our need, not to pick and choose and assimilate
selected objects from the older aesthetics or cultures into our own, but rather to
step outside our own culture – outside the culture of modernism – entirely and
to grasp its relationship to the others and its difference from them by means of
some vaster historical and supracultural model.

Before I suggest one, however, I have an obligation, even in the most
sketchy way, to complete my account of the quarrel between the realists and
the modernists: what both leave out, you will already have guessed, is simply
history itself. Both positions are completely ahistorical, and this in spite of the
fact that *Mimesis* is a history, one of the few great contemporary literary histories
we possess, and in spite of the fact, also, that Lukács is a Marxist (that the
modernists are ahistorical will probably be less surprising, since after all by and
large that is exactly what they set out to be). Briefly, I would suggest that
realism – but also that desacralized, postmagical, common-sense, everyday,
secular reality which is its object – is inseparable from the development of
capitalism, the quantification by the market system of the older hierarchical or
feudal or magical environment, and thus that both are intimately linked to the
bourgeoisie as its product and its commodity (and this is, it seems to me, where
Lukács himself is ahistorical, in not positing an exclusive link between realism
and the life of commerce, in suggesting that a wholly different social order like
that of socialism or communism will still want to maintain this particular –
historically dated – mode of reality-construction). And when in our own time
the bourgeoisie begins to decay as a class, in a world of social anomie and
fragmentation, then that active and conquering mode of the representation of
reality which is realism is no longer appropriate; indeed, in this new social
world which is ours today, we can go so far as to say that the very object of
realism itself – secular reality, objective reality – no longer exists either. Far
from being the world's final and definitive face, it proves to have been simply
one historical and cultural form among many others, such that one might argue
a kind of ultimate paradox of reality itself: there once was such a thing as
objective truth, objective reality, but now that "real world" is itself a thing of
the past. Objective reality – or the various possible objective realities – are in
other words, the function of genuine group existence or collective vitality; and

when the dominant group disintegrates, so also does the certainty of some common truth or being. Thus the problem about realism articulates in the cultural realm that profound ambivalence that Marx and Engels have about the bourgeoisie in history in general: the secularization and systematization that capitalism brought about is both more brutal and alienating, *and* more humane and liberating, than the effects of any previous social system. Capitalism destroys genuine human relationships, but also for the first time liberates humankind from village idiocy and the tyranny and intolerance of tribal life. This simultaneous positive and negative coding of capitalism appears everywhere in the works of Marx, but most strikingly and programmatically perhaps in the *Communist Manifesto*; and it is this very complex and ambivalent, profoundly dialectical assessment of capitalism that is reflected in the notion of the historical necessity of capitalism as a stage; whereas in the literary realm it takes the form of the hesitations just expressed about the realistic mode that corresponds to classic nineteenth-century capitalism, hesitations which can be measured in all their ambiguity by the simultaneous assertion that realism is the most complex epistemological instrument yet devised for recording the truth of social reality, and also, at one and the same time, that it is a lie in the very form itself, the prototype of aesthetic false consciousness, the appearance that bourgeois ideology takes on in the realm of narrative literature.

The model I now want to submit to you derives no doubt ultimately from Engels also, who had it himself from Morgan's *Ancient Society*, who in turn drew it from a still older anthropological tradition. But the form in which I am going to use this model – which in essence is nothing more than the old classification of cultures and social forms into the triad of savage, barbarian, and civilized types – comes more directly from a recent French work that gives us the means of transforming this otherwise purely historical typology into a rather sensitive instrument of practical literary analysis.

Now I should preface all this by saying that I don't intend here to give anything like a complete account, let alone a critique, of this more recent work – the *Anti-Oedipus* of Gilles Deleuze and Félix Guattari[3] – around which there has been a great deal of controversy, and whose usefulness for us lies in its reintroduction of genuinely historical preoccupations into the hitherto resolutely a- or antihistorical problematics of structuralism. Deleuze and Guattari, indeed, give us a vision of history based once more firmly on the transformation of fundamental social forms, and on the correlation between shifts in meaning and conceptual categories, and the various types of socioeconomic infrastructures.

[...]

Let me quickly resume their hypothesis: the savage state is the moment of the coding of the original or primordial schizophrenic flux; in barbarism we have, then, to do with a more complex construction on this basis, which will be called an overcoding of it; under capitalism, reality undergoes a new type of operation or manipulation, and the desacralization and laicization, the quantification and rationalization of capitalism will be characterized by Deleuze and Guattari precisely as a decoding of these earlier types of realities or code-constructions; and finally, our own time – whatever it may be thought to be as a separate social form in its own right, and it is obviously to this question on that we will want to return shortly – our own time is marked by nothing quite so much as a recoding of this henceforth decoded flux – by *attempts* to recode, to reinvent the sacred, to go back to myth (now understood in Frye's archetypal sense) – in brief, that whole host of recoding strategies which characterize the various modernisms, and of which the most revealing and authentic, as far as Deleuze and Guattari are concerned, is surely the emergence of schizophrenic literature, or the attempt to come to terms with the pure primordial flux itself.

Now I will try, not so much to explain these various moments, as to show why this way of thinking and talking about them may be of use to us (and if it is not, of course we have been mistaken in our choice of a model, and there remains nothing but to jettison this one and to find some paradigm better able to do the work we require from it).

The application of the terminology of flux and codes to primitive life and storytelling may be overhastily described in terms of symbolism or of Lévi-Strauss' conception of the "primitive mind," of that *pensée sauvage* or primitive thought which has not yet invented abstraction, for which the things of the outside world are, in themselves, meanings, or are indistinguishable from meanings. The medieval conception of the world as God's book, in which, for example, the beasts are so many sentences in a bestiary, is still close enough to this naïve coding to convey its atmosphere to us. Yet in the primitive world, the world of the endless oral stories and of the simple and naïvely or, if you prefer, "naturally" coded flux, none of those things are really organized systematically; it is only when this omnipresent and decentered primitive coding is somehow ordered and the body of the world *territorialized*, as Deleuze and Guattari put it, that we find ourselves in the next stage of the social (but also the literary) order, namely that of barbarism, or of the despotic machine. Here the world-book is reorganized into what Lewis Mumford calls a megamachine, and the coded flux, now overcoded, acquires a center; certain signifiers become privileged over others in the same way that the despot himself gradually emerges from tribal indistinction to become the very center of the world and the meeting place of the four points of the compass; so a kind of awesome Forbidden City of language comes into being, which is not yet abstraction in our sense either, but far more aptly characterized, in my opinion, by that peculiar phenomenon we call allegory, and in which a single coded object or item of the outside world is suddenly overloaded with meaning, lifted up into a crucial element of a new and complicated object-language or overcoding erected on the basis of the older, simpler, "natural" sign-system. So in the passage from savagery to barbarism, it may be said that we pass from the *production* of coded elements to the *representation* of them, a representation that indicates itself and affirms its own splendor as privilege and as sacred meaning.

Civilization, capitalism, then come as an attempt to annual this barbaric overcoding, this despotic and luxurious sign-system erected parasitically upon the basis of the older "natural" codes; and the new social form, the capitalist one, thus aims at working its way back to some even more fundamental and uncoded reality — scientific or objective — behind the older signs. This change-over is, of course, a familiar historical story, of which we possess a number of different versions, and I have the obligation clearly enough to explain what advantages there are to us — in our practical work as teachers and students of literature — in the one I am proposing here. For we know that the ideologues of the rising bourgeoisie — in that movement called the Enlightenment — set themselves the explicit task of destroying religion and superstition of extirpating the sacred in all of its forms; they were then quite intensely aware of the struggle to *decode*, even if they did not call it that and even if subsequent generations of a bourgeoisie complacently installed in power preferred to forget the now rather frightening corrosive power of that ambitious effort of negativity and destructive criticism.

So gradually the bourgeoise invents a more reassuring, more positive account of the transformation: in this view, the older superstitious remnants simply give way to the new positivities of modern *science*; or, if you prefer — now that a model-building science in our own time has seemed a less reliable ally — to the positive achievements of modern technology and invention. But both these accounts — that of the Enlightenment itself and that of positivism — are concerned more with abstract knowledge and control than with the facts of individual existence. From the point of view of our particular discipline, in other words, this positive science- or technology-oriented account of the secularization of the world seems more appropriate to the history of ideas than to narrative analysis. The dialectical version of the story — that of Hegel as well as of Marx and Engels — still seems to provide the most adequate synthesis of these older purely negative or purely positive accounts. Here the changeover is seen in terms of a passage from quality to quantity: in other words, the gradual substitution of a market economy for the older forms of barter or payment in kind amounts to the increasing primacy of the principle of generalized equivalence, as it is embodied in the money system. This means that where before there was a qualitative difference between the objects of production, between, say, shoes and beef, or oil paintings and leather belts or sacks of grain — all of them, in the older systems, coded in unique and qualitative ways, as objects of quite different and incommensurable desires, invested each with a unique libidinal content of its own – now suddenly they all find themselves absolutely interchangeable, and through equivalence and the common measure of a money system reduced to the gray tastelessness of abstraction.

The advantage now of the addition to this view of Deleuze and Guattari's concept of the decoded flux is that we will come to understand quantification, the pure equivalence of the exchange world, henceforth no longer as a reality in its own right, but rather as a process, an outer limit, a secular ideal, a kind of absence of quality that can never really be reached once and for all in any definitive form, but only approached in that infinite and teasing approximation of the asymptote to a curve with which it will never completely coincide. This is why the periodization of the ideologues of modernism, when they talk about the break with the classical novel, or the realistic novel or the traditional nineteenth-century novel, always proves so embarrassing, because, of course, as a positive phenomenon the classical novel is not there at all when you look for it, realism proving to be, as Darko Suvin put it, simply the zero degree of allegory itself.

Now I can give only two brief illustrations of the usefulness of the view for practical criticism of these so-called realistic novels. In the first place, it seems to me that the idea of a decoded flux for the first time gives content to the very formalistic suggestions – in the Jakobson–Tynianov theses on realism, for instance – that each realism constitutes a demystification of some preceding ideal or illusion. Obviously, the prototype for such a paradigm is the *Quijote* of Cervantes, but it would seem to me that the idea of realism as a decoding tends to direct our attention far more insistently to the very nature of the codes thus canceled, the older barbaric or savage signifiers thus dismantled; this view, in other words, forces us to attend far more closely to the page-by-page and incident-by-incident operations, whereby the novel effectuates this desacralization, thus effectively preserving us, at the same time, from any illusion that secular reality could be anything but provisional terminus of the narrative process.

The other point I want to make is the close identity between realism and historical thinking, an identity revealed by the model of decoded flux. It has been claimed – by the tenets of the rise-of-science explanation I mentioned a moment ago – that the new scientific values, particularly those of causality and causal explanation, are responsible for the new perspectivism shown by critics like Auerbach to constitute the very web of the new realistic narrative texture. Let me suggest, on the contrary, that causality is not a positive but rather a negative or privative concept: causality is simply the form taken by chronology itself when it falls into the world of quantification, of the indifferently equival-

privative

ent and the decoded flux. Angus Fletcher's book *Allegory* (1964) gives us an excellent picture of the literary phenomena that played the role in the older high allegory or barbaric overcoding of what will later become causality in realism: action by contiguity, emanation, magical contamination, the hypnotic and in-gathering spell of a kosmos or spatial form – all of these must then disappear from the decoded narrative, and the continuity of time must be dealt with in some more secular way, if it is not to decay and disintegrate back into the random sequence of unrelated instants which is the very nature of the primordial schizophrenic flux itself. Historical thinking, causality, is now a way of making things yield up their own meanings immanently, without any appeal to transcendental or magical outside forces; the process by which a single item deteriorates in time is now seen to be meaningful in itself, and when you have shown it, you have no further need of any external or transcendental hypotheses. Thus realism is par excellence the moment of the discovery of changing time, of the generation-by-generation and year-by-year dynamics of a new kind of social history. Realism is at one, I am tempted to say, with a world of *worn things*, things among which, of course, one must number people as well, and those discarded objects that are used-up human lives.

At length, as the nineteenth century itself wears on, we begin to detect signs of a kind of fatigue with the whole process of decoding; indeed, as the very memory of feudalism and the ancien régime grows dim, there appear perhaps to be fewer and fewer codes in the older sacred sense to serve as the object of such semiotic purification. This is, of course, the moment of the emergence of modernism, or rather, of the various modernisms, for the subsequent attempts to *recode* the henceforth decoded flux of the realistic, middle-class, secular era are many and varied, and we cannot hope even to give a sense of their variety here. So I will simply attempt to make one point, which seems to me absolutely fundamental for the analysis of modern literature, and which, to my mind, constitutes the most useful contribution to our future work of the model here under consideration. It is simply this: that it follows, from what we have said, and from the very notion of a recoding of secular reality or of the decoded flux, that all modernistic works are essentially simply cancelled realistic ones, that they are, in other words, not apprehended directly, in terms of their own symbolic meanings, in terms of their own mythic or sacred immediacy, the way an older primitive or overcoded work would be, but rather indirectly only, by way of the relay of an imaginary realistic narrative of which the symbolic and modernistic one is then seen as a kind of stylization; and this is a type of reading, and a literary structure, utterly unlike anything hitherto known in the history of literature, and one to which we have been insufficiently attentive until now. Let me suggest, in other words, to put it very crudely, that when you make sense of something like Kafka's *Castle*, your process of doing so involves the

a truth / *postulate*

substitution for that recoded flux of a realistic narrative of your own devising – one which may be framed in terms of Kafka's supposed personal experience – psychoanalytic, religious, or social – or in terms of your own, or in terms of some hypothetical destiny of "modern man" in general. Whatever the terms of the realistic narrative appealed to, however, I think it's axiomatic that the reading of such a work is always a two-stage affair, first, substituting a realistic hypothesis – in narrative form – then interpreting that secondary and invented or projected core narrative according to the procedures we reserved for the older realistic novel in general. And I suggest that this elaborate process is at work everywhere in our reception of contemporary works of art, all the way from those of Kafka down to, say, *The Exorcist*.

And since I mentioned chronology a moment ago, let me briefly use the fate of chronology in the new artistic milieu of the recoded flux to give you a clearer sense of what is meant by the process. It has been said, for instance, that in Robbe-Grillet's novel *La Jalousie*, chronology is abolished: there are two separate sets of events that ought to permit us to reestablish the basic facts of the story in their proper order, only they do not: "the crushing of the centipede which, in a novel telling a story, would provide a good point of reference around which to situate the other events in time, is [in fact] made to occur *before* the trip taken by Franck and A., *during* their trip, and *after* it."[4] Yet it would be wrong to conclude that Robbe-Grillet had really succeeded thereby in shaking our belief in chronology, and along with it, in that myth of a secular, objective, "realistic" reality of which it is a sign and a feature. On the contrary, as every reader of Robbe-Grillet knows, this kind of narrative exasperates our obsession with chronology to a veritable fever pitch, and the absence of any realistic "solution," far from being a return to the older non-causal narrative conscious-ness of primitive peoples, as in allegory for instance, in fact drives us only deeper into the contradictions of our own scientific and causal thought-modes. So it is quite wrong to say that Robbe-Grillet has abolished the story; on the contrary, we read *La Jalousie* by substituting for it a realistic version of one of the oldest stories in the world, and its force and value come from the paradoxical fact that by canceling it, the new novel tells this realistic story more forcefully than any genuinely realistic, old-fashioned, decoded narrative could.

Now from a sociological point of view it is clear why this had to happen with the breakdown of a homogeneous public, with the social fragmentation and anomie of the bourgeoisie itself, and also its refraction among the various national situations of Western or Nato capitalism, each of which then speaks its own private language and demands its own particular frame of reference. So the modern work comes gradually to be constructed as a kind of multipurpose object, Umberto Eco's so-called *opera aperta* or open form,[5] designed to be used by each subgroup after its own fashion and needs, so that its realistic core, that "concrete" emotion, but also situation, which we call, simply, *jealousy*, seems the most abstract and empty starting point of all, inasmuch as every private audience is obliged to recode it afresh in terms of its own sign-system.

The first conclusion one would draw from this peculiar historical and aesthetic situation is that Lukács (whose limits I hope I have already admitted) turns out in the long run to have been right after all about the nature of modernism: very far from a break with that older overstuffed Victorian bourgeois reality, it simply reinforces all the latter's basic presuppositions, only in a world so thoroughly subjectivized that they have been driven underground, beneath the surface of the work, forcing us to reconfirm the concept of a secular reality at the very moment when we imagine ourselves to be demolishing it.

This is a social and historical contradiction, but for the writer it is an agonizing dilemma, and perhaps that would be the most dramatic way of expressing what we have been trying to say. No one here, after all, seriously wants to return to the narrative mode of nineteenth-century realism; the latter's rightful inheritors are the writers of bestsellers, who – unlike Kafka or Robbe-Grillet – really do concern themselves with the basic secular problems of our existence, namely, money, power, position, sex, and all those humdrum daily preoccupations that continue to form the substance of our daily lives all the while that art literature considers them unworthy of its notice. I am not suggesting that we go back and read or write in the older way, only that in their heart of hearts – as the Goldwater people used to say – everyone knows that John O'Hara's novels still give a truer picture of the facts of life in the United States than anything of Hemingway or Faulkner, with all their tourist or magnolia exoticism. Yet – yet – the latter are palpably the greater writers. So we slowly begin to grasp the enormity of a historical situation in which the truth of our social life as a whole – Lukács would have said, as a totality – is increasingly irreconcilable with the aesthetic quality of language or of individual expression; of a situation about which it can be asserted that if we can make a work of art from our experience, if we can tell it in the form of a story, it is no longer true; and if we can grasp the truth about our world as totality, as something transcending mere individual experience, we can no longer make it accessible in narrative or literary form. So a strange malediction hangs over art in our time, and for the writer this dilemma is felt as an increasing (structural) incapacity to generalize or universalize private or lived experience. The dictates, not only of realism, but of narrative in general, tend gradually to restrict writing to sheer autobiography, at the same time that they transform even autobiographical discourse itself into one more private language among others: reduced to the telling of the truth of a private situation alone, that no longer engages the fate of a nation, but merely a single locality; and no longer even for that, but a particular neighborhood – and even that only as long as it still remains a neighborhood in the traditional, ethnic or ghetto, sense; even therein, speaking henceforth only for a specific family, and then not even for its older generations; at length reduced to a single household, and finally, within it, to a single gender. So little by little the writer is reduced to so private a speech that it is henceforth bereft of any public consequences or resonances, so that only symbolic recoding holds out the hope of saying something meaningful to a wider and more heterogeneous public. Yet, as we have seen, that new kind of meaning is quite different from the old one. But in this wholly subjectivized untruth, the modern writer nonetheless in another sense remains profoundly true and profoundly representative: for everyone else is equally locked into his or her private language, imprisoned in those serried ranks of monads that are the ultimate result of the social fragmentation inherent in our system.

Many are the images of this profound subjectivization and fragmentation of our social life, and of our very existences, in the world of late monopoly capitalism. Some strike terror and inspire us with a kind of metaphysical pathos at our condition, like that persona of Lautréamont sealed since birth in an airtight, soundproof membrane, dreaming of the shriek destined to rupture his isolation and to admit for the first time the cries of pain of the world outside.

All are, of course, figures, and it is a measure of our dilemma that we cannot convey the situation in other than a figurative way; yet some figures seem more liberating than others [. . .]. [L]et us conclude with a Platonic vision, which was once itself the foundation of a metaphysic, but which now, today, and owing to historical developments quite unforeseeable in Plato's time, seems – like the gravest of all figures and metaphors – henceforth to have been intended in the most *literal* sense.

Imagine [says Socrates], an underground chamber, like a cave with an entrance open to the daylight and running a long way underground. In this chamber are men who have been prisoners there since they were children, their legs and necks being so fastened that they can only look straight ahead of them and cannot turn their heads. Behind them and above them a fire is burning, and between the fire and the prisoners runs a road, in front of which a curtain-wall has been built, like the screen at puppet-shows . . . Imagine further that there are men carrying all sorts of artefacts along behind the curtain-wall, including figures of men and animals made of wood and stone and other materials . . .

An odd picture [responds Socrates' listener] and an odd sort of prisoner.

They are drawn from life, I replied. For tell me, do you think our prisoners could see anything of themselves or their fellows save the shadows thrown by the fire upon the wall of the cave opposite?[6]

There are, of course, ways of breaking out of this isolation, but they are not literary ways and require complete and thoroughgoing transformation of our economic and social system, and the invention of new forms of collective living. Our task − specialists that we are in the reflections of things − is a more patient and modest, more diagnostic one. Yet even such a task as the analysis of literature and culture will come to nothing unless we keep the knowledge of our own historical situation vividly present to us: for we are least of all, in our position, entitled to the claim that we did not understand, that we thought all those things were real, that we had no way of knowing we were living in a cave.

Notes

1 *Marxism and Form* (Princeton, NJ, Princeton University Press, 1972) pp. 309–26.
2 The modernist position is resumed in Renato Poggioli, *Theory of the Avant-Garde* (Cambridge, Mass., 1968) and eloquently defended in Nathalie Sarraute, *The Age of Suspicion* (New York, 1963). I should add that any really consequent treatment of it would also have necessarily to come to terms with what might be called the left-wing modernism of Brecht or of the *Tel Quel* group.
3 Gilles Deleuze and Félix Guattari, *Anti-Oedipe* (Paris, 1972); translated as *Anti-Oedipus* by R. Hurley, M. Seem, and H. R. Lane (Minneapolis, 1983).
4 Gerald Prince, *A Grammar of Stories* (The Hague, 1973), p. 23.
5 See Umberto Eco, *Opera Aperta* (Milan, 1962).
6 *The Republic*, Book VII, trans. H. D. P. Lee (Baltimore, 1955), pp. 278–9.

12

Postmodernism, or The Cultural Logic of Late Capitalism

This chapter was published in *New Left Review* (1984). A revised version appears as the lead essay in Jameson's *Postmodernism, or, The Cultural Logic of Late Capitalism* (1991), the other chapters of which extend the study of postmodern culture to a variety of domains, such as architecture, video, film, and economic theory.

The last few years have been marked by an inverted millenarianism, in which premonitions of the future, catastrophic or redemptive, have been replaced by senses of the end of this or that (the end of ideology, art, or social class; the "crisis" of Leninism, social democracy, or the welfare state, etc., etc.): taken together, all of these perhaps constitute what is increasingly called postmodernism. The case for its existence depends on the hypothesis of some radical break or *coupure*, generally traced back to the end of the 1950s or the early 1960s. As the word itself suggests, this break is most often related to notions of the waning or extinction of the hundred-year-old modern movement (or to its ideological or aesthetic repudiation). Thus, abstract expressionism in painting, existentialism in philosophy, the final forms of representation in the novel, the films of the great *auteurs*, or the modernist school of poetry (as institutionalized and canonized in the works of Wallace Stevens): all these are now seen as the final, extraordinary flowering of a high modernist impulse which is spent and exhausted with them. The enumeration of what follows then at once becomes empirical, chaotic, and heterogeneous: Andy Warhol and pop art, but also photorealism, and beyond it, the "new expressionism"; the moment, in music, of John Cage, but also the synthesis of classical and "popular" styles found in composers like Phil Glass and Terry Riley, and also punk and new wave rock (the Beatles and the Stones now standing as the high-modernist moment of that more recent and rapidly evolving tradition); in film, Godard, post-Godard and experimental cinema and video, but also a whole new type of commercial film (about which more below); Burroughs, Pynchon, or Ishmael Reed, on the one hand, and the French *nouveau roman* and its succession on the other, along with alarming new kinds of literary criticism, based on some new aesthetic of textuality or *écriture* . . . The list might be extended indefinitely; but does it imply any more fundamental change or break than the periodic style- and fashion–changes determined by an older high-modernist imperative of stylistic innovation?[1]

The Rise of Aesthetic Populism

It is in the realm of architecture, however, that modifications in aesthetic production are most dramatically visible, and that their theoretical problems have been most centrally raised and articulated; it was indeed from architectural debates that my own conception of postmodernism — as it will be outlined in the following pages — initially began to emerge. More decisively than in the other arts or media, postmodernist positions in architecture have been insepar- able from an implacable critique of architectural high modernism and of the so- called International Style (Frank Lloyd Wright, Le Corbusier, Mies), where formal criticism and analysis (of the high-modernist transformation of the building into a virtual sculpture, or monumental "duck", as Robert Venturi puts it) are at one with reconsiderations on the level of urbanism and of the aesthetic institution. High modernism is thus credited with the destruction of the fabric of the traditional city and of its older neighbourhood culture (by way of the radical disjunction of the new Utopian high-modernist building from its surrounding context); while the prophetic elitism and authoritarianism of the modern movement are remorselessly denounced in the imperious gesture of the charismatic Master.

Postmodernism in architecture will then logically enough stage itself as a kind of aesthetic populism, as the very title of Venturi's influential manifesto *Learning from Las Vegas*, suggests. However we may ultimately wish to evaluate this populist rhetoric, it has at least the merit of drawing our attention to one fundamental feature of all the postmodernisms enumerated above: namely, the effacement in them of the older (essentially high-modernist) frontier between high culture and so-called mass or commercial culture, and the emergence of new kinds of texts infused with the forms, categories and contents of that very Culture Industry so passionately denounced by all the ideologues of the modern, from Leavis and the American New Criticism all the way to Adorno and the Frankfurt School. The postmodernisms have in fact been fascinated precisely by this whole "degraded" landscape of schlock and kitsch, of TV series and *Readers' Digest* culture, of advertising and motels, of the late show and the grade-B Hollywood film, of so-called paraliterature with its airport paperback categories of the gothic and the romance, the popular biography, the murder mystery and science-fiction or fantasy novel: materials they no longer simply "quote", as a Joyce or a Mahler might have done, but incorporate into their very substance.

Nor should the break in question be thought of as a purely cultural affair: indeed, theories of the postmodern – whether celebratory or couched in the language of moral revulsion and denunciation – bear a strong family resemblance to all those more ambitious sociological generalizations which, at much the same time, bring us the news of the arrival and inauguration of a whole new type of society, most famously baptized "post-industrial society" (Daniel Bell), but often also designated consumer society, media society, information society, electronic society or "high tech", and the like. Such theories have the obvious ideological mission of demonstrating, to their own relief, that the new social formation in question no longer obeys the laws of classical capitalism, namely the primacy of industrial production and the omnipresence of class struggle. The Marxist tradition has therefore resisted them with vehemence, with the signal exception of the economist Ernest Mandel, whose book *Late Capitalism* sets out not merely to anatomize the historic originality of this new society (which he sees as a third stage or moment in the evolution of capital), but also to demonstrate that it is, if anything, a *purer* stage of capitalism than any of the moments that preceded it. I will return to this argument later; suffice it for the moment to emphasize a point I have defended in greater detail elsewhere,[2] namely that every position on postmodernism in culture – whether apologia or stigmatization – is also at one and the same time, and *necessarily*, an implicitly or explicitly political stance on the nature of multinational capitalism today.

Postmodernism as Cultural Dominant

A last preliminary word on method: what follows is not to be read as stylistic description, as the account of one cultural style or movement among others. I have rather meant to offer a periodizing hypothesis, and that at a moment in which the very conception of historical periodization has come to seem most problematical indeed. I have argued elsewhere that all isolated or discrete cultural analysis always involves a buried or repressed theory of historical periodization; in any case, the conception of the "genealogy" largely lays to rest traditional theoretical worries about so-called linear history, theories of "stages", and teleological historiography. In the present context, however, lengthier theoretical discussion of such (very real) issues can perhaps be replaced by a few substantive remarks.

One of the concerns frequently aroused by periodizing hypotheses is that these tend to obliterate difference, and to project an idea of the historical period as massive homogeneity (bounded on either side by inexplicable "chronological" metamorphoses and punctuation marks). This is, however, precisely why it seems to me essential to grasp "postmodernism" not as a style, but rather as a cultural dominant: a conception which allows for the presence and coexistence of a range of very different, yet subordinate features.

Consider, for example, the powerful alternative position that postmodernism is itself little more than one more stage of modernism proper (if not, indeed, of the even older romanticism); it may indeed be conceded that all of the features of postmodernism I am about to enumerate can be detected, full-blown, in this or that preceding modernism (including such astonishing genealogical precursors as Gertrude Stein, Raymond Roussel, or Marcel Duchamp, who may be considered outright postmodernists, *avant la lettre*). What has not been taken into account by this view is, however, the social position of the older modernism, or better still, its passionate repudiation by an older Victorian and post-Victorian bourgeoisie, for whom its forms and ethos are received as being variously ugly, dissonant, obscure, scandalous, immoral, subversive and generally "anti-social". It will be argued here that a mutation in the sphere of culture has rendered such attitudes archaic. Not only are Picasso and Joyce no longer ugly; they now strike us, on the whole, as rather "realistic"; and this is the result of a canonization and an academic institutionalization of the modern movement generally, which can be traced to the late 1950s. This is indeed surely one of the most plausible explanations for the emergence of postmodernism itself, since the younger generation of the 1960s will now confront the formerly oppositional modern movement as a set of dead classics, which "weigh like a nightmare on the brains of the living", as Marx once said in a different context.

As for the postmodern revolt against all that, however, it must equally be stressed that its own offensive features – from obscurity and sexually explicit material to psychological squalor and overt expressions of social and political defiance, which transcend anything that might have been imagined at the most extreme moments of high modernism – no longer scandalize anyone and are not only received with the greatest complacency but have themselves become institutionalized and are at one with the official culture of Western society.

What has happened is that aesthetic production today has become integrated into commodity production generally: the frantic economic urgency of producing fresh waves of ever more novel-seeming goods (from clothing to airplanes), at ever greater rates of turnover, now assigns an increasingly essential structural function and position to aesthetic innovation and experimentation. Such economic necessities then find recognition in the institutional support of all kinds available for the newer art, from foundations and grants to museums and other forms of patronage. Architecture is, however, of all the arts that closest constitutively to the economic, with which, in the form of commissions and land values, it has a virtually unmediated relationship: it will therefore not be surprising to find the extraordinary flowering of the new postmodern architecture grounded in the patronage of multinational business, whose expansion and development is strictly contemporaneous with it. That these two new phenomena have an even deeper dialectical interrelationship than the simple one-to-one financing of this or that individual project we will try to suggest later on. Yet this is the point at which we must remind the reader of the obvious, namely that this whole global, yet American, postmodern culture is the internal and superstructural expression of a whole new wave of American military and economic domination throughout the world: in this sense, as throughout class history, the underside of culture is blood, torture, death and horror.

The first point to be made about the conception of periodization in dominance, therefore, is that even if all the constitutive features of postmodernism were identical and continuous with those of an older modernism – a position I feel to be demonstrably erroneous but which only an even lengthier analysis of modernism proper could dispel – the two phenomena would still remain utterly distinct in their meaning and social function, owing to the very different positioning of postmodernism in the economic system of late capital, and beyond that, to the transformation of the very sphere of culture in contemporary society.

More on this point at the conclusion of the present [chapter]. I must now briefly address a different kind of objection to periodization, a different kind of concern about its possible obliteration of heterogeneity, which one finds most often on the Left. And it is certain that there is a strange quasi-Sartrean irony – a "winner loses" logic – which tends to surround any effort to describe a "system", a totalizing dynamic, as these are detected in the movement of contemporary society. What happens is that the more powerful the vision of some increasingly total system or logic – the Foucault of the prisons book is the obvious example – the more powerless the reader comes to feel. Insofar as the theorist wins, therefore, by constructing an increasingly closed and terrifying machine, to that very degree he loses, since the critical capacity of his work is thereby paralysed, and the impulses of negation and revolt, not to speak of those of social transformation, are increasingly perceived as vain and trivial in the face of the model itself.

I have felt, however, that it was only in the light of some conception of a dominant cultural logic or hegemonic norm that genuine difference could be measured and assessed. I am very far from feeling that all cultural production today is "postmodern" in the broad sense I will be conferring on this term. The postmodern is however the force field in which very different kinds of cultural impulses – what Raymond Williams has usefully termed "residual" and "emergent" forms of cultural production – must make their way. If we do not achieve some general sense of a cultural dominant, then we fall back into a view of present history as sheer heterogeneity, random difference, a coexistence of a host of distinct forces whose effectivity is undecidable. This has been at any rate the political spirit in which the following analysis was devised: to project some conception of a new systemic cultural norm and its reproduction, in order to reflect more adequately on the most effective forms of any radical cultural politics today.

The exposition will take up in turn the following constitutive features of the postmodern: a new depthlessness, which finds its prolongation both in contemporary "theory" and in a whole new culture of the image or the simulacrum; a consequent weakening of historicity, both in our relationship to public History and in the new forms of our private temporality, whose "schizophrenic" structure (following Lacan) will determine new types of syntax or syntagmatic relationships in the more temporal arts; a whole new type of emotional ground tone – what I will call "intensities" – which can best be grasped by a return to older theories of the sublime; the deep constitutive relationships of all this to a whole new technology, which is itself a figure for a whole new economic world system; and, after a brief account of postmodernist mutations in the lived experience of built space itself, some reflections on the mission of political art in the bewildering new world space of late multinational capital.

The Deconstruction of Expression

Peasant shoes

We will begin with one of the canonical works of high modernism in visual art, Van Gogh's well-known painting of the peasant shoes, an example which as you can imagine has not been innocently or randomly chosen. I want to propose two ways of reading this painting, both of which in some fashion reconstruct the reception of the work in a two-stage or double-level process.

I first want to suggest that if this copiously reproduced image is not to sink to the level of sheer decoration, it requires us to reconstruct some initial situation out of which the finished work emerges. Unless that situation – which has vanished into the past – is somehow mentally restored, the painting will remain an inert object, a reified end-product, and be unable to be grasped as a symbolic act in its own right, as praxis and as production.

This last term suggests that one way of reconstructing the initial situation to which the work is somehow a response is by stressing the raw materials, the initial content, which it confronts and which it reworks, transforms, and appropriates. In Van Gogh, that content, those initial raw materials, are, I will suggest, to be grasped simply as the whole object world of agricultural misery, of stark rural poverty, and the whole rudimentary human world of backbreaking peasant toil, a world reduced to its most brutal and menaced, primitive and marginalized state.

Fruit trees in this world are ancient and exhausted sticks coming out of poor soil; the people of the village are worn down to their skulls, caricatures of some ultimate grotesque typology of basic human feature types. How is it then that in Van Gogh such things as apple trees explode into a hallucinatory surface of colour, while his village stereotypes are suddenly and garishly overlaid with hues of red and green? I will briefly suggest, in this first interpretative option, that the willed and violent transformation of a drab peasant object world into the most glorious materialization of pure colour in oil paint is to be seen as a Utopian gesture: as an act of compensation which ends up producing a whole new Utopian realm of the senses, or at least of that supreme sense – sight, the visual, the eye – which it now reconstitutes for us as a semi-autonomous space in its own right – part of some new division of labour in the body of capital, some new fragmentation of the emergent sensorium which replicates the specializations and divisions of capitalist life at the same time that it seeks in precisely such fragmentation a desperate Utopian compensation for them.

There is, to be sure, a second reading of Van Gogh which can hardly be ignored when we gaze at this particular painting, and that is Heidegger's central analysis in *Der Ursprung des Kunstwerkes*, which is organized around the idea that the work of art emerges within the gap between Earth and World, or what I would prefer to translate as the meaningless materiality of the body and nature and the meaning-endowment of history and of the social. We will return to that particular gap or rift later on; suffice it here to recall some of the famous phrases, which model the process whereby these henceforth illustrious peasant shoes slowly recreate about themselves the whole missing object-world which was once their lived context. "In them," says Heidegger, "there vibrates the silent call of the earth, its quiet gift of ripening corn and its enigmatic self-refusal in the fallow desolation of the wintry field." "This equipment," he goes on, "belongs to the *earth* and it is protected in the *world* of the peasant woman ... Van Gogh's painting is the disclosure of what the equipment, the pair of peasant shoes, *is* in truth ... This entity emerges into the unconcealment of its being", by way of the mediation of the work of art, which draws the whole absent world and earth into revelation around itself, along with the heavy tread of the peasant woman, the loneliness of the field path, the hut in the clearing, the worn and broken instruments of labour in the furrows and at the hearth. Heidegger's account needs to be completed by insistence on the renewed materiality of the work, on the transformation of one form of materiality – the earth itself and its paths and physical objects – into that other materiality of oil paint affirmed and foregrounded in its own right and for its own visual pleasures; but has nonetheless a satisfying plausibility.

Diamond Dust Shoes

At any rate, both of these readings may be described as *hermeneutical*, in the sense in which the work in its inert, objectal form, is taken as a clue or a symptom for some vaster reality which replaces it as its ultimate truth. Now we need to look at some shoes of a different kind, and it is pleasant to be able to draw for such an image on the recent work of the central figure in contemporary visual art. Andy Warhol's *Diamond Dust Shoes* evidently no longer speaks to us with any of the immediacy of Van Gogh's footgear: indeed, I am tempted to say that it does not really speak to us at all. Nothing in this painting organizes even a minimal place for the viewer, who confronts it at the turning of a museum corridor or gallery with all the contingency of some inexplicable natural object. On the level of the content, we have to do with what are now far more clearly fetishes, both in the Freudian and in the Marxian sense (Derrida remarks, somewhere, about the Heideggerian *Paar Bauernschuhe,* that the Van Gogh footgear are a heterosexual pair, which allows neither for perversion nor for fetishization). Here, however, we have a random collection of dead objects, hanging together on the canvas like so many turnips, as shorn of their earlier life-world as the pile of shoes left over from Auschwitz, or the remainders and tokens of some incomprehensible and tragic fire in a packed dancehall. There is therefore in Warhol no way to complete the hermeneutic gesture, and to restore to these oddments that whole larger lived context of the dance hall or the ball, the world of jetset fashion or of glamour magazines. Yet this is even more paradoxical in the light of biographical information: Warhol began his artistic career as a commercial illustrator for shoe fashions and a designer of display windows in which various pumps and slippers figured prominently. Indeed, one is tempted to raise here – far too prematurely – one of the central issues about postmodernism itself and its possible political dimensions: Andy Warhol's work in fact turns centrally around commodification, and the great billboard images of the Coca-cola bottle or the Campbell's Soup Can, which explicitly foreground the commodity fetishism of a transition to late capital, *ought* to be powerful and critical political statements. If they are not that, then one would surely want to know why, and one would want to begin to wonder a little more seriously about the possibilities of political or critical art in the postmodern period of late capital.

But there are some other significant differences between the high-modernist and the postmodernist moment, between the shoes of Van Gogh and the shoes of Andy Warhol, on which we must now very briefly dwell. The first and most evident is the emergence of a new kind of flatness or depthlessness, a new kind of superficiality in the most literal sense – perhaps the supreme formal feature of all the postmodernisms to which we will have occasion to return in a number of other contexts.

Then we must surely come to terms with the role of photography and the photographic negative in contemporary art of this kind: and it is this indeed which confers its deathly quality on the Warhol image, whose glacéd x-ray elegance mortifies the reified eye of the viewer in a way that would seem to have nothing to do with death or the death obsession or the death anxiety on the level of content. It is indeed as though we had here to do with the inversion of Van Gogh's Utopian gesture: in the earlier work, a stricken world is by some Nietzschean fiat and act of the will transformed into the stridency of Utopian colour. Here, on the contrary, it is as though the external and coloured surface of things – debased and contaminated in advance by their assimilation to glossy advertising images – has been stripped away to reveal the deathly black-and-white substratum of the photographic negative which subtends them. Although this kind of death of the world of appearance becomes thematized in certain of Warhol's pieces – most notably, the traffic accidents or the electric chair series – this is not, I think, a matter of content any longer but of some more fundamental mutation both in the object world itself – now become a set of texts or simulacra – and in the disposition of the subject.

Simulacrum

Pastiche

The waning of affect

All of which brings me to the third feature I had in mind to develop here briefly, namely what I will call the waning of affect in postmodern culture. Of course, it would be inaccurate to suggest that all affect, all feeling or emotion, all subjectivity, has vanished from the newer image. Indeed, there is a kind of return of the repressed in *Diamond Dust Shoes*, a strange compensatory decorative exhilaration, explicitly designated by the title itself although perhaps more difficult to observe in the reproduction. This is the glitter of gold dust, the spangling of gilt sand, which seals the surface of the painting and yet continues to glint at us. Think, however, of Rimbaud's magical flowers "that look back at you", or of the august premonitory eye-flashes of Rilke's archaic Greek torso which warn the bourgeois subject to change his life: nothing of that sort here, in the gratuitous frivolity of this final decorative overlay.

The waning of affect is, however, perhaps best initially approached by way of the human figure, and it is obvious that what we have said about the commodification of objects holds as strongly for Warhol's human subjects, stars – like Marilyn Monroe – who are themselves commodified and transformed into their own images. And here too a certain brutal return to the older period of high modernism offers a dramatic shorthand parable of the transformation in question. Edvard Munch's painting *The Scream* is of course a canonical expression of the great modernist thematics of alienation, anomie, solitude and social fragmentation and isolation, a virtually programmatic emblem of what used to be called the age of anxiety. It will here be read not merely as an embodiment of the expression of that kind of affect, but even more as a virtual deconstruction of the very aesthetic of expression itself, which seems to have dominated much of what we call high modernism, but to have vanished away – for both practical and theoretical reasons – in the world of the postmodern. The very concept of expression presupposes indeed some separation within the subject, and along with that a whole metaphysics of the inside and the outside, of the wordless pain within the monad and the moment in which, often cathartically, that "emotion" is then projected out and externalized, as gesture or cry, as desperate communication and the outward dramatization of inward feeling. And this is perhaps the moment to say something about contemporary theory, which has among other things been committed to the mission of criticizing and discrediting this very hermeneutic model of the inside and the outside and of stigmatizing such models as ideological and metaphysical. But what is today called contemporary theory – or better still, theoretical discourse – is also, I would want to argue, itself very precisely a postmodernist phenomenon. It would therefore be inconsistent to defend the truth of its theoretical insights in a situation in which the very concept of "truth" itself is part of the metaphysical baggage which poststructuralism seeks to abandon. What we can at least suggest is that the poststructuralist critique of the hermeneutic, of what I will shortly call the depth model, is useful for us as a very significant symptom of the very postmodernist culture which is our subject here.

Overhastily, we can say that besides the hermeneutic model of inside and outside which Munch's painting develops, there are at least four other fundamental depth models which have generally been repudiated in contemporary theory: the dialectical one of essence and appearance (along with a whole range of concepts of ideology or false consciousness which tend to accompany it); the Freudian model of latent and manifest, or of repression (which is of course the target of Michel Foucault's programmatic and symptomatic pamphlet *La Volonté de savoir*); the existential model of authenticity and inauthenticity, whose heroic or tragic thematics are closely related to that other great opposition between alienation and disalienation, itself equally a casualty of the post-structural or postmodern period; and finally, latest in time, the great semiotic opposition between signifier and signified, which was itself rapidly unravelled and deconstructed during its brief heyday in the 1960s and 1970s. What replaces these various depth models is for the most part a conception of practices, discourses and textual play, whose new syntagmatic structures we will examine later on: suffice it merely to observe that here too depth is replaced by surface, or by multiple surfaces (what is often called intertextuality is in that sense no longer a matter of depth).

Nor is this depthlessness merely metaphorical: it can be experienced physically and literally by anyone who, mounting what used to be Raymond Chandler's Beacon Hill from the great Chicano markets on Broadway and 4th St in downtown Los Angeles, suddenly confronts the great free-standing wall of the Crocker Bank Center (Skidmore, Owings and Merrill) – a surface which seems to be unsupported by any volume, or whose putative volume (rectangular, trapezoidal?) is ocularly quite undecidable. This great sheet of windows, with its gravity-defying two-dimensionality, momentarily transforms the solid ground on which we climb into the contents of a stereopticon, pasteboard shapes profiling themselves here and there around us. From all sides, the visual effect is the same: as fateful as the great monolith in Kubrick's *2001* which confronts its viewers like an enigmatic destiny, a call to evolutionary mutation. If this new multinational downtown (to which we will return later in another context) effectively abolished the older ruined city fabric which it violently replaced, cannot something similar be said about the way in which this strange new surface in its own peremptory way renders our older systems of perception of the city somehow archaic and aimless, without offering another in their place?

Euphoria and self-annihilation

Returning now for one last moment to Munch's painting, it seems evident that *The Scream* subtly but elaborately deconstructs its own aesthetic of expression, all the while remaining imprisoned within it. Its gestural content already underscores its own failure, since the realm of the sonorous, the cry, the raw vibrations of the human throat, are incompatible with its medium (something underscored within the work by the homunculus' lack of ears). Yet the absent scream returns more closely towards that even more absent experience of atrocious solitude and anxiety which the scream was itself to "express". Such loops inscribe themselves on the painted surface in the form of those great concentric circles in which sonorous vibration becomes ultimately visible, as on the surface of a sheet of water – in an infinite regress which fans out from the sufferer to become the very geography of a universe in which pain itself now speaks and vibrates through the material sunset and the landscape. The visible world now becomes the wall of the monad on which this "scream running through nature" (Munch's words) is recorded and transcribed: one thinks of that character of Lautréamont who, growing up inside a sealed and silent membrane, on sight of the monstrousness of the deity, ruptures it with his own scream and thereby rejoins the world of sound and suffering.

All of which suggests some more general historical hypothesis: namely, that concepts such as anxiety and alienation (and the experiences to which they correspond, as in *The Scream*) are no longer appropriate in the world of the postmodern. The great Warhol figures – Marilyn herself, or Edie Sedgewick – the notorious burn-out and self-destruction cases of the ending 1960s, and the great dominant experiences of drugs and schizophrenia – these would seem to have little enough in common anymore, either with the hysterics and neurotics of Freud's own day, or with those canonical experiences of radical isolation and solitude, anomie, private revolt, Van Gogh-type madness, which dominated the period of high modernism. This shift in the dynamics of cultural pathology can be characterized as one in which the alienation of the subject is displaced by the fragmentation of the subject.

Such terms inevitably recall one of the more fashionable themes in contemporary theory – that of the "death" of the subject itself = the end of the autonomous bourgeois monad or ego or individual – and the accompanying stress, whether as some new moral ideal or as empirical description, on the *decentring* of that formerly centred subject or psyche. (Of the two possible formulations of this notion – the historicist one, that a once-existing centred subject, in the period of classical capitalism and the nuclear family, has today in the world of organizational bureaucracy dissolved; and the more radical post-structuralist position for which such a subject never existed in the first place but constituted something like an ideological mirage – I obviously incline towards the former; the latter must in any case take into account something like a "reality of the appearance".)

We must add that the problem of expression is itself closely linked to some conception of the subject as a monad-like container, within which things are felt which are then expressed by projection outwards. What we must now stress, however, is the degree to which the high-modernist conception of a unique *style*, along with the accompanying collective ideals of an artistic or political vanguard or *avant-garde*, themselves stand or fall along with that older notion (or experience) of the so-called centred subject.

Here too Munch's painting stands as a complex reflexion on this complicated situation: it shows us that expression requires the category of the individual monad, but it also shows us the heavy price to be paid for that precondition, dramatizing the unhappy paradox that when you constitute your individual subjectivity as a self-sufficient field and a closed realm in its own right, you thereby also shut yourself off from everything else and condemn yourself to the windless solitude of the monad, buried alive and condemned to a prison-cell without egress.

Postmodernism will presumably signal the end of this dilemma, which it replaces with a new one. The end of the bourgeois ego or monad no doubt brings with it the end of the psychopathologies of that ego as well – what I have generally here been calling the waning of affect. But it means the end of much more – the end for example of style, in the sense of the unique and the personal, the end of the distinctive individual brushstroke (as symbolized by the emergent primacy of mechanical reproduction). As for expression and feelings or emotions, the liberation, in contemporary society, from the older *anomie* of the centred subject may also mean, not merely a liberation from anxiety, but a liberation from every other kind of feeling as well, since there is no longer a self present to do the feeling. This is not to say that the cultural products of the postmodern era are utterly devoid of feeling, but rather that such feelings – which it may be better and more accurate to call "intensities" – are now free-floating and impersonal, and tend to be dominated by a peculiar kind of euphoria to which I will want to return at the end of this [chapter].

The waning of affect, however, might also have been characterized, in the narrower context of literary criticism, as the waning of the great high-modernist thematics of time and temporality, the elegiac mysteries of *durée* and of memory (something to be understood fully as a category of literary criticism associated as much with high modernism as with the works themselves). We have often been told, however, that we now inhabit the synchronic rather than the diachronic, and I think it is at least empirically arguable that our daily life, our psychic experience, our cultural languages, are today dominated by cat-egories of space rather than by categories of time, as in the preceding period of high modernism proper.

The Postmodern and the Past

Pastiche eclipses parody

The disappearance of the individual subject, along with its formal consequence, the increasing unavailability of the personal *style*, engender the well-nigh universal practice today of what may be called pastiche. This concept, which we owe to Thomas Mann (in *Doktor Faustus*), who owed it in turn to Adorno's great work on the two paths of advanced musical experimentation (Schoenberg's innovative planification, Stravinsky's irrational eclecticism), is to be sharply distinguished from the more readily received idea of parody.

This last found, to be sure, a fertile area in the idiosyncrasies of the moderns and their "inimitable" styles: the Faulknerian long sentence with its breathless gerundives, Lawrentian nature imagery punctuated by testy colloquialism, Wallace Stevens' inveterate hypostasis of non-substantive parts of speech ("the intricate evasions of as"), the fateful, but finally predictable, swoops in Mahler from high orchestral pathos into village accordion sentiment, Heidegger's meditative-solemn practice of the false etymology as a mode of "proof" ... All these strike one as somehow "characteristic', insofar as they ostentatiously deviate from a norm which then reasserts itself, in a not necessarily unfriendly way, by a systematic mimicry of their deliberate eccentricities.

Yet, in the dialectical leap from quantity to quality, the explosion of modern literature into a host of distinct private styles and mannerisms has been followed by a linguistic fragmentation of social life itself to the point where the norm itself is eclipsed: reduced to a neutral and reified media speech (far enough from the Utopian aspirations of the inventors of Esperanto or Basic English), which itself then becomes but one more idiolect among many. Modernist styles thereby become postmodernist codes: and that the stupendous proliferation of social codes today into professional and disciplinary jargons, but also into the badges of affirmation of ethnic, gender, race, religious, and class-fraction adhesion, is also a political phenomenon, the problem of micropolitics sufficiently demonstrates. If the ideas of a ruling class were once the dominant (or hegemonic) ideology of bourgeois society, the advanced capitalist countries today are now a field of stylistic and discursive heterogeneity without a norm. Faceless masters continue to inflect the economic strategies which constrain our existences, but no longer need to impose their speech (or are henceforth unable to); and the postliteracy of the late capitalist world reflects, not only the absence of any great collective project, but also the unavailability of the older national language itself.

In this situation, parody finds itself without a vocation; it has lived, and that strange new thing .pastiche slowly comes to take its place. Pastiche is, like parody, the imitation of a peculiar mask, speech in a dead language: but it is a neutral practice of such mimicry, without any of parody's ulterior motives, amputated of the satiric impulse, devoid of laughter and of any conviction that alongside the abnormal tongue you have momentarily borrowed, some healthy linguistic normality still exists. Pastiche is thus blank parody, a statue with blind eyeballs: it is to parody what that other interesting and historically original modern thing, the practice of a kind of blank irony, is to what Wayne Booth calls the "stable ironies" of the eighteenth century.

It would therefore begin to seem that Adorno's prophetic diagnosis has been realized, albeit in a negative way: not Schoenberg (the sterility of whose achieved system he already glimpsed) but Stravinsky is the true precursor of the postmodern cultural production. For with the collapse of the high-modernist ideology of style – what is as unique and unmistakable as your own fingerprints, as incomparable as your own body (the very source, for an early Roland Barthes, of stylistic invention and innovation) – the producers of culture have nowhere to turn but to the past: the imitation of dead styles, speech through all the masks and voices stored up in the imaginary museum of a now global culture.

"Historicism" effaces history

This situation evidently determines what the architecture historians call "historicism", namely the random cannibalization of all the styles of the past, the play of random stylistic allusion, and in general what Henri Lefebvre has called the increasing primacy of the "neo". This omnipresence of pastiche is, however, not incompatible with a certain humour (nor is it innocent of all passion) or at least with addiction – with a whole historically original con-sumers' appetite for a world transformed into sheer images of itself and for pseudo-events and "spectacles" (the term of the Situationists). It is for such objects that we may reserve Plato's conception of the "simulacrum" – the identical copy for which no original has ever existed. Appropriately enough, the culture of the simulacrum comes to *life* in a society where exchange-value has been generalized to the point at which the very memory of use-value is effaced, a society of which Guy Debord has observed, in an extraordinary phrase, that in it "the image has become the final form of commodity reification" (*The Society of the Spectacle*).

The new spatial logic of the simulacrum can now be expected to have a momentous effect on what used to be historical time.

The past is thereby itself modified: what was once, in the historical novel as Lukács defines it, the organic genealogy of the bourgeois collective project – what is still, for the redemptive historiography of an E. P. Thompson or of American "oral history", for the resurrection of the dead of anonymous and silenced generations, the retrospective dimension indispensable to any vital reorientation of our collective future – has meanwhile itself become a vast collection of images, a multitudinous photographic simulacrum. Guy Debord's powerful slogan is now even more apt for the "prehistory" of a society bereft of all historicity, whose own putative past is little more than a set of dusty spectacles. In faithful conformity to poststructuralist linguistic theory, the past as "referent" finds itself gradually bracketed, and then effaced altogether, leaving us with nothing but texts.

wiped out

The nostalgia mode

Yet it should not be thought that this process is accompanied by indifference: on the contrary, the remarkable current intensification of an addiction to the photographic image is itself a tangible symptom of an omnipresent, omnivorous and well-nigh libidinal historicism. The architects use this (exceedingly polysemous) word for the complacent eclecticism of postmodern architecture, which randomly and without principle but with gusto cannibalizes all the architectural styles of the past and combines them in overstimulating ensembles. Nostalgia does not strike one as an altogether satisfactory word for such fascination (particularly when one thinks of the pain of a properly modernist nostalgia with a past beyond all but aesthetic retrieval), yet it directs our attention to what is a culturally far more generalized manifestation of the process in commercial art and taste, namely the so-called "nostalgia film" (or what the French call *la mode rétro*).

These restructure the whole issue of pastiche and project it onto a collective and social level, where the desperate attempt to appropriate a missing past is now refracted through the iron law of fashion change and the emergent ideology of the "generation". *American Graffiti* (1973) set out to recapture, as so many films have attempted since, the henceforth mesmerizing lost reality of the Eisenhower era: and one tends to feel that for Americans at least, the 1950s remain the privileged lost object of desire – not merely the stability and prosperity of a pax Americana, but also the first naïve innocence of the countercultural impulses of early rock-and-roll and youth gangs (Coppola's *Rumble Fish* will then be the contemporary dirge that laments their passing, itself, however, still contradictorily filmed in genuine "nostalgia film" style). With this initial breakthrough, other generational periods open up for aesthetic colonization: as witness the stylistic recuperation of the American and the Italian 1930s, in Polanski's *Chinatown* and Bertolluci's *Il Conformista* respectively. What is more interesting, and more problematical, are the ultimate attempts, through this new discourse, to lay siege either to our own present and immediate past, or to a more distant history that escapes individual existential memory.

Faced with these ultimate objects – our social, historical and existential present, and the past as "referent" – the incompatibility of a postmodernist "nostalgia" art language with genuine historicity becomes dramatically apparent. The contraction propels this model, however, into complex and interesting new formal inventiveness: it being understood that the nostalgia film was never a matter of some old-fashioned "representation" of historical content, but approached the "past" through stylistic connotation, conveying "pastness" by the glossy qualities of the image, and "1930s-ness" or "1950s-ness" by the attributes of fashion (therein following the prescription of the Barthes of *Mythologies*, who saw connotation as the purveying of imaginary and stereotypical idealities, "Sinité", for example, as some Disney-EPCOT "concept" of China).

The insensible colonization of the present by the nostalgia mode can be observed in Lawrence Kazdan's elegant film, *Body Heat*, a distant "affluent society" remake of James M. Cain's *The Postman Always Rings Twice*, set in a contemporary Florida small town not far from Miami. The word "remake" is, however, anachronistic to the degree to which our awareness of the pre-existence of other versions, previous films of the novel as well as the novel itself, is now a constitutive and essential part of the film's structure: we are now, in other words, in "intertextuality" as a deliberate, built-in feature of the aesthetic effect, and as the operator of a new connotation of "pastness" and pseudo-historical depth, in which the history of aesthetic styles displaces "real" history.

Yet from the outset a whole battery of aesthetic signs begins to distance the officially contemporary image from us in time: the art deco scripting of the credits, for example, serves at once to programme the spectator for the appropriate "nostalgia" mode of reception (art deco quotation has much the same function in contemporary architecture, as in Toronto's remarkable Eaton Centre). Meanwhile, a somewhat different play of connotations is activated by complex (but purely formal) allusions to the institutions of the star system itself. The protagonist, William Hurt, is one of a new generation of film "stars" whose status is markedly distinct from that of the preceding generation of male superstars, such as Steve McQueen or Jack Nicholson (or even, more distantly, Brando), let alone of earlier moments in the evolution of the institution of the star. The immediately preceding generation projected their various roles through, and by way of, well-known "off-screen" personalities, who often connoted rebellion and non-conformism. The latest generation of starring actors continues to assure the conventional functions of stardom (most notably, sexuality) but in the utter absence of "personality" in the older sense, and with something of the anonymity of character acting (which in actors like Hurt reaches virtuoso proportions, yet of a very different kind from the virtuosity of the older Brando or Olivier). This "death of the subject" in the institution of the star, however, opens up the possibility of a play of historical allusions to much older roles – in this case to those associated with Clark Gable – so that the very style of the acting can now also serve as a "connotator" of the past.

Finally, the setting has been strategically framed, with great ingenuity, to eschew most of the signals that normally convey the contemporaneity of the United States in its multinational era: the small-town setting allows the camera to elude the high-rise landscape of the 1970s and 1980s (even though a key episode in the narrative involves the fatal destruction of older buildings by land speculators); while the object world of the present-day – artifacts and appliances, even automobiles, whose styling would at once serve to date the image – is elaborately edited out. Everything in the film, therefore, conspires to blur its official contemporaneity and to make it possible for you to receive the narrative as though it were set in some eternal Thirties, beyond real historical time. The approach to the present by way of the art language of the simulacrum, or of the pastiche of the stereotypical past, endows present reality and the openness of present history with the spell and distance of a glossy mirage. But this mesmerizing new aesthetic mode itself emerged as an elaborated symptom of the waning of our historicity, of our lived possibility of experiencing history in some active way: it cannot therefore be said to produce this strange occultation of the present by its own formal power, but merely to demonstrate, through these inner contradictions, the enormity of a situation in which we seem increasingly incapable of fashioning representations of our own current experience.

The fate of "real history"

As for "real history" itself – the traditional object, however it may be defined, of what used to be the historical novel – it will be more revealing now to turn back to that older form and medium and to read its postmodern fate in the work of one of the few serious and innovative Left novelists at work in the United States today, whose books are nourished with history in the more traditional sense, and seem, so far, to stake out successive generational moments in the "epic" of American history. E. L. Doctorow's *Ragtime* gives itself officially as a panorama of the first two decades of the century; his most recent novel, *Loon Lake*, addresses the Thirties and the Great Depression; while *The Book of Daniel* holds up before us, in painful juxtaposition, the two great moments of the Old Left and the New Left, of Thirties and Forties Communism and the radicalism of the 1960s (even his early Western may be said to fit into this scheme and to designate in a less articulated and formally self-conscious way the end of the frontier of the late nineteenth century).

The Book of Daniel is not the only one of these three major historical novels to establish an explicit narrative link between the reader's and the writer's present and the older historical reality which is the subject of the work; the astonishing last page of *Loon Lake*, which I will not disclose, also does this in a very different way; while it is a matter of some interest to note that the first sentence of the first version of *Ragtime* positions us explicitly in our own present, in the novelist's house in New Rochelle, New York, which will then at once become the scene of its own (imaginary) past in the 1900s. This detail has been suppressed from the published text, symbolically cutting its moorings and freeing the novel to float in some new world of past historical time whose relationship to us is problematical indeed. The authenticity of the gesture, however, may be measured by the evident existential fact of life that there no longer does seem to be any organic relationship between the American history we learn from the schoolbooks and the lived experience of the current multinational, high-rise, stagflated city of the newspapers and of our own daily life.

A crisis in historicity, however, inscribes itself symptomally in several other curious formal features within this text. Its official subject is the transition from a pre-World-War I radical and working-class politics (the great strikes) to the technological invention and new commodity production of the 1920s (the rise of Hollywood and of the image as commodity): the interpolated version of Kleist's *Michael Kohlhaas*, the strange tragic episode of the Black protagonist's revolt, may be thought to be a moment related to this process. My point, however, is not some hypothesis as to the thematic coherence of this decentred narrative; but rather just the opposite, namely the way in which the kind of reading this novel imposes makes it virtually impossible for us to reach and to thematize those official "subjects" which float above the text but cannot be integrated into our reading of the sentences. In that sense, not only does the novel resist interpretation, it is organized systematically and formally to short-circuit an older type of social and historical interpretation which it perpetually holds out and withdraws. When we remember that the theoretical critique and repudiation of interpretation as such is a fundamental component of poststructuralist theory, it is difficult not to conclude that Doctorow has somehow deliberately built this very tension, this very contradiction, into the flow of his sentences.

As is well known, the book is crowded with real historical figures – from Teddy Roosevelt to Emma Goldman, from Harry K. Thaw and Sandford White to J. Pierpont Morgan and Henry Ford, not to speak of the more central role of Houdini – who interact with a fictive family, simply designated as Father, Mother, Older Brother, and so forth. All historical novels, beginning with Scott himself, no doubt in one way or another involve a mobilization of previous historical knowledge, generally acquired through the schoolbook history manuals devised for whatever legitimizing purpose by this or that national tradition – thereafter instituting a narrative dialectic between what we already "know" about The Pretender, say, and what he is then seen to be concretely in the pages of the novel. But Doctorow's procedure seems much more extreme than this; and I would argue that the designation of both types of characters – historical names or capitalized family roles – operates powerfully and systematically to reify all these characters and to make it impossible for us to receive their representation without the prior interception of already-acquired knowledge or doxa – something which lends the text an extraordinary sense of déjà-vu and a peculiar familiarity one is tempted to associate with Freud's "return of the repressed" in "The Uncanny", rather than with any solid historiographic formation on the reader's part.

Loss of the radical past

Meanwhile, the sentences in which all this is happening have their own specificity, which will allow us a little more concretely to distinguish the moderns' elaboration of a personal style from this new kind of linguistic innovation, which is no longer personal at all but has its family kinship rather with what Barthes long ago called "white writing". In this particular novel, Doctorow has imposed upon himself a rigorous principle of selection in which only simple declarative sentences (predominantly mobilized by the verb "to be") are received. The effect is, however, not really one of the condescending simplification and symbolic carefulness of children's literature, but rather something more disturbing, the sense of some profound subterranean violence done to American English which cannot, however, be detected empirically in any of the perfectly grammatical sentences with which this work is formed. Yet other more visible technical "innovations" may supply a clue to what is happening in the language of *Ragtime*: it is for example well-known that the source of many of the characteristic effects of Camus' novel *L'étranger* can be traced back to that author's wilful decision to substitute, throughout, the French tense of the *passé composé* for the other past tenses more normally employed in narration in that language. I will suggest that it is *as if* something of that sort were at work here (without committing myself further to what is obviously an outrageous leap): it is, I say, *as though* Doctorow had set out systematically to produce the effect or the equivalent, in his language, of a verbal past tense we do not possess in English, namely the French preterite (or *passé simple*), whose "perfective" movement, as Émile Benveniste taught us, serves to separate events from the present of enunciation and to transform the stream of time and action into so many finished, complete, and isolated punctual event-objects which find themselves sundered from any present situation (even that of the act of story-telling or enunciation).

E. L. Doctorow is the epic poet of the disappearance of the American radical past, of the suppression of older traditions and moments of the American radical tradition: no one with left sympathies can read these splendid novels without a poignant distress which is an authentic way of confronting our own current political dilemmas in the present. What is culturally interesting, however, is that he has had to convey this great theme formally (since the waning of the content is very precisely his subject), and, more than that, has had to elaborate his work by way of that very cultural logic of the postmodern which is itself the mark and symptom of his dilemma. *Loon Lake* much more obviously deploys the strategies of the pastiche (most notably in its reinvention of Dos Passos); but *Ragtime* remains the most peculiar and stunning monument to the aesthetic situation engendered by the disappearance of the historical referent. This historical novel can no longer set out to represent the historical past; it can only "represent" our ideas and stereotypes about that past (which thereby at once becomes "pop history"). Cultural production is thereby driven back inside a mental space which is no longer that of the old monadic subject, but rather that of some degraded collective "objective spirit": it can no longer gaze directly on some putative real world, at some reconstruction of a past history which was once itself a present; rather, as in Plato's cave, it must trace our mental images of that past upon its confining walls. If there is any realism left here, therefore, it is a "realism" which is meant to derive from the shock of grasping that confinement, and of slowly becoming aware of a new and original historical situation in which we are condemned to seek History by way of our own pop images and simulacra of that history, which itself remains forever out of reach.

The Breakdown of the Signifying Chain

The crisis in historicity now dictates a return, in a new way, to the question of temporal organization in general in the postmodern force field, and indeed, to the problem of the form that time, temporality and the syntagmatic will be able *dependent on chance*

to take in a culture increasingly dominated by space and spatial logic. If, indeed, the subject has lost its capacity actively to extend its pro-tensions and re-tensions across the temporal manifold, and to organize its past and future into coherent experience, it becomes difficult enough to see how the cultural productions of such a subject could result in anything but "heaps of fragments" and in a practice of the randomly heterogeneous and fragmentary and the aleatory. These are, however, very precisely some of the privileged terms in which postmodernist cultural production has been analysed (and even defended, by its own apologists). Yet they are still privative features; the more substantive formulations bear such names as textuality, *écriture*, or schizophrenic writing, and it is to these that we must now briefly turn.

I have found Lacan's account of schizophrenia useful here, not because I have any way of knowing whether it has clinical accuracy, but chiefly because – as description rather than diagnosis – it seems to me to offer a suggestive aesthetic model. (I am obviously very far from thinking that any of the most significant postmodernist artists – Cage, Ashbery, Sollers, Robert Wilson, Ishmael Reed, Michael Snow, Warhol or even Beckett himself – are schizophrenics in any clinical sense.) Nor is the point some culture-and-personality diagnosis of our society and its art, as in culture critiques of the type of Christopher Lasch's influential *The Culture of Narcissism,* from which I am concerned radically to distance the spirit and the methodology of the present remarks: there are, one would think, far more damaging things to be said about our social system than are available through the use of psychological categories.

Very briefly, Lacan describes schizophrenia as a breakdown in the signifying chain, that is, the interlocking syntagmatic series of signifiers which constitutes an utterance or a meaning. I must omit the familial or more orthodox psycho-analytic background to this situation, which Lacan transcodes into language by describing the Oedipal rivalry in terms, not so much of the biological individual who is your rival for the mother's attention, but rather of what he calls the Name-of-the-Father, paternal authority now considered as a linguistic function. His conception of the signifying chain essentially presupposes one of the basic principles (and one of the great discoveries) of Saussurean structuralism, namely the proposition that meaning is not a one-to-one relationship between signifier and signified, between the materiality of language, between a word or a name, and its referent or concept. Meaning on the new view is generated by the movement from Signifier to Signifier: what we generally call the Signified – the meaning or conceptual content of an utterance – is now rather to be seen as a meaning-effect, as that objective mirage of signification generated and pro-jected by the relationship of Signifiers among each other. When that relation-ship breaks down, when the links of the signifying chain snap, then we have schizophrenia in the form of a rubble of distinct and unrelated Signifiers. The connection between this kind of linguistic malfunction and the psyche of the schizophrenic may then be grasped by way of a two-fold proposition: first, that personal identity is itself the effect of a certain temporal unification of past and future with the present before me; and second, that such active temporal unification is itself a function of language, or better still of the sentence, as it moves along its hermeneutic circle through time. If we are unable to unify the past, present and future of the sentence, then we are similarly unable to unify the past, present and future of our own biographical experience or psychic life.

With the breakdown of the signifying chain, therefore, the schizophrenic is reduced to an experience of pure material Signifiers, or in other words of a series of pure and unrelated presents in time. We will want to ask questions about the aesthetic or cultural results of such a situation in a moment; let us first see what it feels like:

I remember very well the day it happened. We were staying in the country and I had gone for a walk alone as I did now and then. Suddenly, as I was passing the school, I heard a German song; the children were having a singing lesson. I stopped to listen, and at that instant a strange feeling came over me, a feeling hard to analyse but akin to something I was to know too well later – a disturbing sense of unreality. It seemed to me that I no longer recognized the school, it had become as large as a barracks; the singing children were prisoners, compelled to sing. It was as though the school and the children's song were set apart from the rest of the world. At the same time my eye encountered a field of wheat whose limits I could not see. The yellow vastness, dazzling in the sun, bound up with the song of the children imprisoned in the smooth stone school-barracks, filled me with such anxiety that I broke into sobs. I ran home to our garden and began to play "to make things seem as they usually were," that is, to return to reality. It was the first appearance of those elements which were always present in later sensations of unreality: illimitable vastness, brilliant light, and the gloss and smoothness of material things.[3]

In our present context, this experience suggests the following remarks: first, the breakdown of temporality suddenly releases this present of time from all the activities and the intentionalities that might focus it and make it a space of praxis; thereby isolated, that present suddenly engulfs the subject with inde-scribable vividness, a materiality of perception properly overwhelming, which effectively dramatizes the power of the material – or better still, the literal – Signifier in isolation. This present of the world or material Signifier comes before the subject with heightened intensity, bearing a mysterious charge of affect, here described in the negative terms of anxiety and loss of reality, but which one could just as well imagine in the positive terms of euphoria, the high, the intoxicatory or hallucinogenic intensity.

"China"

What will happen in textuality or schizophrenic art is strikingly illuminated by such clinical accounts, although in the cultural text, the isolated Signifier is no longer an enigmatic state of the world or an incomprehensible yet mesmerizing fragment of language, but rather something closer to a sentence in free-standing isolation. Think, for example, of the experience of John Cage's music, in which a cluster of material sounds (on the prepared piano for example) is followed by a silence so intolerable that you cannot imagine another sonorous chord coming into existence, and cannot imagine remembering the previous one well enough to make any connection with it fit it does. Some of Beckett's narratives are also of this order, most notably *Watt*, where a primacy of the present sentence in time ruthlessly disintegrates the narrative fabric that attempts to reform around it. My example will, however, be a less sombre one, a text by a younger San Francisco poet whose group or school – so-called Language Poetry or the New Sentence – seems to have adopted schizophrenic fragmentation as its fundamental aesthetic.

China
We live on the third world from the sun. Number three. Nobody tells us
   what to do.
The people who taught us to count were being very kind.
It's always time to leave.
If it rains, you either have your umbrella or you don't.
The wind blows your hat off.
The sun rises also.
I'd rather the stars didn't describe us to each other; I'd rather we do it
   for ourselves.
Run in front of your shadow.
A sister who points to the sky at least once a decade is a good sister.
The landscape is motorized.
The train takes you where it goes.
Bridges among water.
Folks straggling along vast stretches of concrete, heading into the plane.
Don't forget what your hat and shoes will look like when you are
   nowhere to be found.
Even the words floating in air make blue shadows.
If it tastes good we eat it.
The leaves are falling. Point things out.
Pick up the right things.
Hey guess what? What? I've learned how to talk. Great.

The person whose head was incomplete burst into tears.
As it fell, what could the doll do? Nothing.
Go to sleep.
You look great in shorts. And the flag looks great too.
Everyone enjoyed the explosions.
Time to wake up.
But better get used to dreams.
                    Bob Perelman from *Primer* (Berkeley, This Press).

Many things could be said about this interesting exercise in discontinuities: not the least paradoxical is the reemergence here across these disjoined sentences of some more unified global meaning. Indeed, insofar as this is in some curious and secret way a political poem, it does seem to capture something of the excitement of the immense, unfinished social experiment of the New China – unparalleled in world history – the unexpected emergence, between the two super-powers, of "number three", the freshness of a whole new object world produced by human beings in some new control over their collective destiny, the signal event, above all, of a collectivity which has become a new "subject of history" and which, after the long subjection of feudalism and imperialism, again speaks in its own voice, for itself as though for the first time.

I mainly wanted to show, however, the way in which what I have been calling schizophrenic disjunction or *écriture*, when it becomes generalized as a cultural style, ceases to entertain a necessary relationship to the morbid content we associate with terms like schizophrenia, and becomes available for more joyous intensities, for precisely that euphoria which we saw displacing the older affects of anxiety and alienation.

Consider, for example, Jean-Paul Sartre's account of a similar tendency in Flaubert: "His sentence", Sartre tells us about Flaubert:

closes in on the object, seizes it, immobilizes it, and breaks its back, wraps itself around it, changes into stone and petrifies its object along with itself. It is blind and deaf, bloodless, not a breath of life; a deep silence separates it from the sentence which follows; it falls into the void, eternally, and drags its prey down into that infinite fall. Any reality, once described, is struck off the inventory. (Sartre, *What is Literature?*)

Yet I am tempted to see this reading as a kind of optical illusion (or photographic enlargement) of an unwittingly genealogical type: in which certain latent or subordinate, properly postmodernist features of Flaubert's style are anachronistically foregrounded. Yet it affords another interesting lesson in periodization, and in the dialectical restructuring of cultural dominants and subordinates. For these features, in Flaubert, were symptoms and strategies in that whole posthumous life and resentment of praxis which is denounced (with increasing sympathy) throughout the three thousand pages of Sartre's *Family Idiot*. When such features become themselves the cultural norm, they shed all such forms of negative affect and become available for other, more decorative uses.

But we have thereby not fully exhausted the structural secrets of Perelman's poem, which turns out to have little enough to do with that referent called China. The author has in fact related how, strolling through Chinatown, he came across a book of photographs whose idiogrammatic captions remained a dead letter to him (or perhaps one should say, a material signifier). The sentences of the poem in question are then Perelman's own captions to those pictures, their referents another image, another absent text; and the unity of the poem is no longer to be found within its language, but outside itself, in the bound unity of another, absent book. There is here a striking parallel to the dynamics of so-called photorealism, which looked like a return to representation and figuration after the long hegemony of the aesthetics of abstraction, until it became clear that its objects were not to be found in the "real world" either, but were themselves photographs of that real world, this last now transformed into images, of which the "realism" of the photorealist painting is now the simulacrum.

Collage and radical difference

This account of schizophrenia and temporal organization might, however, have been formulated in a different way, which brings us back to Heidegger's notion of a gap or rift, albeit in a fashion that would have horrified him. I would like, indeed, to characterize the postmodernist experience of form with what will seem, I hope, a paradoxical slogan: namely the proposition that "difference relates". Our own recent criticism, from Macherey on, has been concerned to stress the heterogeneity and profound discontinuities of the work of art, no longer unified or organic, but now virtual grab-bag or lumber room of disjoined subsystems and random raw materials and impulses of all kinds. The former work of art, in other words, has now turned out to be a text, whose reading proceeds by differentiation rather than by unification. Theories of difference, however, have tended to stress disjunction to the point at which the materials of the text, including its words and sentences, tend to fall apart into random and inert passivity, into a set of elements which entertain purely external separations from one another.

In the most interesting postmodernist works, however, one can detect a more positive conception of relationship which restores its proper tension to the notion of differences itself. This new mode of relationship through difference may sometimes be an achieved new and original way of thinking and perceiving; more often it takes the form of an impossible imperative to achieve that new mutation in what can perhaps no longer be called consciousness. I believe that the most striking emblem of this new mode of thinking relationships can be found in the work of Nam June Paik, whose stacked or scattered television screens, positioned at intervals within lush vegetation, or winking down at us from a ceiling of strange new video stars, recapitulate over and over again prearranged sequences or loops of images which return at dysynchronous moments on the various screens. The older aesthetic is then practised by viewers, who, bewildered by this discontinuous variety, decide to concentrate on a single screen, as though the relatively worthless image sequence to be followed there had some organic value in its own right. The postmodernist viewer, however, is called upon to do the impossible, namely to see all the screens at once, in their radical and random difference; such a viewer is asked to follow the evolutionary mutation of David Bowie in *The Man Who Fell to Earth*, and to rise somehow to a level at which the vivid perception of radical difference is in and of itself a new mode of grasping what used to be called relationship: something for which the word *collage* is still only a very feeble name.

The Hysterical Sublime

Now we need to complete this exploratory account of postmodernist space and time with a final analysis of that euphoria or those intensities which seem so often to characterize the newer cultural experience. Let us stress again the enormity of a transition which leaves behind it the desolation of Hopper's buildings or the stark Midwest syntax of Sheeler's forms, replacing them with the extraordinary surfaces of the photorealist cityscape, where even the automobile wrecks gleam with some new halluncinatory splendour. The exhilaration of these new surfaces is all the more paradoxical in that their essential content – the city itself – has deteriorated or disintegrated to a degree surely still inconceivable in the early years of the twentieth century, let alone in the previous era. How urban squalor can be a delight to the eyes, when expressed in commodification, and how an unparalleled quantum leap in the alienation of daily life in the city can now be experienced in the form of a strange new hallucinatory exhilaration – these are some of the questions that confront us in this moment of our inquiry. Nor should the human figure be exempted from investigation, although it seems clear that for the newer aesthetic the representation of space itself has come to be felt as incompatible with the representation of the body: a kind of aesthetic division of labour far more pronounced than in any of the earlier generic conceptions of landscape, and a most ominous symptom indeed. The privileged space of the newer art is radically anti-anthropomorphic, as in the empty bathrooms of Doug Bond's work. The ultimate contemporary fetishization of the human body, however, takes a very different direction in the statues of Duane Hanson – what I have already called the simulacrum, whose peculiar function lies in what Sartre would have called the *derealization* of the whole surrounding world of everyday reality. Your moment of doubt and hesitation as to the breath and warmth of these polyester figures, in other words, tends to return upon the real human beings moving about you in the museum, and to transform them also for the briefest instant into so many dead and flesh-coloured simulacra in their own right. The world thereby momentarily loses its depth and threatens to become a glossy skin, a stereoscopic illusion, a rush of filmic images without density. But is this now a terrifying or an exhilarating experience?

It has proved fruitful to think such experience in terms of what Susan Sontag once, in an influential statement, isolated as "camp". I propose a somewhat different cross-light on it, drawing on the equally fashionable current theme of the "sublime", as it has been rediscovered in the works of Edmund Burke and Kant; or perhaps, indeed, one might well want to yoke the two notions together in the form of something like a camp or "hysterical" sublime. The sublime was for Burke, as you will recall, an experience bordering on terror, the fitful glimpse, in astonishment, stupor and awe, of what was so enormous as to crush human life altogether: a description then refined by Kant to include the question of representation itself – so that the object of the sublime is now not only a matter of sheer power and of the physical incommensurability of the human organism with Nature, but also of the limits of figuration and the incapacity of the human mind to give representation to such enormous forces. Such forces Burke, in his historical moment at the dawn of the modern bourgeois state, was only able to conceptualize in terms of the divine; while even Heidegger continues to entertain a fantasmatic relationship with some organic precapitalist peasant landscape and village society, which is the final form of the image of Nature in our own time.

Today, however, it may be possible to think all this in a different way, at the moment of a radical eclipse of Nature itself: Heidegger's "field path" is after all irredeemably and irrevocably destroyed by late capital, by the green revolution, by neocolonialism and the megapopolis, which runs its superhighways over the older fields and vacant lots, and turns Heidegger's "house of being" into condominiums, if not the most miserable unheated rat-infested tenement buildings. The *other* of our society is in that sense no longer Nature at all, as it was in precapitalist societies, but something else which we must now identify.

The apotheosis of capitalism

I am anxious that this other thing should not overhastily be grasped as technology per se, since I will want to show that technology is here itself a figure for something else. Yet technology may well serve as adequate shorthand to designate that enormous properly human and anti-natural power of dead human labour stored up in our machinery, an alienated power, what Sartre calls the counterfinality of the practico-inert, which turns back on and against us in unrecognizable forms and seems to constitute the massive dystopian horizon of our collective as well as our individual praxis.

Technology is, however, on the Marxist view the result of the development of capital, rather than some primal cause in its own right. It will therefore be appropriate to distinguish several generations of machine power, several stages of technological revolution within capital itself. I here follow Ernest Mandel who outlines three such fundamental breaks or quantum leaps in the evolution of machinery under capital:

The fundamental revolutions in power technology – the technology of the production of motive machines by machines – thus appears as the determinant moment in revolutions of technology as a whole. Machine production of steam-driven motors since 1848; machine production of electric and combustion motors since the 90s of the 19th century; machine production of electronic and nuclear-powered apparatuses since the 40s of the 20th century – these are the three general revolutions in technology engendered by the capitalist mode of production since the "original" industrial revolution of the later 18th century. (*Late Capitalism*, p. 18)

The periodization underscores the general thesis of Mandel's book *Late Capitalism*, namely that there have been three fundamental moments in capitalism, each one marking a dialectical expansion over the previous stage: these are market capitalism, the monopoly stage or the stage of imperialism, and our own – wrongly called post industrial, but what might better be termed multinational capital. I have already pointed out that Mandel's intervention in the postindustrial involves the proposition that late or multinational or consumer capitalis, far from being inconsistent with Marx's great nineteenth-century analysis, constitutes on the contrary the purest form of capital yet to have emerged, a prodigious expansion of capital into hitherto uncommodified areas. This purer capitalism of our own time thus eliminates the enclaves of precapitalist organization it had hitherto tolerated and exploited in a tributary way: one is tempted to speak in this connection of a new and historically original penetration and colonization of Nature and the Unconscious: that is, the destruction of precapitalist third world agriculture by the green revolution, and the rise of the media and the advertising industry. At any rate, it will also have been clear that my own cultural periodization of the stages of realism, modernism and postmodernism is both inspired and confirmed by Mandel's tripartite scheme.

We may speak therefore of our own age as the Third (or even Fourth) Machine Age; and it is at this point that we must reintroduce the problem of aesthetic representation already explicitly developed in Kant's earlier analysis of the sublime – since it would seem only logical that the relationship to, and representation of, the machine could be expected to shift dialectically with each of these qualitatively different stages of technological development.

It is appropriate therefore to recall the excitement of machinery in the preceding moment of capital, the exhilaration of futurism most notably, and of Marinetti's celebration of the machine gun and the motor car. These are still visible emblems, sculptural nodes of energy which give tangibility and figuration to the motive energies of that earlier moment of modernization. The prestige of these great streamlined shapes can be measured by their metaphorical presence in Le Corbusier's buildings, vast Utopian structures which ride like so many gigantic steamshipliners upon the urban scenery of an older fallen earth. Machinery exerts another kind of fascination in artists like Picabia and Duchamp, whom we have no time to consider here; but let me mention, for the sake of completeness, the ways in which revolutionary or communist artists of the 1930s also sought to reappropriate this excitement of machine energy for a Promethean reconstruction of human society as a whole, as in Fernand Léger and Diego Rivera.

What must then immediately be observed is that the technology of our own moment no longer possesses this same capacity for representation: not the turbine, nor even Sheeler's grain elevators or smokestacks, not the baroque elaboration of pipes and conveyor belts nor even the streamlined profile of the railroad train – all vehicles of speed still concentrated at rest – but rather the computer, whose outer shell has no emblematic or visual power, or even the casings of the various media themselves, as with that home appliance called television which articulates nothing but rather implodes, carrying its flattened image surface within itself.

Such machines are indeed machines of reproduction rather than of production, and they make very different demands on our capacity for aesthetic representation than did the relatively mimetic idolatry of the older machinery of the futurist moment, of some older speed-and-energy sculpture. Here we have less to do with kinetic energy than with all kinds of new reproductive processes; and in the weaker productions of postmodernism the aesthetic embodiment of such processes often tends to slip back more comfortably into a mere thematic representation of content – into narratives which are *about* the processes of reproduction, and include movie cameras, video, tape recorders, the whole technology of the production and reproduction of the simulacrum. (The shift from Antonioni's modernist *Blowup* to DePalma's postmodernist *Blowout* is here paradigmatic.) When Japanese architects, for example, model a building on the decorative imitation of stacks of cassettes, then the solution is at best a thematic and allusive, although often humorous, one.

Yet something else does tend to emerge in the most energetic postmodernist texts, and it is the sense that beyond all thematics or content the work seems somehow to tap the networks of reproductive process and thereby to afford us some glimpse into a postmodern or technological sublime, whose power or authenticity is documented by the success of such works in evoking a whole new postmodern space in emergence around us. Architecture therefore remains in this sense the privileged aesthetic language; and the distorting and fragmenting reflexions of one enormous glass surface to the other can be taken as paradigmatic of the central role of process and reproduction in postmodernist culture.

As I have said, however, I want to avoid the implication that technology is in any way the "ultimately determining instance" either of our present-day social life or of our cultural production: such a thesis is of course ultimately at one with the post-Marxist notion of a "postindustrialist" society. Rather, I want to suggest that our faulty representations of some immense communicational and computer network are themselves but a distorted figuration of something even deeper, namely the whole world system of present-day multinational capitalism. The technology of contemporary society is therefore mesmerizing and fascinating, not so much in its own right, but because it seems to offer some privileged representational shorthand for grasping a network of power and control even more difficult for our minds and imaginations to grasp – namely the whole new decentred global network of the third stage of capital itself. This is a figural process presently best observed in a whole mode of contemporary entertainment literature, which one is tempted to characterize as "high-tech paranoia", in which the circuits and networks of some putative global computer hook-up are narratively mobilized by labyrinthine conspiracies of autonomous but deadly interlocking and competing information agencies in a complexity often beyond the capacity of the normal reading mind. Yet conspiracy theory (and its garish narrative manifestations) must be seen as a degraded attempt – through the figuration of advanced technology – to think the impossible totality of the contemporary world system. It is therefore in terms of that enormous and threatening, yet only dimly perceivable, other reality of economic and social institutions that in my opinion the postmodern sublime can alone be adequately theorized.

Postmodernism and the City

Now, before I try to offer a somewhat more positive conclusion, I want to sketch the analysis of a full-blown postmodern building – a work which is in many ways uncharacteristic of that postmodern architecture whose principal names are Robert Venturi, Charles Moore, Michael Graves, and more recently Frank Gehry, but which to my mind offers some very striking lessons about the originality of postmodernist space. Let me amplify the figure which has run through the preceding remarks, and make it even more explicit: I am proposing the motion that we are here in the presence of something like a mutation in built space itself. My implication is that we ourselves, the human subjects who happen into this new space, have not kept pace with that evolution; there has been a mutation in the object, unaccompanied as yet by any equivalent mutation in the subject; we do not yet possess the perceptual equipment to match this new hyperspace, as I will call it, in part because our perceptual habits were formed in that older kind of space I have called the space of high modernism. The newer architecture therefore – like many of the other cultural products I have evoked in the preceding remarks – stands as something like an imperative to grow new organs, to expand our sensorium and our body to some new, as yet unimaginable, perhaps ultimately impossible, dimensions.

The Bonaventura Hotel

The building whose features I will very rapidly enumerate in the next few moments is the Bonaventura Hotel, built in the new Los Angeles downtown by the architect and developer John Portman, whose other works include the various Hyatt Regencies, the Peachtree Center in Atlanta, and the Renaissance Center in Detroit. I have mentioned the populist aspect of the rhetorical defence of postmodernism against the elite (and Utopian) austerities of the great architectural modernisms: it is generally affirmed, in other words, that these newer buildings are popular works on the one hand; and that they respect the vernacular of the American city fabric on the other, that is to say, that they no longer attempt, as did the masterworks and monuments of high modernism, to insert a different, a distinct, an elevated, a new Utopian language into the tawdry and commercial sign-system of the surrounding city, but rather, on the contrary, seek to speak that very language, using its lexicon and syntax as that has been emblematically "learned from Las Vegas".

On the first of these counts, Portman's Bonaventura fully confirms the claim: it is a popular building, visited with enthusiasm by locals and tourists alike (although Portman's other buildings are even more successful in this respect). The populist insertion into the city fabric is, however, another matter, and it is with this that we will begin. There are three entrances to the Bonaventura, one from Figueroa, and the other two by way of elevated gardens on the other side of the hotel, which is built into the remaining slope of the former Beacon Hill. None of these is anything like the old hotel marquee, or the monumental porte cochere with which the sumptuous buildings of yester year were wont to stage your passage from city street to the older interior. The entryways of the Bonaventura are as it were lateral and rather backdoor affairs: the gardens in the back admit you to the sixth floor of the towers, and even there you must walk down one flight to find the elevator by which you gain access to the lobby. Meanwhile, what one is still tempted to think of as the front entry, on Figueroa, admits you, baggage and all, onto the second-storey shopping balcony, from which you must take an escalator down to the main registration desk. More about these elevators and escalators in a moment. What I first want to suggest about these curiously unmarked ways-in is that they seem to have been imposed by some new category of closure governing the inner space of the hotel itself (and this over and above the material constraints under which Portman had to work). I believe that, with a certain number of other characteristic postmodern buildings, such as the Beaubourg in Paris, or the Eaton Centre in Toronto, the Bonaventura aspires to being a total space, a complete world, a kind of miniature city (and I would want to add that to this new total space corresponds a new collective practice, a new mode in which individuals move and congregate, something like the practice of a new and historically original kind of hyper-crowd). In this sense, then, ideally the mini-city of Portman's Bonaventura ought not to have entrances at all, since the entryway is always the seam that links the building to the rest of the city that surrounds it: for it does not wish to be a part of the city, but rather its equivalent and its replacement or substitute. That is, however, obviously not possible or practical, whence the deliberate downplaying and reduction of the entrance function to its bare minimum. But this disjunction from the surrounding city is very different from that of the great monuments of the International Style: there, the act of disjunction was violent, visible, and had a very real symbolic significance – as in Le Corbusier's great *pilotis* whose gesture radically separates the new Utopian space of the modern from the degraded and fallen city fabric which it thereby explicitly repudiates (although the gamble of the modern was that this new Utopian space, in the virulence of its Novum, would fan out and transform that eventually by the very power of its new spatial language). The Bonaventura, however, is content to "let the fallen city fabric continue to be in its being" (to parody Heidegger); no further effects, no larger protopolitical Utopian transformation, is either expected or desired.

This diagnosis is to my mind confirmed by the great reflective glass skin of the Bonaventura, whose function I will now interpret rather differently than I did a moment ago when I saw the phenomenon of reflexion generally as developing a thematics of reproductive technology (the two readings are however not incompatible). Now one would want rather to stress the way in which the glass skin repels the city outside; a repulsion for which we have analogies in those reflector sunglasses which make it impossible for your interlocutor to see your own eyes and thereby achieve a certain aggressivity towards and power over the Other. In a similar way, the glass skin achieves a peculiar and placeless dissociation of the Bonaventura from its neighbourhood: it is not even an exterior, inasmuch as when you seek to look at the hotel's outer walls you cannot see the hotel itself, but only the distorted images of everything that surrounds it.

Now I want to say a few words about escalators and elevators: given their very real pleasures in Portman, particularly these last, which the artist has termed "gigantic kinetic sculptures" and which certainly account for much of the spectacle and the excitement of the hotel interior, particularly in the Hyatts, where like great Japanese lanterns or gondolas they ceaselessly rise and fall – given such a deliberate marking and foregrounding in their own right, I believe one has to see such "people movers" (Portman's own term. adapted from Disney) as something a little more than mere functions and engineering components. We know in any case that recent architectural theory has begun to borrow from narrative analysis in other fields, and to attempt to see our physical trajectories through such buildings as virtual narratives or stories, as dynamic paths and narrative paradigms which we as visitors are asked to fulfil and to complete with our own bodies and movements. In the Bonaventura, however, we find a dialectical heightening of this process: it seems to me that the escalators and elevators here henceforth replace movement but also and above all designate themselves as new reflexive signs and emblems of movement proper (something which will become evident when we come to the whole question of what remains of older forms of movement in this building, most notably walking itself). Here the narrative stroll has been underscored, symbolized, reified and replaced by a transportation machine which becomes the allegorical signifier of that older promenade we are no longer allowed to conduct on our own: and this is a dialectical intensification of the autoreferentiality of all modern culture, which tends to turn upon itself and designate its own cultural production as its content.

I am more at a loss when it comes to conveying the thing itself, the experience of space you undergo when you step off such allegorical devices into the lobby or atrium, with its great central column, surrounded by a miniature lake, the whole positioned between the four symmetrical residential towers with their elevators, and surrounded by rising balconies capped by a kind of greenhouse roof at the sixth level. I am tempted to say that such space makes it impossible for us to use the language of volume or volumes any longer, since these last are impossible to seize. Hanging streamers indeed suffuse this empty space in such a way as to distract systematically and deliberately from whatever form it might be supposed to have; while a constant busyness gives the feeling that emptiness is here absolutely packed, that it is an element within which you yourself are immersed, without any of that distance that formerly enabled the perception of perspective or volume. You are in this hyperspace up to your eyes and your body; and if it seemed to you before that that suppression of depth I spoke of in postmodern painting or literature would necessarily be difficult to achieve in architecture itself, perhaps you may now be willing to see this bewildering immersion as the formal equivalent in the new medium.

Yet escalator and elevator are also in this context dialectical opposites; and we may suggest that the glorious movement of the elevator gondolas is also a dialectical compensation for this filled space of the atrium – it gives us the chance at a radically different, but complementary, spatial experience, that of rapidly shooting up through the ceiling and outside, along one of the four symmetrical towers, with the referent, Los Angeles itself, spread out breath-takingly and even alarmingly before us. But even this vertical movement is contained: the elevator lifts you to one of those revolving cocktail lounges, in which you, seated, are again passively rotated about and offered a contempla-tive spectacle of the city itself, now transformed into its own images by the glass windows through which you view it.

Let me quickly conclude all this by returning to the central space of the lobby itself (with the passing observation that the hotel rooms are visibly margin-alized: the corridors in the residential sections are low-ceilinged and dark, most depressingly functional indeed; while one understands that the rooms are in the worst of taste). The descent is dramatic enough, plummeting back down through the roof to splash down in the lake; what happens when you get there is something else, which I can only try to characterize as milling confu-sion, something like the vengeance this space takes on those who still seek to walk through it. Given the absolute symmetry of the four towers, it is quite impossible to get your bearings in this lobby; recently, colour coding and directional signals have been added in a pitiful and revealing, rather desperate attempt to restore the coordinates of an older space. I will take as the most dramatic practical result of this spatial mutation the notorious dilemma of the shopkeepers on the various balconies: it has been obvious, since the very opening of the hotel in 1977, that nobody could ever find any of these stores, and even if you located the appropriate boutique, you would be most unlikely to be as fortunate a second time; as a consequence, the commercial tenants are in despair and all the merchandise is marked down to bargain prices. When you recall that Portman is a businessman as well as an architect, and a millionaire developer, an artist who is at one and the same time a capitalist in his own right, one cannot but feel that here too something of a "return of the repressed" is involved.

So I come finally to my principal point here, that this latest mutation in space – postmodern hyperspace – has finally succeeded in transcending the capacities of the individual human body to locate itself, to organize its immediate surroundings perceptually, and cognitively to map its position in a mappable external world. And I have already suggested that this alarming disjunction point between the body and its built environment – which is to the initial bewilderment of the older modernism as the velocities of space craft are to those of the automobile – can itself stand as the symbol and analogue of that even sharper dilemma which is the incapacity of our minds, at least at present, to map the great global multinational and decentred communicational network in which we find ourselves caught as individual subjects.

The new machine

But as I am anxious that Portman's space not be perceived as something either exceptional or seemingly marginalized and leisure-specialized on the order of Disneyland, I would like in passing to juxtapose this complacent and entertaining (although bewildering) leisure-time space with its analogue in a very different area, namely the space of postmodern warfare, in particular as Michael Herr evokes it in his great book on the experience of Vietnam, called *Dispatches*. The extraordinary linguistic innovations of this work may still be considered postmodern, in the eclectic way in which its language impersonally fuses a whole range of contemporary collective idiolects, most notably rock language and Black language: but the fusion is dictated by problems of content. This first terrible postmodernist war cannot be told in any of the traditional paradigms of the war novel or movie – indeed that breakdown of all previous narrative paradigms is, along with the breakdown of any shared language through which a veteran might convey such experience, among the principal subjects of the book and may be said to open up the place of a whole new reflexivity. Benjamin's account of Baudelaire, and of the emergence of modernism from a new experience of city technology which transcends all the older habits of bodily perception, is both singularly relevant here, and singularly antiquated, in the light of this new and virtually unimaginable quantum leap in technological alienation:

He was a moving–target–survivor subscriber, a true child of the war; because except for the rare times when you were pinned or stranded the system was geared to keep you mobile, if that was what you thought you wanted. As a technique for staying alive it seemed to make as much sense as anything, given naturally that you were there to begin with and wanted to see it close; it started out sound and straight but it formed a cone as it progressed, because the more your moved the more you saw, the more you saw the more besides death and mutilation you risked, and the more you risked of that the more you would have to let go of one day as a "survivor". Some of us moved around the war like crazy people until we couldn't see which way the run was taking us anymore, only the war all over its surface with occasional, unexpected penetration. As long as we could have choppers like taxis it took real exhaustion or depression near shock or a dozen pipes of opium to keep us even apparently quiet, we'd still be running around inside our skins like something was after us, ha ha, La Vida Loca. In the months after I got back the hundreds of helicopters I'd flown in began to draw together until they'd formed a collective meta-chopper, and in my mind it was the sexiest thing going; saver–destroyer, provider–waster, right hand–left hand, nimble, fluent, canny and human; hot steel, grease, jungle-saturated canvas webbing, sweat cooling and warming up again, cassette rock and roll in one ear and door-gun fire in the other, fuel, heat, vitality and death, death itself, hardly an intruder.[4]

In this new machine, which does not, like the older modernist machinery of the locomotive or the airplane, represent motion, but which can only be represented *in motion*, something of the mystery of the new postmodernist space is concentrated.

The Abolition of Critical Distance

The conception of postmodernism outlined here is a historical rather than a merely stylistic one. I cannot stress too greatly the radical distinction between a view for which the postmodern is one (optional) style among many others available, and one which seeks to grasp it as the cultural dominant of the logic of late capitalism: the two approaches in fact generate two very different ways of conceptualizing the phenomenon as a whole, on the one hand moral judgements (about which it is indifferent whether they are positive or negative), and on the other a genuinely dialectical attempt to think our present of time in History.

Of some positive moral evaluation of postmodernism little needs to be said: the complacent (yet delirious) camp-following celebration of this aesthetic new world (including its social and economic dimension, greeted with equal enthusiasm under the slogan of "post-industrial society") is surely unacceptable – although it may be somewhat less obvious the degree to which current fantasies about the salvational nature of high technology, from chips to robots – fantasies entertained not only by left as well as right governments in distress, but also by many intellectuals – are essentially of a piece with more vulgar apologies for postmodernism.

But in that case it is also logical to reject moralizing condemnations of the postmodern and of its essential triviality, when juxtaposed against the Utopian "high seriousness" of the great modernisms: these are also judgements one finds both on the Left and on the radical Right. And no doubt the logic of the simulacrum, with its transformation of older realities into television images, does more than merely replicate the logic of late capitalism; it reinforces and intensifies it. Meanwhile, for political groups which seek actively to intervene in history and to modify its otherwise passive momentum (whether with a view towards channelling it into a socialist transformation of society or diverting it into the regressive reestablishment of some simpler fantasy past), there cannot but be much that is deplorable and reprehensible in a cultural form of image addiction which, by transforming the past visual mirages, stereotypes or texts, effectively abolishes any practical sense of the future and of the collective project, thereby abandoning the thinking of future change to fantasies of sheer catastrophe and inexplicable cataclysm – from visions of "terrorism" on the social level to those of cancer on the personal. Yet if postmodernism is a historical phenomenon, then the attempt to conceptualize it in terms of moral or moralizing judgements must finally be identified as a category-mistake. All of which becomes more obvious when we interrogate the position of the cultural critic and moralist: this last, along with all the rest of us, is now so deeply immersed in postmodernist space, so deeply suffused and infected by its new cultural categories, that the luxury of the old-fashioned ideological critique, the indignant moral denunciation of the other, becomes unavailable.

The distinction I am proposing here knows one canonical form in Hegel's differentiation of the thinking of individual morality or moralizing (*Moralität*) from that whole very different realm of collective social values and practices (*Sittlichkeit*). But it finds its definitive form in Marx's demonstration of the materialist dialectic, most notably in those classic pages of the *Manifesto* which teach the hard lesson of some more genuinely dialectical way to think historical development and change. The topic of the lesson is, of course, the historical development of capitalism itself and the deployment of a specific bourgeois culture. In a well-known passage, Marx powerfully urges us to do the impossible, namely to think this development positively *and* negatively all at once; to achieve, in other words, a type of thinking that would be capable of grasping the demonstrably baleful features of capitalism along with its extraordinary and liberating dynamism simultaneously, within a single thought, and without attenuating any of the force of either judgement. We are, somehow, to lift our minds to a point at which it is possible to understand that capitalism is at one and the same time the best thing that has ever happened to the human race, and the worst. The lapse from this austere dialectical imperative into the more comfortable stance of the taking of moral positions is inveterate and all too human: still, the urgency of the subject demands that we make at least some effort to think the cultural evolution of late capitalism dialectically, as catastrophe and progress all together.

Such an effort suggests two immediate questions, with which we will conclude these reflextions. Can we in fact identify some "moment of truth" within the more evident "moments of falsehood" of postmodern culture? And, even if we can do so, is there not something ultimately paralysing in the dialectical view of historical development proposed above; does it not tend to demobilize us and to surrender us to passivity and helplessness, by systematically obliterating possibilities of action under the impenetrable fog of historical inevitability? It will be appropriate to discuss these two (related) issues in terms of current possibilities for some effective contemporary cultural politics and for the construction of a genuine political culture.

To focus the problem in this way is of course immediately to raise the more genuine issue of the fate of culture generally, and of the function of culture specifically, as one social level or instance, in the postmodern era. Everything in the previous discussion suggests that what we have been calling postmodernism is inseparable from, and unthinkable without the hypothesis of, some fundamental mutation of the sphere of culture in the world of late capitalism, which includes a momentous modification of its social function. Older discussions of the space, function or sphere of culture (most notably Herbert Marcuse's classic essay on "The Affirmative Character of Culture") have insisted on what a different language would call the "semi-autonomy" of the cultural realm: its ghostly, yet Utopian, existence, for good or ill, above the practical world of the existent, whose mirror image it throws back in forms which vary from the legitimations of flattering resemblance to the contestatory indictments of critical satire or Utopian pain.

What we must now ask ourselves is whether it is not precisely this "semi-autonomy" of the cultural sphere which has been destroyed by the logic of late capitalism. Yet to argue that culture is today no longer endowed with the relative autonomy it once enjoyed as one level among others in earlier moments of capitalism (let alone in pre-capitalist societies) is not necessarily to imply its disappearance or extinction. On the contrary: we must go on to affirm that the dissolution of an autonomous sphere of culture is rather to be imagined in terms of an explosion: a prodigious expansion of culture throughout the social realm, to the point at which everything in our social life – from economic value and state power to practices and to the very structure of the psyche itself – can be said to have become "cultural" in some original and as yet untheorized sense. This perhaps startling proposition is, however, substantively quite consistent with the previous diagnosis of a society of the image or the simulacrum, and a transformation of the "real" into so many pseudo-events.

It also suggests that some of our most cherished and time-honoured radical conceptions about the nature of cultural politics may thereby find themselves outmoded. However distinct those conceptions may have been – which range from slogans of negativity, opposition, and subversion to critique and reflexivity – they all shared a single, fundamentally spatial, presupposition, which may be resumed in the equally time-honoured formula of "critical distance". No theory of cultural politics current on the Left today has been able to do without one notion or another of a certain minimal aesthetic distance, of the possibility of the positioning of the cultural act outside the massive Being of capital, which then serves as an Archimedean point from which to assault this last. What the burden of our preceding demonstration suggests, however, is that distance in general (including "critical distance" in particular) has very precisely been abolished in the new space of postmodernism. We are submerged in its henceforth filled and suffused volumes to the point where our now postmodern bodies are bereft of spatial coordinates and practically (let alone theoretically) incapable of distantiation; meanwhile, it has already been observed how the prodigious new expansion of multinational capital ends up penetrating and colonizing those very pre-capitalist enclaves (Nature and the Unconscious) which offered extraterritorial and Archimedean footholds for critical effectivity. The short-hand language of "cooptation" is for this reason omnipresent on the Left; but offers a most inadequate theoretical basis for understanding a situation in which we all, in one way or another, dimly feel that not only punctual and local countercultural forms of cultural resistance and guerrilla warfare, but also even overtly political interventions like those of *The Clash*, are all somehow secretly disarmed and reabsorbed by a system of which they themselves might well be considered a part, since they can achieve no distance from it.

What we must now affirm is that it is precisely this whole extraordinarily demoralizing and depressing original new global space which is the "moment of truth" of postmodernism. What has been called the postmodernist "sublime" is only the moment in which this content has become most explicit. has moved the closest to the surface of consciousness, as a coherent new type of space in its own right – even though a certain figural concealment or disguise is still at work here, most notably in the high-technological thematics in which the new spatial content is still dramatized and articulated. Yet the earlier features of the postmodern which were enumerated above can all now be seen as themselves partial (yet constitutive) aspects of the same general spatial object.

The argument for a certain authenticity in these otherwise patently ideo-logical productions depends on the prior proposition that what we have now been calling postmodern (or multinational) space is not merely a cultural ideology or fantasy, but has genuine historical (and socio-economic) reality as a third great original expansion of capitalism around the globe (after the earlier expansions of the national market and the older imperialist system, which each had their own cultural specificity and generated new types of space appropriate to their dynamics). The distorted and unreflexive attempts of newer cultural production to explore and to express this new space must then also, in their own fashion, be considered as so many approaches to the representation of (a new) reality (to use a more antiquated language). As paradoxical as the terms may seem, they may thus, following a classic interpretive option, be read as peculiar new forms of realism (or at least of the mimesis of reality), at the same time that they can equally well be analysed as so many attempts to distract and to divert us from that reality or to disguise its contradictions and resolve them in the guise of various formal mystifications.

As for that reality itself, however – the as yet untheorized original space of some new "world system" of multinational or late capitalism (a space whose negative or baleful aspects are only too obvious), the dialectic requires us to hold equally to a positive or "progressive" evaluation of its emergence, as Marx did for the newly unified space of the national markets, or as Lenin did for the older imperialist global network. For neither Marx nor Lenin was socialism a matter of returning to small (and thereby less repressive and comprehensive) systems of social organization; rather, the dimensions attained by capital in their own times were grasped as the promise, the framework, and the precondition for the achievement of some new and more comprehensive socialism. How much the more is this not the case with the even more global and totalizing space of the new world system, which demands the invention and elaboration of an internationalism of a radically new type? The disastrous realignment of socialist revolution with the older nationalisms (not only in Southeast Asia), whose results have necessarily aroused much serious recent Left reflexion, can be adduced in support of this position.

The need for maps

But if all this is so, then at least one possible form of a new radical cultural politics becomes evident: with a final aesthetic proviso that must quickly be noted. Left cultural producers and theorists – particularly those formed by bourgeois cultural traditions issuing from romanticism and valorizing spontan-eous, instinctive or unconscious forms of "genius" – but also for very obvious historical reasons such as Zhdanovism and the sorry consequences of political and party interventions in the arts – have often by reaction allowed themselves to be unduly intimidated by the repudiation, in bourgeois aesthetics and most notably in high modernism, of one of the age-old functions of art – namely the pedagogical and the didactic. The teaching function of art was, however, always stressed in classical times (even though it there mainly took the form of *moral* lessons); while the prodigious and still imperfectly understood work of Brecht reaffirms, in a new and formally innovative and original way, for the moment of modernism proper, a complex new conception of the relationship between culture and pedagogy. The cultural model I will propose similarly foregrounds the cognitive and pedagogical dimensions of political art and culture, dimensions stressed in very different ways by *both* Lukács *and* Brecht (for the distinct moments of realism and modernism, respectively).

We cannot, however, return to aesthetic practices elaborated on the basis of historical situations and dilemmas which are no longer ours. Meanwhile, the conception of space that has been developed here suggests that a model of political culture appropriate to our own situation will necessarily have to raise spatial issues as its fundamental organizing concern. I will therefore provisionally define the aesthetic of such new (and hypothetical) cultural form as an aesthetic of *cognitive mapping*.

In a classic work, *The Image of the City*, Kevin Lynch taught us that the alienated city is above all a space in which people are unable to map (in their minds) either their own positions or the urban totality in which they find themselves: grids such as those of Jersey City, in which none of the traditional markers (monuments, nodes, natural boundaries, built perspectives) obtain, are the most obvious examples. Disalienation in the traditional city, then, involves the practical reconquest of a sense of place, and the construction or reconstruction of an articulated ensemble which can be retained in memory and which the individual subject can map and remap along the moments of mobile, alternative trajectories. Lynch's own work is limited by the deliberate restriction of his topic to the problems of the city form as such; yet it becomes extraordinarily suggestive when projected outwards onto some of the larger national and global spaces we have touched on here. Nor should it be too hastily assumed that his model – while it clearly raises very central issues of representation as such – is in any way easily vitiated by the conventional poststructuralist critiques of the "ideology of representation" or mimesis. The cognitive map is not exactly mimetic, in that older sense; indeed the theoretical issues it poses allow us to renew the analysis of representation on a higher and much more complex level.

There is, for one thing, a most interesting convergence between the empirical problems studied by Lynch in terms of city space and the great Althusserian (and Lacanian) redefinition of ideology as "the representation of the subject's *Imaginary* relationship to his or her *Real* conditions of existence". Surely this is exactly what the cognitive map is called upon to do, in the narrower framework of daily life in the physical city: to enable a situational representation on the part of the individual subject to that vaster and properly unrepresentable totality which is the ensemble of the city's structure as a whole.

Yet Lynch's work also suggests a further line of development insofar as cartography itself constitutes its key mediatory instance. A return to the history of this science (which is also an art) shows us that Lynch's model does not yet in fact really correspond to what will become map-making. Rather, Lynch's subjects are clearly involved in pre-cartographic operations whose results traditionally are described as itineraries rather than as maps; diagrams organized around the still subject-centred or existential journey of the traveller, along which various significant key features are marked – oases, mountain ranges, rivers, monuments and the like. The most highly developed form of such diagrams is the nautical itinerary, the sea chart or *portulans*, where coastal features are noted for the use of Mediterranean navigators who rarely venture out into the open sea.

Yet the compass at once introduces a new dimension into sea charts, a dimension that will utterly transform the problematic of the itinerary and allow us to pose the problem of a genuine cognitive mapping in a far more complex way. For the new instruments – compass, sextant and theodolite – do not merely correspond to new geographic and navigational problems (the difficult matter of determining longitude, particularly on the curving surface of the planet, as opposed to the simpler matter of latitude, which European navigators can still empirically determine by ocular inspection of the African coast); they also introduce a whole new coordinate – that of relationship to the totality, particularly as it is mediated by the stars and by new operations like that of triangulation. At this point, cognitive mapping in the broader sense comes to require the coordination of existential data (the empirical position of the subject) with unlived, abstract conceptions of the geographic totality.

Finally, with the first globe (1490) and the invention of the Mercator projection around the same period, yet a third dimension of cartography emerges, which at once involves what we would today call the nature of representational codes, the intrinsic structures of the various media, the intervention, into more naïve mimetic conceptions of mapping, of the whole new fundamental question of the languages of representation itself: and in particular the unresolvable (well-nigh Heisenbergian) dilemma of the transfer of curved space to flat charts; at which point it becomes clear that there can be no true maps (at the same time in which it also becomes clear that there can be scientific progress, or better still, a dialectical advance, in the various historical moments of map-making).

Social cartography and symbol

Transcoding all this now into the very different problematic of the Althusserian definition of ideology, one would want to make two points. The first is that the Althusserian concept now allows us to rethink these specialized geographical and cartographic issues in terms of social space, in terms, for example, of social class and national or international context, in terms of the ways in which we all necessarily *also* cognitively map our individual social relationship to local, national and international class realities. Yet to reformulate the problem in this way is also to come starkly up against those very difficulties in mapping which are posed in heightened and original ways by that very global space of the postmodernist or multinational moment which has been under discussion here. These are not merely theoretical issues, but have urgent practical political consequences: as is evident from the conventional feelings of First World subjects that existentially (or "empirically") they really do inhabit a "postindustrial society", from which traditional production has disappeared and in which social classes of the classical type no longer exist – a conviction which has immediate effects on political praxis.

The second observation to be proposed is that a return to the Lacanian underpinnings of Althusser's theory can afford some useful and suggestive methodological enrichments. Althusser's formulation remobilizes an older and henceforth classical Marxian distinction between science and ideology, which is still not without value for us. The existential – the positioning of the individual subject, the experience of daily life, the monadic "point of view" on the world to which we are necessarily, as biological subjects, restricted – is in Althusser's formula implicitly opposed to the realm of abstract knowledge, a realm which as Lacan reminds us is never positioned in or actualized by any concrete subject but rather by that structural void called *"le sujet supposé savoir"*, "the subject supposed to know", a subject-place of knowledge: what is affirmed is not that we cannot know the world and its totality in some abstract or "scientific" way – Marxian "science" provides just such a way of knowing and conceptualizing the world abstractly, in the sense in which, e.g. Mandel's great book offers a rich and elaborated *knowledge* of that global world system, of which it has never been said here that it was unknowable, but merely that it was unrepresentable, which is a very different matter. The Althusserian formula in other words designates a gap, a rift, between existential experience and scientific knowledge: ideology has then the function of somehow inventing a way of articulating those two distinct dimensions with each other. What a historicist view of this "definition" would want to add is that such coordination, the production of functioning and living ideologies, is distinct in different historical situations, but above all, that there may be historical situations in which it is not possible at all – and this would seem to be our situation in the current crisis.

But the Lacanian system is three-fold and not dualistic. To the Marxian–Althusserian opposition of ideology and science correspond only two of Lacan's tripartite functions, the Imaginary and the Real, respectively. Our digression on cartography, however, with its final revelation of a properly representational dialectic of the codes and capacities of individual languages or media, reminds us that what has until now been omitted was the dimension of the Lacanian Symbolic itself.

An aesthetic of cognitive mapping – a pedagogical political culture which seeks to endow the individual subject with some new heightened sense of its place in the global system – will necessarily have to respect this now enormously complex representational dialectic and to invent radically new forms in order to do it justice. This is not, then, clearly a call for a return to some older kind of machinery, some older and more transparent national space, or some more traditional and reassuring perspectival or mimetic enclave: the new political art – if it is indeed possible at all – will have to hold to the truth of postmodernism, that is, to say, to its fundamental object – the world space of multinational capital – at the same time at which it achieves a breakthrough to some as yet unimaginable new mode of representing this last, in which we may again begin to grasp our positioning as individual and collective subjects and regain a capacity to act and struggle which is at present neutralized by our spatial as well as our social confusion. The political form of postmodernism, if there ever is any, will have as its vocation the invention and projection of a global cognitive mapping, on a social as well as a spatial scale.

Notes

1   [This chapter] draws on lectures and on material previously published in *The Anti-Aesthetic*, edited by Hal Foster (Port Townsend, Washington, Bay Press, 1983) and in *Amerika Studien/American Studies*, 29(1) (1984).
2   In "The politics of theory", *New German Critique*, 32 (Spring/Summer 1984).
3   Marguerite Séchehaye, *Autobiography of a Schizophrenic Girl*, trans. G. Rubin-Rabson (New York, 1968), p. 19.
4   Michael Herr, *Dispatches* (New York 1978), pp. 8–9.

13

The Antinomies of Postmodernity

"The Antinomies of Postmodernity," which appears in Jameson's book, *The Seeds of Time* (1994) is divided into four sections. This selection consists of the brief introduction and the first two sections. Please note that the fourth section of this essay appears in chapter 22 of this volume.

It is conventional to distinguish an antinomy from a contradiction, not least because folk wisdom implies that the latter is susceptible of a solution or a resolution, whereas the former is not. In that sense, the antinomy is a cleaner form of language than the contradiction. With it, you know where you stand; it states two propositions that are radically, indeed absolutely, incompatible, take it or leave it. Whereas the contradiction is a matter of partialities and aspects; only some of it is incompatible with the accompanying proposition; indeed, it may have more to do with forces, or the state of things, than with words or logical implications. Contradictions are supposed, in the long run, to be productive; whereas antinomies − take Kant's classic one: the world has a beginning, the world has no beginning − offer nothing in the way of a handle, no matter how diligently you turn them around and around.

All of which probably implies that the contradiction is a singular substance, about which several different, seemingly contradictory, things get said; a little sweat and ingenuity then suffices to show that the two contradictory things are somehow related, or the same − the one implied by the other, or following from it in some unsuspected way. In that case, it is the situation that accounts for the disparity, in its very incompleteness generating the multiple perspectives that make us think the matter at hand is now *x*, or *y*; or better still, *x*-like and *y*-like all at the same time. Whereas the antinomy is clearly and unequivocally two separate things: *y* or *x*; and that in such a way that the question of a situation or a context fades away altogether.

The age is clearly enough more propitious for the antinomy than the contradiction. Even in Marxism itself, the latter's spiritual homeland, the most advanced tendencies have nagged and worried at the contradiction, as at some last inexpungeable remnant of idealism capable of reinfecting the system in some fatally old-fashioned way (like vapors or brain fever). Thus the most brilliant of all Marx's commentators, Lucio Colletti, began to play Kant off against the dialectic, and to persuade himself (and us) that contradictions were not in nature, since there all phenomena are positive. I think he was wrong about this, as far as Kant was concerned, since in Kant it is precisely only "in nature" (or rather, in what he calls the "real in appearance") that oppositions do exist; in fact, the critical position with which Colletti began to flirt here is called positivism, and it led him out of Marxism altogether. (There can be no doubt, however, that the return to Kant, today, has generally had the value of an antidialectical move.)

A still greater and more influential Marxian theorist, Louis Althusser, seems to have conceived of his mission as a resolutely modernizing (or postmodernizing) one; as the intent to cleanse Marxism of all its Hegelian – which is to say Germanic and idealist – baggage. He went so far as to cast doubt on the concept of mediation (which might, indeed, in a pinch be substituted by that of transcoding), but one has it on good evidence that he meant to forge ahead and ultimately to stigmatize and exorcize the very notion of contradiction itself: something he in fact inspired his more distant anti-Marxist followers Hindess and Hirst to go on and do. Their example makes one wonder whether any other way of doing it could have left Marxism as such intact either.

If these were the most advanced trends at work within Marxism, what was going on outside it need perhaps not be imagined. Equivalents of the general notion of contradiction persisted in the various psychoanalyses; structuralism itself – even while Lévi-Strauss continued to emphasize the importance for him of both the Marxist and the Freudian conceptions of contradiction – tended rather, along with emergent semiotics, to reinforce the slippage of the category of contradiction toward the more logical one of the antinomy. But the currency of this second term (itself equally of no interest to the prevailing forms of positivism) we seem to owe primarily to deconstruction, where it became, particularly in the hands of Paul de Man, an instrument for showing up everything that was self-conflicted about a thought and its language at the same time that its essential paralysis and nonproductivity was foregrounded in a kind of conceptual freeze-frame. Something of a return toward the contradiction, however, seems on the agenda today, in Hegelian Lacanianism, where Slavoj Žižek's notion of the "symptom" proposes a rethinking of both Freud and Marx.

My own feeling has been that, rather than positing a situation in which we have to choose between these two categories (contradiction standing for the modernist option perhaps, while antinomy offers a more postmodern one), it might be worthwhile using them both concurrently and against one other, insofar as each is uniquely equipped to problematize the other in its most vital implications. The pair do not themselves form an opposition, exactly (although it would be an amusing logical exercise to pretend they do, and to try to decide whether their difference amounts to an antinomy or is itself merely one more contradiction); rather, they stand as each other's bad conscience, and as a breath of suspicion that clings to the concept itself. To wonder whether an antinomy is not really a contradiction in disguise; to harbor the nagging thought that what we took to be a contradiction was really little more than an antinomy – these pointed reciprocal doubts can do the mind no harm and may even do it some good.

That being said, I will organize my symptomatology accordingly, and operate as though an antinomy were a *symptom* of a contradiction: this may presuppose a multidimensional model or image, as well as the notion that our own age – that of technocratic positivism and experiential nominalism – is one- or two-dimensional by choice just as much as by historical development. So it is that depth forms (if any exist, like prehistoric monsters) tend to be projected up upon the surface in the anamorphic flatness of a scarcely recognizable afterimage, lighting up on the board in the form of a logical paradox or a textual paralogism. We have to swim in both these worlds at once; learn to work the remote-control glove within the contamination chamber; posit a noumenal shadow world of seismographic movements and shoulderings that inscribes itself with grotesque delicacy as minute and pencil-thin lines on the graph.

These figures suggest that the deeper problem with the concept of contradiction – a problem that cannot be resolved and that has no equivalent in anything surrounding the concept of the antinomy – is representational. Contradiction is always one step before representation: if you show it in its conflicted moment, you freeze it over so rigidly that it tends to take on the form of the antinomy. If on the contrary you anticipate its resolution, you empty it of all its negativity and generate the impression of a rigged ballot, a put-up job, a sham conflict whose outcome has already carefully been arranged in advance. Or, if you prefer, the sheer fact of having each foot in a different irreconcilable world – Antigone versus Creon – means that a representation that wants to remain true to those distinct worlds and their laws can only show its credentials and document its authenticity by failing to provide some third representational language in which they both seem falsely reconciled. This situation means, however, that the philosophical languages in which contradiction is accounted for will always be deficient and arouse a properly philosophical dissatisfaction: even Hegel's grand architectonic stages tend to fall on one side or another of the central tension, and seem to intensify into pictures of a dramatic or historical, essentially narrative scene on the one hand, or else to thin out into those formal abstractions of identity and difference that are finally the domain of the antinomy rather than of the contradiction itself.

Such tendencies are everywhere in contemporary thought, and they can be explained as the results and consequences of the latter's fundamental trends, which I have characterized as positivism and nominalism (leaving aside the interesting matter of the relationship between these two things, which can be thought of as objective and subjective respectively, as the realms of the system and of the subject). This "explanation" is, of course, one always wants to hasten to add, in current language, only one of the narratives we can tell about the current situation. But it is a good story, which can be foreshadowed by way of Adolf Loos's notorious attack on ornament in architecture and design, in which such figuration was assimilated to crime and the antisocial on the one hand, and degeneracy (still a popular concept in that period) on the other. After positivism and pragmatism, indeed, abstraction itself comes to be thought of as something like ornament: superfluous and unpractical, self-indulgent, "speculative" and metaphysical, the signs and indices of a slovenly and sinful leisure and privilege. Getting rid of the old names, of all those abstractions that still reek of universalism or generality, cleaving with even greater determination to the empirical and the actual, stigmatizing the residual as philosophical in the bad sense, which is to say as sheer idealism, without thereby lapsing into a materialism equally occult and metaphysical – these are the postmodern watchwords, which were once a guide to a kind of Wittgensteinian witch-hunt in the name of the health and purity of the language, but now circulate through the economy as effortlessly as the deliveries at your corner supermarket.

It is a reduction that can presumably not succeed; but its current hegemony not only means that much of what characterized classical philosophy must disappear but also that there can remain very little, in the way of the syncategoremic abstraction, to bind together the disparate words and syllables of a nominalistic and fragmented set of perceptions. This is the situation and the crisis from which two large and crude sorting systems tend to reemerge, from archaic time, like the return of the repressed. They are the grandest and most empty of all abstractions whose earliest (Western) avatar can be witnessed in formation in the primal indistinctions of the first forms of secular thought in the pre-Socratics: the categories of Identity and Difference (which Kant and Hegel knew as concepts or categories of *reflexion*), the most formal of all, which now survive to constitute the last extant evolutionary conceptual species, insofar as they have the advantage of seeming to offer virtually no content in their own right, no smuggled philosophical contraband, as neutral and value-free as technology or the market.

These are nondialectical categories, and you would have to bend them out of shape with some violence to appropriate them for Hegel's "identity of identity and non-identity." Identity and Difference are, rather, the realm and the domain of the antinomy as such: something they readily offer to demonstrate by effortlessly turning into one another at the slightest pretext. Rather than as dialectical, even as an arrested or paralyzed dialectic, it might be better to characterize them in terms of a kind of reversal of Freud's (modernist) conception of the "antithetical sense of primal words," which drew our attention to the way in which, etymologically X-rayed, a single term proved to carry within itself, along with its primordial meaning, the latter's negation or opposite (most famously, *heimlich*, what is most familiar and homely, also turns out to mean the same thing as *unheimlich*, what is most uncanny, weird and strange). Here, on the contrary, as for example in that specific postmodern antinomy whereby what is anti-Utopian turns out to be Utopian in its most fundamental significance, it is (as we shall see) the antitheses that turn out to be, somehow, "the same." Paradoxes of this kind are not, however, in postmodern discourse, the telltale scandals or anomalies (the failure of a star to correspond infinitestimally to its predicted trajectory) that used to incite to the rethinking of the paradigm as a whole. Here, rather, they provide the bread-and-butter concepts of all of so-called contemporary theory (or theoretical discourse), and offer training in state-of-the-art mental gymnastics not unrelated to the verbal games and logical tricks rehearsed by the sophists (as Lyotard has pointed out).

In what follows, however, we will collect a few of these paradoxes for examination as symptoms rather than as occasions for demonstrating something about the structural incapacity of the mind itself, or of its languages. This will take the form of brief evocations of [...] distinct postmodern antinomies, about which one is of course free to wonder whether they are not all fundamentally the same thing [...]. The first two antinomies concern Kant's "a priori representations," namely time and space, which we have generally come to think of in historical terms as implicit formal frames that nonetheless vary according to the mode of production. We may presumably, then, learn something about our own mode of production from the ways in which we tend to think of change and permanence, or variety and homogeneity – ways that prove to have as much to do with space as with time.

[...]

I

But time is today a function of speed, and evidently perceptible only in terms of its rate, or velocity as such: as though the old Bergsonian opposition between measurement and life, clock time and lived time, had dropped out, along with that virtual eternity or slow permanence without which Valéry thought the very idea of a work as such was likely to die out (something he seems to have been confirmed in thinking). What emerges then is some conception of change without its opposite: and to say so is then helplessly to witness our first two antinomies folding back into each other, since from the vantage point of change it becomes impossible to distinguish space from time, or object from subject. The eclipse of inner time (and its organ, the "intimate" time sense) means that we read our subjectivity off the things outside: Proust's old hotel rooms, like old retainers, respectfully reminded him every morning how old he was, and whether he was on vacation or "at home," and where – that is to say, they told him his name and issued him an identity, like a visiting card on a silver salver. As for habit, memory, recognition, material things do that for us (the way the servants were supposed to do our living, according to Villiers de l'Isle Adam). Subjectivity is an objective matter, and it is enough to change the scenery and the setting, refurnish the rooms, or destroy them in an aerial bombardment for a new subject, a new identity, miraculously to appear on the ruins of the old.

The end of the subject–object dualism, however – for which so many ideologues have yearned for so long – carries with it hidden retroparadoxes, like concealed explosives: Virilio's, for example, which shows how the seeming speed of the outside world is itself a function of the demands of representation. Not, perhaps, the result of some new subjective idea of velocity that projects itself onto an inert exterior, as in stereotypes of classical idealism, but rather technology versus nature. The apparatus – and very specifically the photographic and filmic one – makes its own demands on reality, which, as in the Gulf War, reality then scrambles to fulfill (like a time-lapse photo in which the photographer himself can be seen breathlessly sliding into place at the end of the row of already posing faces):

[T]he disappearance of the proximity effect in the prosthesis of accelerated travel made it necessary to create a wholly simulated appearance that would restore three-dimensionality to the message in full. Now a holographic prosthesis of the military commander's inertia was to be communicated to the viewer, extending his look in time and space by means of constant flashes, here and there, today and yesterday... Already evident in the flashback and then in feedback, this miniaturization of chronological meaning was the direct result of a military technology in which events always unfolded in theoretical time.[1]

Such a "return of the repressed" (an old-fashioned, now relatively metaphorical name for it to be sure) means that eliminating the subject does not leave us with the object *wie es eigentlich gewesen*, but rather with a multiplicity of simulacra. Virilio's point, like that of so many others today, is that it is the cinema that is the truly decentered subject, perhaps indeed the only one: the Deleuzian schizo being only a confused and contradictory idea alongside this apparatus that absorbs the former subject–object pole triumphantly into itself. But it raises the embarrassing secondary question of whether, in that case, there ever was a (centered) subject to begin with: did we ever have to wait? Is boredom a figment of the imagination along with its cousin eternity? Was there a time when things did not seem to change? What did we do before machines? All flesh is grass: and life in the ancient *polis* strikes us as being more fragile and ephemeral than anything in the modern city, even though we ought to be able to remember how many changes this last has undergone. It is as though an illusion of slower permanence accompanies the lived present like an optical projection, masking a change that only becomes visible when it falls outside the temporal frame.

But to put it this way is to measure a gap and to assure ourselves of everything that is radically different from the modernist form-projects and the modernist "time-senses" in the postmodern dispensation, where the formerly classical has itself been unmasked as sheer fashion, albeit the fashion of a slower, vaster world that took ages to cross by caravan or caravel, and through whose thickened time, as through a viscous element, items descended so slowly as to acquire a patina that seemed to transform their contingencies into the necessities of a meaningful tradition. For a world population, the languages of Periclean Athens can no longer be any more normative than that of other tribal styles (although it is very easy to imagine a cultural United Nations Security Council operation in which the "great civilizations" pooled their various classical traditions with a view toward imposing some more generally "human" classical canon): time thereby also becomes multicultural, and the hitherto airtight realms of demography and of industrial momentum begin to seep into each other, as though there were some analogies between great crowds of people and dizzying rates of speed. Both then spell the end of the modern in some renewed and paradoxical conjunction, as when the new styles seem exhausted by virtue of their very proliferation, while their bearers, the individual creators, prophets, geniuses, and seers, suddenly find themselves unwanted owing to sheer population density (if not the realization of the democratic ethos as such).

That the new absolute temporality has everything to do with the urban my references have suggested, without under scoring the requirement in that case of revising traditional notions of the urban as such, in order to accommodate its postnaturality to technologies of communication as well as of production and to mark the decentered, well-nigh global, scale on which what used to be the city is deployed. The modern still had something to do with the arrogance of city people over against the provincials, whether this was a provinciality of peasants, other and colonized cultures, or simply the pre-capitalist past itself: that deeper satisfaction of being "*absolument moderne*" is dissipated when modern technologies are everywhere, there are no longer any provinces, and even the past comes to seem like an alternate world, rather than an imperfect, privative stage of this one. Meanwhile, those "modern" city dwellers or metropolitans of earlier decades themselves came from the country or at least could still register the coexistence of uneven worlds; they could measure change in ways that become impossible once modernization is even relatively completed (and no longer some isolated, unnatural, and unnerving process that stands out to the naked eye). It is an unevenness and a coexistence that can also be registered in a sense of loss, as with the slow partial changes and demolitions of Baudelaire's Paris, which almost literally serve as the objective correlative of his experience of passing time: in Proust all this, although apparently more intensely elegiac (and in any case surcharging the text of Baudelaire itself), has already been subjectivized, as though it were the self and its past that were regretted and not its houses (but Proust's language knows better: "*la muraille de l'escalier, où je vis monter le reflet de sa bougie, n'existe plus depuis longtemps*,"[2] as does his spatial plot construction). Today the very meaning of demolition as such has been modified, along with that of building: it has become a generalized postnatural process that calls into question the very concept of change itself and the inherited notion of time that accompanied it.

These paradoxes are perhaps easier to dramatize in the philosophical and critical realm, than in the aesthetic one, let alone in urbanism as such. For demolition has surely defined the modern intellectual's vocation ever since the ancien régime tended to identify its mission with critique and opposition to established institutions and ideas: what better figure to characterize the strong form of the cultural intellectual from the Enlightenment *philosophes* all the way to Sartre (who has been called the last of the classical intellectuals), if not beyond? It is a figure that has seemed to presuppose an omnipresence of Error, variously defined as superstition, mystification, ignorance, class ideology, and philosophical idealism (or "metaphysics"), in such a way that to remove it by way of the operations of demystification leaves a space in which therapeutic anxiety goes hand in hand with heightened self-consciousness and reflexivity in a variety of senses, if not, indeed, with Truth as such. By attempting to restore, alongside this negative tradition, the intellectual's older mission of the restoration of meaning, Ricoeur sharply dramatized everything the various strands of what he called "the hermeneutics of suspicion" had in common, from the Enlightenment and its relationship to religion all the way to the deconstructive relation to "Western metaphysics," emphasizing above all the three great formative moments of Marx, Nietzsche, and Freud, to which even postmodern intellectuals still owe joint allegiance in one form or another.

What has changed is then perhaps the character of the terrain in which these operations are carried out: just as the transitional period between aristocratic and clerical, ancien-régime societies and mass-democratic industrial capitalist ones has been must longer and slower than we tend to believe (Arno Mayer suggests that significant remnants of the former survived in Europe until the end of World War II), so also the objective role of intellectuals to implement modernization's cultural revolution long remained a progressive one. But the process itself has often tended to impress observers and participants alike by its self-perpetuating and indeed self-devouring energies. It is not only the Revolution that eats its own children; any number of visions of pure negativity as such, from Hegel's account of freedom and the Terror to the Frankfurt School's grim theory of the "dialectic of enlightenment" as an infernal machine, bent on extirpating all traces of transcendence (including critique and negativity itself).

Such visions seem even more relevant for one-dimensional societies like our own, from which the residual, in the forms of habits and practices of older modes of production, has been tendentially eliminated, so that it might be possible to hypothesize a modification or displacement in the very function of ideology-critique itself. This is at least the position of Manfredo Tafuri, who offers a kind of functionalist analysis of the avant-garde intellectual, whose "anti-institutional phase" essentially involved "the criticism of outworn values."[3] The very success of such a mission, however, coterminous with the modernizing struggles of capital itself, "serves to prepare a clean-swept platform from which to depart in discovery of the new 'historic tasks' of intellectual work."[4] Not surprisingly, Tafuri identifies these new "modernizing" tasks with rationalization as such: "what the ideologies of the avant-grade introduced as a proposal for social behavior was the transformation of traditional ideology into Utopia, as a pre-figuration of an abstract final moment of development coincident with a global rationalization, with a positive realization of the dialectic;"[5] Tafuri's formulations become less cryptic when one understands that for him Keynesianism is to be understood as a planification, a rationalization, of the future as such.

Thus seen, demystification in the contemporary period has its own secret "ruse of history," its own inner function and concealed world-historical mission; namely, by destroying traditional societies (not merely the Church and the old aristocracies but above all the peasants and their modes of agricultural production, their common lands, and their villages), to sweep the globe clean for the manipulations of the great corporations: to prepare a purely *fungible* present in which space and psyches alike can be processed and remade at will, with a "flexibility" with which the creativity of the ideologues busy coining glowing new adjectives to describe the potentialities of "post-Fordism" can scarcely keep up. Demolition, under these circumstances, begins to take on new and ominously urbanistic overtones, and to connote the speculations of the developers far more than the older heroic struggles of oppositional intellectuals; while just such objections to and critiques of demolition itself are relegated to a tiresome moralizing and undermine themselves by virtue of their vivid dramatization of outmoded mentalities that are better off being demolished anyhow ("*denn alles, was entsteht,/Ist wert, dass es zugrunde geht*").

These are now media paradoxes, which result from the speed and tempo of the critical process, as well as the way in which all ideological and philosophical positions as such have in the media universe been transformed into their own "representations" (as Kant might put it) – in other words into images of themselves and caricatures in which identifiable slogans substitute for traditional beliefs (the beliefs having indeed been forced to transform themselves into just such recognizable ideological positions in order to operate in the media market-place). This is the situation in which it is easier to grasp the progressive value of conservative or residual modes of resistance to the new thing than to evaluate the range of ostensibly left-liberal positions (which, as in Tafuri's model, often functionally prove to be indistinguishable from the structural requirements of the system itself). The diagnosis also projects the mirage of some possible sound barrier, like a telltale line blurring away against the sky; [. . .] while the new fact itself does seem to offer a fleeting but vivid dramatization of Engels's old law about the transformation of quantity into quality (or at least of that "law"'s afterimage).

In this form, the paradox from which we must set forth is the equivalence between an unparalleled rate of change on all the levels of social life and an unparalleled standardization of everything – feelings along with consumer goods, language along with built space – that would seem incompatible with just such mutability. It is a paradox that can still be conceptualized, but in inverse ratios: that of modularity, for example, where intensified change is enabled by standardization itself, where prefabricated modules, everywhere from the media to a henceforth standardized private life, from commodified nature to uniformity of equipment, allow miraculous rebuildings to succeed each other at will, as in fractal video. The module would then constitute the new form of the object (the new result of reification) in an informational universe: that Kantian point in which raw material is suddenly organized by categories into an appropriate unit.

But the paradox can also incite us to rethink our conception of change itself. If absolute change in our society is best represented by the rapid turnover in storefronts, prompting the philosophical question as to what has really changed when video stores are replaced by T-shirt shops, then Barthes's structural formulation comes to have much to recommend it, namely, that it is crucial to distinguish between rhythms of change inherent to the system and programmed by it, and a change that replaces one entire system by another one altogether. But that is a point of view that revives paradoxes of Zeno's sort, which derive from the Parmenidean conception of Being itself, which, as it *is* by definition, cannot be thought of as even momentarily becoming, let alone failing to be for the slightest instant.

The "solution" to this particular paradox lies of course in the realization (strongly insisted on by Althusser and his disciples) that each system – better still, each "mode of production" – produces a temporality that is specific to it: it is only if we adopt a Kantian and ahistorical view of time as some absolute and empty category that the peculiarly repetitive temporality of our own system can become an object of puzzlement and lead to the reformulation of these old logical and ontological paradoxes.

Yet it may not be without its therapeutic effects to continue for one long moment to be mesmerized by the vision attributed to Parmenides, which however little it holds for nature might well be thought to capture a certain truth of our social and historical moment: a gleaming science-fictional stasis in which appearances (simulacra) arise and decay ceaselessly, without the momentous stasis of everything that is flickering for the briefest of instants or even momentarily wavering in its ontological prestige.

Here, it is as if the logic of fashion had, accompanying the multifarious penetration of its omnipresent images, begun to bind and identify itself with the social and psychic fabric in some ultimately inextricable way, which tends to make it over into the very logic of our system as a whole. The experience and the value of perpetual change thereby comes to govern language and feelings, fully as much as the buildings and the garments of this particular society, to the point at which even the relative meaning allowed by uneven development (or "nonsynchronous synchronicity") is no longer comprehensible, and the supreme value of the New and of innovation, as both modernism and modernization grasped it, fades away against a steady stream of momentum and variation that at some outer limit seems stable and motionless.

What then dawns is the realization that no society has ever been so standardized as this one, and that the stream of human, social, and historical temporality has never flowed quite so homogeneously. Even the great boredom or ennui of classical modernism required some vantage point or fantasy subject position outside the system; yet our seasons are of the post-natural and post-astronomical television or media variety, triumphantly artificial by way of the power of their National Geographic or Weather Channel images: so that their great rotations – in sports, new model cars, fashion, television, the school year or *rentrée*, etc. – simulate formerly natural rhythms for commercial convenience and reinvent such archaic categories as the week, the month, the year imperceptibly, without any of the freshness and violence of, say, the innovations of the French revolutionary calendar.

What we now begin to feel, therefore – and what begins to emerge as some deeper and more fundamental constitution of postmodernity itself, at least in its temporal dimension – is that henceforth, where everything now submits to the perpetual change of fashion and media image, nothing can change any longer. This is the sense of the revival of that "end of History" Alexandre Kojève thought he could find in Hegel and Marx, and which he took to mean some ultimate achievement of democratic equality (and the value equivalence of individual economic and juridical subjects) in both American capitalism and Soviet communism, only later identifying a significant variant of it in what he called Japanese "*snobisme*," but that we can today identify as postmodernity itself (the free play of masks and roles without content or substance). In another sense, of course, this is simply the old "end of ideology" with a vengeance, and cynically plays on the waning of collective hope in a particularly conservative market climate. But the end of History is also the final form of the temporal paradoxes we have tried to dramatize here: namely that a rhetoric of absolute change (or "permanent revolution" in some trendy and meretricious new sense) is, for the postmodern, no more satisfactory (but not less so) than the language of absolute identity and unchanging standardization cooked up by the great corporations, whose concept of innovation is best illustrated by the neologism and the logo and their equivalents in the realm of built space, "lifestyle," corporate culture, and psychic programming. The persistence of the Same through absolute Difference – the same street with different buildings, the same culture through momentous new sheddings of skin – discredits change, since henceforth the only conceivable radical change would consist in putting an end to change itself. But here the antinomy really does result in the blocking or paralysis of thought, since the impossibility of thinking another system except by way of the cancellation of this one ends up discrediting the Utopian imagination itself, which is fantasized [see chapter 22 of the present volume] as the loss of everything we know experientially, from our libidinal investments to our psychic habits, and in particular the artificial excitements of consumption and fashion.

Parmenidean stasis or Being to be sure knows at least one irrevocable event, namely death and the passage of the generations: insofar as the system of Parmenidean simulacrum or illusion is a very recent one, constituted in what we call postmodernity, the temporality of the generations in all their mortal discontinuity is not yet visible in results, except retroactively and as a materialist historiographic imperative. But death itself, as the very violence of absolute change, in the form of the nonimage – not even bodies rotting off stage but rather something persistent like an odor that circulates through the luminous immobility of this world without time – is inescapable and meaningless, since any historical framework that would serve to interpret and position individual deaths (at least for their survivors) has been destroyed. A kind of absolute violence then, the abstraction of violent death, is something like the dialectical correlative to this world without time or history.

But it is more appropriate to conclude this section with a remark about the relationship of this temporal paradox – absolute change equals stasis – to the dynamics of the new global system itself, for here too we can observe an effacement of the temporalities that seemed to govern an older period of modernity, of modernism and modernization alike. For in that older period, most Third World societies were torn by a penetration of Western moderni-zation that generated over against itself – in all the variety of cultural forms characteristic of those very different societies – a counterposition that could generally be described as traditionalism: the affirmation of a cultural (and sometimes religious) originality that had the power to resist assimilation by Western modernity and was indeed preferable to it. Such traditionalism was of course a construction in its own right, brought into being as it were, by the very activities of the modernizers themselves (in some more limited and specific sense than the one now, widely accepted, that all traditions and historical pasts are themselves necessarily invented and constructed). At any rate, what one wants to affirm today is that this second reactive or antimodern term of tradition and traditionalism has everywhere vanished from the reality of the former Third World or colonized societies; where a neotraditionalism (as in certain recent Chinese revivals of Confucianism, or in religious fundamental-isms) is now rather perceived as a deliberate political and collective choice, in a situation in which little remains of a past that must be completely reinvented.

This is to say that, on the one hand, nothing but the modern henceforth exists in Third World societies; but it is also to correct this statement, on the other, with the qualification that under such circumstances, where only the modern exists, "modern" must now be rebaptised postmodern (since what we call modern is the consequence of incomplete modernization and must neces-sarily define itself against a nonmodern residuality that no longer obtains in postmodernity as such – or rather, whose absence defines this last). Here too then, but on a social and historical level, the temporality that modernization promised (in its various capitalist and communist, productivist forms) has been eclipsed to the benefit of a new condition in which that older temporality no longer exists, leaving an appearance of random changes that are mere stasis, a disorder after the end of history. Meanwhile, it is as though what used to be characterized as the Third World has entered the interstices of the First one, as the latter also demodernizes and deindustrializes, lending the former colonial otherness something of the centered identity of the former metropolis.

With this extension of the temporal paradox on a global scale something else becomes clear as well, a kind of second paradox or antinomy that begins to make its presence felt behind and perhaps even within the first. Indeed, the repeated spatial characterizations of temporality here – from Proust to store-fronts, from urban change to global "development" – now begin to remind us that if it is so that postmodernity is characterized by some essential spatializa-tion, then everything we have here been trying to work out in terms of temporality will necessarily have passed through a spatial matrix to come to expression in the first place. If time has in effect been reduced to the most punctual violence and minimal irrevocable change of an abstract death, then we can perhaps affirm that in the postmodern time has become space anyhow. The foundational antinomy of postmodern description lies then in the fact that this former binary opposition, along with identity and difference themselves, no longer is an opposition as such, and ceaselessly reveals itself to have been at one with its other pole in a rather different way than the old dialectical projection back and forth, the classic dialectical metamorphosis. In order to see what this involves, we now necessarily turn to the other spatial antinomy, which appar-ently we have been rehearsing all along in its temporal version, with a view toward determining whether spatiality has any genuine thematic priority.

II

It is at least certain that the form by which one dimension of the antithesis necessarily expresses itself by way of the figurality of the other, time being required to express itself in spatial terms, is not repeated here; nor is the time–space antithesis symmetrical or reversible in this sense. Space does not seem to require a temporal expression; if it is not what absolutely does without such temporal figurality, then at the very least it might be said that space is what represses temporality and temporal figurality absolutely, to the benefit of other figures and codes. If Difference and Identity are at stake in both the temporal and the spatial antinomy, then the difference preeminent in considerations of space is not so much that of change in any temporal understanding of the form, as rather variety and infinity, metonymy, and – to reach some more influential and seemingly definitive and all-encompassing version – heterogeneity.

Historically, the adventures of homogeneous and heterogeneous space have most often been told in terms of the quotient of the sacred and of the folds in which it is unevenly invested: as for its alleged opposite number, the profane, however, one supposes that it is a projection backward in time of postsacred and commercial peoples to imagine that it was itself any single thing or quality (a nonquality, rather); a projection indeed to think that anything like a simple dualism of the profane and the sacred ever existed as such in the first place. For the sacred can be supposed to have meant heterogeneity and multiplicity in the first place: a nonvalue, an excess, something irreducible to system or to thought, to identity, to the degree to which it not merely explodes itself, but its opposite number, positing the spaces for normal village living alongside the chthonic garbage heaps of the *im-monde* (Lefebvre) but also the empty spaces of waste and desert, the sterile voids that punctuate so many naturally expressive landscapes. For by definition there must also have been as many types or kinds of the sacred as there were powers, and one must drain these words of their feeble archaic overtones before we realize that abstractions such as *sacred* or *power* have, in the face of the realities they were meant to designate, about the same expressive force as the abstraction *color* for the variety of intensities that absorb our gaze.

This also bears on the meaning of landscape, whose secular and painted modern version is a very recent development, as interpreters such as Deleuze or Karatani have so often reminded us. I hesitate to lapse into the fantasies of Romantics like Runge, with his languages of the plants; but they are certainly attractive fantasies, at least until they become socially stabilized in the form of kitsch (with its "language of flowers"). Such notions of a space that is somehow meaningfully organized and on the very point of speech, a kind of articulated thinking that fails to reach its ultimate translation in proposition or concepts, in messages, ultimately find their justification and theoretical defense in Lévi-Strauss's description, in *La Pensée sauvage*, of prephilosophical "perceptual science"; while their aesthetic reaches at least one kind of climax in the anthropologist's classic reading of the Pacific Northwest Coast Indian *Epic of Asdiwal*, where the various landscapes, from frozen inland wastes to the river and the coast itself, speak multiple languages (including those of the economic mode of production itself and of the kinship structure) and emit a remarkable range of articulated messages.

This kind of analysis effectively neutralizes the old opposition between the rational and the irrational (and all the satellite oppositions – primitive versus civilized, male versus female, West versus East – that are grounded on it) by locating the dynamics of meaning in texts that precede conceptual abstraction: a multiplicity of levels is thereby at once opened up that can no longer be assimilated to Weberian rationalization, instrumental thought, the reifications and repressions of the narrowly rational or conceptual. It is thereby to be characterized as heterogeneity; and we can go on to describe the sensory articulations of its object, in the mobile landscapes of *Asdiwal*, as heterogeneous space. As Derrida has famously shown, in one of the inaugural documents of what later comes to be called poststructuralism, Lévi-Strauss's analysis remains somehow centered around homologous meanings: it fails to reach the ultimately aleatory and undecideable; it persists in clinging for dear life to the very concept of meaning proper; and in a situation that ought to put an end to that concept, it does not even attain the openness of Bakhtinian polyphony or heteroglossia, since there is still a collective agency – the tribe – that speaks through its multiplicities.

But that then becomes the failure of Lévi-Strauss to reach true heterogeneity rather than the historical insufficiency of this latter concept as such, about which Bataille's whole life's work demonstrates that it exists in situation and is, like the surrealism from which it derived and that it repudiates, a strategic reaction against a modern state of things. This leads one to wonder whether heterogeneity can in fact mean anything suitably subversive until homogeneity has historically emerged, to confer upon it the value and the force of a specific oppositional tactic. What has to be described, therefore, is not so much the prestige of such forms of multiplicity and excess that overspill the rational modern mind and rebuke it, as rather their values as reactions against it whose projection into the past is at best a doubtful and suspicious matter. The prior object of description is rather the gradual colonization of the world by precisely that homogeneity that it was Bataille's historical mission (as of so many others) to challenge: its tendential conquests, the setting in place of forms of identity that only after the fact allow the anachronistic illusion of heterogeneity and difference to come to seem the logic of what they organized and flattened out.

That process, as far as space is concerned, can surely be identified with some precision: it is the moment in which a Western system of private property in real estate displaces the various systems of land tenure it confronts in the course of its successive enlargements (or, in the European situation itself, from which it gradually emerges for the first time in its own right). Nor does a language of violence – otherwise perfectly appropriate for these supercessions and still observable in course in settler colonies such as Israel and also in the various "transitions to capitalism" in Eastern Europe – convey the way in which the substitution of one legal system for another, more customary one is a matter of calculation and elaborate political strategy.[6] The violence was no doubt always implicit in the very conception of ownership as such when applied to the land; it is a peculiarly ambivalent mystery that mortal beings, generations of dying organisms, should have imagined they could somehow *own* parts of the earth in the first place. The older forms of land tenure (as well as the more recent socialist forms, equally varied from country to country) at least posited the collectivity as the immortal governor into whose stewardship portions of the soil are given over; nor has it ever been a simple or easy matter to undo these social relationships and replace them with the apparently more obvious and manageable ones based on individualized ownership and a juridical system of equivalent subjects – East Germany in this respect today rather resembles what the American North had to do to the conquered South after the Civil War; while the Israeli settlements often remind one of the brutal displacement of Native American societies in the West of the United States.

The point is, however, that where the thematic opposition of heterogeneity and homogeneity is invoked, it can only be this brutal process that is the ultimate referent: the effects that result from the power of commerce and then capitalism proper – which is to say, sheer number as such, number now shorn and divested of its own magical heterogeneities and reduced to equivalencies – to seize upon a landscape and flatten it out, reorganize it into a grid of identical parcels, and expose it to the dynamic of a market that now reorganizes space in terms of an identical value. The development of capitalism then distributes that value most unevenly indeed, until at length, in its postmodern moment, sheer speculation, as something like the triumph of spirit over matter, the liberation of the form of value from any of its former concrete or earthly content, now reigns supreme and devastates the very cities and countrysides it created in the process of its own earlier development. But all such later forms of abstract violence and homogeneity derive from the initial parcelization, which translates the money form and the logic of commodity production for a market back onto space itself.

Our own period also teaches us that the fundamental contradiction in this reorganization of space, which seeks to stamp out older and customary forms of collective land tenure (that then swim back into the modern historical imagination in the form of religious or anthropological conceptions of "the sacred" or of archaic heterogeneity), is to be identified as what we equally used to call agriculture itself, when that was associated with a peasantry or even yeoman farmers. In a postmodern global system, in which the tendency of a hitherto overwhelming peasant population to drop to some 7 or 8 percent of the nation can be observed everywhere in the modernizing fully as much as in the "advanced" countries, the relationship between peasant agriculture and traditional culture has become only too clear: the latter follows the former into extinction, and all the great precapitalist cultures prove to have been peasant ones, except where they were based on slavery. (Meanwhile, as for what has until today passed for a capitalist culture – a specifically capitalist "high culture," that is – it can also be identified as the way in which a bourgeoisie imitated and aped the traditions of its aristocratic feudal predecessors, tending also to be eclipsed along with their memory and to give way, along with the older classical bourgeois class consciousness itself, to mass culture – indeed to a specifically American mass culture at that.)

But the very possibility of a new globalization (the expansion of capital beyond its earlier limits in its second, or "imperialist," stage) depended on an agricultural reorganization (sometimes called the green revolution owing to its technological and specifically chemical and biological innovations) that effectively made peasants over into farm workers and great estates or latifundia (as well as village enclaves) over into agribusiness. Pierre-Philippe Rey has indeed suggested that we understand the relationship of modes of production to one another as one of imbrication or articulation, rather than as one of simple supercession: in this respect, he suggests the second or "modern" moment of capital – the stage of imperialism – retained an older precapitalist mode of production in agriculture and kept it intact, exploiting it in tributary fashion, deriving capital by extensive labor, inhuman hours and conditions, from essentially precapitalist relations. The new multinational stage of capital is then characterized by the sweeping away of such enclaves and their utter assimilation into capitalism itself, with its wage labor and working conditions: at this point, agriculture – culturally distinctive and identified in the superstructure as the Other of Nature – now becomes an industry like any other, and the peasants simple workers whose labor is classically commodified in terms of value equivalencies. This is not to say that commodification is evenly distributed over the entire globe or that all areas have been equally modernized or postmodernized; rather, that the tendency toward global commodification is far more visible and imaginable than it was in the modern period, in which tenacious premodern life realities still existed to impede the process. Capital, as Marx showed in the *Grundrisse*, necessarily tends toward the outer limit of a global market that is also its ultimate crisis situation (since no further expansion is then possible): this doctrine is for us today much less abstract than it was in the modern period; it designates a conceptual reality that neither theory nor culture can any longer postpone to some future agenda.

But to say so is to evoke the obliteration of difference on a world scale, and to convey a vision of the irrevocable triumph of spatial homogeneity over whatever heterogeneities might still have been fantasized in terms of global space. I want to stress this as an ideological development, which includes all the ecological fears awakened in our own period (pollution and its accompaniments also standing as a mark of universal commodification and commercialization): for in this situation ideology is not false consciousness but itself a possibility of knowledge, and our constitutive difficulties in imagining a world beyond global standardization are very precisely indices and themselves features of just that standardized reality or being itself.

Such ideological limits, invested with a certain affective terror as a kind of dystopia, are then compensated by other ideological possibilities that come into view when we no longer take the countryside as our vantage point but rather the city and the urban itself. This is of course already an opposition that has left significant traces in the science-fictional or Utopian tradition: the antithesis between a pastoral Utopia and an urban one, and in particular the apparent supercession in the last years of images of a village or tribal Utopia (Ursula Le Guin's *Always Coming Home* of 1985 was virtually the last of those) by visions of an unimaginably dense urban reality (therein nonetheless somehow imagined) that is either explicitly placed on the Utopian agenda, as in Samuel Delany's *Triton* (1976) (or Raymond Williams' prescient forecast that socialism, if it is possible, will not be simpler than all this but far more complicated) or by masquerades under a dystopian appearance whose deeper libidinal excitement, however, is surely profoundly Utopian in spirit (as in most current cyberpunk).

Once again, however, we have to do with the conceptual difficulties in which we are plunged by the disappearance of one of the terms of a formerly functioning binary opposition. The disappearance of Nature – the commodi-fication of the countryside and the capitalization of agriculture itself all over the world – now begins to sap its other term, the formerly urban. Where the world system today tends toward one enormous urban system – tendentially ever more complete modernization promised that, which has however been ratified and delivered in an unexpected way by the communications revolution and its new technologies: a development of which the immediately physical visions, nightmares of the "sprawl" from Boston to Richmond, or the Japanese urban agglomeration, are the merest allegories – the very conception of the city itself and the classically urban loses its significance and no longer seems to offer any precisely delimited objects of study, any specifically differentiated realities. Rather, the urban becomes the social in general, and both of them constitute and lose themselves in a global that is not really their opposite either (as it was in the older dispensation) but something like their outer reach, their prolongation into a new kind of infinity.

Ideologically, what this dissolution of the boundaries of the traditional city and the classically urban enables is a slippage, a displacement, a reinvestment of older urban ideological and libidinal connotations under new conditions. The city always seemed to promise freedom, as in the medieval conception of the urban as the space of escape from the land and from feudal labor and serfdom, from the arbitrary power of the lord: "city air" from this perspective now becomes the very opposite of what Marx famously characterized as "rural idiocy," the narrowness of village manners and customs, the provinciality of the rural, with its fixed ideas and superstitions and its hatred of difference. Here, in contrast to the dreary sameness of the countryside (which is also, however inaccurately, fantasized as a place of sexual repression), the urban classically promised variety and adventure, often linked to crime just as the accompanying visions of pleasure and sexual gratification are inseparable from transgression and illegality.

What happens, then, when even that countryside, even that essentially provincial reality, disappears, becomes standardized, hears the same English, sees the same programs, consumes the same consumer goods, as the former metropolis to which, in the old days, these same provincials and country people longed to go as to a fundamental liberation? I think that the missing second term – provincial boredom, rural idiocy – was preserved, but simply transferred to a different kind of city and a different kind of social reality, namely the Second World city and the social realities of a nonmarket or planned economy. Everyone remembers the overwhelming power of such Cold War iconography, which has perhaps proved even more effective today, after the end of the Cold War and in the thick of the current offensive of market propaganda and rhetoric, than it was in a situation of struggle where visions of terror were more quintessentially operative. Today, however, it is the memory of the imagined drabness of the classic Second World city – with its meager shelves of consumer goods in empty centrals from which the points of light of advertising are absent, streets from which small stores and shops are missing, standardization of clothing fashions (as most emblematically in Maoist China) – that remains ideologically operative in the campaigns for privatization. Jane Jacobs's fundamental identification of a genuine urban fabric and street life with small business is ceaselessly rehearsed ideologically, without any reminder that she thought the diagnosis applied fully as much to the North American or capitalist city in which corporations have equally, but in a different fashion, driven small business out of existence, and created canyons of institutional high-rises without any urban personality at all.

This urban degradation, which characterizes the First World, has, however, been transferred to a separate ideological compartment called postmodernism, where it duly takes its place in the arsenal of attacks on modern architecture and its ideals. As for the Second World city, its vision is rather enlisted in the service of a rather different operation, namely to serve as the visual and experiential *analogon* of a world utterly programmed and directed by human intention, a world therefore from which the contingencies of chance – and thereby the promise of adventure and real life, of libidinal gratification – are also excluded. Conscious intention, the "plan," collective control, are then fantasized as being at one with repression and renunciation, with instinctual impoverishment: and as in the related postmodern polemic, the absence of ornament from the

Second World city – as it were the involuntary enactment of Adolf Loos's program – serves as a grim caricature of the puritanical Utopian values of a revolutionary society (just as it had served as that of the equally puritanical Utopian values of high modernism in the other campaign that in certain recent theory in the Eastern countries – in particular Groys' *Gesamtkunstwerk Stalin* – is explicitly linked to this one in an instructive and revealing way).

Only the spatial features of this particular ideological tactic are new: Edmund Burke was of course the first to develop the great antirevolutionary figure, according to which what people consciously and collectively do can only be destructive and a sign of fatal hubris: that only the slow "natural" growth of traditions and institutions can be trusted to form a genuinely human world (a deep suspicion of the will and of unconscious intention that then passes over into a certain Romantic tradition in aesthetics). But Burke's pathbreaking attack on the Jacobins aimed at the middle-class construction and formation of market society itself, about whose commercialism it essentially expressed the fears and anxieties of an older social formation in the process of being superceded. The market people today, however, marshall the same fantasies in defense of a market society now supposed itself to be somehow "natural" and deeply rooted in human nature; they do so against the Promethean efforts of human beings to take collective production into their own hands and, by planning, to control or at least to influence and inflect their own future (something that no longer seems particularly meaningful in a postmodernity in which the very experience of the future as such has come to seem enfeebled, if not deficient).

But this is precisely the ideological and imaginary background against which it is possible to market and to sell the contemporary capitalist city as a well-nigh Bakhtinian carnival of heterogeneities, of differences, libidinal excitement, and a hyperindividuality that effectively decenters the old individual subject by way of individual hyperconsumption. Now the associations or connotations of provincial misery and renunciation, of petty bourgeois impoverishment, of cultural and libidinal immiseration, systematically reinvested in our images of the urban space of the Second World, are pressed into service as arguments against socialism and planning, against collective ownership and what is fantasized as centralization, at the same time that they serve as powerful stimuli to the peoples of Eastern Europe to plunge into the freedoms of Western consumption. This is no small ideological achievement in view of the difficulties, a priori, in staging the collective control over their destinies by social groups in a negative way and investing those forms of autonomy with all the fears and anxieties, the loathing and libidinal dread, which Freud called counterinvestment or anticathexis and that must constitute the central effect of any successful anti-Utopianism.

This is then also the point at which everything most paradoxical about the spatial form of the antinomy under discussion here becomes vivid and inescapable; our conceptual exhibit comes more sharply into view when we begin to ask ourselves how it is possible for the most standardized and uniform social reality in history, by the merest ideological flick of the thumbnail, the most imperceptible of displacements, to reemerge as the rich oil-smear sheen of absolute diversity and of the most unimaginable and unclassifiable forms of human freedom. Here homogeneity has become heterogeneity, in a movement complementary to that in which absolute change turned into absolute stasis, and without the slightest modification of a real history that there was thought to be at an end, while here it has seemed finally to realize itself. [. . .]

Notes

1 Paul Virilio, *War and Cinema* (London, Verso, 1989), pp. 59–60.
2 Marcel Proust, *A La recherche du temps perdu*, vol. 1 (Paris, Bibliotheque de la Pléïade, 1987), p. 36.
3 Manfredo Tafuri, *Architecture and Utopia* (Cambridge, Mass., MIT Press, 1976), p. 70.
4 Ibid.
5 Ibid., p. 62.
6 See Ranajit Guha, *A Rule of Property for Bengal* (Paris and The Hague, Mouton, 1963).

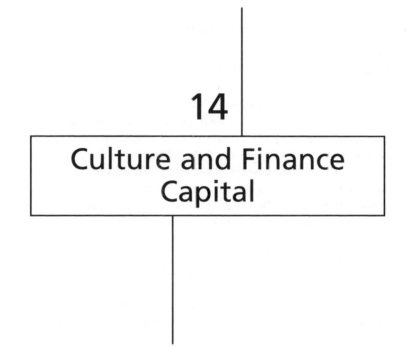

14

Culture and Finance Capital

This chapter was originally published in *Critical Inquiry* in 1997.

Giovanni Arrighi's *The Long Twentieth Century* is remarkable for, among many other things, producing a problem we did not know we had, in the very process of crystallizing a solution to it: the problem of finance capital.[1] No doubt it swarmed around our heads in the form of vague perplexities, quizzicalities that we never paused long enough over to form into real questions: Why monetarism? Why is investment and the stock market getting more attention than an industrial production that seems on the point of disappearing anyway? How can you have profit without production in the first place? Where does all this excessive speculation come from? Does the new form of the city (including postmodern architecture) have anything to do with a mutation in the very dynamic of land values (ground rent)? Why should land speculation and the stock market come to the fore as dominant sectors in advanced societies, where *advanced* certainly has something to do with technology but presumably ought to have something to do with production as well? All of these nagging questions were also secret doubts about the Marxian model of production, as well as about the turn of history in the 1980s, stimulated by the Reaganite/Thatcherite tax cuts. We seemed to be returning to the most fundamental form of class struggle, one so basic that it spelled the end of all those Western Marxist and theoretical subtleties that the Cold War had called forth. During the long period of the Cold War and of Western Marxism − a period one really needs to date from 1917 – a complex analysis of ideology needed to be developed in order to unmask the persistent substitutions of incommensurate dimensions, the passing off of political arguments in the place of economic ones, and the appeal to alleged traditions: freedom and democracy, God, Manichaeism, the values of the West and of the Judeo-Christian or Roman-Christian heritage as answers to new and unpredictable social experiments. This analysis was also needed to accommodate the new conceptions of the operation of the unconscious dis-covered by Freud and presumably at work in the layering of social ideology. In those days the theory of ideology constituted the better mousetrap. Every self-respecting theorist felt the obligation to invent a new one, only to be met with ephemeral acclaim by curious spectators always ready to move on to the next model at a moment's notice, even when that next model meant revamping the very name of ideology itself and substituting episteme, metaphysics, practices, or whatever.

But today many of these complexities seem to have disappeared, and faced with the Reagan–Kemp and Thatcher utopias of immense investments and increases in production to come, based on deregulation, privatization, and the obligatory opening of markets, we sense that the problems of ideological analysis are enormously simplified, and the ideologies themselves far more transparent. Now that, following master thinkers like Hayek, it has become customary to identify political freedom with market freedom, the motivations behind ideology no longer seem to need an elaborate machinery of decoding and hermeneutic reinterpretation; and the guiding thread of all contemporary politics seems much easier to grasp, namely, that the rich want their taxes lowered. This means that an older vulgar Marxism may once again be more relevant to our situation than the newer models; but we also face more objective problems about money itself, which had seemed less relevant in the cold war period.

The rich were certainly doing something with all this new income that no longer needed to be wasted on social services; rather than go into new factories, it seemed to get invested in the stock market. Whence a second perplexity: The Soviets used to joke about the miracle of their system, whose edifice seemed comparable only to those houses kept standing by the swarm of termites eating away inside them. But some of us had the same feeling about the United States. After the disappearance (or brutal downsizing) of heavy industry, the only thing that seemed to keep it going (besides the two prodigious American industries of food and entertainment) was the stock market. How was this possible, and where did the money keep coming from? And if money itself rested on so fragile a basis, why did "fiscal responsibility" matter so much in the first place, and on what was the very logic of monetarism itself grounded?

The dawning suspicion that we were in a new period of finance capitalism was not given much theoretical encouragement or nourishment by the tradition. One old book, Rudolf Hilferding's *Finance Capital* of 1910, seemed to give a historical analysis of an economic and a structural situation: the techniques of the great German trusts of the pre-World War I period and their relations with the banks and eventually the *Flottenbau* required the concept of monopoly, which Lenin appropriated in this sense for his 1916 pamphlet *Imperialism: The Highest Stage of Capitalism*.[2] It too seemed to do away with finance capital by changing its name and displacing it onto the power relations and competition between the great capitalist states. But these "highest stages" now lie well in our own past; imperialism is gone, replaced by neocolonialism and globalization; the great international financial centers do not (yet) seem the locus of ferocious competition among the nations of the capitalist First World, despite a few complaints about the Bundesbank and its interest policies; imperial Germany meanwhile has been replaced by a Federal Republic that may or may not be more powerful than its predecessor but that is now part of an allegedly united Europe. So these historical descriptions do not seem to do us much good, and here the teleological ("highest stage") does seem fully to merit all the opprobrium called down upon it in recent years.

But where the economist could only give us empirical history, it remained for a historical narrative to give us the structural and economic theory we needed to solve this conundrum. Finance capital has to be something like a stage in the way it distinguishes itself from other moments of the development of capitalism. Arrighi's luminous insight was that this peculiar kind of telos need not lie in a straight line but might well organize itself in a spiral (a figure that also avoids the mythical overtones of the various cyclical visions).

It is a picture that unites various traditional requirements. Capitalism's movement must be seen as discontinuous but expansive. With each crisis, it mutates into a larger sphere of activity and a wider field of penetration, of control, investment, and transformation. This doctrine, most forcefully argued by Ernest Mandel in his great book *Late Capitalism*, has the merit of accounting for capitalism's resiliency,[3] which Marx himself already posited in the *Grundrisse* (but which is less evident in *Capital* itself) and which has repeatedly unsettled left prognostications (immediately after World War II and then again in the 1980s and 1990s). But the objection to Mandel's positions has turned on the latent teleology of his slogan *late capitalism*, as though this were the last stage conceivable, or as though the process were some uniform historical progression. (My own use of the term is meant as a homage to Mandel and not particularly as a prophetic forecast; Lenin does say "highest," as we have seen, while Hilferding, more prudently, simply calls it the "jüngste," the latest or most recent, which is obviously preferable.)

The cyclical scheme now allows us to coordinate these features. If we position discontinuity not only in time but also in space, and if we add back in the historian's perspective, which clearly enough needs to reckon with the national situations and the uniquely idiosyncratic developments within the national states, let alone within the greater regional groupings (Third versus First Worlds, for example), then the local teleologies of the capitalist process can be reconciled with its own spasmodic historical developments and mutations as they leap from geographical space to space.

Thus, the system is better seen as a kind of virus (not Arrighi's figure), and its development is something like an epidemic (better still, a rash of epidemics, an epidemic of epidemics). The system has its own logic, which powerfully undermines and destroys the logic of more traditional or precapitalist societies and economies. Deleuze and Guattari call this an axiomatic, as opposed to the older precapitalist, tribal, or imperial codes.[4] But epidemics also play themselves out, like a fire for want of oxygen; and they also leap to new and more propitious settings, in which the preconditions are favorable to renewed development. (I hasten to add that Arrighi's complex political and economic articulation of these paradoxical turns, whereby winners lose and losers sometimes win, is far more dialectical than my figures suggest.)

Thus, in the new scheme of The Long Twentieth Century, capitalism has known any number of false starts and fresh starts, on an ever larger scale. Bookkeeping in Renaissance Italy, the nascent commerce of the great city-states: these phenomena and others evidently occurred in a petri dish of modest proportions, which does not allow the new thing much in the way of scope but which offers a still relatively restricted and sheltered environment. The political form, here, the city-state itself, stands as an obstacle and a limit to development, although this observation should not be extrapolated into a thesis about the way in which form (the political) restricts content (the economic). Then the process that is capitalism leaps over into Spain, where Arrighi's great insight lies in the analysis of this leap as an essentially symbiotic moment. We knew that Spain had an earlier form of capitalism, of course, which was disastrously undermined by the conquest of the New World and the fleets of silver. But Arrighi stresses the way in which Spanish capitalism is to be understood in close functional and symbiotic relationship to Genoa, which financed the empire and which was thus a full participant in the new moment. It is a kind of dialectical link to the earlier Italian city-state moment, which will not be reproduced in the later discontinuous history, unless one is also willing to posit a kind of propagation by rivalry and negation, that is, the way in which the enemy is led to take on your own development, to match it, to succeed where you fell short.

Such is the next moment, the leap to Holland and the Dutch, to a system more resolutely based on the commercialization of the ocean and the waterways. After that, the story becomes more familiar; the limits of the Dutch system pave the way for a more successful English development along the same lines. The United States becomes the center of capitalist development in the twentieth century, and Arrighi, fraught with doubts, leaves a question mark about the capacity of Japan to constitute yet another cycle and another stage, to replace an American "empire" in full internal contradiction (the word is not strictly appropriate, according to Wallerstein). At this point, perhaps, Arrighi's model is no longer useful, and the complex realities of contemporary globalization may now demand something else, of a wholly different synchronic mode.

Yet we have not come to the most exciting feature of Arrighi's history, namely, the internal stages of the cycle itself, the way in which capitalist development in each of these moments replicates itself and reproduces a series of three moments (this may be taken to be the local teleological content of his new "universal history"). These are modeled on the famous formula of *Capital*: M–C–M', in which money is transformed into capital, which then generates supplementary money, in an expanding dialectic of accumulation. The first phase of the tripartite process has to do with trade, which, in one way or another, and often by way of the violence and brutality of primitive accumulation, brings into being a quantity of money for eventual capitalization. In the second classic moment, then, that money becomes capital and is invested in agriculture and manufacture. It is territorialized and transforms its associated area into a center of production. But this second stage knows internal limits, which weigh on production, distribution, and consumption alike. They are worked by a falling rate of profit endemic to the second stage in general: "profits are still high, but *it is a condition for their maintenance that they should not be invested in further expansion.*"[5]

At this point, the third stage begins, which is the moment that primarily interests us here. Arrighi's treatment of this – the recurrent moment of a cyclical finance capitalism – is inspired by Braudel's remark that "the stage of financial expansion" is always "*a sign of autumn.*"[6] Speculation – the withdrawal of profits from the home industries, the increasingly feverish search, not so much for new markets (those are also saturated) as for the new kind of profits available in financial transactions themselves and as such – is the way in which capitalism now reacts to and compensates for the closing of its productive moment. Capital itself becomes free-floating. It separates from the concrete context of its productive geography. Money becomes in a second sense and to a second degree abstract (it always was abstract in the first and basic sense), as though somehow in the national moment money still had a content. It was cotton money, or wheat money, textile money, railroad money, and the like. Now, like the butterfly stirring within the chrysalis, it separates itself from that concrete breeding ground and prepares to take flight. We know today only too well (but Arrighi shows us that this contemporary knowledge of ours only replicates the bitter experience of the dead, of disemployed workers in the older moments of capitalism, of local merchants and dying cities as well) that the term is literal. We know that there exists such a thing as capital flight: the disinvestment, the pondered or hasty moving on to the greener pastures of higher rates of investment return and cheaper labor. This free-floating capital, in its frantic search for more profitable investments (a process prophetically described for the US as long ago as Paul Baran and Paul Sweezy's *Monopoly Capital* of 1966),[7] will begin to live its life in a new context: no longer in the factories and the spaces of extraction and production, but on the floor of the stock market, jostling for more intense profitability. But it won't be as one industry competing with another branch, nor even one productive technology against another more advanced one in the same line of manufacturing, but rather in the form of speculation itself: specters of value, as Derrida might put it, vying against each other in a vast, world-wide, disembodied phantasmagoria.[8] This is of course the moment of finance capital as such, and it now becomes clear how, according to Arrighi's extraordinary analysis, finance capital is not only a kind of "highest stage" but the highest and last stage of every moment of capital itself. During its cycles capital exhausts its returns in the new national and international capitalist zone and seeks to die and be reborn in some "higher" incarnation, a vaster and immeasurably more productive one, in which it is fated to live through again the three fundamental stages: its implantation, its productive development, and its financial or speculative final stage.

All of which, as I suggested above, might be dramatically heightened, for our own period, by a reminder of the results of the cybernetic "revolution," the intensification of communications technology to the point at which capital transfers today abolish space and time, virtually instantaneously effectuated across national spaces. The results of these lightninglike movements of immense quantities of money around the globe are incalculable, yet already they have clearly produced new kinds of political blockage and also new and unrepresentable symptoms in late-capitalist everyday life.

For the problem of abstraction – of which this one of finance capital is a part – must also be grasped in its cultural expressions. Real abstractions in an older period – the effects of money and number in the big cities of nineteenth-century industrial capitalism, the very phenomena analyzed by Hilferding and culturally diagnosed by Georg Simmel in his pathbreaking essay "The Metropolis and Mental Life"[9] – had as one significant offshoot the emergence of what we call modernism in all the arts. In this sense, modernism faithfully – even "realistically" – reproduced and represented the increasing abstraction and deterritorialization of Lenin's "imperialist stage." Today, what is called postmodernity articulates the symptomatology of yet another stage of abstraction, qualitatively and structurally distinct from the previous one, which I have drawn on Arrighi to characterize as our own moment of finance capitalism: the finance capital moment of globalized society, the abstractions brought with it by cybernetic technology (which it is a misnomer to call postindustrial except as a way of distinguishing its dynamic from the older, "productive" moment). Thus any comprehensive new theory of finance capitalism will need to reach out into the expanded realm of cultural production to map its effects; indeed, mass cultural production and consumption itself – at one with globalization and the new information technology – are as profoundly economic as the other productive areas of late capitalism and as fully a part of the latter's generalized commodity system.

Now I want to speculate on the potential uses of this new theory for cultural and literary interpretation, and in particular for the understanding of the historical or structural sequence of realism, modernism, and postmodernism, which has interested many of us in recent years. For better or for worse, only the first of these – realism – has been the object of much serious attention and analysis in the Marxist tradition, the attacks on modernism being on the whole largely negative and contrastive, although not without their occasional local suggestivity (particularly in the work of Lukács). I want to show how Arrighi's work now puts us in a position to frame a better and more global theory of these three cultural stages or moments, it being understood that the analysis will be staged on the level of the mode of production (or in brief, that of the economic) rather than on social classes, a level of interpretation which I argued in *The Political Unconscious* we need to separate from the economic frame in order to avoid category mistakes.[10] Arrighi's work gives us new themes and materials to work with in this area; and it is worth vulgarizing that work by suggesting that it offers us a new, or perhaps we should simply say a more complex and satisfying, account of the role of money in these processes.

Indeed, the classical political thinkers of the period, from Hobbes to Locke and including those of the Scottish Enlightenment, all identified money far more clearly than we do as the central novelty, the central mystery, at the heart of the transition to modernity, taken in its largest sense as capitalist society (and not merely in narrower cultural terms). In his classic work, C. B. MacPherson has shown how Locke's vision of history turns on the transition to a money economy, while the ambiguous richness of Locke's ideological solution was predicated on the positioning of money in both places, in the modernity that follows the social contract of civilized society, but also in the state of nature itself. Money, MacPherson demonstrates, is what allows Locke his extraordinary dual and superimposed systems, of nature and of history, of equality and of class conflict at the same time, or, if you prefer, the peculiar nature of money is what allows Locke to operate simultaneously as a philosopher of human nature and as a historical analyst of social and economic change.[11]

Money has continued to play this kind of role in the traditions of a Marxian analysis of culture, where it is less often a purely economic category than a social one. In other words, Marxist literary criticism – to limit ourselves to that – has less often tried to analyze its objects in terms of capital and value, in terms of the system of capitalism itself, than it has in terms of class, and most often of one class in particular, namely, the bourgeoisie. This is obviously something of a paradox. One would have expected an engagement of the literary critics with the very center of Marx's work, the structural account of the historic originality of capitalism, but such efforts seem to have involved too many mediations (no doubt in the spirit in which Oscar Wilde complained that socialism required too many evenings). It was thus much simpler to establish the more direct mediation of a merchant and business class, with its emergent class culture, and the forms and texts themselves. Money enters the picture here only insofar as exchange, merchant activity and the like, and, later on, nascent capitalism determine the coming into being of some historically original burgher or city merchant, and, more generally, bourgeois class life. (Meanwhile, the aesthetic dilemmas of modern times are for Marxism almost exclusively linked to the problem of imagining some equivalent and parallel class culture and art for that other emergent group, the industrial working class.)

This means that Marxian cultural theory has almost exclusively turned on the question of realism, insofar as that is associated with a bourgeois class culture. And for the most part (with some famous and signal exceptions) the analyses of modernism have taken a negative and critical form: how and why does the latter deviate from the realistic path? (It is true that in the hands of Lukács this kind of question can produce enlightening and sometimes significant results.) At any rate, I would briefly illustrate this traditional Marxian focus on realism by way of Arnold Hauser's *The Social History of Art*.[12] I refer, for example, to the moment in which Hauser notes the naturalistic tendencies in the Egyptian art of the Middle Kingdom at the moment of Ikhnaton's abortive revolution. These tendencies stand out sharply against the hieratic tradition so familiar to us and therefore suggest the influence of new factors. Indeed, if one persists in a much older anthropological and philosophical tradition for which religion determines the spirit of a given society, Ikhnaton's abortive attempt to substitute mono-theism would probably be explanation enough. Hauser rightly feels that the religious determination requires a further social determination in its turn, and unsurprisingly he proposes a heightened influence of commerce and money on social life and on the emergence of new kinds of social relations. But there is a hidden mediation here, which Hauser does not articulate: the matter of the history of perception as such and the emergence of new kinds of perceptions.

Herein lies the unorthodox kernel of these orthodox explanations, for it is tacitly assumed that with the emergence of exchange value a new interest in the physical properties of objects comes into being. Their equivalence by way of the money form (which in standard Marxian economics is grasped as the supercession of concrete use and function by an essentially idealistic and abstract fetishism of commodities) here rather leads to a more realistic interest in the body of the world and in the new and more lively human relationships developed by trade. The merchants and their consumers need to take a keener interest in the sensory nature of their wares as well as in the psychological and characterological traits of their interlocutors. These new interests develop new kinds of perceptions, both physical and social – new kinds of seeing, new types of behavior – and in the long run create the conditions in which more realistic art forms are not only possible but desirable, and encouraged by their new publics.

It is an epochal explanation or account, which will not be satisfying for anyone seeking to scrutinize the individual text. The proposition is also subject to radical and unexpected dialectical reversals in the later stages. Above all, except for the obviously suggestive implications for plot and character, the relevance of the account for language itself is less clear. It would be abusive to assimilate the one great theoretician of the relations between realism and language, Erich Auerbach, to this schema, even though a notion of expanding social democratization tactfully underpins his work and informs an insistence on the transfer of popular language to writing, which is however by no means his central emphasis. This is no Wordsworthian emphasis on plain speech and speakers but rather, I would like to suggest, an immense *Bildungsroman* whose protagonist is Syntax itself, as it develops throughout the Western European languages. He does not cite Mallarmé: "*Quel pivot, j'entends, dans ces contrastes, à l'intelligibilité? Il faut une garantie – La Syntaxe –.*"[13] Yet the adventures of syntax down the ages, from Homer to Proust are the deeper narrative of *Mimesis:* the gradual unlimbering of hierarchical sentence structure, and the differential evolution of the incidental clauses of the new sentence in such a way that each can now register a hitherto unperceived local complexity of the Real. This is the great narrative and teleological thread of Auerbach's history, whose multiple determinants remain to be worked out but clearly include many of the social features already mentioned.[14]

It should also be noted that in both these theories of realism the new artistic and perceptual categories are grasped as being absolutely and fundamentally linked to modernity (if not yet modernism, of which however realism can be seen here as a kind of first stage). They also include the great modernist topos of the break and the Novum, for whether it is with the older hieratic conventions of a formulaic art, or the cumbersome inherited syntax of a previous literary period, both insist on the necessarily subversive and critical, destructive, character of their realisms, which must clear away a useless and jumbled monumentality in order to develop their new experimental instruments and laboratories.

This is the point at which, without false modesty, I want to register the two contributions I have felt able to make to some as yet unformulated and properly Marxian theory of modernism. The first of these proposes a dialectical theory of the paradox we have just encountered, namely, realism as modernism, or a realism that is so fundamentally a part of modernity that it demands description in some of the ways we have traditionally reserved for modernism itself: the break, the Novum, the emergence of new perceptions, and the like. What I proposed was to see these historically distinct and seemingly incompatible modes of realism and modernism as so many stages in a dialectic of reification, which seizes on the properties and the subjectivities, the institutions and the forms of an older precapitalist lifeworld in order to strip them of their hierarchical or religious content. Realism and secularization are a first Enlightenment moment in that process; it is dialectical when it leaps and turns from quantity to quality. With the intensification of the forces of reification, their suffusion through ever greater zones of social life (including individual subjectivity), it is as though the force that generated the first realism now turns against it and devours it in its turn. The ideological and social preconditions of realism – its naïve belief in a stable social reality, for example – are now themselves unmasked, demystified, and discredited; and modernist forms – generated by the very same pressure of reification – take their place. And, in this narrative, the supercession of modernism by the postmodern is, predictably enough, read in the same way as a further intensification of the forces of reification, which has utterly unexpected and dialectical results for the now hegemonic modernisms themselves.

As for my other contribution, it posited a specific formal process in the modern that seemed to me much less significantly influential in either realism or postmodernism but that can be linked dialectically to both. For this "theory" of modernist formal processes I wanted to follow Lukács (and others) in seeing modernist reification in terms of analysis, decomposition, and, above all, internal differentiation. Thus, in the course of hypothesizing modernism in various contexts, I found it interesting and productive to see this particular process in terms of autonomization: what were formerly parts of a whole become independent and self-sufficient. It is something that can be observed in the chapters and their subepisodes in *Ulysses*, and also in the Proustian sentence. I wanted to establish a kinship here, not so much with the sciences (as is customarily done when people talk about the sources of modernity), but with the labor process itself. And here the great phenomenon of Taylorization (contemporaneous with modernism) slowly imposes itself: a division of labor (theorized as long ago as Adam Smith) now becoming a method of mass production in its own right by way of the separation of different stages and their reorganization around principles of efficiency (to use the ideological word for it). Harry Braverman's classic *Labor and Monopoly Capital* remains the cornerstone of any approach to that labor process and seems to me full of suggestions for the cultural and structural analysis of modernism as such.[15]

But now, in the period some people like to call post-Fordist, this particular logic no longer seems to obtain; just as in the cultural sphere, forms of abstraction that in the modern period seemed ugly, dissonant, scandalous, indecent, or repulsive have also entered the mainstream of cultural consumption (in the largest sense, from advertising to commodity styling, from visual decoration to artistic production) and no longer shock anyone. Our entire system of commodity production and consumption today is based on those older, once antisocial modernist forms. Nor does the conventional notion of abstraction seem very appropriate in the postmodern context; and yet, as Arrighi teaches us, nothing is quite so abstract and deterritorialized as the finance capital that underpins and sustains postmodernity as such.

At the same time, it also seems clear that if autonomization characterizes the modern, it is still very much with us in postmodernity. The Europeans were the first, for example, to be struck by the rapidity of the editing and the sequence of shots that characterized classical American film. It is a process that has everywhere intensified in television editing, where an advertisement lasting only half a minute can today include an extraordinary number of distinct shots or images without in the least provoking the modernist estrangement and bewilderment of the work of a great modernist independent filmmaker like Stan Brakhage. So a process and a logic of extreme fragmentation still seems to obtain here but without any of its earlier effects. Is one then to imagine, with Deleuze and Guattari, that we here confront a recording of hitherto decoded or axiomatic materials, something they posit as an operation inseparable from late capitalism, whose intolerable axiomatics are everywhere locally turned back into private gardens, private religions, vestiges of older or even archaic local coding systems? It is however an interpretation that raises embarrassing questions. In particular, how different is this opposition that Deleuze and Guattari develop between the axiomatic and the code from classical existentialism – the loss of meaning everywhere in the modern world, followed by the attempt locally to reendow it, either by regressing to religion or making an absolute out of the private and the contingent?

What also militates against the concept of recoding is that it is not a local but a general process; the languages of postmodernity are universal, in the sense in which they are media languages. They are thus very different from the solitary

obsessions and private thematic hobbies of the great moderns, which achieved
their universalization, indeed their very socialization, only through a process of
collective commentary and canonization. Unless entertainment and visual
consumption are to be thought of as essentially religious practices, then, the
notion of recoding seems to lose its force here. Put another (more existential)
way, it can be said that the scandal of the death of God and the end of religion
and metaphysics placed the moderns in a situation of anxiety and crisis, which
now seems to have been fully absorbed by a more fully humanized and
socialized, "culturalized" society. Its voids have been saturated and neutralized,
not by new values, but by the visual culture of consumerism as such. So the
anxieties of the absurd, to take only one example, are themselves recaptured
and recontained by a new and postmodern cultural logic, which offers them for
consumption fully as much as its other seemingly more anodyne exhibits.

It is thus to this new break that we must turn our attention, and it is in its
theorization that Arrighi's analysis of finance capitalism makes a signal contribution, which I first propose to examine in terms of the category of abstraction itself and in particular of the peculiar form of abstraction that is money.
Worringer's pathbreaking essay on abstraction linked it to distinct cultural
impulses and concluded that it finally drew its force from the intensifying
assimilation of more ancient and nonfigurative visual materials into the West's
"imaginary museum," which he associates with a kind of death drive. But the
crucial intervention for our purposes is Simmel's "The Metropolis and Mental
Life," in which the processes of the new industrial city, very much including
the abstract flows of money, determine a whole new and more abstract way of
thinking and perceiving, radically different from the object world of the older
merchant cities and countryside. What is at stake here is a dialectical transformation of the effects of exchange value and monetary equivalence; if the latter
had once announced and provoked a new interest in the properties of objects,
now in this new stage equivalence has as its result a withdrawal from older
notions of stable substances and their unifying identifications. Thus, if all these
objects have become equivalent as commodities, if money has leveled their
intrinsic differences as individual things, one may now purchase as it were their
various, henceforth semiautonomous qualities or perceptual features; and both
color and shape free themselves from their former vehicles and come to live
independent existences as fields of perception and as artistic raw materials. This
is then a first stage, but only a first one, in the onset of an abstraction that
becomes identified as aesthetic modernism but that in hindsight should be
limited to the historical period of the second stage of capitalist industrialization
– that of oil and electricity, the combustion engine and the new velocities and
technologies of the motorcar, the steamship and the flying machine – in the
decades immediately preceding and following the turn of the century.

But before continuing this dialectical narrative, we need to return to Arrighi for a moment. We have already spoken of the imaginative way in which Arrighi exfoliates Marx's famous formula M-C-M' into a supple and cyclical historical narrative. Marx began, as will be remembered, with an inversion of another formula C-M-C, which characterizes commerce as such: "the simple circulation of commodities begins with a sale and ends with a purchase."[16] The merchant sells a commodity and with the money received buys another commodity: "the whole process begins when money is received in return for commodities, and comes to an end when money is given up in return for commodities."[17] It is not, as one can readily imagine, a very profitable trajectory, except in those instances between trading regions in which very special commodities such as salt or spice can be transformed into money as exceptions to the general law of equivalence. Besides this, as has already been said, the centrality of the physical commodities themselves determines a kind of perceptual attention, along with the philosophical categories of the substance, that can only lead to a more realistic aesthetic.

It is however the other formula that interests us, M-C-M', which will be the dialectical space in which commerce (or if you prefer, merchant capital) is transformed into capital tout court. I abridge Marx's explanation (in chapter 4 of the first volume of *Capital*) and merely observe the gradual imposition of the prime on the second M: the moment in which the focus of the operation is no longer on the commodity but on money, and in which its impulse now lies in the investment of money in commodity production, not for its own sake, but to increase the return of M, now M'. In other words, riches transform into capital itself; this is the autonomization of the process of capital accumulation, which asserts its own logic over that of the production and consumption of goods as such, as well as over the individual entrepreneur and the individual worker.

Now I want to introduce a Deleuzian neologism (this time very relevant and his most famous and successful, I believe), which seems to me dramatically to enhance our sense of what is at stake in this momentous transformation. "Deterritorialization," which will immensely clarify the meaning of Arrighi's story, has become very widely used for all kinds of different phenomena; but I wish to assert that its first and as it were foundational meaning lies in this very emergence of capitalism itself, as any patient reconstruction of the central role of Marx in *Capitalism and Schizophrenia* would demonstrate. The first and most fateful deterritorialization is then this one: what Deleuze and Guattari call the axiomatic of capitalism decodes the terms of the older precapitalist coding systems and "liberates" them for new and more functional combinations. The resonance of the new term can be measured against an altogether more frivolous and even more successful current media word, decontextualization;

it properly suggests that anything wrenched out of its original context (if you can imagine one) will always be recontextualized in new areas and situations. But deterritorialization is far more absolute than that (although its results can indeed be recaptured and even occassionally "recoded" in new historical situations). For it rather implies a new ontological and free-floating state, one in which the content (to revert to Hegelian language) has definitively been suppressed in favor of the form, in which the inherent nature of the product becomes insiginficant, a mere marketing pretext, while the goal of production no longer lies in any specific market, any specific set of consumers or social and individual needs, but rather in its transformation into that element which by definition has no context or territory, and indeed no use value as such, namely, money. So it is that in any specific region of production, as Arrighi shows us, there comes a moment in which the logic of capitalism – faced with the saturation of local and even foreign markets – determines an abandonment of that kind of specific production, along with its factories and trained workforce, and, leaving them behind in ruins, takes its flight to other more profitable ventures.

Or rather that moment is a dual one, and it is in this demonstration of the two stages of deterritorialization that I see Arrighi's most fundamental orig-inality and also his most suggestive contribution for cultural analysis today. There is a deterritorialization in which capital shifts to other and more profitable forms of production, often enough in new geographical regions. Then there is the grimmer conjuncture, in which the capital of an entire center or region abandons production altogether in order to seek maximization in nonproduc-tive spaces, which as we have seen are those of speculation, the money market, and finance capital in general. Of course, here the word *deterritorialization* can celebrate its own kinds of ironies; for one of the privileged forms of speculation today is that of land and city space. The new postmodern informational or global cities (as they have been called) thus result very specifically from the ultimate deterritorialization, that of territory as such – the becoming abstract of land and the earth, the transformation of the very background or context of commodity exchange into a commodity in its own right. Land speculation is therefore one face of a process whose other one lies in the ultimate deterritor-ialization of globalization itself, where it would be a great mistake to imagine something like the globe as yet a new and larger space replacing the older national or imperial ones. Globalization is rather a kind of cyberspace in which money capital has reached its ultimate dematerialization, as messages that pass instantaneously from one nodal point to another across the former globe, the former material world.

I now want to offer some speculations as to the way in which this new logic of finance capital – its radically new forms of abstraction, in particular, which are sharply to be distinguished from those of modernism as such – can be observed to operate in cultural production today or, in other words, in what people have come to call postmodernity. What is wanted is an account of abstraction in which the new deterritorialized postmodern contents are to an older modernist autonomization as global financial speculation is to an older kind of banking and credit, or as the stock market frenzies of the eighties are to the Great Depression. I don't particularly want to introduce the theme of the gold standard here, which fatally suggests a solid and tangible kind of value as opposed to various forms of paper and plastic (or information on your computer). Or, perhaps, the theme of gold would become relevant again only to the degree that it was also grasped as an artificial and contradictory system in its own right. What we want to be able to theorize is a modification in the very nature of cultural tokens and the systems they operate in. If modernism is a kind of canceled realism, as I have suggested. one which segments and differentiates some initial mimetic starting point, then it might be likened to a largely accepted paper money, whose inflationary ups and downs suddenly lead to the introduction of financial and speculative instruments and vehicles.

I want to examine this point of historical change in terms of the fragment and its destiny throughout these various cultural moments. The rhetoric of the fragment has been with us since the dawn of what the Schlegels identified as modernism. It will be understood that I think it is something of a misnomer, since the image contents in question are the result, not of breakage, incompletion, or extreme wear and tear, but rather of analysis. But the word is convenient for want of a better one, and I'll go on using it in this brief final discussion. I want to begin by recalling Ken Russell's seemingly jocular remark that in the twenty-first century all fiction films will last no longer than fifteen minutes apiece; the implication is that in a *Late Show* culture like our own, the elaborate preparations we used to require in order to apprehend a series of images as a story of some kind will be, for whatever reason, unnecessary. But actually I think this can be documented by our own experience. Everyone who still visits movie theaters has become aware of the way in which intensified competition by the film industry for now-inveterate television viewers has led to a transformation in the very structure of the preview. It has had to be developed and expanded, becoming a far more comprehensive teaser for the film than it formerly was. At length the viewer of these enforced coming attractions (five or six of them precede every feature presentation and replace the older kinds of shorts) is led to make a momentous discovery, namely, that the preview is really all you need. You no longer need to see the "full" two-hour version (unless the object is to kill time, which it so often is). Nor is this something that has to do with the quality of the film (although it may have something to do with the quality of the preview, the better ones being cunningly arranged in such a way that the story they seem to tell is not the same as the "real story" in the "real film"). Nor does this new development have much to do with knowing the plot or the story, for, in any case, in contemporary action films, the story has become little more than a pretext on which to suspend a perpetual present of thrills and explosions. Thus these images are provided in the seemingly brief anthology of shots and highlights offered by the preview, and they are fully satisfying in themselves, without the benefit of the laborious threads and connections of the former plot. At that point it would seem that the preview, as a structure and a work in its own right, bears something of the same relationship to its supposed final product, as a novelized film, written after the fact of the movie and published later on as a kind of xeroxed reminder, is to the filmic original it replicates. The difference is that in the case of the feature film and its book version we are dealing with completed narrative structures of a similar type, structures similarly antiquated by these new developments. Whereas the preview is a new form, a new kind of minimalism, whose generic satisfactions are distinct from the older kind. It would thus seem that Russell was imperfectly prophetic in his forecast: not in the twenty-first century, but already in this one; and not fifteen minutes, but only two or three!

Of course, what he had in mind was something rather different, for he was evoking MTV, whose imaginative representations of music in visual analogues find their immediate predecessors, less in Disney and in music animation, than in television commercials as such, which can at their best achieve an aesthetic quality of great intensity. I want however to turn in a more familiar direction (partly because of the difficulty of illustrating ephemera of that kind) and to juxtapose an older practice of the image fragment with this newer one. It thus seems instructive to contrast the full currency of Buñuel's surrealist films, *An Andalusian Dog* (1928) and *The Golden Age* (1930), or of the very different experimental filmmaking of Stan Brakhage's *Dog Star Man* (1965), with the junk bonds of Derek Jarman's epic *Last of England* (1987).

As a matter of fact, we ought to note in passing that Jarman also expressed the same formal interest in the innovations of MTV as Russell, but, unlike him, Jarman deplored the temporal restrictions of the new mode and dreamed of an immense epic-length deployment of this image language, something he was to put into practice in just such a work as the ninety-minute *Last of England* (the longer films by Buñuel and Brakhage run some sixty-two and seventy-five minutes respectively, but it is the comparative quality of their interminabilities that is here in question). Yet, even in the modern, the practice of the fragment resulted in two distinct and antithetical tendencies or strategies: the minimalism of Webern or Beckett on the one hand, and the infinite temporal expansion of Mahler or Proust on the other. Here, in what some people call the postmodern, we might want to juxtapose the brevity of the Russell conception of MTV with the epic temptations of Jarman or the literal interminability of a text like *Gravity's Rainbow*.

But what I want to bring out, for this speculative discussion of the cultural impact of finance capital, is a rather different property of such image fragments. It seems appropriate to characterize those of Buñuel, working at the very center of the classical modern movement, as a practice of the symptom. Deleuze has indeed brilliantly characterized them in his only apparently idiosyncratic classification of Buñuel (along with Stroheim) under what he calls naturalism: "The naturalist image, the impulse-image [the image as drive or libido], has in fact two kinds of signs: symptoms, and idols or fetishes."[18] The image fragments in Buñuel are thus forever incomplete, markers of incomprehensible psychic catastrophe, obsessions and eruptions, the symptom in its pure form as an incomprehensible language that cannot be translated into any other. Brakhage's practice is completely different from this one, as befits a different historical period and also virtually a different medium, that of experimental film (which I have elsewhere suggested is to be inserted into a kind of ideal genealogy of experimental video rather than of cinema). This could be described, in analogy with music, as a deployment of quarter tones, of analytic segments of the image that are somehow visually incomplete to eyes still trained for and habituated to our Western visual languages: something like an art of the phoneme rather than of the morpheme or the syllable. Both of these practices, however, share the will to confront us with the structurally incomplete, which however dialectically affirms its constitutive relationship with an absence, with something else that is not given and perhaps never can be.

In Jarman's *Last of England*, however, about which words like *surrealist* have loosely been bandied, what we really confront is the commonplace, the cliche. A feeling tone is certainly developed here: the impotent rage of its punk heroes smashing about themselves with lead pipes, the disgust with the royal family and with traditional trappings of an official English life. But these feelings are themselves clichés, and disembodied ones at that. One can certainly speak of the death of the subject here, if by that is meant the substitution for some agonizing personal subjectivity (as in Buñuel) or some organizing aesthetic direction (as in Brakhage), a Flaubertian autonomous life of banal media entities floating through the empty public realm of a galactic Objective Spirit. But everything here is impersonal on the mode of the stereotype, including the rage itself. We see the most familiar and hackneyed shots of a dystopian future: terrorists, canned music classical and popular, along with Hitler's speeches, and a predictable parody of the royal wedding. All of this is processed by a painterly eye in order to generate mesmerizing sequences that alternate between black and white and color for purely visual reasons. The narrative or pseudonarrative segments are certainly longer than anything in Buñuel or Brakhage, yet they sometimes alternate and oscillate, overprint each other as in *Dog Star Man*, while generating an oneiric feeling that is a kind of cliché in its own right and radically different from the obsessive precision of Buñuel.

How to account for these qualitative differences, which surely themselves imply structural ones? I find myself reverting to Roland Barthes's extraordinary insights in *Mythologies*: Jarman's fragments are meaningful or intelligible, Buñuel's or Brakhage's are not.[19] Barthes's great dictum, that in the contemporary world there is an incompatibility between meaning and experience or the existential, was richly exercised in his *Mythologies*, which denounces the excess of meaning in his clichés and ideologies, and the nausea that sheer meaning brings with itself. Authentic language- or image-practice then tries to keep faith with some more fundamental contingency of meaninglessness, a proposition that holds either from an existential or a semiotic perspective. Barthes meanwhile tried to account for the overdose of meaning in the stereotypical by way of the notion of connotation as a kind of second-degree meaning built up provisionally on more literal ones. It is a theoretical tool that he was later to abandon but that we have every interest in reconsidering, particularly in the present context.

For I want to suggest that in the modern moment, of both Buñuel and Brakhage, the play of autonomized fragments remains meaningless. The Buñuel symptom is no doubt meaningful as such, but only at a distance and not for us, meaningful no doubt as a kind of other side of the carpet we will never see. Brakhage's descent into the fractional states of the image is also meaningless, although in a different way. But Jarman's total flow is only too meaningful, for in him the fragments have been reendowed with a cultural mediative meaning; and here I think we need a concept of the renarrativization of these fragments to complement Barthes's diagnosis of connotation at an earlier stage of mass culture. What happens here is that each former fragment of a narrative, which was once incomprehensible without the narrative context as a whole, has now become capable of emitting a complete narrative message in its own right. It has become autonomous, not in the formal sense I attributed to modernist processes, but rather in its newly acquired capacity to soak up content and to project it in a kind of instant reflex – whence the vanishing away of affect in the postmodern. The situation of contingency or meaninglessness, of alienation, has been superseded by this cultural renarrativization of the broken pieces of the image world.

What does all this have to do with finance capital? Modernist abstraction, I believe, is less a function of capital accumulation as such than of money itself in a situation of capital accumulation. Money is here both abstract (making everything equivalent) and empty and uninteresting, since its interest lies outside itself. It is thus incomplete like the modernist images I have been evoking; it directs attention elsewhere, beyond itself, towards what is supposed to complete (and also abolish) it. It knows a semiautonomy, certainly, but not a full autonomy in which it would constitute a language or a dimension in its own right. But that is precisely what finance capital brings into being: a play of monetary entities that need neither production (as capital does) nor consumption (as money does), which supremely, like cyberspace, can live on their own internal metabolisms and circulate without any reference to an older type of content. But so do the narrativized image fragments of a stereotypical postmodern language; they suggest a new cultural realm or dimension that is independent of the former real world, not because as in the modern (or even the romantic) period culture withdrew from that real world into an autonomous space of art, but rather because the real world has already been suffused with culture and colonized by it, so that it has no outside in terms of which it could be found lacking. Stereotypes are never lacking in that sense, and neither is the total flow of the circuits of financial speculation. That each of these also steers unwittingly towards a crash I leave for another essay and another time.

Notes

1 See Giovanni Arrighi, *The Long Twentieth Century: Money, Power, and the Origins of our Times* (New York, 1994).
2 See Rudolf Hilferding, *Finance Capital*, trans. Morris Watnick and Sam Gordon (1910; Boston, 1981), and V. I. Lenin, *Imperialism: The Highest Stage of Capitalism*, trans. pub. (New York, 1939).
3 See Ernest Mandel, *Late Capitalism*, trans. Joris De Bres (New York, 1975).
4 See Gilles Deleuze and Félix Guattari, *A Thousand Plateaus*, trans. Brian Massumi, vol. 2 of *Capitalism and Schizophrenia* (Minneapolis, 1987), p. 461.
5 John Hicks, *A Theory of Economic History* (Oxford, 1969); quoted in Arrighi, *The Long Twentieth Century*, p. 94.
6 Fernand Braudel, *The Perspective of the World* (New York, 1984); quoted in Arrighi, *The Long Twentieth Century*, p. 6.
7 See Paul A. Baran and Paul M. Sweezy, *Monopoly Capital: An Essay on the American Economic and Social Order* (New York, 1966).
8 See Jacques Derrida, *Specters of Marx: The State of the Debt, the Work of Mourning, and the New International*, trans. Peggy Kamuf (New York, 1994).
9 See Georg Simmel, "The metropolis and mental life," in Donald N. Levine (ed.), *On Individuality and Social Forms: Selected Writings* (Chicago, 1971), pp. 324–39.
10 See Fredric Jameson, *The Political Unconscious: Narrative as a Socially Symbolic Act* (Ithaca, NY, 1981).

11 See C. B. MacPherson, *The Political Theory of Possessive Individualism: Hobbes to Locke* (Oxford, 1964).

12 See Arnold Hauser, *The Social History of Art*, trans. Arnold Hauser and Stanley Godman (2 vols, New York, 1951).

13 Stéphane Mallarmé, "Le Mystère dans les lettres," *Divagations* (Paris, 1917), p. 289; trans. Bradford Cook, under the title "Mystery in literature," *Mallarmé: Selected Prose Poems, Essays, and Letters* (Baltimore, 1956), p. 32: "What sure guide is there to intelligibility in the midst of these contrasts? What guarantee? Syntax."

14 See Erich Auerbach, *Mimesis: The Representation of Reality in Western Literature*, trans. Willard Trask (Garden City, NY, 1953).

15 See Harry Braverman, *Labor and Monopoly Capital: The Degradation of Work in the Twentieth Century* (New York, 1974).

16 Karl Marx, *Capital: A Critique of Political Economy*, trans. Ben Fowkes (2 vols, Harmondsworth, 1976), vol. 1, p. 249.

17 Ibid.

18 Gilles Deleuze, *Cinema 1: The Movement-Image*, trans. Hugh Tomlinson and Barbara Habberjam (Minneapolis, 1986), p. 125.

19 See Roland Barthes, *Mythologies*, trans. Annette Lavers (New York, 1972).

Part IV

Exercises in Cognitive Mapping

15

Cognitive Mapping

This text was originally presented at a 1983 conference on Marxism and the interpretation of culture. It was published in 1988.

[...] In the project for a spatial analysis of culture that I have been engaged in sketching for the teaching institute that preceded this conference, I have tried to suggest that the three historical stages of capital have each generated a type of space unique to it, even though these three stages of capitalist space are obviously far more profoundly interrelated than are the spaces of other modes of production. The three types of space I have in mind are all the result of discontinuous expansions or quantum leaps in the enlargement of capital, in the latter's penetration and colonization of hitherto uncommodified areas. You will therefore note in passing that a certain unifying and totalizing force is presupposed here — although it is not the Hegelian Absolute Spirit, nor the party, nor Stalin, but simply capital itself; and it is on the strength of such a view that a radical Jesuit friend of mine once publicly accused me of monotheism. It is at least certain that the notion of capital stands or falls with the notion of some unified logic of this social system itself, that is to say, in the stigmatized language I will come back to later, that both are irrecoverably totalizing concepts.

I have tried to describe the first kind of space of classical or market capitalism in terms of a logic of the grid, a reorganization of some older sacred and heterogeneous space into geometrical and Cartesian homogeneity, a space of infinite equivalence and extension of which you can find a kind of dramatic or emblematic shorthand representation in Foucault's book on prisons. The example, however, requires the warning that a Marxian view of such space grounds it in Taylorization and the labor process rather than in that shadowy and mythical Foucault entity called "power." The emergence of this kind of space will probably not involve problems of figuration so acute as those we will confront in the later stages of capitalism, since here, for the moment, we witness that familiar process long generally associated with the Enlightenment, namely, the desacralization of the world, the decoding and secularization of the older forms of the sacred or the transcendent, the slow colonization of use value by exchange value, the "realistic" demystification of the older kinds of transcendent narratives in novels like *Don Quixote*, the standardization of both subject and object, the denaturalization of desire and its ultimate displacement by commodification or, in other words, "success," and so on.

The problems of figuration that concern us will only become visible in the next stage, the passage from market to monopoly capital, or what Lenin called the "stage of imperialism"; and they may be conveyed by way of a growing contradiction between lived experience and structure, or between a phenomenological description of the life of an individual and a more properly structural model of the conditions of existence of that experience. Too rapidly we can say that, while in older societies and perhaps even in the early stages of market capital, the immediate and limited experience of individuals is still able to encompass and coincide with the true economic and social form that governs that experience, in the next moment these two levels drift ever further apart and really begin to constitute themselves into that opposition the classical dialectic describes as *Wesen* and *Erscheinung*, essence and appearance, structure and lived experience.

At this point the phenomenological experience of the individual subject – traditionally, the supreme raw materials of the work of art – becomes limited to a tiny corner of the social world, a fixed-camera view of a certain section of London or the countryside or whatever. But the truth of that experience no longer coincides with the place in which it takes place. The truth of that limited daily experience of London lies, rather, in India or Jamaica or Hong Kong; it is bound up with the whole colonial system of the British Empire that determines the very quality of the individual's subjective life. Yet those structural coordinates are no longer accessible to immediate lived experience and are often not even conceptualizable for most people.

There comes into being, then, a situation in which we can say that if individual experience is authentic, then it cannot be true; and that if a scientific or cognitive model of the same content is true, then it escapes individual experience. It is evident that this new situation poses tremendous and crippling problems for a work of art; and I have argued that it is as an attempt to square this circle and to invent new and elaborate formal strategies for overcoming this dilemma that modernism or, perhaps better, the various moderisms as such emerge: in forms that inscribe a new sense of the absent global colonial system on the very syntax of poetic language itself, a new play of absence and presence that at its most simplified will be haunted by the erotic and be tattooed with foreign place names, and at its most intense will involve the invention of remarkable new languages and forms.

At this point I want to introduce another concept that is basic to my argument, that I call the "play of figuration." This is an essentially allegorical concept that supposes the obvious, namely, that these new and enormous global realities are inaccessible to any individual subject or consciousness – not even to Hegel, let alone Cecil Rhodes or Queen Victoria – which is to say that those fundamental realities are somehow ultimately unrepresentable or, to use the Althusserian phrase, are something like an absent cause, one that can never emerge into the presence of perception. Yet this absent cause can find figures through which to express itself in distorted and symbolic ways: indeed, one of our basic tasks as critics of literature is to track down and make conceptually available the ultimate realities and experiences designated by those figures, which the reading mind inevitably tends to reify and to read as primary contents in their own right.

Since we have evoked the modernist moment and its relationship to the great new global colonial network, I will give a fairly simple but specialized example of a kind of figure specific to this historical situation. Everyone knows how, toward the end of the nineteenth century, a wide range of writers began to invent forms to express what I will call "monadic relativism." In Gide and Conrad, in Fernando Pessoa, in Pirandello, in Ford, and to a lesser extent in Henry James, even very obliquely in Proust, what we begin to see is the sense that each consciousness is a closed world, so that a representation of the social totality now must take the (impossible) form of a coexistence of those sealed subjective worlds and their peculiar interaction, which is in reality a passage of ships in the night, a centrifugal movement of lines and planes that can never intersect. The literary value that emerges from this new formal practice is called "irony"; and its philosophical ideology often takes the form of a vulgar appropriation of Einstein's theory of relativity. In this context, what I want to suggest is that these forms, whose content is generally that of privatized middle-class life, nonetheless stand as symptoms and distorted expressions of the penetration even of middle-class lived experience by this strange new global relativity of the colonial network. The one is then the figure, however deformed and symbolically rewritten, of the latter; and I take it that this figural process will remain central in all later attempts to restructure the form of the work of art to accommodate content that must radically resist and escape artistic figuration.

If this is so for the age of imperialism, how much more must it hold for our own moment, the moment of the multinational network, or what Mandel calls "late capitalism," a moment in which not merely the older city but even the nation-state itself has ceased to play a central functional and formal role in a process that has in a new quantum leap of capital prodigiously expanded beyond them, leaving them behind as ruined and archaic remains of earlier stages in the development of this mode of production.

At this point I realize that the persuasiveness of my demonstration depends on your having some fairly vivid perceptual sense of what is unique and original in postmodernist space – something I have been trying to convey in my course, but for which it is more difficult here to substitute a shortcut. Briefly, I want to suggest that the new space involves the suppression of distance (in the sense of Benjamin's aura) and the relentless saturation of any remaining voids and empty places, to the point where the postmodern body – whether wandering through a postmodern hotel, locked into rock sound by means of headphones, or undergoing the multiple shocks and bombardments of the Vietnam War as Michael Herr conveys it to us – is now exposed to a perceptual barrage of immediacy from which all sheltering layers and intervening mediations have been removed. There are, of course, many other features of this space one would ideally want to comment on – most notably, Lefebvre's concept of abstract space as what is simultaneously homogeneous and fragmented – but I think that the peculiar disorientation of the saturated space I have just mentioned will be the most useful guiding thread.

You should understand that I take such spatial peculiarities of postmodernism as symptoms and expressions of a new and historically original dilemma, one that involves our insertion as individual subjects into a multidimensional set of radically discontinuous realities, whose frames range from the still surviving spaces of bourgeois private life all the way to the unimaginable decentering of global capital itself. Not even Einsteinian relativity, or the multiple subjective worlds of the older modernists, is capable of giving any kind of adequate figuration to this process, which in lived experience makes itself felt by the so-called death of the subject, or, more exactly, the fragmented and schizophrenic decentering and dispersion of this last (which can no longer even serve the function of the Jamesian reverberator or "point of view"). And although you may not have realized it, I am talking about practical politics here: since the crisis of socialist internationalism, and the enormous strategic and tactical difficulties of coordinating local and grassroots or neighborhood political actions with national or international ones, such urgent political dilemmas are all immediately functions of the enormously complex new international space I have in mind.

Let me here insert an illustration, in the form of a brief account of a book that is, I think, not known to many of you but in my opinion of the greatest importance and suggestiveness for problems of space and politics. The book is nonfiction, a historical narrative of the single most significant political experience of the American 1960s: *Detroit: I Do Mind Dying*, by Marvin Surkin and Dan Georgakis. (I think we have now come to be sophisticated enough to understand that aesthetic, formal, and narrative analyses have implications that far transcend those objects marked as fiction or as literature.) *Detroit* is a study of the rise and fall of the League of Black Revolutionary Workers in that city in the late 1960s.[1] The political formation in question was able to conquer power in the workplace, particularly in the automobile factories; it drove a substantial wedge into the media and informational monopoly of the city by way of a student newspaper; it elected judges; and finally it came within a hair's breadth of electing the mayor and taking over the city power apparatus. This was, of course, a remarkable political achievement, characterized by an exceedingly sophisticated sense of the need for a multilevel strategy for revolution that involved initiatives on the distinct social levels of the labor process, the media and culture, the juridical apparatus, and electoral politics.

Yet it is equally clear – and far clearer in virtual triumphs of this kind than in the earlier stages of neighborhood politics – that such strategy is bound and shackled to the city form itself. Indeed, one of the enormous strengths of the superstate and its federal constitution lies in the evident discontinuities between city, state, and federal power: if you cannot make socialism in one country, how much more derisory, then, are the prospects for socialism in one city in the United States today? Indeed, our foreign visitors may not be aware that there exist in this country four or five socialist communes, near one of which, in Santa Cruz, California, I lived until recently; no one would want to belittle these local successes, but it seems probable that few of us think of them as the first decisive step toward the transition to socialism.

If you cannot build socialism in one city, then suppose you conquer a whole series of large key urban centers in succession. This is what the League of Black Revolutionary Workers began to think about; that is to say, they began to feel that their movement was a political model and ought to be generalizable. The problem that arises is spatial: how to develop a *national* political movement on the basis of a *city* strategy and politics. At any rate, the leadership of the League began to spread the word in other cities and traveled to Italy and Sweden to study workers' strategies there and to explain their own model; reciprocally, out-of-town politicos came to Detroit to investigate the new strategies. At this point it ought to be clear that we are in the middle of the problem of representation, not the least of it being signaled by the appearance of that ominous American word "leadership." In a more general way, however, these trips were more than networking, making contacts, spreading informa-tion: they raised the problem of how to represent a unique local model and experience to people in other situations. So it was logical for the League to make a film of their experience, and a very fine and exciting film it is.

Spatial discontinuities, however, are more devious and dialectical, and they are not overcome in any of the most obvious ways. For example, they returned on the Detroit experience as some ultimate limit before which it collapsed. What happened was that the jet-setting militants of the League had become media stars; not only were they becoming alienated from their local constitu-encies, but, worse than that, nobody stayed home to mind the store. Having acceded to a larger spatial plane, the base vanished under them; and with this the most successful social revolutionary experiment of that rich political decade in the United States came to a sadly undramatic end. I do not want to say that it left no traces behind, since a number of local gains remain, and in any case every rich political experiment continues to feed the tradition in underground ways. Most ironic in our context, however, is the very success of their failure: the representation – the model of this complex spatial dialectic – triumphantly survives in the form of a film and a book, but in the process of becoming an image and a spectacle, the referent seems to have disappeared, as so many people from Debord to Baudrillard always warned us it would.

Yet this very example may serve to illustrate the proposition that successful spatial representation today need not be some uplifting socialist-realist drama of revolutionary triumph but may be equally inscribed in a narrative of defeat, which sometimes, even more effectively, causes the whole architectonic of postmodern global space to rise up in ghostly profile behind itself, as some ultimate dialectical barrier or invisible limit. This example also may have given a little more meaning to the slogan of cognitive mapping to which I now turn.

I am tempted to describe the way I understand this concept as something of a synthesis between Althusser and Kevin Lynch – a formulation that, to be sure, does not tell you much unless you know that Lynch is the author of a classic work, *The Image of the City*, which in its turn spawned the whole low-level subdiscipline that today takes the phrase "cognitive mapping" as its own designation.[2] Lynch's problematic remains locked within the limits of phenom-enology, and his book can no doubt be subjected to many criticisms on its own terms (not the least of which is the absence of any conception of political agency or historical process). My use of the book will be emblematic, since the mental map of city space explored by Lynch can be extrapolated to that mental map of the social and global totality we all carry around in our heads in variously garbled forms. Drawing on the downtowns of Boston, Jersey City, and Los Angeles, and by means of interviews and questionnaires in which subjects were asked to draw their city context from memory, Lynch suggests that urban alienation is directly proportional to the mental unmapability of local cityscapes. A city like Boston, then, with its monumental perspectives, its markers and monuments, its combination of grand but simple spatial forms, including dramatic boundaries such as the Charles River, not only allows people to have, in their imaginations, a generally successful and continous location to the rest of the city, but in addition gives them something of the freedom and aesthetic gratification of traditional city form.

I have always been struck by the way in which Lynch's conception of city experience – the dialectic between the here and now of immediate perception and the imaginative or imaginary sense of the city as an absent totality – presents something like a spatial analogue of Althusser's great formulation of ideology itself, as "the Imaginary representation of the subject's relationship to his or her Real conditions of existence." Whatever its defects and problems, this positive conception of ideology as a necessary function in any form of social life has the great merit of stressing the gap between the local positioning of the individual subject and the totality of class structures in which he or she is situated, a gap between phenomenological perception and a reality that transcends all individual thinking or experience; but this ideology, as such, attempts to span or coordinate, to map, by means of conscious and unconscious representations. The conception of cognitive mapping proposed here therefore involves an extrapolation of Lynch's spatial analysis to the realm of social structure, that is to say, in our historical moment, to the totality of class relations on a global (or should I say multinational) scale. The secondary premise is also maintained, namely, that the incapacity to map socially is as crippling to political experience as the analogous incapacity to map spatially is for urban experience. It follows that an aesthetic of cognitive mapping in this sense is an integral part of any socialist political project.

In what has preceded I have infringed so many of the taboos and shibboleths of a faddish post-Marxism that it becomes necessary to discuss them more openly and directly before proceeding. They include the proposition that class no longer exists (a proposition that might be clarified by the simple distinction between class as an element in small-scale models of society, class consciousness as a cultural event, and class analysis as a mental operation); the idea that this society is no longer motored by production but rather reproduction (including science and technology) – an idea that, in the midst of a virtually completely built environment, one is tempted to greet with laughter; and, finally, the repudiation of representation and the stigmatization of the concept of totality and of the project of totalizing thought. Practically, this last needs to be sorted into several different propositions – in particular, one having to do with capitalism and one having to do with socialism or communism. The French *nouveaux philosophes* said it most succinctly, without realizing that they were reproducing or reinventing the hoariest American ideological slogans of the Cold War: totalizing thought is totalitarian thought; a direct line runs from Hegel's Absolute Spirit to Stalin's Gulag.

As a matter of self-indulgence, I will open a brief theoretical parenthesis here, particularly since Althusser has been mentioned. We have already experienced a dramatic and instructive melt-down of the Althusserian reactor in the work of Barry Hindess and Paul Hirst, who quite consequently observe the incompat-ibility of the Althusserian attempt to secure semiautonomy for the various levels of social life, and the more desperate effort of the same philosopher to retain the old orthodox notion of an "ultimately determining instance" in the form of what he calls "structural totality." Quite logically and consequently, then, Hindess and Hirst simply remove the offending mechanism, whereupon the Althusserian edifice collapses into a rubble of autonomous instances without any necessary relationship to each other whatsoever – at which point it follows that one can no longer talk about or draw practical political consequences from any conception of social structure; that is to say, the very conceptions of something called capitalism and something called socialism or communism fall of their own weight into the ash can of History. (This last, of course, then vanishes in a puff of smoke, since by the same token nothing like History as a total process can any longer be conceptually entertained.) All I wanted to point out in this high theoretical context is that the baleful equation between a philosophical conception of totality and a political practice of totalitarianism is itself a particularly ripe example of what Althusser calls "expressive causality," namely, the collapsing of two semiautonomous (or, now, downright autono-mous) levels into one another. Such an equation, then, is possible for unre-constructed Hegelians but is quite incompatible with the basic positions of any honest post-Althusserian post-Marxism.

To close the parenthesis, all of this can be said in more earthly terms. The conception of capital is admittedly a totalizing or systemic concept: no one has ever seen or met the thing itself; it is either the result of scientific reduction (and it should be obvious that scientific thinking always reduces the multiplicity of the real to a small-scale model) or the mark of an imaginary and ideological vision. But let us be serious: anyone who believes that the profit motive and the logic of capital accumulation are not the fundamental laws of this world, who believes that these do not set absolute barriers and limits to social changes and transformations undertaken in it – such a person is living in an alternative universe; or, to put it more politely, in this universe such a person – assuming he or she is progressive – is doomed to social democracy, with its now abundantly documented treadmill of failures and capitulations. Because if capital does not exist, then clearly socialism does not exist either. I am far from suggesting that no politics at all is possible in this new post-Marxian

Nietzschean world of micropolitics – that is observably untrue. But I do want to argue that without a conception of the social totality (and the possibility of transforming a whole social system), no properly socialist politics is possible.

About socialism itself we must raise more troubling and unsolved dilemmas that involve the notion of community or the collective. Some of the dilemmas are very familiar, such as the contradiction between self-management on the local level and planning on the global scale; or the problems raised by the abolition of the market, not to mention the abolition of the commodity form itself. I have found even more stimulating and problematical the following propositions about the very nature of society itself: it has been affirmed that, with one signal exception (capitalism itself, which is organized around an economic mechanism), there has never existed a cohesive form of human society that was not based on some form of transcendence or religion. Without brute force, which is never but a momentary solution, people cannot in this vein be asked to live cooperatively and to renounce the omnivorous desires of the id without some appeal to religious belief or transcendent values, something absolutely incompatible with any conceivable socialist society. The result is that these last achieve their own momentary coherence only under seige circumstances, in the wartime enthusiasm and group effort provoked by the great blockades. In other words, without the nontranscendent economic mechanism of capital, all appeals to moral incentives (as in Che) or to the primacy of the political (as in Maoism) must fatally exhaust themselves in a brief time, leaving only the twin alternatives of a return to capitalism or the construction of this or that modern form of "oriental despotism." You are certainly welcome to believe this prognosis, provided you understand that in such a case any socialist politics is strictly a mirage and a waste of time, which one might better spend adjusting and reforming an eternal capitalist landscape as far as the eye can see.

In reality this dilemma is, to my mind the most urgent task that confronts Marxism today. I have said before that the so-called crisis in Marxism is not a crisis in Marxist science, which has never been richer, but rather a crisis in Marxist ideology. If ideology – to give it a somewhat different definition – is a vision of the future that grips the masses, we have to admit that, save in a few ongoing collective experiments, such as those in Cuba and in Yugoslavia, no Marxist or Socialist party or movement anywhere has the slightest conception of what socialism or communism as a social system ought to be and can be expected to look like. That vision will not be purely economic, although the Marxist economists are as deficient as the rest of us in their failure to address this Utopian problem in any serious way. It is, as well, supremely social and cultural, involving the task of trying to imagine how a society without hierarchy, a society of free people, a society that has at once repudiated the economic mechanisms of the market, can possibly cohere. Historically, all forms of hierarchy have always been based ultimately on gender hierarchy and on the building block of the family unit, which makes it clear that this is the true juncture between a feminist problematic and a Marxist one – not an antagonistic juncture, but the moment at which the feminist project and the Marxist and socialist project meet and face the same dilemma: how to imagine Utopia.

Returning to the beginning of this lengthy excursus, it seems unlikely that anyone who repudiates the concept of totality can have anything useful to say to us on this matter, since for such persons it is clear that the totalizing vision of socialism will not compute and is a false problem within the random and undecidable world of microgroups. Or perhaps another possibility suggests itself, namely, that our dissatisfaction with the concept of totality is not a thought in its own right but rather a significant symptom, a function of the increasing difficulties in thinking of such a set of interrelationships in a complicated society. This would seem, at least, to be the implication of the remark of the Team X architect Aldo van Eyck, when, in 1966, he issued his version of the death of modernism thesis: "We know nothing of vast multiplicity – we cannot come to terms with it – not as architects or planners or anybody else." To which he added, and the sequel can easily be extrapolated from architecture to social change itself: "But if society has no form – how can architects build its counterform?"[3]

You will be relieved to know that at this point we can return both to my own conclusion and to the problem of aesthetic representation and cognitive mapping, which was the pretext of this [chapter]. The project of cognitive mapping obviously stands or falls with the conception of some (unrepresentable, imaginary) global social totality that was to have been mapped. I have spoken of form and content, and this final distinction will allow me at least to say something about an aesthetic, of which I have observed that I am, myself, absolutely incapable of guessing or imagining its form. That postmodernism gives us hints and examples of such cognitive mapping on the level of content is, I believe, demonstrable.

I have spoken elsewhere of the turn toward a thematics of mechanical reproduction, of the way in which the autoreferentiality of much of postmodernist art takes the form of a play with reproductive technology – film, tapes, video, computers, and the like – which is, to my mind, a degraded figure of the great multinational space that remains to be cognitively mapped. Fully as striking on another level is the omnipresence of the theme of paranoia as it expresses itself in a seemingly inexhaustible production of conspiracy plots of the most elaborate kinds. Conspiracy, one is tempted to say, is the poor person's cognitive mapping in the postmodern age; it is a degraded figure of the total logic of late capital, a desperate attempt to represent the latter's system, whose failure is marked by its slippage into sheer theme and content.

Achieved cognitive mapping will be a matter of form, and I hope I have shown how it will be an integral part of a socialist politics, although its own possibility may well be dependent on some prior political opening, which its task would then be to enlarge culturally. Still, even if we cannot imagine the productions of such an aesthetic, there may, nonetheless, as with the very idea of Utopia itself, be something positive in the attempt to keep alive the possibility of imagining such a thing.

Notes

1 Dan Georgakis and Marvin Surkin, *Detroit: I Do Mind Dying, A Study in Urban Revolution* (New York, St Martin's Press, 1975).
2 Kevin Lynch, *The Image of the City* (Cambridge, Mass., MIT Press, 1960).
3 Quoted in Kenneth Frampton, *Modern Architecture: A Critical History* (New York, Oxford University Press, 1980), pp. 276–7.

16

Class and Allegory in Contemporary Mass Culture: *Dog Day Afternoon* as a Political Film

This chapter was originally published in 1977. The present version, which includes a brief afterword, appears in Jameson's book, *Signatures of the Visible* (1992).

One of the most persistent leitmotivs in liberalism's ideological arsenal, one of the most effective anti–Marxist arguments developed by the rhetoric of liberalism and anticommunism, is the notion of the disappearance of class. The argument is generally conveyed in the form of an empirical observation, but can take a number of different forms, the most important ones for us being either the appeal to the unique development of social life in the United States (so called American exceptionalism), or the notion of a qualitative break, a quantum leap, between the older industrial systems and what now comes to be called "post–industrial" society. In the first version of the argument, we are told that the existence of the frontier (and, when the real frontier disappeared, the persistence of that "inner" frontier of a vast continental market unimaginable to Europeans) prevented the formation of the older, strictly European class antagonisms, while the absence from the United States of a classical aristocracy of the European type is said to account for the failure of a classical bourgeoisie to develop in this country – a bourgeoisie which would then, following the continental model, have generated a classical proletariat over against itself. This is what we may call the American mythic explanation, and seems to flourish primarily in those American Studies programs which have a vested interest in preserving the specificity of their object and in preserving the boundaries of their discipline.

The second version is a little less parochial and takes into account what used to be called the Americanization, not only of the older European societies, but also, in our time, that of the Third World as well. It reflects the realities of the transition of monopoly capitalism into a more purely consumer stage on what is for the first time a global scale; and it tries to take advantage of the emergence of this new stage of monopoly capitalism to suggest that classical Marxist economics is no longer applicable. According to this argument, a social homogenization is taking place in which the older class differences are disappearing, and which can be described either as the embourgeoisement of the worker, or better still, the transformation of both bourgeois and worker into that new grey organization person known as the consumer. Meanwhile, although most of the ideologues of a post-industrial stage would hesitate to claim that value as such is no longer being produced in consumer society, they are at least anxious to suggest that ours is becoming a "service economy" in which production of the classical types occupies an ever dwindling percentage of the work force.

Now if it is so that the Marxian concept of social class is a category of nineteenth-century European conditions, and no longer relevant to our situation today, then it is clear that Marxism may be sent to the museum where it can be dissected by Marxologists (there are an increasing number of those at work all around us today) and can no longer interfere with the development of that streamlined and postmodern legitimation of American economic evolution in the seventies and beyond, which is clearly the most urgent business on the agenda now that the older rhetoric of a classical New Deal type liberalism has succumbed to unplanned obsolescence. On the left, meanwhile, the failure of a theory of class seemed less important practically and politically during the anti-war situation of the 1960s, in which attacks on authoritarianism, racism, and sexism had their own internal justification and logic, and were lent urgency by the existence of the war, and content by the collective practice of social groups, in particular students, blacks, browns, and women. What is becoming clearer today is that the demands for equality and justice projected by such groups are not (unlike the politics of social class) intrinsically subversive. Rather, the slogans of populism and the ideals of racial justice and sexual equality were already themselves part and parcel of the Enlightenment itself, inherent not only in a socialist denunciation of capitalism, but even and also in the bourgeois revolution against the ancien régime. The values of the civil rights movement and the women's movement and the anti-authoritarian egalitarianism of the student's movement are thus preeminently cooptable because they are already – as ideals – inscribed in the very ideology of capitalism itself; and we must take into account the possibility that these ideals are part of the internal logic of the system, which has a fundamental interest in social equality to the degree to which it needs to transform as many of its subjects or its citizens into identical consumers interchangeable with everybody else. The Marxian position – which includes the ideals of the Enlightenment but seeks to ground them in a materialist theory of social evolution – argues on the contrary that the system is structurally unable to realize such ideals even where it has an economic interest in doing so.

This is the sense in which the categories of race and sex as well as the generational ones of the student movement are theoretically subordinate to the categories of social class, even where they may seem practically and politically a great deal more relevant. Yet it is not adequate to argue the importance of class on the basis of an underlying class reality beneath a relatively more classless appearance. There is, after all, a reality of the appearance just as much as a reality behind it; or, to put it more concretely, social class is not merely a structural fact but also very significantly a function of class consciousness, and the latter, indeed, ends up producing the former just as surely as it is produced by it. This is the point at which dialectical thinking becomes unavoidable, teaching us that we cannot speak of an underlying "essence" of things, of a fundamental class structure inherent in a system in which one group of people produces value for another group, unless we allow for the dialectical possibility that even this fundamental "reality," may be "realer" at some historical junctures than at others, and that the underlying object of our thoughts and representations – history and class structure – is itself as profoundly historical as our own capacity to grasp it. We may take as the motto for such a process the following still extremely Hegelian sentence of the early Marx: "It is not enough that thought should seek to realize itself; reality must also strive towards thought."

In the present context, the "thought" towards which reality strives is not only or even not yet class consciousness: it is rather the very preconditions for such class consciousness in social reality itself, that is to say, the requirement that, for people to become aware of the class, the classes be already in some sense perceptible as such. This fundamental requirement we will call, now borrowing a term from Freud rather than from Marx, the requirement of *figurability*, the need for social reality and everyday life to have developed to the point at which its underlying class structure becomes *representable* in tangible form. The point can be made in a different way by underscoring the unexpectedly vital role that culture would be called on to play in such a process, culture not only as an instrument of self-consciousness but even before that as a symptom and a sign of possible self-consciousness in the first place. The relationship between class consciousness and figurability, in other words, demands something more basic than abstract knowledge, and implies a mode of experience that is more visceral and existential than the abstract certainties of economics and Marxian social science: the latter merely continue to convince us of the informing presence, behind daily life, of the logic of capitalist production. To be sure, as Althusser tells us, the concept of sugar does not have to taste sweet. Nonetheless, in order for genuine class consciousness to be possible, we have to begin to sense the abstract truth of class through the tangible medium of daily life in vivid and experiential ways; and to say that class structure is becoming representable means that we have now gone beyond mere abstract understanding and entered that whole area of personal fantasy, collective storytelling, narrative figurability – which is the domain of culture and no longer that of abstract sociology or economic analysis. To become figurable – that is to say, visible in the first place, accessible to our imaginations – the classes have to be able to become in some sense characters in their own right: this is the sense in which the term allegory in our title is to be taken as a working hypothesis.

We will have thereby also already begun to justify an approach to commercial film, as that medium where, if at all, some change in the class character of social reality ought to be detectable, since social reality and the stereotypes of our experience of everyday social reality are the raw material with which commercial film and television are inevitably forced to work. This is my answer, in advance, to critics who object a priori that the immense costs of commercial films, which inevitably place their production under the control of multinational corporations, make any genuinely political content in them unlikely, and on the contrary ensure commercial film's vocation as a vehicle for ideological manipulation. No doubt this is so, if we remain on the level of the intention of the filmmaker who is bound to be limited consciously or unconsciously by the objective situation. But it is to fail to reckon with the political content of daily life, with the political logic which is already inherent in the raw material with which the filmmaker must work: such political logic will then not manifest itself as an overt political message, nor will it transform the film into an unambiguous political statement. But it will certainly make for the emergence of profound formal contradictions to which the public cannot not be sensitive, whether or not it yet possesses the conceptual instruments to understand what those contradictions mean.

In any case, *Dog Day Afternoon* (1975) would seem to have a great deal more overt political content than we would normally expect to find in a Hollywood production. In fact, we have only to think of the CIA-type espionage thriller, or the police show on television, to realize that overt political content of that kind is so omnipresent as to be inescapable in the entertainment industry. It is indeed as though the major legacy of the sixties was to furnish a whole new code, a whole new set of thematics – that of the political – with which, after that of sex, the entertainment industry could reinvest its tired paradigms without any danger to itself or to the system; and we should take into account the possibility that it is the overtly political or contestatory parts of *Dog Day Afternoon* which will prove the least functional from a class point of view.

But before this becomes clear, we will want to start a little further back, with the anecdotal material in which the film takes its point of departure. The event itself is not so far removed in time that we cannot remember it for what it was; or more precisely, remember what the media found interesting about it, what made it worthwhile transforming into a feature story in its own right an otherwise banal bank robbery and siege with hostages, of the type with which countless newscasts and grade-B movies have familiarized us in the past. Three novelties distinguished the robbery on which *Dog Day Afternoon* was to be based: first, the crowd sympathized with the bank robber, booing at the police and evoking the then still very recent Attica massacre; second, the bank robber turned out to be a homosexual, or, more properly, to have gone through a homosexual marriage ceremony with a transsexual, and indeed later claimed to have committed the robbery in order to finance his partner's sex-change operation; finally, the television cameras and on the spot telephone interviews were so heavily involved in the day-long negotiations as to give a striking new twist to the concept of the "media-event": and to this feature, we should probably add the final sub-novelty that the robbery took place on the climactic day of the Nixon–Agnew nominating convention (August 22, 1972).[1]

A work of art that had been able to do justice to any one of these peculiarities by itself would have been assured of an unavoidably political resonance. The Sidney Lumet film, "faithfully" incorporating all three, ended up having very little – and it is probably too easy, although not incorrect, to say that they cancel each other out by projecting a set of circumstances too unique to have any generalizable meaning: literature, as Aristotle tells us, being more philosophical than history in that it shows us what can happen, where the latter only shows us what did happen. Indeed, I believe a case can be made for the ideological function of overexposure in commercial culture: the repeated stereotypical use of otherwise disturbing and alien phenomena in our present social conjuncture – political militancy, student revolt, drugs, resistance to and hatred of authority – has an effect of containment for the system as a whole. To name something is to domesticate it, to refer to it repeatedly is to persuade a fearful and

beleaguered middle-class public that all of that is part of a known and cata-
logued world and thus somehow in order. Such a process would then be the
equivalent, in the realm of everyday social life, of that cooptation by the media,
that exhaustion of novel raw material, which is one of our principal techniques
for defusing threatening and subversive ideas. If something like this is the case,
then clearly *Dog Day Afternoon*, with its wealth of anti-social detail, may be
thought to work overtime in the reprocessing of alarming social materials for
the reassurance of suburban moviegoers.

Turning to those raw materials themselves, it is worth taking a passing glance
at what the film did not become. Ours is, after all, a period and a public with an
appetite for the documentary fact, for the anecdotal, the *vécu*, the *fait divers*, the
true story in all its sociological freshness and unpredictability. Not to go as far
back as the abortive yet symptomatic "non-fiction novel," nor even the
undoubted primacy of non-fiction over fiction on the best-seller lists, we find
a particularly striking embodiment of this interest in a whole series of recent
experiments on American television with the fictional documentary (or docu-
drama): narrative reports, played by actors, of sensational crimes, like the
Manson murders or the Shepherd case or the trial of John Henry Faulk, or of
otherwise curious *fait divers* – like a flying saucer sighting by a bi-racial couple,
Truman's climactic confrontation with MacArthur, or an ostracism at West
Point. We would have understood a great deal if we could explain why *Dog
Day Afternoon* fails to have anything in common with these fictional document-
aries, which are far and away among the best things achieved by American
commercial television, their success at least in part attributable to the distance
which such pseudo-documentaries maintain between the real-life fact and its
representation. The more powerful of them preserve the existence of a secret in
their historical content, and, at the same time that they purport to give us a
version of the events, exacerbate our certainty that we will never know for sure
what really did happen. (This structural disjunction between form and content
clearly projects a very different aesthetic strategy from those of classical Grier-
sonian documentary, of Italian neo-realism, or of Kino-pravda or ciné-vérité,
to name only three of the older attempts to solve the problem of the relationship between movies and fact or event, attempts which now seem closed to us.)

While it is clear that *Dog Day Afternoon* has none of the strengths of any of
these strategies and does not even try for them, the juxtaposition has the benefit
of dramatizing and reinforcing all of the recent French critiques of representation as an ideological category. What sharply differentiates the Lumet film from
any of the TV pseudo-documentaries just mentioned is precisely, if you will, its
unity of form and content: we are made secure in the illusion that the camera is
witnessing everything exactly as it happened and that what it sees is all there is.
The camera is absolute presence and absolute truth: thus, the aesthetic of

representation collapses the density of the historical event, and flattens it back out into fiction. The older values of realism, living on in commercial film, empty the anecdotal raw material of its interest and vitality; while, paradoxically, the patently degraded techniques of television narrative, irremediably condemned by their application to and juxtaposition with advertising, end up preserving the truth of the event by underscoring their own distance from it. Meanwhile, it is the very splendor of Al Pacino's virtuoso performance which marks it off from any possibility of *verismo* and irreparably condemns it to remain a Hollywood product: the star system is fundamentally, structurally, irreconcilable with neo-realism.

This is indeed the basic paradox I want to argue and to deepen in the following remarks: that what is good about the film is what is bad about it, and what is bad about it is, on the contrary, rather good in many ways; that everything which makes it a first-rate piece of filmmaking, with bravura actors, must render it suspect from another point of view, while its historical originality is to be sought in places that must seem accidental with respect to its intrinsic qualities. Yet this is not a state of things that could have been remedied by careful planning: it is not a mismatch that could have been avoided had the producers divided up their material properly, and planned a neo-realist documentary on the one hand, and a glossy robbery film on the other. Rather, we have to do here with that unresolvable, profoundly symptomatic thing which is called a contradiction, and which we may expect, if properly managed and interrogated, to raise some basic issues about the direction of contemporary culture and contemporary social reality.

What is clear from the outset is that *Dog Day Afternoon* is an ambiguous product at the level of reception; more than that, that the film is so structured that it can be focused in two quite distinct ways which seem to yield two quite distinct narrative experiences. I've promised to show that one of these narratives suggests an evolution, or at least a transformation, in the figurable class articulation of everyday life. But this is certainly not the most obvious or the most accessible reading of the film, which initially seems to inscribe itself in a very different, and for us today surely much more regressive tradition. This is what we may loosely call the existential paradigm, in the non-technical sense of this term, using it in that middle-brow media acceptation in which in current American culture it has come to designate *Catch-22* or Mailer's novels. Existentialism here means neither Heidegger nor Sartre, but rather the anti-hero of the sad sack, Saul Bellow type, and a kind of self-pitying vision of alienation (also meant in its media rather than its technical sense), frustration, and above all – yesterday's all-American concept – the "inability to communicate." Whether this particular narrative paradigm be the cause or the effect of the systematic psychologization and privatization of the ideology of the fifties and early sixties, it is clear that things change more slowly in the cultural and narrative realm than they do in the more purely ideological one, so that writers and filmmakers tend to fall back on paradigms such as this who would otherwise have no trouble recognizing a dated, no-longer-fashionable idea. Meanwhile, this "unequal development" of the narrative paradigms through which we explain daily life to ourselves is then redoubled by another trend in contemporary consumerism, namely the return to the fifties, the nostalgia fad or what the French call *la mode rétro*, in other words the deliberate substitution of the pastiche and imitation of past styles for the impossible invention of adequate contemporary or post-contemporary ones (as in a novel like *Ragtime*).

Thus, as if it were not enough that the political and collective urgencies of the sixties consigned the anti-hero and the anti-novel to the ash-can of history, we now find them being revived as a paradoxical sign of the good old days when all we had to worry about were psychological problems, momism, and whether television would ruin American culture. I would argue, for instance, not only that Miloš Forman's 1975 *One Flew over the Cuckoo's Nest* (from the Kesey novel of 1962) is a typical fifties nostalgia film, which revives all of the stereotypical protests of that bygone individualistic era, but also that, virtually a Czech film in disguise, it reduplicates that particular time lag by another, more characteristically Central European form of "unequal development."

Method acting was the working out of the ideology of the anti-hero in that relatively more concrete realm of theatrical style, voice, gesture, which borders on the behavioral stances and gestural idiom, the interpersonal languages, of everyday life, where it is indeed the stylization and effect of elements already present in the parts of the American community, and also the cause and model of newer kinds of behavior that adapt it to the street and to the real world. Here for the first time perhaps we can understand concretely how what is best about *Dog Day Afternoon* is also what is least good about it: for Al Pacino's performance as Sonny by its very brilliance thrusts the film further and further back into the antiquated paradigm of the anti-hero and the method actor. Indeed, the internal contradiction of his performance is even more striking than that: for the anti-hero, as we suggested, was predicated on non-communication and inarticulacy, from Frédéric Moreau and Kafka's K's all the way to Bellow, Malamud, Roth, and the rest; and the agonies and exhalations of method acting were perfectly calculated to render this asphyxiation of the spirit that cannot complete its sentence. But in Pacino's second-generation reappropriation of this style something paradoxical happens, namely, that the inarticulate becomes the highest form of expressiveness, the wordless stammer proves voluble, and the agony over uncommunicability suddenly turns out to be everywhere fluently comprehensible.

At this point, then, something different begins to happen, and Sonny's story ceases to express the pathos of the isolated individual or the existential loner in much the same way that the raw material from which it is drawn – that of marginality or deviancy – has ceased to be thought of as anti-social and has rather become a new social category in its own right. The gesture of revolt and the cry of rage begin to lose their frustration – the expression "impotent rage" had been a stereotype of American storytelling from Faulkner, indeed, from Norris and Dreiser, on – and to take on another meaning. Not because of any new political content to be sure: for Sonny's robbery, the politics of marginality, is not much more than part of the wild-cat strikes of contemporary everyday life; but rather simply because the gesture "projects" and is understood. We mentioned the support of the crowd (both in real life and in the Lumet movie), but that is only the most conventional inscription of this tangible resonance of Sonny's gesture within the film. More significant, it seems to me, is the manifest sympathy of the suburban moviegoing audience itself, which from within the tract housing of the *société de consommation* clearly senses the relevance to its own daily life of the reenactment of this otherwise fairly predictable specimen of urban crime. Unlike the audience of the Bogart films, who had to stand by and watch the outcast mercilessly destroyed by the monolithic and omnipotent institution of Society, this one has witnessed the collapse of the system's legitimacy (and the sapping of the legitimations on which it was based): not only Vietnam, least of all Watergate, most significantly surely the experience of inflation itself, which is the privileged phenomenon through which a middle-class audience suddenly comes to an unpleasant consciousness of its own historicity – these are some of the historical reasons for that gradual crumbling of those older protestant-ethic-type values (respect for law and order, for property, and institutions) which allows a middle-class audience to root for Sonny. In the longer run, however, the explanation must be sought in the very logic of the commodity system itself, whose programming ends up liquidating even those ideological values (respect for authority, patriotism, the ideal of the family, obedience to the law) on which the social and political order of the system rests. Thus ideal consumers – compared to their protestant-ethic ancestors, with their repressive ethics of thrift and work and self-denial – turn out to be a far more doubtful quantity than their predecessors were when it comes to fighting foreign wars or honoring your debts or cheating on your income taxes. For the citizens of some multinational stage of post-monopoly capitalism, the practical side of daily life is a test of ingenuity and a game of wits waged between the consumer and the giant faceless corporation.

These, then, are the people who understand Sonny's gesture, and whose sympathies are strangely intersected and at least arrested by the whole quite different countercultural theme of homosexuality. Yet such viewers have their counterpart within the film, not so much in the street crowd, which is only a chorus-like sign of this implicit public for Sonny's act, as rather in the hostages themselves, the women employees of the branch bank, whose changing attitudes towards Sonny thus become a significant part of what the film has to show us. Indeed, I would argue that on a second reading of the film, the relationship of form and background reverses itself, and the Sonny character – the hero, as we have seen, of a more conventional anti-hero plot – now becomes a simple pretext for the emergence and new visibility of something more fundamental in what might otherwise simply seem the background itself. This more fundamental thing is the sociological equivalent of that wholesale liquidation of older ideological values by consumer society on which we have already commented: but here it takes the more tangible form of the ghettoization of the older urban neighborhoods. The phenomenon is not an historically extremely recent one; nor is it unknown either to sociological journalism or to literature itself, where in one sense its representation may be said to go all the way back to Balzac's description of the corrosive and solvent effect of the money economy and the market system on the sleepy *Gemeinschaften* of the older provincial towns.

What is less well understood is the degree to which this process, which in the United States was significantly accelerated after the end of World War II, and thus contemporaneous with the introduction of television and the launching of the Cold War, was the result of deliberate political decisions that can be identified and dated. The post-war federal highway program and the momentum given to the construction of individual family dwellings by veterans' housing bills are essential components in the new corporate strategy:

The 1949 Housing Act introduced the idea of federal assistance for private development of the center cities, an approach to urban renewal vigorously pushed by the General Electric Company, large banks and insurance companies. The center cities were not to be the site of housing development for working class people ... These political and economic decisions effectively determined the pattern of individual and residential development for the next generation. The white working class was fated for dispersal; the center cities were to be reserved for the very poor and the relatively affluent. In the circumstances, durable goods purchases – cars, washing machines, one-family houses – began to absorb an increasing proportion of workers' incomes and had an enormous impact on work patterns.[2]

We may add that this vision of the future was first systematically tried out on Newark, New Jersey, which may thus fairly lay claim to something of the ominous and legendary quality which surrounds the names of the targets of the World War II strategic bombing experiments.

But there is a fundamental distortion in the way in which we have traditionally tended to deplore such developments in contemporary American
society as the destruction of the inner city and the rise of shopping center
culture. On the whole I would think it would be fair to say that we have
thought of these developments as inevitable results of a logic of consumer
society which neither individuals nor politicians could do very much to reverse;
even radicals have been content to stress the continuity between the present-
day atomization of the older communities and social groups and Marx's analysis
of the destructive effects of classical capitalism, from the enclosure stage all the
way to the emergence of the factory system. What is new today, what can be
sensed in the excerpt from Stanley Aronowitz's *False Promises* quoted above
just as much as in *Dog Day Afternoon* itself, is the dawning realization that
someone was responsible for all that, that such momentous social transformations were not merely part of the on-going logic of the system – although they
are certainly that too – but were also, and above all, the consequences of the
decisions of powerful and strategically placed individuals and groups. Yet the
reemergence of these groups – the renewed possibility of once again catching
sight of what Lukács would have called the *subject* that history of which the rest
of us are still only just the *objects* – this is not to be understood as the result of
increased information on our part of so-called revisionist historians; rather, our
very possibility of rewriting history in this way is itself to be understood as the
function of a fundamental change in the historical situation itself, and of the
power and class relations that underlie it.

Before we say what that change is, however, we want to remember how
vividly *Dog Day Afternoon* explores the space which is the result of these
historical changes, the ghettoized neighborhood with its decaying small busi-
nesses gradually being replaced by parking lots or chain stores. It is no accident
indeed that the principal circuit of communications of the film passes between
the mom-and-pop store in which the police have set up their headquarters, and
the branch bank – the real-life original was appropriately enough a branch of
Chase Manhattan – in which Sonny is holding his hostages. Thus it is possible
for the truth of recent urban history to be expressed within the framework of
the bank scenes themselves; it is enough to note, first, that everyone in the
branch is nothing but a salaried employee of an invisible multi-national empire,
and then, as the film goes on, that the work in this already peripheral and
decentered, fundamentally colonized, space is done by those doubly second-
class and under-payable beings who are women, and whose structurally marginal situation is thus not without analogy to Sonny's own, or at least reflects it
in much the same way that a Third World proletariat might reflect minority
violence and crime in the First. One of the more realistic things about recent
American commercial culture, indeed, has been its willingness to recognize and

to represent at least in passing the strange coexistence and superposition of the America of today of social worlds as rigidly divided from each other as in a caste system, a kind of post-Bowery and/or permanent Third World existence at the heart of the First World itself.

Yet this kind of perception does not in itself constitute that renewed class consciousness we evoked at the beginning of this [chapter], but as such merely provides the material for a rhetoric of marginality, for a new and more virulent populism. The Marxian conception of class, indeed, must be distinguished from the academic bourgeois sociological one above all by its emphasis on relationality. For academic sociology, the social classes are understood in isolation from each other, on the order of sub-cultures or independent group "life styles": the frequently used term "stratum" effectively conveys this view of independent social units, which implies in turn that each can be studied separately, without reference to one another, by some researcher who goes out into the field. So we can have monographs on the ideology of the professional stratum, on the political apathy of the secretarial stratum, and so forth. For Marxism, however, these empirical observations do not yet penetrate to the structural reality of the class system which it sees as being essentially dichotomous, at least in that latest and last social formation of prehistory which is capitalism: "The whole of society," a famous sentence of the *Communist Manifesto* tells us, "is increasingly split into two great hostile camps, into two great classes directly confronting one another: the bourgeoisie and the proletariat." To which we must only add (1) that this underlying starkly dichotomous class antagonism only becomes fully visible empirically in times of absolute crises and polarization, that is to say, in particular, at the moment of social revolution itself; and (2) that in a henceforth worldwide class system the oppositions in question are evidently a good deal more complicated and difficult to reconstruct than they were within the more representational, or figurable, framework of the older nation state.

This said, it is evident that a Marxian theory of classes involves the restructuring of the fragmentary and unrelated data of empirical bourgeois sociology in a holistic way: in terms, Lukács would say, of the social totality, or, as his antagonist Althusser would have it, of a "pre-given complex hierarchical structure of dominant and subordinate elements." In either case, the random sub-groupings of academic sociology would find their place in determinate, although sometimes ambivalent, structural positions with respect to the dichotomous opposition of the two fundamental social classes themselves, about which innovative recent work — I'm thinking, for the bourgeoisie, of Sartre's Flaubert trilogy; for the proletariat, of the Aronowitz book already quoted from — has demonstrated the mechanisms by which each class defines itself in terms of the other and constitutes a virtual anti-class with respect to the other, and this, from overt ideological values all the way down to the most apparently non-political, "merely" cultural features of everyday life.

The difference between the Marxian view of structurally dichotomous classes and the academic sociological picture of independent strata is however more than a merely intellectual one: once again, consciousness of social reality, or on the other hand the repression of the awareness of such reality, is itself "determined by social being" in Marx's phrase and is therefore a function of the social and historical situation. A remarkable sociological investigation by Ralf Dahrendorf has indeed confirmed the view that these two approaches to the social classes – the academic and the Marxist – are themselves class-conditioned and reflect the structural perspectives of the two fundamental class positions themselves. Thus it is those on the higher rungs of the social ladder who tend to formulate their view of the social order, looking down at it, as separate strata; while those on the bottom looking up tend to map their social experience in terms of the stark opposition of "them" and "us."[3]

But if this is so, then the representation of victimized classes in isolation – whether in the person of Sonny himself as a marginal, or the bank's clerical workers as an exploited group – is not enough to constitute a class system, let alone to precipitate a beginning consciousness of class in its viewing public. Nor are the repeated references to the absent bank management sufficient to transform the situation into a genuine class relationship, since this term does not find concrete representation – or *figuration*, to return to our earlier term – within the filmic narrative itself. Yet such representation is present in *Dog Day Afternoon*, and it is this unexpected appearance, in a part of the film where one would not normally look for it, that constitutes its greatest interest in the present context – our possibility of focusing it being as we have argued directly proportional to our ability to let go of the Sonny story and to relinquish those older narrative habits that program us to follow the individual experiences of a hero or an anti-hero, rather than the explosion of the text and the operation of meaning in other, random narrative fragments.

If we can do this – and we have begun to do so when we are willing to reverse the robbery itself, and read Sonny's role as that of a mere pretext for the revelation of that colonized space which is the branch bank, with its peripheralized or marginalized work force – then what slowly comes to occupy the film's center of gravity is the action outside the bank itself, and in particular the struggle for precedence between the local police and the FBI officials. Now there are various ways of explaining this shift of focus, none of them wrong: for one thing, we can observe that, once Sonny has been effectively barricaded inside the bank, he can no longer initiate events, the center of gravity of the narrative as such then passing to the outside. More pertinently still, since the operative paradox of the film – underscored by Al Pacino's acting – is the fundamental likeability of Sonny, this external displacement of the acting can be understood as the narrative attempt to generate an authority figure who can deal directly with him without succumbing to his charm. But this is not just a matter of narrative dynamics; it also involves an ideological answer to the fundamental question: how to imagine authority today, how to conceive imaginatively – that is in non-abstract, non-conceptual form – of a principle of authority that can express the essential impersonality and post-individualistic structure of the power structure of our society while still operating among real people, in the tangible necessities of daily life and individual situations of repression?

It is clear that the figure of the FBI agent (James Broderick) represents a narrative solution to this ideological contradiction, and the nature of the solution is underscored by the characterological styles of the FBI agents and the local police chief, Maretti (Charles Durning), whose impotent rages and passionate incompetence are there, not so much to humanize him, as rather to set off the cool and technocratic expertise of his rival. In one sense, of course, this contrast is what has nowadays come to be called an intertextual one: this is not really the encounter of two characters, who represent two "individuals," but rather the encounter of two narrative paradigms, indeed, of two narrative stereotypes: the clean-cut Efrem Zimbalist-type FBI agents, with their fifties haircuts, and the earthy urban cop whose television embodiments are so multiple as to be embarrassing: FBI meets Kojak! Yet one of the most effective things in the film, and the most haunting impression left by *Dog Day Afternoon* in the area of performance, is surely not so much the febrile heroics of Al Pacino as rather their stylistic opposite, the starkly blank and emotionless, expressionless, coolness of the FBI man himself. This gazing face, behind which decision-making is reduced to (or developed into) pure technique, yet whose judgments and assessments are utterly inaccessible to spectators either within or without the filmic frame, is one of the most alarming achievements of recent American moviemaking, and may be said to embody something like the truth of a rather different but equally actual genre, the espionage thriller, where it has tended to remain obfuscated by the cumbersome theological apparatus of a dialectic of Good and Evil.

Meanwhile, the more existential and private-tragic visions of this kind of figure – I'm thinking of the lawman (Denver Pyle) in Arthur Penn's *Bonnie and Clyde* (1967) – project a nemesis which is still motivated by personal vindictiveness, so that the process of tracking the victim down retains a kind of passion of a still recognizable human type; Penn's more recent *The Missouri Breaks* (1976) tried to make an advance on this personalized dramatization of the implacability of social institutions by endowing its enforcer with a generalized paranoia (and, incidentally, furnishing Marlon Brando with the occasion of one of his supreme bravura performances); but it is not really much of an improvement and the vision remains locked in the pathos of a self-pitying and individualistic vision of history.

In *Dog Day Afternoon*, however, the organization man is neither vindictive nor paranoid; he is in this sense quite beyond the good and evil of conventional melodrama, and inaccessible to any of the psychologizing stereotypes that are indulged in most of the commercial representations of the power of institutions; his anonymous features mark a chilling and unexpected insertion of the real into the otherwise relatively predictable framework of the fiction film – and this, not, as we have pointed out earlier, by traditional documentary or montage techniques, but rather through a kind of dialectic of connotations on the level of the style of acting, a kind of silence or charged absence in a sign-system in which the other modes of performance have programmed us for a different kind of expressiveness.

Now the basic contrast, that between the police chief and the FBI agent, dramatizes a social and historical change which was once an important theme of our literature but to which we have today become so accustomed as to have lost our sensitivity to it: in their very different ways, the novels of John O'Hara and the sociological investigations of C. Wright Mills documented a gradual but irreversible erosion of local and state-wide power structures and leadership or authority networks by national, and, in our own time, multinational ones. Think of the social hierarchy of Gibbsville coming into disillusioning contact with the new wealth and the new political hierarchies of the New Deal era; think – even more relevantly for our present purposes – of the crisis of figurability implied by this shift of power from the face-to-face small-town life situations of the older communities to the abstraction of nation-wide power (a crisis already suggested by the literary representation of "politics" as a specialized theme in itself).

The police lieutenant thus comes to incarnate the very helplessness and impotent agitation of the local power structure; and with this inflection of our reading, with this interpretive operation, the whole allegorical structure of *Dog Day Afternoon* suddenly emerges in the light of day. The FBI agent – now that we have succeeded in identifying what he supersedes – comes to occupy the place of that immense and decentralized power network which marks the present multinational stage of monopoly capitalism. The very absence in his features becomes a sign and an expression of the presence/absence of corporate power in our daily lives, all-shaping and omnipotent and yet rarely accessible in figurable terms, that is to say, in the representable form of individual actors or agents. The FBI man is thus the structural opposite of the secretarial staff of the branch bank: the latter present in all their existential individuality, but inessential and utterly marginalized, the former so depersonalized as to be little more than a marker – in the empirical world of everyday life, of *fait divers* and newspaper articles – of the place of ultimate power and control.

Yet with even this shadowy embodiment of the forces of those multinational corporate structures that are the subject of present-day world history, the possibility of genuine figuration, and with it, the possibility of a kind of beginning adequate class consciousness itself, is given. Now the class structure of the film becomes articulated in three tiers: the first, that newly atomized petty bourgeoisie of the cities whose "proletarianization" and marginalization is expressed both by the women employees on the one hand, and by the lumpens on the other (Sonny and his accomplice, Sal [John Cazale], but also the crowd itself, an embodiment of the logic of marginality that runs all the way from the "normal" deviancies of homosexuality and petty crime to the pathologies of Sal's paranoia and Ernie's [Chris Sarandon] transsexuality). A second level is constituted by the impotent power structures of the local neighborhoods, which represent something like the national bourgeoisies of the Third World, colonized and gutted of their older content, left with little more than the hollow shells and external trappings of authority and decision making. Finally, of course, that multinational capitalism into which the older ruling classes of our world have evolved, and whose primacy is inscribed in the spatial trajectory of the film itself as it moves from the ghettoized squalor of the bank interior to that eerie and impersonal science fiction landscape of the airport finale: a corporate space without inhabitants, utterly technologized and functional, a place beyond city and country alike – collective, yet without people, automated and computerized, yet without any of that older utopian or dystopian clamor, without any of those still distinctive qualities that characterized the then still "modern" and streamlined futuristic vision of the corporate future in our own recent past. Here – as in the blank style of acting of the FBI agents – the film makes a powerful non-conceptual point by destroying its own intrinsic effects and canceling an already powerful, yet conventional, filmic and performative language.

Two final observations about this work, the one about its ultimate aesthetic and political effects, the other about its historical conditions of possibility. Let us take the second problem first: we have here repeatedly stressed the dependence of a narrative figuration of class consciousness on the historical situation. We have stressed both the dichotomous nature of the class structure, and the dependence of class consciousness itself on the logic of the social and historical conjuncture. Marx's dictum, that consciousness is determined by social being, holds for class consciousness itself no less than for any other form. We must now therefore try to make good our claim, and say why, if some new and renewed possibility of class consciousness seems at least faintly detectable, this should be the case now and today rather than ten or twenty years ago.

But the answer to this question can be given concisely and decisively; it is implicit in the very expression, "multinational corporation," which – as great a misnomer as it may be (since all of them are in reality expressions of American capitalism) – would not have been invented had not something new suddenly emerged which seemed to demand a new name for itself. It seems to be a fact that after the failure of the Vietnam War, the so-called multinational corporations – what used to be called the "ruling classes" or later on the "power elite" of monopoly capitalism – have once again emerged in public from the wings of history to advance their own interests. The failure of the war "has meant that the advancement of world capitalist revolution now depends more on the initiative of corporations and less on governments. The increasingly political pretensions of the global corporation are thus unavoidable but they inevitably mean more public exposure, and exposure carries with it the risk of increased hostility."[4] But in our terms, the psychological language of the authors of *Global Reach* may be translated as "class consciousness," and with this new historical visibility capitalism becomes objectified and dramatized as an actor and as a subject of history with an allegorical intensity and simplicity that had not been the case since the 1930s.

Now a final word about the political implications of the film itself and the complexities of the kind of allegorical structure we have imputed to it. Can *Dog Day Afternoon* be said to be a political film? Surely not, since the class system we have been talking about is merely implicit in it, and can just as easily be ignored or repressed by its viewers as brought to consciousness. What we have been describing is at best something pre-political, the gradual rearticulation of the raw material of a film of this kind in terms and relationships which are once again, after the anti-political and privatizing, "existential" paradigms of the forties and fifties, recognizably those of class.

Yet we should also understand that the use of such material is much more complicated and problematical than the terminology of representation would suggest. Indeed, in the process by which class structure finds expression in the triangular relationship within the film between Sonny, the police chief, and the FBI man, we have left out an essential step. For the whole qualitative and dialectical inequality of this relationship is mediated by the star system itself, and in that sense – far more adequately than in its overt thematics of the media exploitation of Sonny's hold-up – the film can be said to be about itself. Indeed we reach each of the major actors in terms of his distance from the star system: Sonny's relationship to Maretti is that of superstar to character actor, and our reading of this particular narrative is not a direct passage from one character or actant to another, but passes through the mediation of our identification and decoding of the actors' status as such. Even more interesting and complex than this is our decoding of the FBI agent, whose anonymity in the filmic narrative is expressed very precisely through his anonymity within the framework of the Hollywood star system. The face is blank and unreadable precisely because the actor is himself unidentifiable.

In fact, of course, it is only within the coding of a Hollywood system that he is unfamiliar, for the actor in question soon after became a permanent feature of the durable and well-known television series, *Family* (1976–80). But the point is precisely that in this respect television and its reference is a different system of production, but even more, that television comes itself to figure, with respect to Hollywood films, that new and impersonal multinational system which is coming to supersede the more individualistic one of an older national capitalism and an older commodity culture. Thus, the external, extrinsic sociological fact or system of realities finds itself inscribed within the internal intrinsic experience of the film in what Sartre in a suggestive and too-little known concept in his *Psychology of Imagination* calls the analogon:[5] that structural nexus in our reading or viewing experience, in our operations of decoding or aesthetic reception, which can then do double duty and stand as the substitute and the representative within the aesthetic object of a phenomenon on the outside which cannot in the very nature of things be "rendered" directly. This complex of intra-and extra-aesthetic relationships might then be schematically represented as figure 16.1.

Here then we find an ultimate formal confirmation of our initial hypothesis, that what is bad about the film is what is best about it, and that the work is a paradoxical realization in which qualities and defects form an inextricable dialectical unity. For it is ultimately the star system itself – that commodity phenomenon most stubbornly irreconcilable with any documentary or ciné-verité type of exploration of the real – which is thus responsible for even that limited authenticity which *Dog Day Afternoon* is able to achieve.

Afterword

I would today [1992] say that this [chapter] is a study in what I have come to call *cognitive mapping*.[6] It presupposes a radical incompatibility between the possibilities of an older national language or culture (which is still the framework in which literature is being produced today) and the transnational, worldwide organization of the economic infrastructure of contemporary capitalism. The result of this contradiction is a situation in which the truth of our social life as a whole – in Lukács's terms, as a totality – is increasingly irreconcilable with the possibilities of aesthetic expression or articulation available to us; a situation about which it can be asserted that if we can make a work of art from our experience, if we can give experience the form of a story that can be

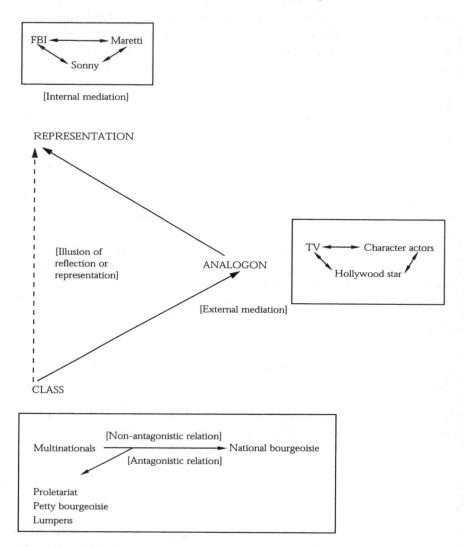

Figure 16.1   Complex of intra- and extra-aesthetic relationships

told, then it is no longer true, even as individual experience; and if we can grasp the truth about our world as a totality, then we may find it some purely conceptual expression but we will no longer be able to maintain an imaginative relationship to it. In current psychoanalytic terminology, we will thus be unable to insert ourselves, as individual subjects, into an ever more massive and impersonal or transpersonal reality outside ourselves. This is the perspective in which it becomes a matter of more than mere intellectual curiosity to interrogate the artistic production of our own time for signs of some new, so far only dimly conceivable, collective forms which may be expected to replace the older individualistic ones (those either of conventional realism or of a now conventionalized modernism); and it is also the perspective in which an indecisive aesthetic and cultural phenomenon like *Dog Day Afternoon* takes on the values of a revealing symptom.

Notes

1 See, for a useful survey of the newspaper coverage of the Wojtowicz robbery, Eric Holm, "Dog Day aftertaste," in *Jump Cut*, 10–11 (June, 1976), pp. 3–4.
2 Stanley Aronowitz, *False Promises* (New York, McGraw-Hill, 1973), p. 383.
3 Ralf Dahrendorf, *Class and Class Conflict in Industrial Society* (Stanford, Stanford University Press, 1959), pp. 280–9.
4 See Richard J. Barnet and Ronald E. Muller, *Global Reach* (New York, Simon and Schuster, 1974), p. 68.
5 Jean-Paul Sartre, *The Psychology of Imagination* (New York: Washington Square Press, 1968), pp. 21–71, where analogon is translated as "the analogue."
6 See my *Postmodernism, or, The Cultural Logic of Late Capitalism* (Durham, Duke University Press, 1991), particularly the first and last chapters.

17

National Allegory in Wyndham Lewis

National allegory is a strategy that figures prominently for Jameson in the practice of cognitive mapping. The following selection is taken from *Fables of Aggression* (1979), Jameson's book-length study of the painter and novelist Wyndham Lewis. In this section Jameson explores the function of national allegory in Lewis's novels.

Lewis, unread, is customarily lumped together for convenience with the great modernists who were his sometime friends or collaborators – Pound, Eliot, Joyce, and Yeats – the latter having come to form an exclusive and overisolated pantheon in that unexamined schema which passes the most often for our notion of literary history. Yet this honor by association does Lewis little good, I think, and only serves to obscure the real nature of his originality.

Unlike the aforementioned writers, he was essentially a *political* novelist. In this role he modeled himself by design as well as by temperament on the most dazzling and successful craftsman in political art whom modern Britain has known – namely, George Bernard Shaw.[1] Lewis wished indeed to become an anti-Shaw, artistic technician (replacing music with painting) and journalist–ideologue all at once, this time using Nietzsche *against* the idea of progress; peopling his works with secondary characters who are his own spokesmen, though the socialist chauffeurs and mechanics of Shaw are here replaced by young and truculent Blackshirts; and like the older man, evolving an idiosyncratic and cantankerous persona in inveterate contradiction with the fashions of the time.

That the parallel runs a little deeper than the role itself may be judged by *Tarr*, which is in this respect a virtual rewrite of *Man and Superman*, with its garrulous overintellectualized hero who succumbs to the invincible power of sex; by *The Childermass*, whose setting in the afterlife bears some striking similarities to the cosomological scheme of the "Don Juan in Hell" sequence of the same play and by *The Human Age*, which, with its reverse evolutionary perspective, it is not without its affinities to the central themes of *Back to Methuselah*. To ask why Lewis did not simply become a fascist Shaw is to place ourselves squarely before the central issues of his work.

At the same time, Lewis was an internationalist, the most European and least insular of all the great contemporary British writers. He felt the impact of Dostoyevsky at a time when Gide was only just introducing the latter to the French-speaking world; the Russian novelist's dramatization of the vagaries of individual consciousness clearly pave the way for the portrait of Kreisler, by general agreement the most remarkable psychological study in all of Lewis, with its grotesque self-revelatory outbursts. (Think only of the moment in which a sluggish and aroused Kreisler murmurs to his half-naked model, "Your arms are like bananas!" [*Tarr*, p. 177][2] or of the climactic duel scene, when, seeing his adversary surreptitiously gulp tranquillizers, he shrieks, with all the ghastly peremptoriness of the winning child, "Give me one! . . . I want a jujube. Ask Herr Soltyk! Tell him not to keep them for himself!" [*Tarr*, p. 250]). In this sense, indeed, *Tarr*, with its double plot, and its twin heroes Tarr and Kreisler, may be described as a work in which a Shavian character contemplates the scandals of a Dostoyevskian social world. Lewis's politics, moreover, are profoundly marked by the book he called "the Bible of counter-revolution," Dostoyevsky's *The Possessed*.

Yet he was also one of the few great Western writers in recent times to have been deeply responsive to the German, as well as the Mediterranean, fact. He had studied in that country and understood it as something other than a symbol. In Kreisler he produced a German figure far more troubled and human than Lawrence's Prussian officer ("Tarr's sympathies were all with Kreisler . . . an atavistic creature whom on the whole he preferred" [*Tarr*, p. 267]). In Lewis's imagination, indeed, the German nation, as the pariah of European politics and the victim of Versailles, tends to figure the *id* rather than that respressive superego which the Prussian manner has generally connoted for foreigners. It is this German component which is no doubt as responsible as anything else for the deliberate cynicism of what is for Lewis as well as for Brecht the comedy of sex, the meaningless and exasperating bondage to desire:

Ob sie wollen oder nicht, – sie sind bereit.
Das ist die sexuelle Hörigkeit.

The pale Shavian situation thereby takes on something of the full-blooded and raucous joviality of *Baal*: it is a note which would have been inconceivable (for opposite reasons) either in the atmosphere of Anglo-Saxon prudishness or in the relatively culinary tradition of French sensuality; and may serve as a useful corrective to present-day Reichian sexual optimism.

Lewis is indeed so keenly aware of these various national traditions that they constitute the very backdrop and organizational framework of the works written before World War I: the stories of *The Wild Body* and *Tarr* itself, with its portrait gallery of international Bohemia in the prewar City of Light. *Tarr* thus takes its place among the most characteristic monuments to the aristo-cratic-bohemian cosmopolitan and multilingual European culture of that per-iod, whose most substantial expression is *The Magic Mountain* of Thomas Mann (1924). Such a juxtaposition reminds us that the use of national types projects an essentially allegorical mode of representation, in which the individual characters figure those more abstract national characteristics which are read as their inner essence. In its simplest form, that of the contemplation of a single foreign national essence alone, such allegory often serves as the instrument of cultural critique: thus Stendhal's heroic images of the Italian or the Spanish tempera-ment are designed to humiliate the conformistic philistinism of the French business classes of his time by juxtaposing it with the *gestus* of a vanished Renaissance.

Yet where, as in *Tarr* or *Der Zauberberg*, the various national types find themselves grouped within a common ballroom or Grand Hotel, a more complex network of interrelations and collisions emerges, and with it a dialecti-cally new and more complicated allegorical system. Now narrative meaning becomes relational, as momentary alliances develop and disintegrate. Fascinat-ing apparitions – the Russo-German Anastasya of *Tarr*, the Polish Clawdia Chauchat of Thomas Mann's sanitorium – criss-cross the field of force, leaving disarray behind them. Figures initially distant – Kreisler and the Englishman – slowly and with mutual wariness and distrust approach each other. Under these circumstances, allegory ceases to be that static decipherment of one-on-one correspondences with which it is still so often identified and opens up that specific and uniquely allegorical space between signifier and signified, in which "the signifier is what represents the subject for another signifier" (Lacan).[3] This is the sense in which the allegorical signified of such narratives is ultimately always World War I, or Apocalypse: not in any punctual prediction or reflec-tion of this conflict as a chronological event, but rather as the ultimate con-flictual "truth" of the sheer, mobile, shifting relationality of national types and of the older nation-states which are their content.

Hence the centrality of Kreisler himself, that "certain disquieting element" which is not without impunity introduced into the concourse of nations.

Kreisler in Paris — that is the stiff and powerful, ungainly, explosive Prussian temperament in the throes of Culture, flinging "a man or a woman on to nine feet of canvas and [pummelling] them on it for a couple of hours, until they promised to remain there or were incapable of moving" (*Tarr*, p. 75). Even Kreisler in love tells the story of a national inferiority complex: paralyzed by the prospect of courting Anastasya, he catches fire at the chance of feeling jealousy, raging inwardly at the sight of her surreptitious conversations with the ill-fated Pole, Soltyk.

It is indeed around Soltyk that Kreisler's most turbid and volcanic emotions organize themselves: Soltyk, who has supplanted him as the borrower-in-chief of his friend Vokt's money; Soltyk, who is inexplicably able to murmur interminable small talk to Anastasya; Soltyk, above all, who with his "hereditary polish of manner," his "self-possession, his ready social accomplishment, depressed Kreisler: for it was not in his nature to respect those qualities, yet he felt they were what he always lacked" (*Tarr*, p. 140).

Soltyk is in fact a virtual double of Kreisler, bearing a distant and mocking physical resemblance to the latter as though he represents some more prosperous and well-favored branch of the family, some far more successful second version, which can but reinforce the envy and resentment of the botched first draft. In cultural terms, then, Kreisler's fury reenacts the humiliation of Germany, not merely before the more sophisticated culture of the West, but even in the face of the Frenchified and Westernized culture of subject Poland as well. Unfortunately, in spite of the Pole's cultural polish, it is the German, along with his even more "alarming" Russian second, who has the real power. The duel scene (compare its anticlimactic equivalent in *Sentimental Education*) is thus a league of the strong against the weak, an acting out by the two great powers of their cultural marginalization, of which history's version is the sequence of Polish partitions, as well as the self-destructive sequels of the various Central and Eastern European war efforts. Lewis's psychopathology of Kreisler may thus be read as the figuration of that complex of German feelings which served as the ideological justification for the War, and as a virtually inexhaustible source of war enthusiasm, while the relational and allegorical structure of his narrative articulates (without conceptualizing it) that "combination of antagonistic principles...that is the essence of imperialism" and that made 1914 inevitable.[4] On Lenin's view, indeed, the war of the nation-states is an ideological appearance ("nationality and fatherland as essential forms of the bourgeois system")[5] which political praxis must both unmask as, and transform into, the reality of transnational civil war and class struggle: Lenin's program thereby corresponds exactly to the "break" in Lewis's own work and to the disintegration of his older national system.

What we must now investigate are the objective preconditions of this initial structure, which we will henceforth call "national allegory." The very unfamiliarity of this now outmoded narrative system suggests that as a formal possibility it is enabled by an objective situation whose modification once again excludes it. To understand the history of forms, as the ideologists of modernism do, as an autonomous dynamic of purely formal innovations, each of which is motivated by the will to replace an establishment form by a novelty at length superseded in its turn, is to think such modifications in an empty, cyclical and ultimately static way. From any point of view, however — whether that of the formal possibilities themselves, or of their content — every great formal innovation is *determinate*, and reflects a situation that cannot immediately be assimilated to those which may precede or follow it.[6]

Meanwhile, it also seems useful to insist that the history of forms is not the only set of coordinates within which artistic production and innovation need to be understood. It should not be forgotten that the very concept of production itself — in wide currency today — entails a consequence which is less often explored, namely the requirement of a preexistent availability of certain specific raw materials, or what I have elsewhere called a specific "logic of content."[7] The question about the objective preconditions of a given form has the strategic advantage of allowing us to cut across the false problems of causality or "determinism": it does not program us into a situation in which we find ourselves obliged to affirm the meaningless proposition that the verbal artifact *Tarr* was somehow "caused" by forces on the quite different levels of political history or socioeconomic organization. Rather, it directs our attention to the more sensible procedure of exploring those semantic and structural givens which are logically prior to this text and without which its emergence is inconceivable. This is of course the sense in which national allegory in general, and *Tarr* in particular, presuppose not merely the nation-state itself as the basic functional unit of world politics, but also the objective existence of a system of nation-states, the international diplomatic machinery of pre-World-War-I Europe which, originating in the sixteenth century, was dislocated in significant ways by the War and the Soviet Revolution.

This account of the preconditions of Lewis's novel is a very different proposition from interpretive statements which might take it as the "reflexion" of the European diplomatic system or see its violent content as betraying some "homology" with World War I. An analysis of the semantic and structural preconditions of a form is not a correspondence theory of art; nor do we mean to see national allegory as an afterimage given off by the international diplomatic system itself. Rather, like any form, it must be read as an instable and provisory solution to an aesthetic dilemma which is itself the manifestation of a social and historical contradiction.

Thus, national allegory should be understood as a formal attempt to bridge the increasing gap between the existential data of everyday life within a given nation-state and the structural tendency of monopoly capital to develop on a worldwide, essentially transnational scale. Nineteenth-century or "classical" realism presupposed the relative intelligibility and self-sufficiency of the national experience from within, a coherence in its social life such that the narrative of the destinies of its individual citizens can be expected to achieve formal completeness. It is this formal possibility which the pan-European allegory of *Tarr* now calls into question, implying the increasing inability of English life to furnish the raw materials for an intelligible narrative code. Tarr himself, with his observer's aloofness from his setting, in this respect dramatizes the security of the liberal and counterrevolutionary class compromise of the British tradition from the seething and politicized history of the continental states. Yet this security is abstract: at the very same moment, owing to its momentary industrial and naval supremacy, the British Empire is inextricably and structurally involved in and dependent on the outside world – whence the rather different, more properly colonial allegory of a novel like Forster's *Passage to India*. Thus the lived experience of the British situation is domestic, while its structural intelligibility is international: it is from this dilemma that *Tarr* as an aesthetic totality seeks to deliver itself.[8] [...]

Notes

1 "I am just as genial a character as Mr Bernard Shaw, to give you an idea. I am rather what Mr Shaw would have been like if he had been an artist – I here use 'artist' in the widest possible sense – if he had not been an Irishman, if he had been a young man when the Great War occurred, if he had studied painting and philosophy instead of economics and Ibsen, and if he had been more richly endowed with imagination, emotion, intellect and a few other things ...;" *Blasting and Bombardiering* (London, Eyre and Spottiswoode, 1937), p. 3.
2 Wyndham Lewis, *Tarr* (London, Calder and Boyars, 1968).
3 Jacques Lacan, "Subversion du sujet et dialectique du désir," in *Écrits* (Paris, Seuil, 1966), p. 819. And compare this other dictum: "Only the relationship of one signifier to another signifier engenders the relationship of signifier to signified;" quoted in A. G. Wilden, *The Language of the Self* (Baltimore, Maryland: Johns Hopkins University Press, 1968), p. 239.
4 V. I. Lenin, *Collected Works* (Moscow, Progress Publishers, 1961), vol. 24, p. 465.
5 Ibid., vol. 21 (1964), p. 38.
6 This is not to exclude more global analyses of the specific dynamic of such cultural and formal innovations, which is obviously closely related to the rhythm of capitalist production itself and which Barthes has described as "that purely formal process of

Exercises in Cognitive Mapping

the rotation of possibles which characterizes Fashion ... here *difference* is the motor, not of history, but of diachrony; history intervenes only when these micro-rhythms are perturbed;" Roland Barthes, *Essais critiques* (Paris, Seuil, 1964), p. 262.

7   Fredric Jameson, *Marxism and Form* (Princeton, NJ, Princeton University Press, 1971), pp. 327–31, and also pp. 164–9.

8   See, for an inventory of the formal consequences of this "break" in English literature, Terry Eagleton's *Exiles and Emigres* (New York, Schocken, 1970): "The process of grasping any culture as a whole, of discerning its essential forms and directions, is always, needless to say, an acutely difficult task; but that difficulty seems significantly exacerbated in modern English Society" (p. 221).

18

Third-world Literature in the Era of Multinational Capitalism

This chapter was originally published in *Social Text* in 1986. In "A Brief Response" (1987) to a critique of the essay, Jameson explained: "The essay was intended as an intervention into a 'first-world' literary and critical situation, in which it seemed important to me to stress the loss of certain literary functions and intellectual commitments in the contemporary American scene. It seemed useful to dramatize that loss by showing the constitutive presence of those things – what I called narrative allegory [...] and also the political role of the cultural intellectual – in other parts of the world."

Judging from recent conversations among third-world intellectuals, there is now an obsessive return of the national situation itself, the name of the country that returns again and again like a gong, the collective attention to "us" and what we have to do and how we do it, to what we can't do and what we do better than this or that nationality, our unique characteristics, in short, to the level of the "people." This is not the way American intellectuals have been discussing "America," and indeed one might feel that the whole matter is nothing but that old thing called "nationalism," long since liquidated here and rightly so. Yet a certain nationalism is fundamental in the third world (and also in the most vital areas of the second world), thus making it legitimate to ask whether it is all that bad in the end.[1] Does in fact the message of some disabused and more experienced first-world wisdom (that of Europe even more than of the United States) consist in urging these nation states to outgrow it as fast as possible? The predictable reminders of Kampuchea and of Iraq and Iran do not really seem to me to settle anything or suggest by what these nationalisms might be replaced except perhaps some global American postmodernist culture.

Many arguments can be made for the importance and interest of non-canonical forms of literature such as that of the third world,[2] but one is peculiarly self-defeating because it borrows the weapons of the adversary: the strategy of trying to prove that these texts are as "great" as those of the canon itself. The object is then to show that, to take an example from another non-canonical form, Dashiell Hammett is really as great as Dostoyevsky, and there-fore can be admitted. This is to attempt dutifully to wish away all traces of that "pulp" format which is constitutive of sub-genres, and it invites immediate failure insofar as any passionate reader of Dostoyevsky will know at once, after a few pages, that those kinds of satisfactions are not present. Nothing is to be gained by passing over in silence the radical difference of non-canonical texts. The third-world novel will not offer the satisfactions of Proust or Joyce; what is more damaging than that, perhaps, is its tendency to remind us of outmoded stages of our own first-world cultural development and to cause us to conclude that "they are still writing novels like Dreiser or Sherwood Anderson."

A case could be built on this kind of discouragement, with its deep existential commitment to a rhythm of modernist innovation if not fashion-changes; but it would not be a moralizing one – a historicist one, rather, which challenges our imprisonment in the present of postmodernism and calls for a reinvention of the radical difference of *our own* cultural past and its now seemingly old-fashioned situations and novelties.

But I would rather argue all this a different way, at least for now;[3] these reactions to third-world texts are at one and the same time perfectly natural, perfectly comprehensible, *and* terribly parochial. If the purpose of the canon is to restrict our aesthetic sympathies, to develop a range of rich and subtle perceptions which can be exercised only on the occasion of a small but choice body of texts, to discourage us from reading anything else or from reading those things in different ways, then it is humanly impoverishing. Indeed our want of sympathy for these often unmodern third-world texts is itself frequently but a disguise for some deeper fear of the affluent about the way people actually live in other parts of the world – a way of life that still has little in common with daily life in the American suburb. There is nothing particularly disgraceful in having lived a sheltered life, in never having had to confront the difficulties, the complications and the frustrations of urban living, but it is nothing to be particularly proud of either. Moreover, a limited experience of life normally does not make for a wide range of sympathies with very different kinds of people (I'm thinking of differences that range from gender and race all the way to those of social class and culture).

The way in which all this affects the reading process seems to be as follows: as western readers whose tastes (and much else) have been formed by our own modernisms, a popular or socially realistic third-world novel tends to come before us, not immediately, but as though already-read. We sense, between ourselves and this alien text, the presence of another reader, of the Other reader, for whom a narrative, which strikes us as conventional or naïve, has a freshness of information and a social interest that we cannot share. The fear and the resistance I'm evoking has to do, then, with the sense of our own non-coincidence with that Other reader, so different from ourselves; our sense that to coincide in any adequate way with that Other "ideal reader" – that is to say, to read this text adequately – we would have to give up a great deal that is individually precious to us and acknowledge an existence and a situation unfamiliar and therefore frightening – one that we do not know and prefer *not* to know.

Why, returning to the question of the canon, *should* we only read certain kinds of books? No one is suggesting we should *not* read those, but why should we not also read other ones? We are not, after all, being shipped to that "desert island" beloved of the devisers of great books lists. And as a matter of fact – and this is to me the conclusive nail in the argument – we all do "read" many different kinds of texts in this life of ours, since, whether we are willing to admit it or not, we spend much of our existence in the force field of a mass culture that is radically different from our "great books" and live at least a double life in the various compartments of our unavoidably fragmented society. We need to be aware that we are even more fundamentally fragmented than that; rather than clinging to this particular mirage of the "centered subject" and the unified personal identity, we would do better to confront honestly the fact of frag-mentation on a global scale; it is a confrontation with which we can here at least make a cultural beginning.

A final observation on my use of the term "third world." I take the point of criticisms of this expression, particularly those which stress the way in which it obliterates profound differences between a whole range of non-western coun-tries and situations (indeed, one such fundamental opposition – between the traditions of the great eastern empires and those of the post-colonial African nation states – is central in what follows). I don't, however, see any comparable expression that articulates, as this one does, the fundamental breaks between the capitalist first world, the socialist bloc of the second world, and a range of other countries which have suffered the experience of colonialism and imperialism. One can only deplore the ideological implications of oppositions such as that between "developed" and "underdeveloped" or "developing" countries; while the more recent conception of northern and southern tiers, which has a very different ideological content and import than the rhetoric of development, and is used by very different people, nonetheless implies an unquestioning acceptance of "convergence theory" – namely the idea that the Soviet Union and the United States are from this perspective largely the same thing. I am using the term "third world" in an essentially descriptive sense, and objections to it do not strike me as especially relevant to the argument I am making.

In these last years of the century, the old question of a properly world literature reasserts itself. This is due as much or more to the disintegration of our own conceptions of cultural study as to any very lucid awareness of the great outside world around us. We may therefore – as "humanists" – acknowledge the pertinence of the critique of present-day humanities by our titular leader, William Bennett, without finding any great satisfaction in his embarrassing solution: yet another impoverished and ethnocentric Graeco-Judaic "great books list of the civilization of the West," "great texts, great minds, great ideas."[4] One is tempted to turn back on Bennett himself the question he approvingly quotes from Maynard Mack: "How long can a democratic nation afford to support a narcissistic minority so transfixed by its own image?" Nevertheless, the present moment does offer a remarkable opportunity to rethink our humanities curriculum in a new way – to re-examine the shambles and ruins of all our older "great books," "humanities," "freshman-introductory" and "core course" type traditions.

Today the reinvention of cultural studies in the United States demands the reinvention, in a new situation, of what Goethe long ago theorized as "world literature." In our more immediate context, then, any conception of world literature necessarily demands some specific engagement with the question of third-world literature, and it is this not necessarily narrower subject about which I have something to say today.

It would be presumptuous to offer some general theory of what is often called third-world literature, given the enormous variety both of national cultures in the third world and of specific historical trajectories in each of those areas. All of this, then, is provisional and intended both to suggest specific perspectives for research and to convey a sense of the interest and value of these clearly neglected literatures for people formed by the values and stereotypes of a first-world culture. One important distinction would seem to impose itself at the outset, namely that none of these cultures can be conceived as anthropologically independent or autonomous, rather, they are all in various distinct ways locked in a life-and-death struggle with first-world cultural imperialism – a cultural struggle that is itself a reflexion of the economic situation of such areas in their penetration by various stages of capital, or as it is sometimes euphemistically termed, of modernization. This, then, is some first sense in which a study of third-world culture necessarily entails a new view of ourselves, from the outside, insofar as we ourselves are (perhaps without fully knowing it) constitutive forces powerfully at work on the remains of older cultures in our general world capitalist system.

But if this is the case, the initial distinction that imposes itself has to do with the nature and development of older cultures at the moment of capitalist penetration, something it seems to me most enlightening to examine in terms of the marxian concept of modes of production.[5] Contemporary historians seem to be in the process of reaching a consensus on the specificity of feudalism as a form which, issuing from the break-up of the Roman Empire or the Japanese Shogunate, is able to develop directly into capitalism.[6] This is not the case with the other modes of production, which in some sense must be disaggregated or destroyed by violence, before capitalism is able to implant its specific forms and displace the older ones. In the gradual expansion of capital-ism across the globe, then, our economic system confronts two very distinct modes of production that pose two very different types of social and cultural resistance to its influence. These are so-called primitive, or tribal society on the one hand, and the Asiatic mode of production, or the great bureaucratic imperial systems, on the other. African societies and cultures, as they became the object of systematic colonization in the 1880s, provide the most striking examples of the symbiosis of capital and tribal societies; while China and India offer the principal examples of another and quite different sort of engagement of capitalism with the great empires of the so-called Asiatic mode. My examples below, then, will be primarily African and Chinese; however, the special case of Latin America must be noted in passing. Latin America offers yet a third kind of development – one involving an even earlier destruction of imperial systems now projected by collective memory back into the archaic or tribal. Thus the earlier nominal conquests of independence open them at once to a kind of indirect economic penetration and control – something Africa and Asia will come to experience only more recently with decolonization in the 1950s and 1960s.

Having made these initial distinctions, let me now, by way of a sweeping hypothesis, try to say what all third-world cultural productions seem to have in common and what distinguishes them radically from analogous cultural forms in the first world. All third-world texts are necessarily, I want to argue, allegorical, and in a very specific way: they are to be read as what I will call *national allegories*, even when, or perhaps I should say, particularly when their forms develop out of predominantly western machineries of representation, such as the novel. Let me try to state this distinction in a grossly oversimplified way: one of the determinants of capitalist culture, that is, the culture of the

western realist and modernist novel, is a radical split between the private and
the public, between the poetic and the political, between what we have come
to think of as the domain of sexuality and the unconscious and that of the public
world of classes, of the economic, and of secular political power: in other
words, Freud versus Marx. Our numerous theoretical attempts to overcome
this great split only reconfirm its existence and its shaping power over our
individual and collective lives. We have been trained in a deep cultural conviction that the lived experience of our private existences is somehow incommensurable with the abstractions of economic science and political dynamics.
Politics in our novels therefore is, according to Stendhal's canonical formulation, a "pistol shot in the middle of a concert."

I will argue that, although we may retain for convenience and for analysis
such categories as the subjective and the public or political, the relations
between them are wholly different in third-world culture. Third-world texts,
even those which are seemingly private and invested with a properly libidinal
dynamic – necessarily project a political dimension in the form of national
allegory: *the story of the private individual destiny is always an allegory of the embattled
situation of the public third-world culture and society.* Need I add that it is precisely
this very different ratio of the political to the personal which makes such texts
alien to us at first approach, and consequently, resistant to our conventional
western habits of reading?

I will offer, as something like the supreme example of this process of
allegorization, the first masterwork of China's greatest writer, Lu Xun, whose
neglect in western cultural studies is a matter of shame which no excuses based
on ignorance can rectify. "Diary of a Madman" (1918) must at first be read by
any western reader as the protocol of what our essentially psychological language terms a "nervous breakdown." It offers the notes and perceptions of a
subject in intensifying prey to a terrifying psychic delusion, the conviction that
the people around him are concealing a dreadful secret, and that that secret can
be none other than the increasingly obvious fact that they are cannibals. At the
climax of the development of the delusion, which threatens his own physical
safety and his very life itself as a potential victim, the narrator understands that
his own brother is himself a cannibal and that the death of their little sister, a
number of years earlier, far from being the result of childhood illness, as he had
thought, was in reality a murder. As befits the protocol of a psychosis, these
perceptions are objective ones, which can be rendered without any introspective machinery: the paranoid subject observes sinister glances around him in the
real world, he overhears tell-tale conversations between his brother and an
alleged physician (obviously in reality another cannibal) which carry all the
conviction of the real, and can be objectively (or "realistically") represented.
This is not the place to demonstrate in any detail the absolute pertinence, to Lu

Xun's case history, of the pre-eminent western or first-world reading of such phenomena, namely Freud's interpretation of the paranoid delusions of Senat-spräsident Schreber: an emptying of the world, a radical withdrawal of libido (what Schreber describes as "world-catastrophe"), followed by the attempt to recathect by the obviously imperfect mechanisms of paranoia. "The delusion-formation," Freud explains, "which we take to be a pathological product, is in reality an attempt at recovery, a process of reconstruction."[7]

What is reconstructed, however, is a grisly and terrifying objective real world beneath the appearances of our own world: an unveiling or deconcealment of the nightmarish reality of things, a stripping away of our conventional illusions or rationalizations about daily life and existence. It is a process comparable, as a literary effect, only to some of the processes of western modernism, and in particular of existentialism, in which narrative is employed as a powerful instrument for the experimental exploration of reality and illusion, an explora-tion which, however, unlike some of the older realisms, presupposes a certain prior "personal knowledge." The reader must, in other words, have had some analogous experience, whether in physical illness or psychic crisis, of a lived and balefully transformed real world from which we cannot even mentally escape, for the full horror of Lu Xun's nightmare to be appreciated. Terms like "depression" deform such experience by psychologizing it and projecting it back into the pathological Other; while the analogous western literary approaches to this same experience – I'm thinking of the archetypal deathbed murmur of Kurtz, in Conrad's "Heart of Darkness," "The horror! the horror!" – recontains precisely that horror by transforming it into a rigorously private and subjective "mood," which can only be designated by recourse to an aesthetic of *expression* – the unspeakable, unnameable inner feeling, whose external formulation can only designate it from without, like a symptom.

But this representational power of Lu Xun's text cannot be appreciated properly without some sense of what I have called its allegorical resonance. For it should be clear that the cannibalism literally apprehended by the sufferer in the attitudes and bearing of his family and neighbors is at one and the same time being attributed by Lu Xun himself to Chinese society as a whole: and if this attribution is to be called "figural," it is indeed a figure more powerful and "literal" than the "literal" level of the text. Lu Xun's proposition is that the people of this great maimed and retarded, disintegrating China of the late and post-imperial period, his fellow citizens, are "literally" cannibals: in their desperation, disguised and indeed intensified by the most traditional forms and procedures of Chinese culture, they must devour one another ruthlessly to stay alive. This occurs at all levels of that exceedingly hierarchical society, from lumpens and peasants all the way to the most privileged elite positions in the mandarin bureaucracy. It is, I want to stress, a social and historical nightmare, a vision of the horror of life specifically grasped through History itself, whose consequences go far beyond the more local western realistic or naturalistic representation of cut-throat capitalist or market competition, and it exhibits a specifically political resonance absent from its natural or mythological western equivalent in the nightmare of Darwinian natural selection.

Now I want to offer four additional remarks about this text, which will touch, respectively, on the libidinal dimension of the story, on the structure of its allegory, on the role of the third-world cultural producer himself, and on the perspective of futurity projected by the tale's double resolution. I will be concerned, in dealing with all four of these topics, to stress the radical structural difference between the dynamics of third-world culture and those of the first-world cultural tradition in which we have ourselves been formed.

I have suggested that in third-world texts such as this story by Lu Xun the relationship between the libidinal and the political components of individual and social experience is radically different from what obtains in the west and what shapes our own cultural forms. Let me try to characterize this difference, or if you like this radical reversal, by way of the following generalization: in the west, conventionally, political commitment is recontained and psychologized or subjectivized by way of the public–private split I have already evoked. Interpretations, for example, of political movements of the 1960s in terms of Oedipal revolts are familiar to everyone and need no further comment. That such interpretations are episodes in a much longer tradition, whereby political commitment is re-psychologized and accounted for in terms of the subjective dynamics of *ressentiment* or the authoritarian personality, is perhaps less well understood, but can be demonstrated by a careful reading of anti-political texts from Nietzsche and Conrad all the way to the latest cold-war propaganda.

What is relevant to our present context is not, however, the demonstration of that proposition, but rather of its inversion in third-world culture, where I want to suggest that psychology, or more specifically, libidinal investment, is to be read in primarily political and social terms. (It is, I hope, unnecessary to add that what follows is speculative and very much subject to correction by specialists: it is offered as a methodological example rather than a "theory" of Chinese culture.) We're told, for one thing, that the great ancient imperial cosmologies identify by analogy what we in the west analytically separate: thus, the classical sex manuals are at one with the texts that reveal the dynamics of political forces, the charts of the heavens at one with the logic of medical lore, and so forth.[8] Here already then, in an ancient past, western antinomies – and most particularly that between the subjective and the public or political – are refused in advance. The libidinal center of Lu Xun's text is, however, not sexuality, but rather the oral stage, the whole bodily question of eating, of ingestion, devoration, incorporation, from which such fundamental categories as the pure and the impure spring. We must now recall, not merely the extraordinary symbolic complexity of Chinese cuisine, but also the central role this art and practice occupies in Chinese culture as a whole. When we find that centrality confirmed by the observation that the very rich Chinese vocabulary for sexual matters is extraordinarily intertwined with the language of eating; and when we observe the multiple uses to which the verb "to eat" is put in ordinary Chinese language (one "eats" a fear or a fright, for example), we may feel in a somewhat better position to sense the enormous sensitivity of this libidinal region, and of Lu Xun's mobilization of it for the dramatization of an essentially social nightmare – something which in a western writer would be consigned to the realm of the merely private obsession, the vertical dimension of the personal trauma.

A different alimentary transgression can be observed throughout Lu Xun's works, but nowhere quite so strikingly as in his terrible little story, "Medicine." The story portrays a dying child – the death of children is a constant in these works – whose parents have the good fortune to procure an "infallible" remedy. At this point we must recall both that traditional Chinese medicine is not "taken," as in the west, but "eaten," and that for Lu Xun traditional Chinese medicine was the supreme locus of the unspeakable and exploitative charlatanry of traditional Chinese culture in general. In his crucially important *Preface* to the first collection of his stories,[9] he recounts the suffering and death of his own father from tuberculosis, while declining family reserves rapidly disappeared into the purchase of expensive and rare, exotic and ludicrous medicaments. We will not sense the symbolic significance of this indignation unless we remember that for all these reasons Lu Xun decided to study western medicine in Japan – the epitome of some new western science that promised collective regeneration – only later to decide that the production of culture – I am tempted to say, the elaboration of a political culture – was a more effective form of political medicine.[10] As a writer, then, Lu Xun remains a diagnostician and a physician. Hence this terrible story, in which the cure for the male child, the father's only hope for survival in future generations, turns out to be one of those large doughy-white Chinese steamed rolls, soaked in the blood of a criminal who has just been executed. The child dies anyway, of course, but it is important to note that the hapless victim of a more properly state violence (the supposed criminal) was a *political* militant, whose grave is mysteriously covered in flowers by absent sympathizers of whom one knows nothing. In the analysis of a story like this, we must rethink our conventional conception of the symbolic levels of a narrative (where sexuality and politics might be in hom-ology to each other, for instance) as a set of loops or circuits which intersect and overdetermine each other – the enormity of therapeutic cannibalism finally intersecting in a pauper's cemetery, with the more overt violence of family betrayal and political repression.

This new mapping process brings me to the cautionary remark I wanted to make about allegory itself – a form long discredited in the west and the specific target of the Romantic revolution of Wordsworth and Coleridge, yet a linguistic structure which also seems to be experiencing a remarkable reawakening of interest in contemporary literary theory. If allegory has once again become somehow congenial for us today, as over against the massive and monumental unifications of an older modernist symbolism or even realism itself, it is because the allegorical spirit is profoundly discontinuous, a matter of breaks and heterogeneities, of the multiple polysemia of the dream rather than the homogeneous representation of the symbol. Our traditional conception of allegory – based, for instance, on stereotypes of Bunyan – is that of an elaborate set of figures and personifications to be read against some one-to-one table of equivalences: this is, so to speak, a one-dimensional view of this signifying process, which might only be set in motion and complexified were we willing to entertain the more alarming notion that such equivalences are themselves in constant change and transformation at each perpetual present of the text.

Here too Lu Xun has some lessons for us. This writer of short stories and sketches, which never evolved into the novel form as such, produced at least one approach to the longer form, in a much lengthier series of anecdotes about a hapless coolie named Ah Q, who comes to serve, as we might have suspected, as the allegory of a certain set of Chinese attitudes and modes of behavior. It is interesting to note that the enlargement of the form determines a shift in tone or generic discourse: now everything that had been stricken with the stillness and emptiness of death and suffering without hope – "the room was not only too silent, it was far too big as well, and the things in it were far too empty"[11] – becomes material for a more properly Chaplinesque comedy. Ah Q's resiliency springs from an unusual – but we are to understand culturally very normal and familiar – technique for overcoming humiliation. When set upon by his persecutors, Ah Q, serene in his superiority over them, reflects: " 'It is as if I were beaten by my own son. What is the world coming to nowadays...?' Thereupon he too would walk away, satisfied at having won."[12] Admit that you are not even human, they insist, that you are nothing but an animal! On the contrary, he tells them, I'm worse than an animal, I'm an insect! There, does that satisfy you? "In less than ten seconds, however, Ah Q would walk away also satisfied that he had won, thinking that he was after all 'number one in self-belittlement,' and that after removing the 'self-belittlement' what remained was still the glory of remaining 'number one.' "[13] When one recalls the remarkable self-esteem of the Manchu dynasty in its final throes, and the serene contempt for foreign devils who had nothing but modern science, gunboats, armies, technology and power to their credit, one achieves a more precise sense of the historical and social topicality of Lu Xun's satire.

Ah Q is thus, allegorically, China itself. What I want to observe, however, what complicates the whole issue, is that his persecutors – the idlers and bullies who find their daily pleasures in getting a rise out of just such miserable victims as Ah Q – they too are China, in the allegorical sense. This very simple example, then, shows the capacity of allegory to generate a range of distinct meanings or messages, simultaneously, as the allegorical tenor and vehicle change places: Ah Q is China humiliated by the foreigners, a China so well versed in the spiritual techniques of self-justification that such humiliations are not even registered, let alone recalled. But the persecutors are also China, in a different sense, the terrible self-cannibalistic China of the "Diary of a Madman," whose response to powerlessness is the senseless persecution of the weaker and more inferior members of the hierarchy.

All of which slowly brings us to the question of the writer himself in the third world, and to what must be called the function of the intellectual, it being understood that in the third-world situation the intellectual is always in one way or another a political intellectual. No third-world lesson is more timely or more urgent for us today, among whom the very term "intellectual" has withered away, as though it were the name for an extinct species. Nowhere has the strangeness of this vacant position been brought home to me more strongly than on a recent trip to Cuba, when I had occasion to visit a remarkable college-preparatory school on the outskirts of Havana. It is a matter of some shame for an American to witness the cultural curriculum in a socialist setting which also very much identifies itself with the third world. Over some three or four years, Cuban teenagers study poems of Homer, Dante's Inferno, the Spanish theatrical classics, the great realistic novels of the nineteenth-century European tradition, and finally contemporary Cuban revolutionary novels, of which, incidentally, we desperately need English translations. But the semester's work I found most challenging was one explicitly devoted to the study of the role of the intellectual as such: the cultural intellectual who is also a political militant, the intellectual who produces both poetry and praxis. The Cuban illustrations of this process – Ho Chi Minh and Augustino Nieto – are obviously enough culturally determined: our own equivalents would probably be the more familiar figures of DuBois and C. L. R. James, of Sartre and Neruda or Brecht, of Kollontai or Louise Michel. But as this whole talk aims implicitly at suggesting a new conception of the humanities in American education today, it is appropriate to add that the study of the role of the intellectual as such ought to be a key component in any such proposals.

I've already said something about Lu Xun's own conception of his vocation, and its extrapolation from the practice of medicine. But there is a great deal more to be said specifically about the *Preface*. Not only is it one of the fundamental documents for understanding the situation of the third-world artist, it is also a dense text in its own right, fully as much a work of art as any of the greatest stories. And in Lu Xun's own work it is the supreme example of the very unusual ratio of subjective investment and a deliberately depersonalized objective narration. We have no time to do justice to those relationships, which would demand a line-by-line commentary. Yet I will quote the little fable by which Lu Xun, responding to requests for publication by his friends and future collaborators, dramatizes his dilemma:

Imagine an iron house without windows, absolutely indestructible, with many people fast asleep inside who will shortly die of suffocation. But you know that since they will die in their sleep, they will not feel the pain of death. Now if you cry aloud to wake a few of the lighter sleepers, making those unfortunate few suffer the agony of irrevocable death, do you think you are doing them a good turn?[14]

The seemingly hopeless situation of the third-world intellectual in this histori-cal period (shortly after the founding of the Chinese Communist Party, but also after the bankruptcy of the middle-class revolution had become apparent) – in which no solutions, no forms of praxis or change, seem conceivable – this situation will find its parallel, as we shall see shortly, in the situation of African intellectuals after the achievement of independence, when once again no political solutions seem present or visible on the historical horizon. The formal or literary manifestation of this political problem is the possibility of narrative closure, something we will return to more specifically.

In a more general theoretical context – and it is this theoretical form of the problem I should now like at least to thematize and set in place on the agenda – we must recover a sense of what "cultural revolution" means, in its strongest form, in the marxist tradition. The reference is not to the immediate events of that violent and tumultuous interruption of the "eleven years" in recent Chinese history, although some reference to Maoism as a doctrine is necessarily implicit. The term, we are told, was Lenin's own, and in that form explicitly designated the literacy campaign and the new problems of universal scholarity and education: something of which Cuba, again, remains the most stunning and successful example in recent history. We must, however, enlarge the conception still further, to include a range of seemingly very different pre-occupations, of which the names of Gramsci and Wilhelm Reich, Frantz Fanon, Herbert Marcuse, Rudolph Bahro, and Paolo Freire, may give an indication of their scope and focus. Overhastily, I will suggest that "cultural revolution" as it is projected in such works turns on the phenomenon of what Gramsci called "subalternity," namely the feelings of mental inferiority and habits of subservience and obedience which necessarily and structurally develop in situations of domination – most dramatically in the experience of colonized peoples. But here, as so often, the subjectivizing and psychologizing habits of first-world peoples such as ourselves can play us false and lead us into misunderstandings. Subalternity is not in that sense a psychological matter, although it governs psychologies; and I suppose that the strategic choice of the term "cultural" aims precisely at restructuring that view of the problem and projecting it outwards into the realm of objective or collective spirit in some non-psychological, but also non-reductionist or non-economistic, materialistic fashion. When a psychic structure is objectively determined by economic and political relationships, it cannot be dealt with by means of purely psychological therapies; yet it equally cannot be dealt with by means of purely objective transformations of the economic and political situation itself, since the habits remain and exercise a baleful and crippling residual effect.[15] This is a more dramatic form of that old mystery, the unity of theory and practice; and it is specifically in the context of this problem of cultural revolution (now so strange and alien to us) that the achievements and failures of third-world intellectuals, writers and artists must be replaced if their concrete historical meaning is to be grasped. We have allowed ourselves, as first-world cultural intellectuals, to restrict our consciousness of our life's work to the narrowest professional or bureaucratic terms, thereby encouraging in ourselves a special sense of subalternity and guilt, which only reinforces the vicious circle. That a literary article could be a political act, with real consequences, is for most of us little more than a curiosity of the literary history of Czarist Russia or of modern China itself. But we perhaps should also consider the possibility that as intellectuals we ourselves are at present soundly sleeping in that indestructable iron room, of which Lu Xun spoke, on the point of suffocation.

The matter of narrative closure, then, and of the relationship of a narrative text to futurity and to some collective project yet to come, is not, merely a formal or literary-critical issue. "Diary of a Madman" has in fact two distinct and incompatible endings, which prove instructive to examine in light of the writer's own hesitations and anxieties about his social role. One ending, that of the deluded subject himself, is very much a call to the future, in the impossible situation of a well-nigh universal cannibalism: the last desperate lines launched into the void are the words, "Save the children . . . " But the tale has a second ending as well, which is disclosed on the opening page, when the older (supposedly cannibalistic) brother greets the narrator with the following cheerful remark: "I appreciate your coming such a long way to see us, but my brother recovered some time ago and has gone elsewhere to take up an official post." So, in advance, the nightmare is annulled; the paranoid visionary, his brief and terrible glimpse of the grisly reality beneath the appearance now vouchsafed, gratefully returns to the realm of illusion and oblivion therein again to take up his place in the space of bureaucratic power and privilege. I want to suggest that it is only at this price, by way of a complex play of simultaneous and antithetical messages, that the narrative text is able to open up a concrete perspective on the real future.

I must interrupt myself here to interpolate several observations before proceeding. For one thing, it is clear to me that *any* articulation of radical difference – that of gender, incidentally, fully as much as that of culture – is susceptible to appropriation by that strategy of otherness which Edward Said, in the context of the Middle East, called "orientalism." It does not matter much that the radical otherness of the culture in question is praised or valorized positively, as in the preceding pages: the essential operation is that of differentiation, and once that has been accomplished, the mechanism Said denounces has been set in place. On the other hand, I don't see how a first-world intellectual can avoid this operation without falling back into some general liberal and humanistic universalism: it seems to me that one of our basic political tasks lies precisely in the ceaseless effort to remind the American public of the radical difference of other national situations.

But at this point one should insert a cautionary reminder about the dangers of the concept of "culture" itself: the very speculative remarks I have allowed myself to make about Chinese "culture" will not be complete unless I add that "culture" in this sense is by no means the final term at which one stops. One must imagine such cultural structures and attitudes as having been themselves, in the beginning, vital responses to infrastructural realities (economic and geographic, for example), as attempts to resolve more fundamental contradictions – attempts which then outlive the situations for which they were devised, and survive, in reified forms, as "cultural patterns." Those patterns themselves then become part of the objective situation confronted by later generations, and, as in the case of Confucianism, having once been part of the solution to a dilemma, then become part of the new problem.

Nor can I feel that the concept of cultural "identity" or even national "identity" is adequate. One cannot acknowledge the justice of the general poststructuralist assault on the so-called "centered subject," the old unified ego of bourgeois individualism, and then resuscitate this same ideological mirage of psychic unification on the collective level in the form of a doctrine of collective identity. Appeals to collective identity need to be evaluated from a historical perspective, rather than from the standpoint of some dogmatic and placeless "ideological analysis." When a third-world writer invokes this (to us) ideological value, we need to examine the concrete historical situation closely in order to determine the political consequences of the strategic use of this concept. Lu Xun's moment, for example, is very clearly one in which a critique of Chinese "culture" and "cultural identity" has powerful and revolutionary consequences – consequences which may not obtain in a later social configuration. This is then, perhaps, another and more complicated way of raising the issue of "nationalism" to which I referred earlier.

As far as national allegory is concerned, I think it may be appropriate to stress its presence in what is generally considered western literature in order to underscore certain structural differences. The example I have in mind is the work of Benito Pérez Galdós – the last and among the richest achievements of nineteenth-century realism. Galdós' novels are more visibly allegorical (in the national sense) than most of their better-known European predecessors:[16] something that might well be explained in terms of Immanuel Wallerstein's world-system terminology.[17] Although nineteenth-century Spain is not strictly *peripheral* after the fashion of the countries we are here designating under the term third world, it is certainly *semi-peripheral* in his sense, when contrasted with England or France. It is therefore not terribly surprising to find the situation of the male protagonist of *Fortunata y Jacinta* (1887) – alternating between the two women of the title, between the wife and the mistress, between the woman of the upper-middle classes and the woman of the "people" – characterized in terms of the nation-state itself, hesitating between the republican revolution of 1868 and the Bourbon restoration of 1873.[18] Here, too, the same "floating" or transferable structure of allegorical reference detected in Ah Q comes into play: for Fortunata is also married, and the alternation of "revolution" and "restoration" is likewise adapted to her situation, as she leaves her legal home to seek her lover and then returns to it in abandonment.

What it is important to stress is not merely the wit of the analogy as Galdós uses it, but also its optional nature: we can use it to convert the entire situation of the novel into an allegorical commentary on the destiny of Spain, but we are also free to reverse its priorities and to read the political analogy as metaphorical decoration for the individual drama, and as a mere figural intensification of this last. Here, far from dramatizing the identity of the political and the individual or psychic, the allegorical structure tends essentially to separate these levels in some absolute way. We cannot feel its force unless we are convinced of the radical difference between politics and the libidinal: so that its operation reconfirms (rather than annuls) that split between public and private which was attributed to western civilization earlier in our discussion. In one of the more powerful contemporary denunciations of this split and this habit, Deleuze and Guattari argue for a conception of desire that is at once social and individual.

How does a delirium begin? Perhaps the cinema is able to capture the movement of madness, precisely because it is not analytical or regressive, but explores a global field of coexistence. Witness a film by Nicholas Ray, supposedly representing the formation of a cortisone delirium: an overworked father, a high-school teacher who works over-time for a radio-taxi service and is being treated for heart trouble. He begins to rave about the educational system in general, the need to restore a pure race, the salvation of the social and moral order, then he passes to religion, the timeliness of a return to the Bible, Abraham. But what in fact did Abraham do? Well now, he killed or wanted to kill his son, and perhaps God's only error lies in having stayed his hand. But doesn't this man, the film's protagonist, have a son of his own? Hmmm . . . What the film shows so well, to the shame of psychiatrists, is that every delirium is first of all the investment of a field that is social, economic, political cultural, racial and racist, pedagogical, and religious: the delirious person applies a delirium to his family and his son that over-reaches them on all sides.[19]

I am not myself sure that the objective consequences of this essentially social and concrete gap, in first-world experience, between the public and the private can be abolished by intellectual diagnosis or by some more adequate theory of their deeper interrelationship. Rather, it seems to me that what Deleuze and Guattari are proposing here is a new and more adequate *allegorical* reading of this film. Such allegorical structures, then, are not so much absent from first-world cultural texts as they are *unconscious*, and therefore they must be deciphered by interpretive mechanisms that necessarily entail a whole social and historical critique of our current first-world situation. The point here is that, in distinc-tion to the unconscious allegories of our own cultural texts, third-world national allegories are conscious and overt: they imply a radically different and objective relationship of politics to libidinal dynamics.

Now, before turning to the African texts, I remind you of the very special occasion of the present talk, which is concerned to honor the memory of Robert C. Elliott and to commemorate his life's work. I take it that the very center of his two most important books, *The Power of Satire* and *The Shape of Utopia*,[20] is to be found in his pathbreaking association of satire and the utopian impulse as two seemingly antithetical drives (and literary discourses), which in reality replicate each other such that each is always secretly active within the other's sphere of influence. All satire, he taught us, necessarily carries a utopian frame of reference within itself; all utopias, no matter how serene or disem-bodied, are driven secretly by the satirist's rage at a fallen reality. When I spoke of futurity a moment ago, I took pains to withhold the world "utopia," which in my language is another word for the socialist project.

But now I will be more explicit and take as my motto an astonishing passage from the novel *Xala*, by the great contemporary Senegalese novelist and film-maker Sembène Ousmane. The title designates a ritual curse or affliction, of a very special kind, which has been visited on a prosperous and corrupt Senegalese businessman at the moment in which, at the height of his fortune, he takes to himself a beautiful young (third) wife. Shades of *The Power of Satire!*, the curse is of course, as you may have guessed, sexual impotence. The Hadj, the unfortunate hero of this novel, desperately explores a number of remedies, both western and tribal, to no avail, and is finally persuaded to undertake a laborious trip into the hinterland of Dakar to seek out a shaman of reputedly extraordinary powers. Here is the conclusion of his hot and dusty journey in a horse-drawn cart:

As they emerged from a ravine, they saw conical thatched roofs, grey-black with weathering, standing out against the horizon in the middle of the empty plain. Free-ranging, skinny cattle with dangerous-looking horns fenced with one another to get at what little grass there was. No more than silhouettes in the distance, a few people were busy around the only well. The driver of the cart was in familiar territory and greeted people as they passed. Sereen Mada's house, apart from its imposing size, was identical in construction with all the others. It was situated in the center of the village whose huts were arranged in a semi-circle, which you entered by a single main entrance. The village had neither shop nor school nor dispensary; there was nothing at all attractive about it in fact [Ousmane concludes, then he adds, as if in afterthought, this searing line:] There was nothing at all attractive about it in fact. Its life was based on the principles of community interdependence.[21]

Here, then, more emblematically than virtually any other text I know, the space of a past and future utopia – a social world of collective cooperation – is dramatically inserted into the corrupt and westernized money economy of the new post-independence national or comprador bourgeoisie. Indeed, Ousmane takes pains to show us that the Hadj is not an industrialist, that his business is in no sense productive, but functions as a middle-man between European multinationals and local extraction industries. To this biographical sketch must be added a very significant fact: that in his youth, the Hadj was political, and spent some time in jail for his nationalist and pro-independence activities. The extraordinary satire of these corrupt classes (which Ousmane will extend to the person of Senghor himself in *The Last of the Empire*) is explicitly marked as the failure of the independence movement to develop into a general social revolution.

The fact of nominal national independence, in Latin America in the nineteenth century, in Africa in the mid-twentieth, puts an end to a movement for which genuine national autonomy was the only conceivable goal. Nor is this symbolic myopia the only problem: the African states also had to face the crippling effects of what Fanon prophetically warned them against – to receive independence is not the same as to take it, since it is in the revolutionary struggle itself that new social relationships and a new consciousness is developed. Here again the history of Cuba is instructive: Cuba was the last of the Latin American nations to win its freedom in the nineteenth century – a freedom which would immediately be taken in charge by another greater colonial power. We now know the incalculable role played in the Cuban Revolution of 1959 by the protracted guerrilla struggles of the late nineteenth century (of which the figure of José Martí is the emblem); contemporary Cuba would not be the same without that laborious and subterranean, one wants to say Thompsonian, experience of the mole of History burrowing through a lengthy past and creating its specific traditions in the process.

So it is that after the poisoned gift of independence, radical African writers like Ousmane, or like Ngugi in Kenya, find themselves back in the dilemma of Lu Xun, bearing a passion for change and social regeneration which has not yet found its agents. I hope it is clear that this is also very much an aesthetic dilemma, a crisis of representation: it was not difficult to identify an adversary who spoke another language and wore the visible trappings of colonial occupation. When those are replaced by your own people, the connections to external controlling forces are much more difficult to represent. The newer leaders may of course throw off their masks and reveal the person of the Dictator, whether in its older individual or newer military form: but this moment also determines problems of representation. The dictator novel has become a virtual genre of Latin American literature, and such works are marked above all by a profound and uneasy ambivalence, a deeper ultimate sympathy for the Dictator, which can perhaps only be properly accounted for by some enlarged social variant of the Freudian mechanism of transference.[22]

The form normally taken by a radical diagnosis of the failures of contemporary third-world societies is, however, what is conventionally designated as "cultural imperialism," a faceless influence without representable agents, whose literary expression seems to demand the invention of new forms: Manuel Puig's *Betrayed by Rita Hayworth* may be cited as one of the most striking and innovative of those. One is led to conclude that under these circumstances traditional realism is less effective than the satiric fable: whence to my mind the greater power of certain of Ousmane's narratives (besides *Xala*, we should mention *The Money-order*) as over against Ngugi's impressive but problematical *Petals of Blood*.

With the fable, however, we are clearly back into the whole question of allegory. *The Money-order* mobilizes the traditional Catch-22 dilemma – its hapless protagonist cannot cash his Parisian check without identity papers, but since he was born long before independence there are no documents, and meanwhile the money-order, uncashed, begins to melt away before an accumulation of new credits and new debts. I am tempted to suggest, anachronistically, that this work, published in 1965, prophetically dramatizes the greatest misfortune that can happen to a third-world country in our time, namely the discovery of vast amounts of oil resources – something which as economists have shown us, far from representing salvation, at once sinks them incalculably into foreign debts they can never dream of liquidating.

On another level, however, this tale raises the issue of what must finally be one of the key problems in any analysis of Ousmane's work, namely the ambiguous role played in it by archaic or tribal elements. Viewers may perhaps remember the curious ending of his first film, *The Black Girl*, in which the European employer is inconclusively pursued by the little boy wearing an archaic mask; meanwhile such historical films as *Ceddo* or *Emitai* seem intent on evoking older moments of tribal resistance either to Islam or to the west, yet in a historical perspective which with few exceptions is that of failure and ultimate defeat. Ousmane cannot, however, be suspected of any archaizing or nostalgic cultural nationalism. Thus it becomes important to determine the significance of this appeal to older tribal values, particularly as they are more subtly active in modern works like *Xala* or *The Money-order*.

I suspect that the deeper subject of this second novel is not so much the evident one of the denunciation of a modern national bureaucracy, but rather the historical transformation of the traditional Islamic value of alms-giving in a contemporary money economy. A Muslim has the duty to give alms – indeed, the work concludes with just such another unfulfilled request. Yet in a modern economy, this sacred duty to the poor is transformed into a frenzied assault by free-loaders from all the levels of society (at length, the cash is appropriated by a westernized and affluent, influential cousin). The hero is literally picked clean by the vultures; better still, the unsought for, unexpected treasure fallen from heaven at once transforms the entire society around him into ferocious and insatiable petitioners, in something like a monetary version of Lu Xun's cannibalism.

The same double historical perspective – archaic customs radically transformed and denatured by the superposition of capitalist relations – seems to me demonstrable in *Xala* as well, in the often hilarious results of the more ancient Islamic and tribal institution of polygamy. This is what Ousmane has to say about that institution (it being understood that authorial intervention, no longer tolerable in realistic narrative, is still perfectly suitable to the allegorical fable as a form):

It is worth knowing something about the life led by urban polygamists. It could be called geographical polygamy, as opposed to rural polygamy, where all the wives and children live together in the same compound. In the town, since the families are scattered, the children have little contact with their father. Because of his way of life the father must go from house to house, villa to villa, and is only there in the evenings, at bedtime. He is therefore primarily a source of finance, when he has work.[23]

Indeed, we are treated to the vivid spectacle of the Hadj's misery when, at the moment of his third marriage, which should secure his social status, he realizes he has no real home of his own and is condemned to shuttle from one wife's villa to the other, in a situation in which he suspects each of them in turn as being responsible for his ritual affliction. But the passage I have just read shows that – whatever one would wish to think about polygamy in and of itself as an institution – it functions here as a twin-valenced element designed to open up historical perspective. The more and more frenzied trips of the Hadj through the great city secure a juxtaposition between capitalism and the older collective tribal form of social life.

These are not as yet, however, the most remarkable feature of *Xala*, which can be described as a stunning and controlled, virtually text-book exercise in what I have elsewhere called "generic discontinuities."[24] The novel begins, in effect, in one generic convention, in terms of which the Hadj is read as a comic victim. Everything goes wrong all at once, and the news of his disability suddenly triggers a greater misfortune: his numerous debtors begin to descend on someone whose bad luck clearly marks him out as a loser. A comic pity and terror accompanies this process, though it does not imply any great sympathy for the personage. Indeed it conveys a greater revulsion against the privileged new westernized society in which this rapid overturning of the wheel of fortune can take place. Yet we have all been in error, as it turns out: the wives have not been the source of the ritual curse. In an abrupt generic reversal and enlargement (comparable to some of the mechanisms Freud describes in "The Uncanny"), we suddenly learn something new and chilling about the Hadj's past:

"Our story goes back a long way. It was shortly before your marriage to that woman there. Don't you remember? I was sure you would not. What I am now" (a beggar in rags is addressing him) "what I am now is your fault. Do you remember selling a large piece of land at Jeko belonging to our clan? After falsifying the clan names with the complicity of people in high places, you took our land from us. In spite of our protests, our proof of ownership, we lost our case in the courts. Not satisfied with taking our land you had me thrown into prison."[25]

Thus the primordial crime of capitalism is exposed: not so much wage labor as such, or the ravages of the money form, or the remorseless and impersonal rhythms of the market, but rather this primal displacement of the older forms of collective life from a land now seized and privatized. It is the oldest of modern tragedies, visited on the Native Americans yesterday, on the Palestinians today, and significantly reintroduced by Ousmane into his film version of *The Money-order* (called *Mandabi*), in which the protagonist is now threatened with the imminent loss of his dwelling itself.

The point I want to make about this terrible "return of the repressed" is that it determines a remarkable generic transformation of the narrative: suddenly we are no longer in satire, but in ritual. The beggars and the lumpens, led by Sereen Mada himself, descend on the Hadj and require him to submit, for the removal of his *xala*, to an abominable ceremony of ritual humiliation and abasement. The representational space of the narrative is lifted to a new generic realm, which reaches back to touch the powers of the archaic even as it foretells the utopian destruction of the fallen present in the mode of prophecy. The word "Brechtian," which inevitably springs to mind, probably does inadequate justice to these new forms which have emerged from a properly third-world reality. Yet in light of this unexpected generic ending, the preceding satiric text is itself retroactively transformed. From a satire whose subject-matter or content was the ritual curse visited on a character within the narrative, it suddenly becomes revealed as a ritual curse in its own right – the entire imagined chain of events becomes Ousmane's own curse upon his hero and people like him. No more stunning confirmation could be adduced for Robert C. Elliott's great insight into the anthropological origins of satiric discourse in real acts of shamanistic malediction.

I want to conclude with a few thoughts on why all this should be so and on the origins and status of what I have identified as the primacy of national allegory in third-world culture. We are, after all, familiar with the mechanisms of autoreferentiality in contemporary western literature: is this not simply to be taken as another form of that, in a structurally distinct social and cultural context? Perhaps. But in that case our priorities must be reversed for proper understanding of this mechanism. Consider the disrepute of social allegory in our culture and the well-nigh inescapable operation of social allegory in the west's Other. These two contrasting realities are to be grasped, I think, in terms of *situational consciousness*, an expression I prefer to the more common term materialism. Hegel's old analysis of the Master–Slave relationship[26] may still be the most effective way of dramatizing this distinction between two cultural logics. Two equals struggle each for recognition by the other: the one is willing to sacrifice life for this supreme value. The other, a heroic coward in the Brechtian, Schweykian sense of loving the body and the material world too well, gives in, in order to continue life. The Master – now the fulfillment of a baleful and inhuman feudal-aristocratic disdain for life without honor – proceeds to enjoy the benefits of his recognition by the other, now become his humble serf or slave. But at this point two distinct and dialectically ironic reversals take place: only the Master is now genuinely human, so that "recognition" by this henceforth sub-human form of life which is the slave evaporates at the moment of its attainment and offers no genuine satisfaction. "The truth of the Master," Hegel observes grimly, "is the Slave; while the truth of the Slave, on the other hand, is the Master." But a second reversal is in process as well: for the slave is called upon to labor for the master and to furnish him with all the material benefits befitting his supremacy. But this means that, in the end, only the slave knows what reality and the resistance of matter really are; only the slave can attain some true materialistic consciousness of his situation, since it is precisely to that that he is condemned. The Master, however, is condemned to idealism – to the luxury of a placeless freedom in which any consciousness of his own concrete situation flees like a dream, like a word unremembered on the tip of the tongue, a nagging doubt which the puzzled mind is unable to formulate.

It strikes me that we Americans, we masters of the world, are in something of that very same position. The view from the top is epistemologically crippling, and reduces its subjects to the illusions of a host of fragmented subjectivities, to the poverty of the individual experience of isolated monads, to dying individual bodies without collective pasts or futures bereft of any possibility of grasping the social totality. This placeless individuality, this structural idealism which affords us the luxury of the Sartrean blink, offers a welcome escape from the "nightmare of history," but at the same time it condemns our culture to psychologism and the "projections" of private subjectivity. All of this is denied to third-world culture, which must be situational and materialist despite itself. And it is this, finally, which must account for the allegorical nature of third-world culture, where the telling of the individual story and the individual experience cannot but ultimately involve the whole laborious telling of the experience of the collectivity itself.

I hope I have suggested the epistemological priority of this unfamiliar kind of allegorical vision; but I must admit that old habits die hard, and that for us such unaccustomed exposure to reality, or to the collective totality, is often intolerable, leaving us in Quentin's position at the end of *Absalom, Absalom!*, murmuring the great denial, "I don't hate the Third World! I don't! I don't! I don't!"

Even that resistance is instructive, however; and we may well feel, confronted with the daily reality of the other two-thirds of the globe, that "there was nothing at all attractive about it in fact." But we must not allow ourselves that feeling without also acknowledging its ultimate mocking completion: "Its life was based on the principles of community interdependence."

Notes

1 The whole matter of nationalism should perhaps be rethought, as Benedict Anderson's interesting essay *Imagined Communities* (London, Verso, 1983), and Tom Nairn's *The Breakup of Britain* (London, New Left Books, 1977) invite us to do.

2 I have argued elsewhere for the importance of mass culture and science fiction. See "Reification and utopia in mass culture," *Social Text*, 1 (1979), pp. 130–48 [see chapter 8 of the present volume].

3 The [chapter] was written for an immediate occasion – the third memorial lecture in honor of my late colleague and friend Robert C. Elliot at the University of California, San Diego. It is essentially reprinted as given.

4 William Bennett "To reclaim a legacy," text of a report on the humanities, *Chronicle of Higher Education*, 29 (14) (November 28, 1984), pp. 16–21.

5 The classic texts are F. Engels, *The Origin of the Family, Private Property and the State* (1884) and the earlier, but only more recently published section of Marx's *Grundrisse*, often called "Pre-capitalist economic formations," trans. Martin Nicolaus (London, NLB/Penguin, 1973), pp. 471–514. See also Emmanuel Terray, *Marxism and "Primitive" Societies*, trans. M. Klopper, (New York, Monthly Review, 1972); Barry Hindess and Paul Hirst, *Pre-Capitalist Modes of Production* (London, Routledge and Kegan Paul, 1975); and Gilles Deleuze and Félix Guattari, "Savages, barbarians, civilized men," in *Anti-Oedipus*, trans. R. Hurley, M. Seem and H. R. Lane (Minneapolis, University of Minnesota Press, 1983), pp. 139–271. Besides mode-of-production theory, whose validity is in any case widely debated, there have also appeared in recent years a number of important synthesizing works on third-world history as a unified field. Three works in particular deserve mention: *Global Rift*, by L. S. Stavrianos (New York, Morrow, 1981); *Europe and the People without History*, by Eric R. Wolf (California, 1982), and *The Three Worlds*, by Peter Worsley (Chicago, 1984). Such works suggest a more general methodological consequence implicit in the present [chapter] but which should be stated explicitly here: first, that the kind of comparative work demanded by this concept of third-world literature involves comparison, not of the individual texts, which are formally and culturally very different from each other, but of the concrete situations from which such texts spring and to which they constitute distinct responses; and second, that such an approach suggests the possibility of a literary and cultural comparatism of a new type, distantly modeled on the new comparative history of Barrington Moore and exemplified in books like Theda Skocpol's *States and Social Revolutions* or Eric Wolf's *Peasant Revolutions of the 20th Century*. Such a new cultural comparatism would juxtapose the study of the differences and similarities of specific literary and cultural texts with a more typological analysis of the various socio-cultural situations from which they spring, an analysis whose variables would necessarily include such features as the interrelationship of social classes, the role of intellectuals, the dynamics of language and writing, the configuration of traditional forms, the relationship to western influences, the development of urban experience and

money, and so forth. Such comparatism, however, need not be restricted to third-world literature.

6   See, for example, Perry Anderson, *Lineages of the Absolutist State* (London, New Left Books, 1974), pp. 435–549.

7   Sigmund Freud, "Psychoanalytic notes on an autobiographical account of a case of paranoia," trans. James Strachey, *The Standard Edition of the Complete Psychological Works of Sigmund Freud* (London, Hogarth Press, 1958), volume XII, p. 457.

8   See, for example, Wolfram Eberhard, *A History of China*, trans. E. W. Dickes (Berkeley, University of California Press, 1977), p. 105: "When we hear of alchemy, or read books about it we should always keep in mind that many of these books can also be read as books of sex; in a similar way, books on the art of war, too, can be read as books on sexual relations."

9   Lu Xun, *Selected Stories of Lu Hsun*, trans. Gladys Yang and Yang Hsien-yi (Beijing, Foreign Languages Press, 1972), pp. 1–6.

10 Ibid., pp. 2–3.

11 Ibid., p. 40.

12 Ibid., p. 72.

13 Ibid. I am indebted to Peter Rushton for some of these observations.

14 Ibid., p. 5.

15 Socialism will become a reality, Lenin observes, "when the *necessity* of observing the simple, fundamental rules of human intercourse" has "become a *habit*"; *State and Revolution* (Beijing, Foreign Languages Press, 1973), p. 122.

16 See the interesting discussions in Stephen Gilman, *Galdós and the Art of the European Novel: 1867–1887* (Princeton, Princeton University Press, 1981).

17 Immanuel Wallerstein, *The Modern World System* (New York, Academic Press, 1974).

18 For example: "El Delfin habia entrado, desde los últimos dias del 74, en aquel periodo sedante que segula infaliblemente a sus desvarios. En realidad, no era aquello virtud, sino casancio del pecado; no era el sentimiento puro y regular del orden, sino el hastio de la revolución. Verificábase en él lo que don Baldomero habia dicho del pais: que padecìa fiebres alternativas de libertad y de paz": *Fortunata y Jacinta* (Madrid, Editorial Hernando, 1968), p. 585 (part III, ch. 2, s. 2).

19 Deleuze and Guattari, in *Anti-Oedipus*, p. 274.

20 Published by Princeton University Press, 1960; and University of Chicago Press, 1970, respectively.

21 Sembène Ousmane, *Xala*, trans. Clive Wake (Westport, Conn., Lawrence Hill, 1976), p. 69.

22 I am indebted to Carlos Blanco Aguinaga for the suggestion that in the Latin American novel this ambivalence may be accounted for by the fact that the archetypal Dictator, while oppressing his own people, is also perceived as *resisting* North American influence.

23 Ousmane, *Xala*, p. 66.

24 "Generic discontinuities in science fiction: Brian Aldiss's *Starship*," *Science Fiction Studies*, 2 (1973), pp. 57–68.

25 Ousmane, *Xala*, pp. 110–11.

26 G. W. F. Hegel, *The Phenomenology of Mind*, trans. A. V. Miller, (Oxford, Oxford
    University Press, 1977), section B, ch. IV, pt A–3, "Lordship and bondage," pp.
    111–19. The other basic philosophical underpinning of this argument is Lukács'
    epistemology in *History and Class Consciousness* according to which "mapping" or
    the grasping of the social totality is structurally available to the dominated rather
    than the dominating classes. "Mapping" is a term I have used in "Postmodernism,
    or the cultural logic of late capitalism," *New Left Review*, 146 (July–August, 1984),
    pp. 53–92 [see chapter 12 of the present volume]. What is here called "national
    allegory" is clearly a form of just such mapping of the totality, so that the present
    [chapter] – which sketches a theory of the cognitive aesthetics of third-world
    literature – forms a pendant to the essay on postmodernism which describes the
    logic of the cultural imperalism of the first world and above all of the United States.

19

Totality as Conspiracy

"Totality as Conspiracy," which appears in Jameson's book, *The Geopolitical Aesthetic* (1992), is divided into four sections. This selection includes the brief introductory pages and the third section of the essay.

In the widespread paralysis of the collective or social imaginary, to which "nothing occurs" (Karl Kraus) when confronted with the ambitious program of fantasizing an economic system on the scale of the globe itself, the older motif of conspiracy knows a fresh lease on life, as a narrative structure capable of reuniting the minimal basic components: a potentially infinite network, along with a plausible explanation of its invisibility; or in other words: the collective and the epistemological.

To put it this way is to understand how this imperfect mediatory and allegorical structure – the conspiracy, not yet even the world system itself – offers the gravest representational dilemmas, since traditional narratives have never been much good at conveying the collective (save in the explosive punctual moments of war or revolution), while the knowledge function as such has never been thought to be particularly compatible with *belles lettres*. Beyond this, the conspiratorial allegory also raises the issue of Value, insofar as it needs to be marked as imperfect in order to serve as a cognitive map (which it would be disastrous to confuse with reality itself, as when Flaubert's Félicité, shown a map of Havana where her sailor nephew has landed, asks to see the house he is staying in).

On the other hand, the cognitive or allegorical investment in this representation will be for the most part an unconscious one, for it is only at that deeper level of our collective fantasy that we think about the social system all the time, a deeper level that also allows us to slip our political thoughts past a liberal and anti-political censorship. But this means, on the one hand, that the cognitive function of the conspiratorial plot must be able to flicker in and out, like some secondary or subliminal after-image; while by the same token the achieved surface of the representation itself must not be allowed to aspire to the monumental status of high art as such (at least until the beginnings of the postmodern, where a new interpenetration of high art and mass culture enables conspiratorial plot-constructions such as those of Pynchon to attain "artistic" or high-brow standing).

As for the collective dimension of this hermeneutic machine, what clearly trips it into another order of things is the dialectical intensification of information and communication as such, which remains unthematized as long as we are in the realm of the mob, or of Victor Hugo's bird's-eye view of the battle of Waterloo (in *Les Misérables*), but which the hardening into technology problematizes, all the way from that thesis topic called "the first appearance of the railroad in English (or French) literature" to Proust's embarrassing Vestal Virgins of the telephone. Since the world system of late capitalism (or postmodernity) is however inconceivable without the computerized media technology which eclipses its former spaces and faxes an unheard-of simultaneity across its branches, information technology will become virtually the representational solution as well as the representational problem of this world system's cognitive mapping, whose allegories can now always be expected to include a communicational third term.

We will therefore want to explore the new symptomatic narratives from three general directions: (1) to interrogate them about the ways in which their object-worlds can be allegorically prepared, disposed, and rewired in order to become the bearers of conspiracy, the existential furniture of daily life thereby finding itself slowly transformed into communications technology; (2) to test the incommensurability between an individual witness – the individual character of a still anthropomorphic narrative – and the collective conspiracy which must somehow be exposed or revealed through these individual efforts; (3) the thing itself, namely, how the local items of the present and the here-and-now can be made to express and to designate the absent, unrepresentable totality; how individuals can add up to more than their sum; what a global or world system might look like after the end of cosmology.

[...]

III

The form-problem that has been tracked thus far, with as much a view towards registering its fitful moments of appearance as its "solutions" – which can never be anything more than provisional – can also be posed in terms of the empirical and the conceptual content (or meanings) one would like it to vehiculate. In principle, indeed, the here-and-now ought to suffice unto itself, and need no further meaning; but that would only be the case in Utopia, in a landscape of sheer immanence, in which social life coincided fully with itself, so that the most insignificant situations of its everyday life were already in and of themselves fully philosophical. This was presumably what Hegel's slogan about the real being the rational and the rational being the real was supposed to designate; while in aesthetics the canonical New Critical vision of an absolute fusion of form and content is ideological to the degree to which it attributes to the actually existing work of art what it is the latter's impossible vocation to strain for without ever achieving (or so runs the more plausible variant of this aesthetic of immanence, in Lukács' *Theory of the Novel*).

In the absence of Utopia, however, things, remaining as they do contingent and "unequal" to their own concepts, have to be pumped back up and patched together with allegory. The characterological traits of the protagonists required by the plot have to be remotivated, and made to mean something of a "supplementary" and symbolic nature. Even the plots themselves must be made to mean something a little extra: a war like Vietnam or El Salvador means the larger imperialist conspiracy, true enough; but as an empirical event, a unique occurrence in that particular latitude and longitude, on that particular date in the calendar, it must also be *made* to mean its meaning: it must in short be *allegorized*, however discreetly, in order to pass for some more general logical class of which it is itself a member. The problem would scarcely be solved by suppressing the mediation: the narrative cannot but remain allegorical, since the object it attempts to represent – namely, the social totality itself – is not an empirical entity and cannot be made to materialize as such in front of the individual viewer. In effect, the new figure we are here asked to supply continues to suggest something other than itself, in the occurrence a conspiracy that is in reality a (class) war.

But we have not yet exhausted the formal possibilities and permutations: leaving aside the victim for the moment, we began from the basic scenario of the classical detective story, in which both the murderer and the detective were individual agents. A first modification and amplification then suggested itself, in which the murderer becomes identified as a collective instance, even while the point of view of the detective remains an individual one. In this modification, certain kinds of social or political investigations (such as the Abdrashitov film) are rarer than the more schematic surface manifestation in terms of civil war: this being, however, from a North American viewing standpoint, as science-fictional as *Videodrome* since it evidently has no equivalent within our own "current situation." Its actantial problems are thereby compounded, since the individual social detective still in question here will in the guerrilla/civil-war film also carry the narrative onus of being a foreigner and a foreign speaker.

But there remain two narrative permutations which have not yet been examined. Suppose, for instance, that the murderer (or indeed the victim) remains an individual, while the detective has somehow already been trans-formed into a collective instance? And even if this peculiar formal possibility can be conceived (let alone empirically realized somewhere), how would it be possible to imagine moving forward to the ultimate and most satisfying trans-formation of the form, in which both crime and detective, murderer and investigator (not to speak of the victim), have finally, like chrysalids, been transmogrified into that final manifestation of which they were supposed to be allegories in the first place, namely, the collective – the group or class – as agent, actor, or communal agency. That would presumably be a civil war, but somehow within the US, and with a domestic rather than a foreign-language cast.[1]

But at least the first of these structural possibilities can readily be identified, if looked for in the right place, since it is one of the most frequently rehearsed motifs or fantasy-narratives, not to say obsessions, of the current political unconscious, namely, *assassination*, which, owing to the mediation of the public sphere and its technologies, is one of the few individual crimes upon which a whole collectivity broods like a many-headed private investigator, noting the insufficiencies of the official police procedures all the while it revels in in-genious speculations of its own devising. Meanwhile, few plot structures so dramatically illustrate the constructional dilemmas of allegory, and the problems that obtain when events of an individual, empirical nature are worked over by force with a view towards endowing them with this or that more general meaning.

From the very outset, indeed, the assassination plot poses two preliminary questions that are virtually unanswerable: not merely why the death of this particular political figure should hold any more general interest – particularly within an aesthetic frame which is commonly supposed to suspend in advance our interests in and commitments to the real political world outside it; but even more fundamentally (and in a question that clearly violates that frame in advance), what relationship this particular fictional assassination plot is supposed to entertain with the one real-life assassination that has, in our time, had general philosophical significance (above and beyond its more immediate practical consequences). I want to argue that these two questions or problems largely transcend the more familiar aesthetic question about the value of "*romans à clef*" or even of topical allusions within the traditional work of art. Or if you prefer, those traditional problems anticipate these, which now – in the context of the new representational issues of the world system – raise questions in their very form about the public and the private spheres which were not yet problems under an older dispensation, problems which can, for example, be glimpsed by asking ourselves whether there still exist sub-genres and narrative classifications such as the "political novel" or "political film."

In another place,[2] I have made the suggestion that the paradigmatic political assassination in (Western) modern times – that of John F. Kennedy – cannot be said to owe its resonance to Kennedy's political meaning, nor even (save for an emergent youth culture) to the deeper social symbolism and fantasy investment associated with him as a figure (in that respect, Malcolm X, or Martin Luther King, or Bobby Kennedy probably generated more intense experiences of mourning). Rather, what ensured the well-nigh permanent association of assassination in general with this particular historical one was the experience of the media, which for the first time and uniquely in its history bound together an enormous collectivity over several days and vouchsafed a glimpse into a Utopian public sphere of the future which remained unrealized.

However that may be, it means that henceforth any structural deployment of the assassination narrative necessarily faces two supplementary problems. First, it must specify its distance from this specific historical referent, that is to say, it must give us the means to determine whether it is meant to offer a commentary on the Kennedy event itself, or whether it is designed to bracket that topical reference point and direct our attention towards other themes. Then, too, it must somehow handle the new and historically original problem of the media which the Kennedy event brought into being for the first time (and this is the deeper sense in which Kennedy's assassination was paradigmatic): henceforth assassination and the question of the media are representationally related and mutually implicit (in ways in which they were not in popular or collective representations of Sarajevo, for example, or of Lincoln's death).

These are, as it were, the new features, the new problems, associated with the assassination narrative. They do not, however, annul the inherited problems associated with political themes as a *genre*. What has to be explained here, in other words, is why we no longer grasp *The Parallax View*, or even *All the President's Men*, as narrative artifacts that can be classed under the rubrics appropriate for, say, *Advise and Consent* (Preminger, 1962) or *Fail-Safe* (Lumet, 1964) or even, perhaps, *The Dead Zone* (Cronenberg, 1983). These last evidently presupposed a specialization of political thematics as a local subject-matter associated with Washington, DC, or with electoral politics, something no longer terribly relevant or meaningful after the 1960s (and a more widely disseminated Marxian view of historical dynamics) enlarged our perception of what is political well beyond this narrowly governmental material. But it would be wrong to grasp this more traditional category of the genre of the political novel (or film) as one uniquely correlated with parliamentary or representative democracy, since specialized notions of the court and its intrigues, in the baroque political drama (or *Haupt-und-Staatsaktion*), for example, played an analogous role in the period of the absolute monarchy (and perhaps in other imperial cultures).

Such a pre-bourgeois genealogy, however, reminds us to take note of a rather different (though in another sense equally "traditional") way of cutting across the generic signals of a specifically "political" literature: Lukács' discussion of the historical novel as such (and the historical drama), which subsumes the narrowly and sociologically "political" back under the more philosophical and universal concept of the "historical." But the newer assassination and conspiratorial narratives under investigation here seem also to have coincided with a significant waning and obsolescence of just such "historical" genres – in film and the novel, fully as much as in drama: only Gore Vidal's remarkable American chronicles have seemed to constitute the straw in the wind of a momentous revival (if not of a whole new type of historical representation). What Lukács' line of reflection reminds us to inscribe is, however, the classical opposition of public and private, which constituted the foundation and the fundamental structural presupposition of the notion of a distinct, specialized "political" literature about public life. The waning and disappearance of this literature may therefore now offer valuable clues as to the specificity of the conspiratorial narrative, whose emergence may indeed equally well stand as a symptom of the tendential end of "civil society" in late capitalism.

What is certain is that both of these categories – the nature of the "political" as a literary, representational or narrative constraint or feature, and the structural opposition of private and public spheres – are decisively modified, if not transformed beyond all recognition, by the enlargement of the social totality or operative context out into the uniquely distended proportions of the new world system of late capitalism. If already, in Brecht's time, the social forces and realities invested in the Krupp works were, as he once put it, no longer susceptible to representation of a photographic sort, how much more is this the case for a kind of production that can scarcely be spatially identified as an individual factory in the first place? Better still, the very problem or theme of its possible photographic reproduction would under post-contemporary circumstances now have to be factored into the attempt itself; while any intent to map a network of just such productive nodes or provisional centers would have to include within the description an account of their mode of communicational relationship and command transmission. Multinational capitalism, in other words, is a concept that has to include within itself reproduction as well as production.

In more political terms, the Nixon tapes may offer some (conspiratorial) equivalent to the "photographic realism" discredited by Brecht, suggesting, as they do, not merely a unity of place and action, but also a strongly representational aesthetic (powered, no doubt, by a Freudian scoptic drive) in which, as in so much historiography and historical fiction, what the reader/spectator really longs for is to be present at the scene: to see, to hear, to find out the secret truth. The limits of such categories of personal or anthropomorphic power are not only evident intellectually – in the incompatibility between a complex bureaucratic system and the arbitrary caprice of individual psychology – but representationally as well: where the dramatization of the most powerful conceivable "world-historical" figure, whether Hitler, Stalin or whatever occupant of the Oval Office, pushed to its extreme, still fails to yield anything more suggestive than the inside of a room – "power" at best manifesting itself in banks of telephones or the arrival and departure of written messages or heralds whose actantial form is shrouded in antiquity. But this is the narrative stock in trade of Oriental Despotism and not of late capitalism: the hold over our imagination of such antiquated narrative categories ought to tell us something about the dilemmas of cognitive mapping in the world system today.

So it is, for example, that one's first thought of an adequate representation of the Cuban Missile Crisis of 1962, inevitably projects a conference in the War Room onto the screen of the mind, with Kennedy and his advisors hunched over enlargements of strategic maps and high altitude surveillance photographs. What we are here really looking at, however, are the formal stereotypes and kitsch narrative paradigms and archetypes inside our own minds: not even the most concrete visuality in detail and reconstruction, nor the historical accuracy and "truth" of the re-enactment, can rescue such images from the realm of simulacra and the imaginary. "Even if it was a fact it wouldn't be true" (Adorno); and the historians have known, at least since the Higher Criticism of the Bible, that familiar paradigms must by definition be wrong, just as Cornford demonstrated the suspicious operation, within the stoic and glacial factuality of Thucydides, of patterns of Athenian tragic drama that are not likely to have shown up, by accident, in nature or in "real life."[3] But are fresh paradigms possible any longer, or even the raucous mockery of the parodic satyr play (Dr Strangelove, for example [Kubrick, 1964]), in which high convention is mimetically remastered by the gross human productivity of farce?

In fact, we do possess a rather different "rendering" of the October Crisis from the point of view, as it were, of the Other. This is Tomás Gutiérrez Alea's now classical *Memories of Underdevelopment* (Cuba, 1968, from the novel by Edmundo Desnois), in which "Kennedy" exists, not as an old-fashioned fictional character in the round (played by the appropriate look-alike movie star), but rather as a well-nigh disembodied television image, inserted, intermittently flickering but full of menace, into the daily life of Cubans in Havana, in an urban routine unchanged in everything but the imminence of the nuclear flash. This is the ominous silence of the new kind of nuclear "phony war" that at best, in First World representations, shows up in pathology or obsession, like that Bergman character muttering darkly and compulsively about the peril of millions of Chinese. The media image or photographic reproduction thus offers a provisional mediation between the category of the old-fashioned narrative character or agent and the information transmissions of the new global communication systems, binding these incommensurable levels punctually together in an unstable kind of ion-exchange: from Kennedy to "Kennedy," not to say from the referent or signified to the simulacrum.

Nixon also remained just such a television image and a constitutive absence in Pakula's *All the President's Men*, which, framed in video close-ups of the protagonist of the convention and the reinauguration, faithfully transmits the more successful dramatic touches of this theatrical president (not the notorious operetta uniforms of the White House guard, but rather the splendidly timed helicopter touchdown at the joint session of Congress staged as the climax of his world journey). Oddly enough, however, this residual Nixoniana does not reintroduce the shadow of a fictional White House redramatization "behind the scenes," as in our imaginary Kennedy scenarios, but rather succeeds triumphantly in here splitting reference from narrativity. Indeed, virtually the most interesting formal feature of Pakula's achievement here lies in its evasion of the traditional category of the costume drama or narrowly "political" film or sub-generic Washington "exposé." "Nixon" here remains an absence: a technical stroke of no little interest that at one blow produces and solves a qualitatively new form-problem, and which, by cutting across the traditional opposition between public and private, has virtually, in Pakula's most successful films, become his trademark.

It is therefore worth looking for the antecedents of this effect in the earlier panels of his so-called paranoia trilogy, in *Klute* of 1971 and *The Parallax View* of 1974, in which the public–private opposition is already rehearsed in unusual and untraditional ways. Indeed, it is precisely this opposition that makes up the originality of *Klute*, not officially a "political" film at all. A neutral plot summary might wildly misrepresent it as the touching story of a love affair between a prostitute and a policeman, omitting the essentials, namely, that it is a question of a big-city prostitute and a small-town policeman. For in this film, exceptionally, the tension between public and private is played out upon the opposition between what is still the city itself, or the urban, and what is no longer the country in any traditional sense but not the suburb either: rather, a kind of bedroom community outside, in the former countryside, where new and presumably high-tech industries have established themselves, their upper-level employees adopting the rural style of the former farming culture just as urban yuppies reinhabit brownstones and appropriate a classical nineteenth-century American city culture for technocracy.

What this means is that, in the powerful reversal of this axis staged in *Klute*, the countryside becomes the public realm and the city the private one. Such is indeed the burden of the mystery's exposition: the respected family man at Thanksgiving dinner with his friends, in the bright sunlight of the small-town community, where this seemingly domestic persona is in reality the public image – Manhattan becoming the place of the hidden perversion and the secret life. The disappearance and possible murder only conceals this spatial axis which was there all along, hidden away within the fragility of a domestic prosperity which is also a corporate one. Nor does it matter much later on when we find that the two lives never did co-exist within the same individual after all. As for the protagonists of this film, a similar (but narratively unrelated) reversal gives their relationship its bite and freshness. For it is the official or professional figure, the policeman John Klute (Donald Sutherland), who is the bearer of private feelings, of love and affection as well as of therapeutic consolation; while the prostitute (Jane Fonda), who might be supposed to be associated with the double life and the sexual underworld, in reality represents professionalism and business life with a well-nigh Brechtian irony (she has her answering service and her own "private life," her hobbies, her therapist, and her career prospects – acting lessons and a possible career in fashion modeling). Such is the hypocrisy of North American culture, however, that, unlike *The Threepenny Opera*, the effect in late capitalism is not to turn the public formalities of business and big-city bureaucratic life to ridicule, but rather to stand as a social statement, with political and even activist consequences, by portraying the hooker as belonging to a genuine sub-group in her own right and thereby deserving of public attention (demonstrations, unions, legal rights, and so on). *Klute* seems to have accomplished this despite the (equally American) thera-peutic overtones (prostitutes are frigid, they want attention and power over others, above all – shades of neo-Freudianism and the soaps! – they are unable to face "serious" relations with others). But I would argue that these social messages, which seemed at the time to mark out the boldness of *Klute*'s subject-matter, are little more than the (necessary) pre-text for the unsettling of our conventional notions of private life and the public sphere. Simmel, indeed, liked to point out that what is scandalous for the middle classes about prostitu-tion is not the degradation of the body, sexuality and love that it seems to imply, but rather, the other way round, the way money finds itself degraded by this association with the sexual functions.

At any rate, in Pakula's trilogy, such Brechtian changing of the valences of private and public does not so much have the effect of defamiliarizing either of these poles (for some specifically satiric purpose) as much as it does of holding them apart and freezing their incompatibility in such a way as to "produce" their incommensurable antagonism as an object of aesthetic contemplation, if I may use this Althusserian way of speaking. What transpires, particularly in the public figures, is an absolute dissociation between their public and private realities, in ways consistent with an image culture but which then block that older kind of "political" genre literature in which the character or personality of the politician remained a substantive issue.

In *The Parallax View*, it is the disparity between the two senatorial victims of assassination that is designed to disjoin and to problematize the mystery of the private–public allegory. (They are of course by no means the only victims, in this greatest of all assassination films, which takes as its premise that famous rumor about the deaths in mysterious circumstances of a high and statistically improbable number of eye-witnesses in the years immediately following the Kennedy assassination. Here it is the public on the Needle that begins to disappear improbably after the equivalent shooting: a fact that determines the newspaperman protagonist to infiltrate the organized conspiracy he thinks he has begun to glimpse. Only too successful in doing so and in passing himself off as a potential assassin, he finds himself trapped in the wings and causeways of the sports arena in which the second senator has just been shot, becoming an only too plausible, indeed a fatal, suspect in the crime.)

Here, then, the representational dilemma is inscribed in the text and thereby acknowledged, rather than repressed or resolved: the gap between the private individual and the public function or meaning is held open and exacerbated; resolution is not even presupposed in advance; and the very problem of representability now becomes in some sense its own solution – the thing being done, as it were, by showing it cannot be done in the first place. Meanwhile, a third term silently associates itself with the other two, and that is assassination or conspiracy itself, which sets private life and public reputation side by side, before sweeping both away into meaningless contingency and externality, thus rendering old-fashioned political questions irrelevant. A new kind of political narrative thereby emerges, which is more consistent with the dynamics of the world system than an older anthropomorphic or "humanist" kind (in which personal agency still had to be attributed to individual politicians by virtue of their narrative significance as characters). Its operation above the level of representative democracy in *The Parallax View* does not, however, lead into the abstractions of the spy thriller, nor even into the science-fictional loops of *Videodrome*, but rather paves the way for the return to what looks like the most classic political intrigue and Washingtoniana in the "victimless" conspiracies of *All the President's Men*.

Meanwhile, its social detective must now also be remotivated, but in a way that somehow transcends sheer reportorial curiosity (the purely epistemological) in order to take root in the ontological, in a world in which conspiracy is the fundamental law. The problem to be solved here is then that characterological one we have already observed in *Salvador*, where the existential messiness of the protagonist's psyche somehow corresponded to the messiness of revolution and civil war itself. But in *Salvador*, the James Woods character's mission was personal redemption, and redemption of a sort – finally nailing a story, putting his personal life back together, saving his career – which does not particularly connect back up with the objective situation; it could not do so, indeed, for that situation speaks Spanish and comes from out of another world (the Third), while the Woods-style neurosis is necessarily a North American product. *The Parallax View*, however, confronts this formal problem head on, by trying to give figuration to the equivalent of a civil war within an "advanced" capitalist society whose contradictions no longer express themselves in that fashion.

Nonetheless, the Warren Beatty character is inscribed in a tradition of North American revolutionary and political literature by way of the characterology that allows his story to be read as the last in that series, if not the beginning of something else. It is not enough to describe him as a rebel, unless we take the trouble of noting the historical disappearance of this kind of figure from a bureaucratic and corporate universe, and also of interrogating the paradoxical sources of such violence, which can also be described as "anti-social" as it brushes the psychotic and the pathological. At the beginning of the century, indeed, in his path-breaking study of the emergence of modern drama, Lukács underscored pathology as a fundamental aspect of the wresting of dramatic action from the complacencies of the new bourgeois social life and culture. The stylization demanded by a contemporary drama, he observed,

can no longer simply be the pathos of an abstract or self-conscious heroism as such. It can only be found in the stylization of a specific character trait, on a gigantic scale beyond anything found in life, and to a degree that dominates the entire human being and his destiny. Or, to put it in the language of everyday life: pathology. For what else can this most extreme form of intensification prove to be but morbidity and the pathological excess of one particular feature over everything else in human life? And this is clearly exaggerated by the motivational compulsion that derives from the style of the drama itself: if the excessiveness is to be confirmed on psychic grounds, these cannot be drawn from the limits of normal psychology, and even less to the very degree that the situation of the character is itself dramatic...If there is no mythology...everything must be based on and derived from character itself. But a motivation thrown back exclusively on character, and the exclusive interiority of that character's destiny, now always drive character to the very borders of pathology.[4]

The dramatic, in other words what shakes the status quo and produces crisis as such, is difficult to derive or produce from out of the status quo of a non-transcendent universe, and must therefore be housed, as a disturbing and unsettling force, within the individual herself. But in the various European national traditions, which are more intensely socialized, the representation of such a force must take into account the class context, and the rebel will either be a sympathizer with another class or else someone viewed as sick or aberrant from the perspective of this one. In the frontier dissolution of the older North American classes, however, the rebel can incarnate sheer unmotivated violence, an energy that blasts open social convention and needs no other ideological justification than the hatred of masters and of the social order: something which shows up in sheer aggressivity as such.

Yet all American political ideologies have sought in one way or another to remotivate that aggressivity and to draw its energies back within their own programs: most recently the great political images of the 1930s and of American socialist realism, in which characterological violence is necessary in order to oppose the whole weight and force of the system itself. But the paradoxes of such violence (dramatized in a film like *Bound for Glory* [Ashby, 1976], based on the life of Woody Guthrie) do not seem to have been registered until the 1960s and the contemporary feminist movement: namely, how anti-social violence can with impunity be tapped for social reconstruction; how a temperament suited for the demolition of the old order can participate in the formation of a new one; how the purifying negative act can be Utopian; how the destructive personality can be productively used. Not only the deeper constitutive tensions between anarchism and communism are resonated here, but also a whole set of Freudian presuppositions about the childhood sources of violence and aggressivity and their possible redirection, as well as the classical ideological arguments about the goodness or irrecuperability of human nature itself.

But in *The Parallax View* a positive contribution on the part of the protagonist is unnecessary, save in whatever resistance is required to overcome the concealment of the conspiracy. The Warren Beatty character's unruly belligerence and temperamental uncooperativeness already stand in the service of the epistemological, and in a bureaucratic world in which cognitive mapping is the supreme remaining form of praxis, aggressivity in following up the truth becomes Utopian, at least for a time. But it also becomes ironic, an irony which may have its deeper origins in the disabused refusal of this political film, as in so many others in recent times, to project even the shadow of some older "positive" hero. The postmodern period generally has been described as the era of universal cynicism, not least because of the triumphant process whereby it has demystified all value and reduced everything to instrumentality: the remnants of value then come before us as so much propaganda or sentimentalism. But the rhetoric of cynical demystification demands a certain modesty. No one should profit from the universal corruption of the system (it is the old paradox of the satirist: if everyone has become tainted, who is left to say so but the misanthrope?), so that only the absence of heroes authenticates the document and proves the point. So also in that muted new version of *The Parallax View* which is Pakula's Watergate film (*All the President's Men*), where the conspiratorial reporter's well-nigh physical pugnaciousness (in the earlier film misleadingly attributed to alcoholism) has instructively been diminished to the characterologically unpleasant traits of the two reporters: everything awkward and inarticulate about Hoffman as a character actor is here mobilized in the service of manipulation, while the Redford figure is so vacuous and shabby as to cast a more fundamental doubt on the very category of the "good guy" in the first place. Meanwhile, their combination in what has elsewhere been termed the pseudo-couple deprives them of all possible dignity (while formally allowing anything resembling subjective experience to be externalized as dialogue and exposition). In any case, the detective story classically required a pair in order to sift through the findings; only here priority status shifts back and forth in order to pre-empt a definitive by-line.

In *The Parallax View*, however, the protagonist's pathological character is functional and is systematically looped back into the narrative: only psychotic candidates are able to pass the screen test (psychologically calibrated reactions to a carefully chosen and suggestive series of images involving family, state, race, violence, and social and psychological inferiority and *ressentiment*) and thus to qualify for the Parallax Corporation's openings as professional assassins. Yet it is the very rebelliousness inherent in his pursuit of the conspiracy that allows him to pass for potentially psychopathic in the first place. But here is the supplementary turn of the screw: everything that qualified him to be a professional killer also confirms his identity as lone assassin, without any ties to an "organized conspiracy"; everything that equips him to penetrate the organization also makes him vulnerable to the latter's manipulation.

What must be stressed is that the institutional construction of the conspirator figures is not to be confused with the essentially satiric portrayal of "organization men" and the new corporate personality which culturally precedes it and of which it is no doubt, in another sense, a kind of structural variant. The allegorical indices that enable the rewriting of individual actors in the register of the collective no longer have anything to do with satire in that older sense in which the structural "opposite" of the faceless corporation man remained the true individual, most often a rebel and a non-conformist in just that great American tradition of individual protest and resistance already evoked.

For, as I have implied above, all forms of opposition are today also collective and organized into political protest groups and movements of various kinds: at which point the corporate fact and the corporate style is somehow no longer merely an aberrant business subculture, but some deeper, quasi-ontological law of the social world itself. In this sense, indeed, the Beatty character in *The Parallax View* can be taken as a comment on, and a definitive dismissal of, the older narrative paradigm of the rebel; for he still looks like that, and the violence and anti-social nature of his personality is here insistently set in place. It is not, to be sure, the tragic fate of this protagonist that differentiates his story from the rebel plot, since those stories draw their heroic qualities from the very sense of the inevitability of doom and failure. The Beatty character, however, ceases to be the rebel figure for which he still takes himself because the oppositional impulses within himself and in his character and unconscious have become the very instruments of the conspiracy proper, which uses and welcomes them specifically for its own purposes. In a kind of Hegelian ruse of reason, it is precisely the will to revolt and to destroy the conspiracy which allows this last to write him into their scenario and to destroy him in the process, something for which the popular term "co-optation" is probably not a very adequate characterization.

The detective is thus murderer and victim all at once: two mirror-image conspiracies begin to confront each other, except that one has more people and is better organized. But this means that finally bureaucracy wins out over the rebel, whose last glimpse in life (as his killers move in on his hiding-place) cancels the definitive closing door of the nineteenth-century carceral imagination, substituting instead the more intense nightmare of an open door that gives onto a world conspiratorially organized and controlled as far as the eye can see. The rebel's paradigmatic narrative is thereby retired along with him. The final silhouette of the enemy of the causeway is if anything grimmer than the blank video-screen of *Videodrome* insofar as it is followed by the Warren Commission-style judicial announcement ("Beatty" acted alone) that translates all this back into new and current events, into that segment of daily life to which we now confine "history" and the public sphere and which, in its rapid obsolescence, becomes associated with the historical referents from which the film had so triumphantly kept its distance; only at this point it is an association as dusty as the closed file or the wastepaper-basket.

Here, then, the motivation of the social detective reaches back into, and is overdetermined by, the "crime" it is his mission and his destiny to detect. In some immense postmodern Hegelianism the same structures contaminate the fields of the subject and of the object alike, making them infinitely substitutable and susceptible to endless transformation into each other – something which is not without its consequences for filmic language as well. For the detective, Benjamin's *Grübler*, the saturnine melancholic brooding among things and reading their fragmentary, allegorical messages – the message of the fragment, in late capitalism, always being the totality itself and the world system – the visual knows a primacy which is congenial indeed to the development of film as medium (as the pivotal constructions of Hitchcock demonstrate).

That both detectives and assassins need to be at least in that respect analogous to documentary film-makers is clear enough. But *The Parallax View* trumps this general thesis about the intimate relations of suspicion and perception with a whole reading test – the Corporation's photographic "fascist reaction scale" – that seems to drop us back into the crudest kind of associationism or experimental psychology (this last, to be sure, remaining a fertile breeding ground for paranoia as well as superstition, as its institutional links with the CIA and various forms of counter-insurgency training testify). Yet the testing sequence in *The Parallax View*, like its predecessor in the programming sequences of *A Clockwork Orange* (Kubrick, 1971), comments on image society and advertising fully as much as it hints at darker sources of manipulation and control; the deck is here shuffled differently than in *Videodrome*, where commodities (television programs and/or pornography) stood in for political conspiracy. Here the fact of consumption is underscored by discontinuity; narrativity is deliberately interrupted by the insertion of still photographic images which are then renarrativized on a second level by the suggestive music that forges them into an allegory of good and evil, family and country versus the enemy, the heroic comic-book persona of the avenging hero, and the pathos of rich and poor, ins and outs, in a oscillation finally becoming so fast as to endow the positive presidential images with the quotient of loathing associated with "evil" Nazi and communist leaders.

The sequence recalls both narrative interpolations – such as the wondrous silent-film flash-back tale of Alma's humiliation in *The Naked Night* (Bergman, 1953) – and the inserted competition with a rival medium: the television monitor itself, or an interruption by photography proper, as in the pack of snapshots that invades *Last Year at Marienbad* (Resnais, 1962). The rivalry with another medium – it has been suggested that it is always staged, in film, to demonstrate the primacy of this one[5] – will return again and again in [my analyses]. Here it is enough to pause on the way in which film here is used against itself and to suggest something beyond itself. As in the euthanasia sequence of *Soylent Green* (Fleischer, 1973), where Edward G. Robinson's last moments are fulfilled with a lush travelogue of the great natural images that no longer exist on the film's near-future polluted earth, the insertion is also distinguished from its narrative context by style as such, that is to say, by a garish bad taste meant (at least in the American context) to signify the popular or mass unconscious in which such images function. In *Parallax*, this unconscious is home-grown American comic-book fascism, as native as apple pie; in *Soylent Green*, it is the deeper longing for *National Geographic* pictures as the most authentic domestic contact with nature itself. To use style as an instrument for Barthesian connotation in this way, as a vehicle for a specific ideological message, is perhaps always to ensure its qualification as bad, meretricious, kitsch, or degraded: only in the various modernisms are there ways distinct from camp of turning the connotative use of such vulgarity back into "art." In *Parallax*, however, the quoted style authenticates the filmic narratives all around it as a reliable kind of realism; while the very excursus through impersonal collective and cultural stereotypes ends on a chilling note indeed, reducing the Beatty character to a sociological type and driving a new kind of wedge between the private and the public by its disclosure of a non-individual unconsciousness made up of thoughts and myths belonging to nobody in particular.

These supplementary images may indeed comment more generally on the filmic language of *The Parallax View*, which is more brassily orchestrated than the other films in the so-called paranoia trilogy. In *Klute* color was used against the nocturnal interiors and closed urban scenery, and it is indeed as if a bright palette there were designed to demystify that floral and pastoral, sunlit suburban village space with which, as I have already observed, the film had to begin. *All the President's Men* [...] must retain a certain drabness as a sign that, like Washington itself, it is beyond the opposition between city and country. But *The Parallax View* enfolds a variety of landscapes within itself by way of documenting its model of the social totality as conspiracy. As with *Videodrome* (and also, in a different way, *North by Northwest*), the multiplicity of landscapes becomes something like an *analogon* for aesthetic as well as epistemological closure: so here we have all the elements – the high seas and a boat in flames, the needle of the Seattle Tower high up in the stratosphere, a raging river in the mountains, a faceless glass modernist office-building in a corporate no man's land, rented rooms in the tenderloin, the classical airport, the classical shopping mall, the classical morgue and also the traditional newspaper office – all of them sewn together, if not by typically US parades and marching bands, then by the miniature train in the zoo where the protagonist learns how to go about changing his identity.

Still, none of this yet tells us the essential: namely, how the villains are to be allegorized in this particular film, how – after the appropriate operations on the victim and the detective – the third position of criminal agent is to be de-individualized, if not collectivized. Here too a totality-effect must be achieved; the conspiracy must not simply be a collection of individual characters, but project something like a corporate structure: in *The Parallax View*, this is achieved by the division of labor between two notable villains, who constitute something like the president of the company and the chairman of the board, respectively. But even that structural collectivity must now be hollowed out and made capable of bearing the weight of allegorical generalization. It is an a priori formal dilemma about which virtually the only thing that can be said in advance is that the recourse to the stock languages of older melodrama is an immediately identifiable sign of failure or of the admission of defeat. What strikes the viewer of *The Parallax View*, however, as well as of the other related films by Pakula already mentioned, is an unexpected solution by displacement, a local innovation in a different zone of the text, where one would not at first have sought the elements of some new kind of compositional allegory. These films are all indeed characterized by a nagging stylistic peculiarity, which can at first distract the viewer: namely, something like an arbitrary decision to work up very close to the actors and to substitute the obsessive close-ups of their faces for the long or medium shots of conventional filmic story-telling. What is imperceptibly unnerving about all this has been astutely registered by James Monaco, who, invoking Dreyer, observes that "a film shot mainly in close-ups . . . deprives us of setting and is therefore disorienting, claustrophobic."[6]

   It is a stylistic mannerism that seems at first to operate indiscriminately, lingering on innocent or guilty alike, and dwelling on the whole range of curious or indifferent, interested or suspicious people in any way involved in the events in question (the camera thereby itself replicating the attention of the conspiracy, since an improbable number of bystanders to the assassination end up dying accidental deaths). The close-up style here therefore signals some outer problematic limit of visual interrogation: the camera seems to look more closely at these people, to examine their features and to surprise their secrets – only the face itself marks the boundary and the limits of what it can explore. Meanwhile, shorn of its bodily and gestural context, facial expression is in the process depersonalized and dehumanized. The variety of human emotions (or more properly, of our concepts of emotion) – that distinct collection of names for the muscle contractions and grimaces of which the human mask is physically capable – now finds itself somehow sharply reduced, everything coming to stand as the changing sign of some deeper underlying mood tone, that can variously be characterized as anxiety, concern, *Sorge*, harassed bewilderment, apprehension, confusion, or disquiet. At the same time, this peculiar standardization by depersonalized fear is accompanied by something rather different – an unpleasant sense of intimacy, as is normal enough (in the Anglo-Saxon world) when faces come too close.

This is the context in which the distinctive treatment of the agents of conspiracy must now be specified: for alone among these troubled faces, the villains, the members of the conspiracy, are calm and unruffled, with a complacency it may not be too hasty to connote as that of corporations and corporate officials. The faces of this second species are male, well-fed, utterly lacking in personal idiosyncrasies, and above all deeply tanned (the connotator, in our society, of privilege).

Yet they are also *sweating* faces: a film of oiliness is always present which marks these faces as haunted by preoccupation, but by a preoccupation of a very different type than the fear that grips their victims. For the agents of conspiracy, *Sorge* is a matter of smiling confidence, and the preoccupation is not personal but corporate, concern for the vitality of the network or the institution, a disembodied distraction or inattentiveness engaging the absent space of the collective organization itself without the clumsy conjectures that sap the energies of the victims. These people *know*, and are therefore able to invest their presence as individual characters in an intense yet complacent attention whose center of gravity is elsewhere: a rapt intentness which is at one and the same time disinterest. Yet this very different type of concern, equally depersonalized, carries its own specific anxiety with it, as it were unconsciously and corporately, without any personal consequences for the individual villains. Sweat does double duty, as the badge of that collective responsibility, and as the tangible locus of everything that is unpleasant in the intimacy of the close-up; an index sometimes projected onto other sensory levels, as in the telephone exchanges of *All the President's Men*, or above all in the murderer's whispering voice in *Klute*, near and hoarse enough to be obscene. What we have here called "intimacy" is the discovery that we are caught in a collective network without knowing it, that people are already up much closer than we realized, even in moments of solitude, their alien body warmth testifying without melodrama to our own vulnerability. From Sartre to Foucault, and beyond them in contemporary feminism, the look has been the privileged ontological space in which our disempowerment as manipulatable objects is dramatized and deployed. Yet the dynamics of the visual and of the gaze always project a space of "power" – the absent Other, the watch-tower of the panopticon – which is somehow itself immune to sight and escapes its own logic by taking refuge behind the recording apparatus. Pakula's world here seems to me to move into a new and more generalized sensory space in which there are no longer any ontological hiding-places of that kind: the conspiracy wins, if it does (as in *The Parallax View*), not because it has some special form of "power" that the victims lack, but simply because it is collective and the victims, taken one by one in their isolation, are not.

Notes

1 I have here omitted gang war films, which, at least during a certain period, might well have been read as visions of internal civil war: see, for example, *Escape from New York* (Carpenter, 1981), *The Warriors* (Hill, 1979), *Fort Apache, The Bronx* (Petrie, 1981). On my view these films shade over into what is called, in Science-Fiction terminology, "near-future" representations and this is a distinctive genre in its own right, its form and structure sharply distinguished by the viewer from "realistic" verisimilitude or immanence.

2 *Postmodernism, or, The Cultural Logic of Late Capitalism* (Durham, NC, Duke University Press, 1990), pp. 355–6.

3 See F. M. Cornford, *Thucydides Mythhistoricus* (London, Cambridge University Press, 1907).

4 Georg Lukács, *Entwicklungsgeschichte des modernen Dramas* (Neuwied, Luchterhand, 1981 [1911], pp. 117–18.

5 Speaking of the power of visual hieroglyph over print and script in Griffith's *Intolerance*, Miriam Hansen notes: "The self-conscious mixing of heterogeneous materials throws into relief a dialectical tension between written characters and images ... In terms of the film's metafictional economy, the hieroglyphic discourse exceeds and unmakes the confines of the book, literalized in the Book of Intolerance (title-card), whose defeat is dramatized in the happy ending of the Modern narrative"; Miriam Hansen, *Babel and Babylon* (Harvard University Press, 1991), pp. 190–4. Meanwhile, speaking of the competition of television in *The China Syndrome* (James Bridges, 1979), Bordwell and Staiger observe: "Classical narration aims to create the impression that it proceeds directly from the story action (owing to multiple motivation and other factors). Television is the perfect foil for this process ... Television mediates reality; it disjoins and fragments. Film, on the other hand, is immediate"; David Bordwell, Janet Staiger and Kristin Thompson, *The Classical Hollywood Cinema* (Columbia University Press, 1985), p. 371. It does not seem abusive to generalize these insights into the general hypothesis that whenever other media appear within film, their deeper function is to set off and demonstrate the latter's ontological primacy.

6 James Monaco, *How to Read a Film* (Oxford, Oxford University Press, 1977), p. 167.

Part V

Utopia

20

Introduction / Prospectus: To Reconsider the Relationship of Marxism to Utopian Thought

This chapter was written as the introduction to a group of essays on Marxism and utopia that appeared in *The Minnesota Review* (1976).

Everyone is familiar with the classical polemic waged by the founders of Marxism (e.g., Engels, "Socialism Utopian and Scientific") against the so-called Utopian socialisms of their day (Saint-Simon, Fourier, Owen, etc.). The spirit of the polemic can only be properly grasped if it is remembered that Engels numbered Utopian socialism among the three fundamental currents of thought whose confluence, in the mid-nineteenth century, furnished the necessary preconditions for the emergence of Marxism itself (the other two currents were, of course, British political economy and the Hegelian dialectic). But this means that for Engels Utopian socialism was a good deal more complicated than mere doctrinal error to be combatted; rather, it amounted to a kind of truth unavailable elsewhere, yet politically and intellectually harmful in its present ("utopian") form, and thus subject to more urgent and vigilant correction than other more obviously antagonistic forms of thought.

Of the two main traditions of Utopian socialism – what we will call the technological or organizational tradition (Saint-Simon, and later Bellamy) and the libidinal or aesthetic one (Fourier, and later Morris and indeed a vital ingredient in the thinking of the New Left) – we will say little here, save for observing that the indispensable feature supplied by the Utopian socialists to the Marxism-to-be of Marx's and Engels' time was simply their vision of the *future* itself (the British economists, meanwhile, supplied the analysis of the present, while Hegel provided the basic mechanism of historical change, the dialectic, or in other words, the pathway that led from Ricardo's present to Fourier's future). What Engels objected to in these thinkers was something Marxists have since that time become accustomed to detecting in the various species of revisionism and liberal reformism, namely the absence of any mechanism for implementing their vision. This must be understood in a two-fold way in accordance with its correction in Marxism. For, on the one hand, the latter understands the future to be *structurally* inherent in the present (the essential features of a socialist economy are gradually developed within the capitalist system itself); on the other, the analysis of class conflict suggests that a monumental transformation of this type can only be achieved by revolutionary means, at the same time that it designates the historical agent (the classical proletariat) required to effectuate such a change. Now the urgency of Engels' strictures on the Utopian socialists becomes clear: without the first of these convictions (the structural relationship of socialism to capitalism) there can be no effective social engineering, no trustworthy guarantee that what emerges from the collapse of capitalism will be anything like a socialist vision of the future. Without the second feature of the Marxian view of the transition – not simply the insistence on social revolution but also on the concrete presence of the appropriate revolutionary actors and classes – the will to change society is deflected into wishful thinking about gradual reforms, appeals to reason and to education (both of the ruling class and of the public at large), and a misplaced confidence in parliamentary democracy. This is the sense in which Engels' attack on Utopian socialism today seems more appropriately addressed to the various non-Marxist or "liberal" critics of the system, such as groups like those of Ralph Nader, the ecologists, Common Cause, and the like.

This is perhaps simply to recognize that in our day and age Utopian socialism as such no longer exists. But that would not be quite true either. Consider the following reflection of Georg Lukács, a few years before his death: "We must essentially compare our [that of Marxists] situation today with that in which people like Fourier or Sismondi found themselves at the beginning of the nineteenth century. We can only achieve effective action when we become aware that we find ourselves in that situation and when it becomes clear to us that there is a sense in which the development from Fourier to Marx remains, both theoretically and practically, a task for the future."[1] This remarkable historical estimate, which suggests that a revolutionary 1848 has not yet even become dimly visible upon the horizon of our own times, reflects, not so much Lukács' increasing pessimism, as rather his sober and critical appraisal both of the development of socialism in Eastern Europe and of the potential of revolutionary movements in the West. Perhaps the French May Events of the following year may be seen as some confirmation of his view, proving more readily comparable to the protest movements of the 1820s and 1830s (Carbonari, conspiracies of student groups, and the like) than to the great and classical class manifestation of June 1848. As for the socialist countries, it is difficult to escape the impression that Lukács is there precisely underscoring a deficiency in Utopian thinking itself, and deploring a situation in which a Marxian social apparatus has inexplicably lost interest in the future.

But of course Lukács' remarks are also a veiled allusion to the revival of Utopian thinking in the West: here what can only be meant are the works of the Frankfurt School, in particular those of Herbert Marcuse and (in a somewhat different way) of Ernst Bloch, to whom Lukács thus strikes as ambivalent an attitude as that complex and by no means purely negative or critical one of Engels to the Utopian socialists of his own day which we have described above. Thus, one would seem entitled to conclude that alongside his critique of their Marxism (scarcely an unexpected reaction from a man for whom party and doctrinal "orthodoxy" was a matter of importance his whole life long) there are signs of a surprisingly positive assessment of the historical necessity and importance of the Frankfurt School in the elaboration of some Marxism of the future. Such an assessment may now perhaps offer a more productive framework in which to examine the crucial question of the degree to which the Frankfurt synthesis remains consistent with so-called orthodox Marxism, and of what, if it does not, it may be considered to be. Perhaps it might even make possible – if the hope itself is not too "Utopian"! – a perspective in which the practical opposition to which this theoretical one corresponds, the antagonism between an "old" and a "New" left, might be superseded.

At any rate, the reflections of the Frankfurt School suggest several further directions in which the present discussion might wish to move. Foremost among these is Marcuse's diagnosis of the atrophy of the Utopian imagination in our society. His own work – along with a slowly increasing number of others in recent years, the latest being Ursula Le Guin's *The Dispossessed* – provides a Utopian blueprint for a liberated society which can be examined in its own terms and also understood, therapeutically, as the attempt to reawaken and to exercise that long-dormant mental and imaginative function which is the active effort to envision the future. Thus, besides a critique of visions of the liberated society like that Marcuse has given us (a critique which could do worse than to force Marxists in turn to reimagine the future in their own right), his work suggests that much remains to be done of a critical and diagnostic nature in examining the various ways in which our society *represses*, to use his expression, the Utopian principle and the Utopian imagination. It has long since become clear that the apparently "realistic" attack of Western thinkers on the old Enlightenment ideal of progress, which for so long constituted the foundation of bourgeois ideology, did not merely express revulsion against the expansion-istic tendencies of imperialism and the irrational internal momentum of capitalism itself, but was also pressed into service as a way of discrediting other, socialistic visions of the future as well (the political function of the so-called dystopia along the lines of *1984* clearly needs no comment). Today, mass culture seems more inclined to dwell on visions of the future consequences of our own system (e.g., pollution, destruction of the ecology, over population, fallout, and the like) than on "preventive" nightmares about the totalitarian future of the various socialist ones; yet even these developments raise ideo-logical problems for Marxists to the degree to which it would seem that it is American business itself which is concerned, for its own interests, to exchange the older consumer optimism for some new and more austere acceptance by the public of collective constraints and communal living. It would be ironic indeed if the Marxist critique of the consumer society proved in the long run to have made a "cultural revolution" for the benefit of Big Business. At any rate, the issue demonstrates the fact that the status of the idea of the future has very real practical as well as theoretical consequences, for the quality of social life itself as well as for the strategy of a cultural politics.

Meanwhile, the work of Ernst Bloch would seem to suggest a proposition almost antithetical to that we have found expressed by Marcuse: for where the latter denounces the repression of the Utopian principle, the former, most systematically in his magnum opus *Das Prinzip Hoffnung*, sees its in-forming presence at work everywhere, in all the objects of culture as well as in all social activities and individual values or more properly psychological phenomena. Marxists impatient with this degree of systematization and with Bloch's idio-syncratic and often provocatively mystical language will overhastily dismiss this work as metaphysical. Yet it suggests still another useful and preeminently practical avenue of exploration for the present symposium, which may perhaps be termed that of Utopian *analysis* or *method*, of the Utopian principle as a hermeneutic or technique of decipherment, in opposition to the examination of the content of individual Utopian visions, or that of the cultural diagnosis we outlined above.

Bloch's work, indeed, suggests that we need a thoroughgoing overhaul of some of our traditional views of the way in which ideology works, and in particular with the view of ideology as mere "false consciousness." Yet we need a historical framework to understand why this view is no longer adequate. The older class society of the nineteenth century, in which such a view of ideology arose and was serviceable, was far more rigidly divided into closed social groups than our own (suffice it to recall the famous description of the proletariat as a "nation within a nation"); at the same time, along with a permanency of physical coercion to which contemporary advanced societies have been less willing to have so obvious and open a recourse, order was maintained through the interiorization of philosophical attitudes and values (of what was then called *ideologies*, in the conscious and systematic sense). Thus, a Victorian who had unsound notions, who was in other words ideologically suspect, at once tended to be socially distanced as well. Under such circumstances, the attack on "bourgeois" ideology could be a far more militant kind of demystification which repudiated the entire system of attitudes and values so characterized as "false consciousness"; by the same token, insofar as such an ideology is only too evidently the cultural property of a completely different group or class, it may thus be repudiated wholesale, and a different ideology (or, in the occurrence, rather, a "science" of socialism) be substituted for it.

Such a description suggests that today, with the immense and thoroughgoing systematization and standardization of monopoly capitalism, programmed by the media, ideas have come to have a somewhat different status. For one thing, the "dominant ideology," if it may still be called that, has been diffused throughout the entire social system by the propagation of consumers' goods. It is thus no longer merely a question of repudiating the values and philosophies of my class enemies, but rather of some much more complicated process of self-analysis whereby I attempt to detect and eradicate the ideological infection inevitably present in myself as well. For another, it may be questioned whether abstract ideas and systems of value of the old type are as functional socially as they used to be: the rapid assimilation by the media culture of "radical" ideas is a text-book demonstration in the absence from the latter of any inherently subversive power. Indeed, it seems as least worth exploring Adorno's speculation that today, in our particular stage of consumer capitalism, "the commodity is its own ideology."

In this new situation, it no longer seems so useful to deal with ideology as "false consciousness" alone. The case of mass culture offers an instructive example of the need for a more complex approach than this. For there can surely be little question that the bulk of the productions of a mass or media culture are precisely "false consciousness" in the traditional sense: that is, they may be considered utterly without content of their own (or with a content so degraded that it is not worth considering in its own right), their fundamental purpose consisting in the way in which they distract their readers and viewers from any genuine thinking about the nature of their own lives and the relationship of the latter to the socioeconomic system in which they live. This said, and apart from a few local effects – e.g., a kind of lateral programming, in which certain attitudes will be systematically programmed into viewer or spectator – such cultural products are seen as virtually interchangeable and of no further interest for analysis.

Into this vacuum, approaches like the analysis of myth then rapidly penetrate, for the latter are willing to see in the mass consumption of, say, comic books, or horror movies, a positive as well as a negative or privative phenomenon: such cultural objects become no longer mere diversions or distractions but the unconscious or semi-conscious exercise of collective fantasy. Indeed, for Leslie Fiedler, they are thereby *more* authentic than the individual expressions of such fantasy in so-called high or art culture. Now Marxists have traditionally been willing to make a (small) place for certain insights like this, provided they have been properly limited: thus, they are willing to see certain cultural products as disguised fantasies which pursue various imaginary scapegoats or collective enemies as projections of the real ones about whom we are unwilling or unable to think. Here the principal instruments of analysis are generally those of Sartrean existentialism, particularly in its reflection on the Other, and on the various fantasy relationships to Otherness, the various modes of symbolic exclusion and castigation, which may so frequently be detected in commercial culture.

Yet even this does not go far enough, and it is here that Bloch's vision has something concrete and productive to offer us. For Bloch's work suggests that even a cultural product whose social function is that of *distracting* us can only realize that aim by fastening and harnessing our attention and our imaginative energies in some positive way and by some type of genuine, albeit disguised and distorted, content. Such content is for him what he calls "Hope," or in other words the permanent tension of human reality towards a radical transformation of itself and everything about it, towards a Utopian transfiguration of its own existence as well as of its social context. To maintain that everything is a "figure of Hope" is to offer an analytical tool for detecting the presence of some Utopian content even within the most degraded and degrading type of com-mercial product.

It is not, of course, necessary to limit ourselves to Bloch's own formula, and Marxists ought to be in a position to identify any number of variations which a Utopian principle might take, from that of a renewal of collective life to that of justice, or instinctual gratification, as well as the nightmare opposites of all of these things. By tapping such powerful sources of collective fantasy, mass and commercial culture not only provides itself with an energy power but also puts itself in a position to manipulate and to control such energies as well.

It is clear that by creating a system of pseudo-gratifications, mass culture functions as a sort of social regulator, attempting to absorb tensions arising out of everyday life and to deflect frustrations which might otherwise actualize themselves in opposition to the system into channels which serve the system. More specifically, these tensions include those generated by the contradictions between the promises of the mass consumption system and the reality of gratification provided and between the increasing socialization of production and the atomization of individuals within the mass society. They manifest themselves typically in the yearning for community and authentic human relationships, in the violent refusal of institutionally defined roles and values.[2]

Such issues, which are the fundamental problems of any genuine Marxist critique of contemporary culture, may serve to dramatize the implications of our current inquiry into the status of Utopian thought, which, far from being merely speculative, thus proves to have concrete methodological implications as well.

Notes

1 Georg Lukács, *Gespräche mit Georg Lukács: Hans Heinz Holz, Leo Kofler, Wolfgang Abendroth*, edited by Theo Pinkus (Hamburg, 1967), p. 93.
2 Stanley Aronowitz, *False Promises* (New York, 1973), pp. 111–12.

21

World-reduction in Le Guin: The Emergence of Utopian Narrative

This chapter was originally published in *Science Fiction Studies* in 1975.

Huddled forms wrapped in furs, packed snow and sweaty faces, torches by day, a ceremonial trowel and a corner stone swung into place...Such is our entry into the *other* world of *The Left Hand of Darkness* (LHD), a world which, like all invented ones, awakens irresistible reminiscences of this the real one – here less Eisenstein's Muscovy, perhaps, than some Eskimo High Middle Ages. Yet this surface exoticism conceals a series of what may be called "generic discontinuities,"[1] and the novel can be shown to be constructed from a heterogeneous group of narrative modes artfully superposed and intertwined, thereby constituting a virtual anthology of narrative strands of different kinds. So we find here intermingled: the travel narrative (with anthropological data), the pastiche of myth, the political novel (in the restricted sense of the drama of court intrigue), straight SF (the Hainish colonization, the spaceship in orbit around Gethen's sun), Orwellian dystopia (the imprisonment on the Voluntary Farm and Resettlement Agency), adventure-story (the flight across the glacier), and finally even, perhaps, something like a multi-racial love-story (the drama of communication between the two cultures and species).

Such structural discontinuities, while accounting for the effectiveness of LHD by comparison with books that can do only one or two of these things, at once raise the basic question of the novel's ultimate unity. In what follows, I want to make a case for a thematic coherence which has little enough to do with plot as such, but which would seem to shed some light on the process of world-construction in fictional narratives in general. Thematically, we may distinguish four different types of material in the novel, the most striking and obvious being that of the hermaphroditic sexuality of the inhabitants of Gethen. The "official" message of the book, however, would seem to be rather different than this, involving a social and historical meditation on the institutions of Karhide and the capacity of that or any other society to mount full-scale organized warfare. After this, we would surely want to mention the peculiar ecology, which, along with the way of life it imposes, makes of LHD something like an anti-*Dune*; and, finally, the myths and religious practices of the planet, which give the book its title.[2]

The question is now whether we can find something that all these themes have in common, or better still, whether we can isolate some essential structural *homology* between them. To begin with the climate of Gethen (known to the Ekumen as Winter), the first Investigator supplies an initial interpretation of it in terms of the resistance of this ice-age environment to human life:

The weather of Winter is so relentless, so near the limit of tolerability even to them with all their cold-adaptations, that perhaps they use up their fighting spirit fighting the cold. The marginal peoples, the races that just get by, are rarely the warriors. And in the end, the dominant factor in Gethenian life is not sex or any other human being: it is their environment, their cold world. Here man has a crueler enemy even than himself. (ch. 7)

However, this is not the only connotation that extreme cold may have; the *motif* may have some other, deeper, disguised symbolic meaning that can perhaps best be illustrated by the related symbolism of the tropics in recent SF, particularly in the novels of J. G. Ballard. Heat is here conveyed as a kind of dissolution of the body into the outside world, a loss of that clean separation from clothes and external objects that gives you your autonomy and allows you to move about freely, a sense of increasing contamination and stickiness in the contact between your physical organism and the surfaces around it, the wet air in which it bathes, the fronds that slap against it. So it is that the jungle itself, with its non- or anti-Wordsworthian nature, is felt to be some immense and alien organism into which our bodies run the risk of being absorbed, the most alarming expression of this anxiety in SF being perhaps that terrible scene in Silverberg's *Downward to Earth* (ch. 8) in which the protagonist discovers a human couple who have become hosts to some unknown parasitic larvae that stir inside their still living torsos like monstrous foetuses.

This loss of physical autonomy – dramatized by the total environment of the jungle into which the European dissolves – is then understood as a figure for the loss of psychic autonomy, of which the utter demoralization, the colonial whisky-drinking and general dissolution of the tropical hero is the canonical symbol in literature. (Even more relevant to the present study is the relationship between extreme heat and sexual anxiety – a theme particularly visible in the non-SF treatments of similar material by Catholic novelists like Graham Greene and François Mauriac, for whom the identification of heat and adolescent sexual torment provides ample motivation for the subsequent desexualization experienced by the main characters.)

Ballard's work is suggestive in the way in which he translates both physical and moral dissolution into the great ideological myth of entropy, in which the historic collapse of the British Empire is projected outwards into some immense cosmic deceleration of the universe itself as well as of its molecular building blocks.[3] This kind of ideological message makes it hard to escape the feeling that the heat symbolism in question here is a peculiarly Western and ethnocentric one. Witness, if proof be needed, Vonnegut's *Cat's Cradle*, where the systematic displacement of the action from Upstate New York to the Caribbean, from dehumanized American scientists to the joyous and skeptical religious practices of Bokononism, suggests a scarcely disguised meditation on the relationship between American power and the Third World, between repression and scientific knowledge in the capitalist world, and a nostalgic and primitivistic evocation of the more genuine human possibilities available in an older and simpler culture. The preoccupation with heat, the fear of sweating as of some dissolution of our very being, would then be tantamount to an unconscious anxiety about tropical field-labor (an analogous cultural symbolism can be found in the historical echo of Northern factory work in the blue jeans and work-shirts of our own affluent society). The nightmare of the tropics thus expresses a disguised terror at the inconceivable and unformulable threat posed by the masses of the Third World to our own prosperity and privilege, and suggests a new and unexpected framework in which to interpret the icy climate of Le Guin's Gethen.

In such a reading the cold weather of the planet Winter must be understood, first and foremost, not so much as a rude environment, inhospitable to human life, as rather a symbolic affirmation of the autonomy of the organism, and a fantasy realization of some virtually total disengagement of the body from its environment or eco-system. Cold *isolates*, and the cold of Gethen is what brings home to the characters (and the reader) their physical detachment, their free-standing isolation as separate individuals, goose-flesh transforming the skin itself into some outer envelope, the sub-zero temperatures of the planet forcing the organism back on its own inner resources and making of each a kind of self-sufficient blast-furnace. Gethen thus stands as an attempt to imagine an experimental landscape in which our being-in-the-world is simplified to the extreme, and in which our sensory links with the multiple and shifting perceptual fields around us are abstracted so radically as to vouchsafe, perhaps, some new glimpse as to the ultimate nature of human reality.

It seems to me important to insist on this cognitive and experimental function of the narrative in order to distinguish it from other, more nightmarish representations of the sealing off of consciousness from the external world (as, e.g. in the "half-life" of the dead in Philip K. Dick's *Ubik*). One of the most significant potentialities of SF as a form is precisely this capacity to provide something like an experimental variation on our own empirical universe; and Le Guin has herself described her invention of Gethenian sexuality along the lines of just such a "thought experiment" in the tradition of the great physicists: "Einstein shoots a light-ray through a moving elevator; Schrödinger puts a cat in a box. There is no elevator, no cat, no box. The experiment is performed, the question is asked, in the mind."[4] Only one would like to recall that "high literature" once also affirmed such aims. As antiquated as Zola's notions of heredity and as naïve as his fascination with Claude Bernard's account of experimental research may have been, the naturalist concept of the *experimental novel* amounted, on the eve of the emergence of modernism, to just such a reassertion of literature's cognitive function. That his assertion no longer seems believable merely suggests that our own particular environment – the total system of late monopoly capital and of the consumer society – feels so massively in place and its reification so overwhelming and impenetrable, that the serious artist is no longer free to tinker with it or to project experimental variations.[5] The historical opportunities of SF as a literary form are intimately related to this paralysis of so-called high literature. The officially "non-serious" or pulp character of SF is an indispensable feature in its capacity to relax that tyrannical "reality principle" which functions as a crippling censorship over high art, and to allow the "paraliterary" form thereby to inherit the vocation of giving us alternate versions of a world that has elsewhere seemed to resist even *imagined* change. (This account of the transfer of one of the most vital traditional functions of literature to SF would seem to be confirmed by the increasing efforts of present-day "art literature" – e.g., Thomas Pynchon – to reincorporate those formal capacities back into the literary novel.)

The principal techniques of such narrative experimentation – of the systematic variation, by SF, of the empirical and historical world around us – have been most conveniently codified under the twin headings of *analogy* and *extrapolation*.[6] The reading we have proposed of Le Guin's experimental ecology suggests, however, the existence of yet a third and quite distinct technique of variation which it will be the task of the remainder of this analysis to describe. It would certainly be possible to see the Gethenian environment as extrapolating one of our own Earth seasons, in an extrapolation developed according to its own inner logic and pushed to its ultimate conclusions – as, for example, when Pohl and Kornbluth project out onto a planetary scale, in *The Space Merchants*, huckstering trends already becoming visible in the nascent consumer society of 1952; or when Brunner, in *The Sheep Look Up*, catastrophically speeds up the environmental pollution already underway. Yet this strikes me as being the least interesting thing about Le Guin's experiment, which is based on a principle of systematic exclusion, a kind of surgical excision of empirical reality, something like a process of ontological attenuation in which the sheer teeming multiplicity of what exists, of what we call reality, is deliberately thinned and weeded out through an operation of radical abstraction and simplification which we will henceforth term *world-reduction*. And once we grasp the nature of this technique, its effects in the other thematic areas of the novel become inescapable, as for instance in the conspicuous absence of other animal species on Gethen. The omission of a whole gridwork of evolutionary phyla can, of course, be accounted for by the hypothesis that the colonization of Gethen, and the anomalous sexuality of its inhabitants, were the result of some forgotten biological experiment by the original Hainish civilization, but it does not make that lack any less disquieting: "There are no communal insects on Winter. Gethenians do not share their earth as Terrans do with those older societies, those innumerable cities of little sexless workers possessing no instinct but that of obedience to the group, the whole" (ch. 13).

But it is in Le Guin's later novel, *The Dispossessed* (TD) that this situation is pushed to its ultimate consequences, providing the spectacle of a planet (Anarres) in which human life is virtually without biological partners:

It's a queer situation, biologically speaking. We Anarresti are unnaturally isolated. On the old World there are eighteen phyla of land animal; there are classes, like the insects, that have so many species they've never been able to count them, and some of these species have populations of billions. Think of it: everywhere you looked animals, other creatures, sharing the earth and air with you. You'd feel so much more a *part*. (ch. 6)

Hence Shevek's astonishment, when, on his arrival in Urras, he is observed by a face "not like any human face...as long as his arm, and ghastly white. Breath jetted in vapor from what must be nostrils, and terrible, unmistakable, there was an eye" (ch.1). Yet the absence, from the Anarres of TD, of large animals such as the donkey which here startles Shevek, is the negative obverse of a far more positive omission, namely that of the Darwinian life-cycle itself, with its predators and victims alike: it is the sign that human beings have surmounted historical determinism, and have been left alone with themselves, to invent their own destinies. In TD, then, the principle of world-reduction has become an instrument in the conscious elaboration of a utopia. On Gethen, however, its effects remain more tragic, and the Hainish experiment has resulted in the unwitting evolution of test-tube subjects rather than in some great and self-conscious social laboratory of revolution and collective self-determination: "Your race is appallingly alone in its world. No other mammalian species. No other ambisexual species. No animal intelligent enough even to domes-ticate as pets. It must color your thinking, this uniqueness . . . to be so solitary, in so hostile a world: it must affect your entire outlook" (ch. 16).

Still, the deeper import of such details, and of the constructional principle at work in them, will become clear only after we observe similar patterns in other thematic areas of the novel, as, for instance, in Gethenian religion. In keeping with the book's antithetical composition, to the two principal national units, Karhide and Orgoreyn, correspond two appropriately antithetical religious cults: the Orgota one of Meshe being something like a heresy or offshoot of the original Karhidish Handdara in much the same way that Christianity was the issue of Judaism. Meshe's religion of total knowledge reflects the mystical experience from which it sprang and in which all of time and history became blindingly co-present: the emphasis on knowing, however, suggests a positiv-istic bias which is as appropriate to the commercial society of Orgoreyn, one would think, as was Protestantism to the nascent capitalism of western Europe. It is, however, the other religion, that of Karhide, which is most relevant to our present argument: the Handdara is, in antithesis to the later sect, precisely a mystique of darkness, a cult of non-knowledge parallel to the drastic reduction-ism of the Gethenian climate. The aim of its spiritual practice is to strip the mind of its non-essentials and to reduce it to some quintessentially simplified function:

The Handdara discipline of Presence . . . is a kind of trance – the Handdarate, given to negatives, call it an untrance – involving self-loss (self-augmentation?) through extreme sensual receptiveness and awareness. Though the technique is the exact opposite of most techniques of mysticism it probably is a mystical discipline, tending towards the experience of Immanence. (ch. 5)

Thus the fundamental purpose of the ritual practice of the foretelling – drama-tized in one of the most remarkable chapters of the novel – is, by answering *ans-verable* questions about the future, "to exhibit the perfect uselessness of knowing the answer to the wrong question" (ch. 5), and indeed, ultimately, of the activity of asking questions in general. What the real meaning of these wrong or unanswerable questions may be, we will try to say later on; but this mystical valorization of ignorance is certainly quite different from the brash commercial curiosity with which the Envoy is so pleasantly surprised on his arrival in Orgoreyn (ch. 10).

Now we must test our hypothesis about the basic constructional principle of LHD against that picture of an ambisexual species – indeed, an ambisexual *society* – which is its most striking and original feature. The obvious defamiliarization with which such a picture confronts the *lecteur moyen sensuel* is not exactly that of the permissive and countercultural tradition of male SF writing, as in Farmer or Sturgeon. Rather than a stand in favor of a wider tolerance for all kinds of sexual behaviour, it seems more appropriate to insist (as does Le Guin herself in [an] article) on the feminist dimension of her novel, and on its demystification of the sex roles themselves. The basic point about Gethenian sexuality is that the sex role does not color everything else in life, as is the case with us, but is rather contained and defused, reduced to that brief period of the monthly cycle when, as with our animal species, the Gethenians are in heat" or "kemmer." So the first Investigator sent by the Ekumen underscores this basic "estrangement-effect" of Gethen on "normally" sexed beings:

The First Mobile, if one is sent, must be warned that unless he is very self-assured, or senile, his pride will suffer. A man wants his virility regarded, a woman wants her femininity appreciated, however indirect and subtle the indications of regard and appreciation. On Winter they will not exist. One is respected and judged only as a human being. It is an appalling experience. (ch. 7)

That there are difficulties in such a representation (e.g., the unavoidable designation of gender by English pronouns), the author is frank to admit in the article referred to.[7] Still, the reader's failures are not all her own, and the inveterate tendency of students to describe the Gethenians as "sexless" says something about the limits imposed by stereotypes of gender on their own imaginations. Far from eliminating sex, indeed, Gethenian biology has the result of eliminating sexual *repression*:

Being so strictly defined and limited by nature, the sexual urge of Gethenians is really not much interfered with by society: there is less coding, channeling, and repressing of sex than in any bisexual society I know of. Abstinence is entirely voluntary; indulgence is entirely acceptable. Sexual fear and sexual frustration are both extremely rare. (ch. 13)

The author was in fact most careful not merely to *say* that these people are not eunuchs, but also – in a particularly terrifying episode, that of the penal farm with its anti-kemmer drugs – to *show* by contrast what eunuchs in this society would look like (ch. 13).

Indeed, the vision of public kemmer-houses (along with the sexual license of utopia in TD) ought to earn the enthusiasm of the most hard-core Fourierist or sexual libertarian. If it does not quite do that, it is because there is another, rather different sense in which my students were not wrong to react as they did and in which we meet, once again, the phenomenon we have called world-reduction. For if Le Guin's Gethen does not do away with sex, it may be suggested that it does away with everything that is *problematical* about it. Essentially, Gethenian physiology *solves* the problem of sex, and that is surely something no human being of our type has ever been able to do (owing largely to the non-biological nature of human desire as opposed to "natural" or instinctual animal need). Desire is permanently scandalous precisely because it admits of no "solution" – promiscuity, repression, or the couple all being equally intolerable. Only a makeup of the Gethenian type, with its limitation of desire to a few days of the monthly cycle, could possibly curb the problem. Such a makeup suggests that sexual desire is something that can be completely removed from other human activities, allowing us to see them in some more fundamental, unmixed fashion. Here again, then, in the construction of this particular projection of desire which is Gethenian ambisexuality, we find a process at work which is structurally analogous to that operation of world-reduction or ontological attenuation we have described above: the experimental production of an imaginary situation by *excision* of the real, by a radical suppression of features of human sexuality which cannot but carry a powerful fantasy-investment in its own right. The dream of some scarcely imaginable freedom from sex, indeed, is a very ancient human fantasy, almost as powerful in its own way as the outright sexual wish-fulfillments themselves. What its more general symbolic meaning in LHD might be, we can only discover by grasping its relationship to that other major theme of the novel which is the nature of Gethenian social systems, and in particular, their respective capacities to wage war.

It would seem on first glance that the parallelism here is obvious and that, on this particular level, the object of what we have been calling world-reduction can only be institutional warfare itself, which has not yet developed in Karhide's feudal system. Certainly Le Guin's work as a whole is strongly pacifistic, and her novella "The Word for World is Forest" is (along with Aldiss' *Dark Light-Years*) one of the major SF denunciations of the American genocide in Vietnam. Yet it remains an ethical, rather than a socioeconomic, vision of imperialism, and its last line extends the guilt of violence to even that war of national liberation of which it has just shown the triumph: " 'Maybe after I die people will be as they were before I was born, and before you came. But I do not think so' " (ch.8). Yet if there is no righteous violence, then the long afternoon and twilight of Earth will turn out to be just that onerous dystopia SF writers have always expected it would.

This properly liberal, rather than radical, position in Le Guin seems to be underscored by her predilection for quietistic heroes and her valorization of an anti-political, anti-activist stance, whether it be in the religion of Karhide, the peaceable traditions of the "creechies," or in Shevek's own reflective temperament. What makes her position more ambiguous and more interesting, however, is that Le Guin's works reject the institutionalization of violence rather than violence itself: nothing is more shocking in TD than the scene in which Shevek is beaten into unconsciousness by a man who is irritated by the similarity between their names:

"You're one of those little profiteers who goes to school to keep his hands clean," the man said. "I've always wanted to knock the shit out of one of you." "Don't call me profiteer!" Shevek said, but this wasn't a verbal battle. Shevet knocked him double. He got in several return blows, having long arms and more temper than his opponent expected: but he was outmatched. Several people paused to watch, saw that it was a fair fight but not an interesting one, and went on. They were neither offended nor attracted by simple violence. Shevek did not call for help, so it was nobody's business but his own. When he came to he was lying on his back on the dark ground between two tents. (ch. 2)

Utopia is, in other words not a place in which humanity is freed from violence, but rather one in which it is released from the multiple determinisms (economic, political, social) of history itself: in which it settles its accounts with its ancient collective fatalisms, precisely in order to be free to do whatever it wants with its interpersonal relationships – whether for violence, love, hate, sex or whatever. All of that is raw and strong, and goes farther towards authenticating Le Guin's vision – as a return to fundamentals rather than some beautification of existence – than any of the explanations of economic and social organization which TD provides.

What looks like conventional liberalism in Le Guin (and is of course still ideologically dubious to the very degree that it continues to "look like" liberalism) is in reality itself a use of the Jeffersonian and Thoreauvian tradition against important political features of that imperializing liberalism which is the dominant ideology of the United States today – as her one contemporary novel, *The Lathe of Heaven*, makes plain. This is surely the meaning of the temperamental opposition between the Tao-like passivity of Orr and the obsession of Haber with apparently reforming and ameliorative projects of all kinds:

The quality of the will to power is, precisely, growth. Achievement is its cancellation. To be, the will to power must increase with each fulfillment, making the fulfillment only a step to a further one. The vaster the power gained, the vaster the appetite for more. As there was no visible limit to the power Haber wielded through Orr's dreams, so there was no end to his determination to improve the world. (ch. 9)

The pacifist bias of LHD is thus part of a more general refusal of the growth-oriented power dynamics of present-day American liberalism, even where the correlations it suggests between institutionalized warfare, centralization, and psychic aggression may strike us as preoccupations of a characteristically liberal type.

I would suggest, however, that beneath this official theme of warfare, there are details scattered here and there throughout the novel which suggest the presence of some more fundamental attempt to reimagine history. What reader has not indeed been struck – without perhaps quite knowing why – by descriptions such as that of the opening cornerstone ceremony: "Masons below have set an electric winch going, and as the king mounts higher the keystone of the arch goes up past him in its sling, is raised, settled, and fitted almost soundlessly, great ton-weight block though it is, into the gap between the two piers, making them one, one thing, an arch" (ch. 1); or of the departure of the first spring caravan towards the fastnesses of the North: "twenty bulky, quiet-running, barge-like trucks on caterpillar treads, going single file down the deep streets of Erhenrang through the shadows of morning" (ch. 5)? Of course, the concept of *extrapolation* in SF means nothing if it does not designate just such details as these, in which heterogenous or contradictory elements of the empirical real world are juxtaposed and recombined into piquant montages. Here the premise is clearly that of a feudal or medieval culture that knows electricity and machine technology. However, the machines do not have the same results as in our own world: "The mechanical-industrial Age of Invention in Karhide is at least three thousand years old, and during those thirty centuries they have developed excellent and economical central-heating devices using steam, electricity, and other principles; but they do not install them in their houses" (ch. 3). What makes all this more complicated than the usual extrapolative projection is, it seems to me, the immense time span involved, and the great antiquity of Karhide's science and technology, which tends to emphasize not so much what happens when we thus combine or amalgamate different historical stages of our own empirical Earth history, but rather precisely *what does not happen*. That is, indeed, what is most significant about the example of Karhide, namely that *nothing* happens, an immemorial social order remains exactly as it was, and the introduction of electrical power fails – quite unaccountably and astonishingly to us – to make any impact whatsoever on the stability of a basically static, unhistorical society.

Now there is surely room for debate as to the role of science and technology in the evolution of the so-called West (i.e., the capitalist countries of western

Europe and North America). For Marxists, science developed as a result both of technological needs and of the quantifying thought-modes inherent in the emergent market system; while an anti-Marxist historiography stresses the fundamental role played by technology and inventions in what now becomes strategically known as the Industrial Revolution (rather than capitalism). Such a dispute would in any case be inconceivable were not technology and capitalism so inextricably intertwined in our own history. What Le Guin has done in her projection of Karhide is to sunder the two in peremptory and dramatic fashion: "Along in those four millennia the electric engine was developed, radios and power looms and power vehicles and farm machinery and all the rest began to be used, and a Machine Age got going, gradually, without any industrial revolution, without any revolution at all" (ch. 2). What is this to say but that Karhide is an attempt to imagine something like a West which would never have known capitalism? The existence of modern technology in the midst of an essentially feudal order is the sign of this imaginative operation as well as the gauge by which its success can be measured: the miraculous presence, among all those furs and feudal *shifgrethor*, of this emblematically quiet, peacefully humming technology is the proof that in Karhide we have to do not with one more specimen of feudal SF, but rather precisely with an alternate world to our own, one in which – by what strange quirk of fate? – capitalism never happened.

It becomes difficult to escape the conclusion that this attempt to rethink Western history without capitalism is of a piece, structurally and in its general spirit, with the attempt to imagine human biology without desire which we have described above; for it is essentially the inner dynamic of the market system which introduces into the chronicle-like and seasonal, cyclical, tempo of pre-capitalist societies the fever and ferment of what we used to call *progress*. The underlying identification between sex as an intolerable, wellnigh gratuitous complication of existence, and capitalism as a disease of change and meaningless evolutionary momentum, is thus powerfully underscored by the very technique – that of world-reduction – whose mission is the utopian exclusion of both phenomena.

Karhide is, of course, not a utopia, and LHD is not in that sense a genuinely utopian work. Indeed, it is now clear that the earlier novel served as something like a proving ground for techniques that are not consciously employed in the construction of a utopia until TD. It is in the latter novel that the device of world-reduction becomes transformed into a sociopolitical hypothesis about the inseparability of utopia and scarcity. The Odonian colonization of barren Anarres offers thus the most thoroughgoing literary application of the technique, at the same time that it constitutes a powerful and timely rebuke to present-day attempts to parlay American abundance and consumers' goods into some ultimate vision of the "great society."[8]

I would not want to suggest that all of the great historical utopias have been constructed around the imaginative operation which we have called world-reduction. It seems possible, indeed, that it is the massive commodity environment of late capitalism that has called up this particular literary and imaginative strategy, which would then amount to a political stance as well. So in William Morris's *News from Nowhere*, the hero – a nineteenth-century visitor to the future – is astonished to watch the lineaments of nature reappear beneath the fading inscription of the grim industrial metropolis, the old names on the river themselves transfigured from dreary slang into the evocation of meadow landscapes, the slopes and streams, so long stifled beneath the pavements of tenement buildings and channeled into sewage gutters, now reemergent in the light of day:

London, which – which I have read about as the modern Babylon of civilization, seems to have disappeared... As to the big murky places which were once, as we know, the centres of manufacture, they have, like the brick and mortar desert of London, disappeared; only, since they were centres of nothing but "manufacture," and served no purpose but that of the gambling market, they have left less signs of their existence than London... On the contrary, there has been but little clearance, though much rebuilding, in the smaller towns. Their suburbs, indeed, when they had any, have melted away into the general country, and space and elbow-room has been got in their centres; but there are the towns still with their streets and squares and market-places; so that it is by means of these smaller towns that we of today can get some kind of idea of what the towns of the older world were alike, – I mean to say, at their best.[9]

Morris's utopia is, then, the very prototype of an aesthetically and libidinally oriented social vision, as opposed to the technological and engineering-oriented type of Bellamy's *Looking Backward* – a vision thus in the line of Fourier rather than Saint Simon, and more prophetic of the values of the New Left rather than those of Soviet centralism, a vision in which we find this same process of weeding out the immense waste-and-junk landscape of capitalism and an artisanal gratification in the systematic excision of masses of buildings from a clogged urban geography. Does such an imaginative projection imply and support a militant political stance? Certainly it did so in Morris's case; but the issue in our time is that of the militancy of ecological politics generally. I would be inclined to suggest that such "no-places" offer little more than a breathing space, a momentary relief from the overwhelming presence of late capitalism. Their idyllic, yet elegiac, sweetness, their pastel tones, the rather pathetic withdrawal they offer from grimier Victorian realities, seems most aptly characterized by Morris's subtitle to *News from Nowhere: "An Epoch of Rest."* It is as though – after the immense struggle to free yourself, even in imagination, from the infection of our very minds and values and habits by an omnipresent consumer capitalism – on emerging suddenly and against all expectation into a narrative space radically other, uncontaminated by all those properties of the old lives and the old preoccupations, the spirit could only lie there gasping in the fresh silence, too weak, too *new*, to do more than gaze wanly about it at a world remade.

Something of the fascination of LHD – as well as the ambiguity of its ultimate message – surely derives from the subterranean drive within it towards a utopian "rest" of this kind, towards some ultimate "no-place" of a collectivity untormented by sex or history, by cultural superfluities or an object-world irrelevant to human life. Yet we must not conclude without observing that in this respect the novel includes its own critique as well.

It is indeed a tribute to the rigor with which the framework has been imagined that history has no sooner, within it, been dispelled, than it sets fatally in again; that Karhide, projected as a social order without development, begins to develop with the onset of the narrative itself. This is, it seems to me, the ultimate meaning of that *motif* of right and wrong questions mentioned above and resumed as follows: "to learn which questions are unanswerable, and *not to answer them*: this skill is most needful in times of stress and darkness." It is no accident that this maxim follows hard upon another, far more practical discussion about politics and historical problems:

To be sure, if you turn your back on Mishnory and walk away from it, you are still on the Mishnory road . . . You must go somewhere else; you must have another goal; then you walk a different road. Yegey in the Hall of the Thirty-Three today: "I unalterably oppose this blockade of grain-exports to Karhide, and the spirit of competition which motivates it." Right enough, but he will not get off the Mishnory road going that way. He must offer an alternative. Orgoreyn and Karhide both must stop following the road they're on, in either direction; they must go somewhere else, and break the circle. (ch. 11)

But, of course, the real alternative to this dilemma, the only conceivable way of breaking out of that vicious circle which is the option between feudalism and capitalism, is a quite different one from the liberal "solution" – the Ekumen as a kind of galactic United Nations – offered by the writer and her heroes. One is tempted to wonder whether the strategy of *not* asking questions ("Mankind," according to Marx, "always [taking] up only such problems as it can solve")[10] is not the way in which the utopian imagination protects itself against a fatal return to just those historical contradictions from which it was supposed to provide relief. In that case, the deepest subject of Le Guin's LHD would not be utopia as such, but rather our own incapacity to conceive it in the first place. In this way too, it would be a proving ground for TD.

Notes

1   See my "Generic discontinuities in science fiction: Brian Aldiss' *Starship*," *Science Fiction Studies*, 1 (1973), pp. 57–68.

2   I find justification for omitting from this list the theme of communication – mind-speech and foretelling – in Ian Watson's important "Le Guin's *Lathe of Heaven* and the role of Dick," *Science Fiction Studies* 2 (1975), pp. 67–75.

3   Entropy is of course a very characteristic late nineteenth-century bourgeois myth (e.g., Henry Adams, Wells, Zola). See, for further justification of this type of interpretation, my "In retrospect," *Science Fiction Studies*, 1 (1974), pp. 272–6.

4   Ursula K. Le Guin, "Is gender necessary?," in Susan J. Anderson and Vonda McIntyre (eds), *Aurora: Beyond Equality* (in press).

5   I have tried to argue an analogous reduction of possibilities for the historical novel in *Marxism and Form* (Princeton, NJ, Princeton University Press, 1971), pp. 248–52.

6   See Darko Suvin, "On the poetics of the science fiction genre," *College English* 34 (1972), pp. 372–82, and "Science fiction and the genological jungle," *Genre* 6 (1973), pp. 251–73.

7   See note 4. Some problems Le Guin does not notice – e.g., synchronization of kemmer and continuity of sex roles between love partners – are pointed out by the relentlessly logical Stanislaw Lem in "Lost opportunities," *SF Commentary*, 24, pp. 22–4.

8   Inasmuch as *The Dispossessed* – sure the most important utopia since Skinner's *Walden Two* – seems certain to play a significant part in political reflection, it seems important to question Le Guin's qualification of Anarres as an "anarchist" Utopia. Thereby she doubtless intends to differentiate its decentralized organization from the classical Soviet model, without taking into account the importance of the "withering away of the state" in Marxism also – a political goal most recently underscored by the Cultural Revolution and the experimental Communes in China and the various types of workers' self-management elsewhere.

9   William Morris, *News from Nowhere* (London, 1903), pp. 91, 95, 96.

10 Karl Marx and Friedrich Engels, *Basic Writings on Politics and Philosophy* ed. Lewis S. Feuer (Garden City, NY, 1959), p. 44.

22

Utopianism and Anti-Utopianism

"The Antinomies of Postmodernity," which appears in Jameson's book, *The Seeds of Time* (1994), is divided into four sections. This selection consists of the fourth section. Please note that the first two sections are included in chapter 13 of this volume.

IV

Utopia was always an ambiguous ideal, urging some on to desperate and impossible realizations about which it reassured the others that they could never come into being in the first place: so it whipped the passionate and the dogmatic into a frenzy while plunging the liberal lukewarm into an immobilizing intellectual comfort. The result is that those who desire action are able to repudiate the Utopian with the same decisiveness as those who desire no action; the converse obviously also being true.

It would seem that the times are propitious for anti-Utopianism; and, particularly in Eastern Europe, but washing all the way back over the reactionary revisions of the French Revolution that have momentarily gained currency in Western Europe, the critique and diagnosis of the evils of the Utopian impulse has become a boom industry. It is a critique compounded of Edmund Burke and of the nineteenth-century additions (which we have wrongly come to think of as Nietzschean, whereas they represent only the most derivative side of his thought, soaked up from standard counterrevolutionary doxa), in which Jacobinism is seen as a form of *ressentiment* (and most frequently the *ressentiment* of intellectuals) that expresses itself in a rage to destroy. As for Utopia, it is not so secretly supposed to manifest a will to power over all those individuals for whom you are plotting an ironclad collective happiness, and the diagnosis thereby, in most recent times, acquires a bad aesthetic dimension, as most dramatically in Boris Groys's remarkable *Gesamtkunstwerk Stalin*, where the dictator is identified as the greatest of modern Utopians and more specifically as a modernist in state-craft, whose monumental "Soviet Union" is as grand a conception as *Finnegans Wake* or *A la recherche du temps perdu*.

At this point, then, anti-Utopianism meets postmodernism, or at least the implacable postmodern critique of high modernism itself as repressive, totalizing, phallocentric, authoritarian, and redolent of an even more sublime and inhuman hubris than anything Burke could have attributed to his Jacobin contemporaries. This inevitable but genial next step, then, coordinates current political doxa with postcontemporary aesthetic attitudes that have coexisted with the former without ever being completely integrated into a new ideological system. Thus, we find expressed a very old (but hitherto Western) Cold-War and, as we have just seen, market rhetoric about hubris and human sinfulness (our old friend human nature again) rehearsed with a view toward the dangers involved in trying to create anything like a new society from scratch, and vividly warning of the Burkean Jacobinism and the Stalinism implicit and inevitable in any Utopian effort to create a new society, or even in any fantasy of doing so. Socialism takes too many evenings, as Oscar Wilde put it; people cannot stand the sustained demands of the political absolute, their human frailty then calling forth the violence of the Jacobin-Stalinist state as it tried to bully them into sustaining this impossible momentum. Artistic modernism is then the expression of this same will to power in the imaginary, in the absence of state power or of the deed: and Le Corbusier will bully his clients into a healthy and strenuous high-modern life style with much the same obsessive single-mindedness, while, with more subtle Nietzschean dissimulations and indirections, Joyce or Mallarmé will try imperiously to appropriate their readers' existential time by way of a commitment to interminable exegesis and a quasi-religious adulation. Perhaps it is too soon to add that diagnoses like these are most often mirror images, denunciations of *ressentiment* most often flung down by people themselves genuinely eaten away by resentments; all the more is this the case with images of political commitment such as those vehiculated by revolutionary and Utopian sympathies, which seem to have a remarkable power of stimulating guilt feelings in the non- or no longer political people who contemplate them.

On the other hand, I want to go further than this here and to argue – as the fourth of my antinomies [the first two antinomies are included in chapter 13 of the present volume] – that the most powerful arguments against Utopia are in reality Utopian ones, expressions of a Utopian impulse *qui s'ignore*. If indeed one believes that the Utopian desire is everywhere, and that some individual or pre-individual Freudian libido is enlarged and completed by a realm of social desire, in which the longing for transfigured collective relationships is no less powerful and omnipresent, then it can scarcely be surprising that this particular political unconscious is to be identified even there where it is the most passionately decried and denounced. But that is not exactly the argument I want to make here, since what is everywhere is just about as good as what is nowhere (the inner name, by the way, of our curious topic).

I also want to caution about the facile deployment of the opposition between Utopia and dystopia: these formal or generic concepts, which have become current since science fiction, seem to lend themselves to a relatively simple play of oppositions in which the enemies of Utopia can easily be sorted out from its friends – Orwell being sent over to that corner, Morris to this one, while some of them (Wells himself, for example) spend their whole lives vacillating between the poles like tender and tough, or hawks and doves. The more dramatic intervention comes then when a Deleuze, examining a similar time-honored opposition, in that case called sadism and masochism, unexpectedly concludes that they are not opposites and in reality have nothing to do with each other (the sadist, Deleuze concludes, is not really the one the masochist seeks and would not participate in the latter's game in any very satisfying way; the reverse also being true in the present instance). I should like to disjoin the pair Utopia/dystopia in much the same definitive way (although it is probably a more complicated operation): it is not merely that the pleasures of the nightmare – evil monks, gulags, police states – have little enough to do with the butterfly temperament of great Utopians like Fourier, who are probably not intent on pleasures at all but rather on some other form of gratification.

A little more to the point is the secondary formal observation that the dystopia is generally a narrative, which happens to a specific subject or character, whereas the Utopian text is mostly nonnarrative and, I would like to say, somehow without a subject-position, although to be sure a tourist-observer flickers through its pages and more than a few anecdotes are disengaged. On my view (but in this form it is a mere opinion), the dystopia is always and essentially what in the language of science-fiction criticism is called a "near-future" novel: it tells the story of an imminent disaster – ecology, overpopulation, plague, drought, the stray comet or nuclear accident – waiting to come to pass in our own near future, which is fast-forwarded in the time of the novel (even if that be then subsequently disguised as some repressive society galactic ages away from us). But the Utopian text does not tell a story at all; it describes a mechanism or even a kind of machine, it furnishes a blueprint rather than lingering upon the kinds of human relations that might be found in a Utopian condition or imagining the kinds of living we wish were available in some stable well-nigh permanent availability; although the great Utopians did that too, notoriously (again, like Fourier above all, who is by way of being the compleat Utopist, the Platonic idea of the Utopian imaginer) reaping the occassional pastoral reward of this or that scene, this or that innocent or not-so-innocent pleasure. Mostly, however, they carefully noted down the precise mechanisms whose construction alone would render those relations and pleasures, those scenes, possible. For the ideals of Utopian living involve the imagination in a contradictory project, since they all presumably aim at illustrating and exerciz-ing that much-abused concept of freedom that, virtually by definition and in its very structure, cannot be defined in advance, let alone exemplified: if you know already what your longed-for exercise in a not-yet-existent freedom looks like, then the suspicion arises that it may not really express freedom after all but only repetition; while the fear of projection, of sullying an open future with our own deformed and repressed social habits in the present, is a perpetual threat to the indulgence of fantasies of the future collectivity.

All authentic Utopias have obscurely felt this deeper figural difficulty and structural contradiction, however much their various authors, like Fourier himself, longed to give us a picture of what they thought life really ought to be like (and to watch our sympathetic astonishment and admiration); they have for the most part rigorously restricted their textual production to a very different kind of operation, namely the construction of material mechanisms that would alone enable freedom to come into existence all around them. The mechanism itself has nothing to do with freedom, except to release it; it exists to neutralize what blocks freedom, such as matter, labor, and the requirements of their accompanying human social machinery (such as power, training and discipline, enforcement, habits of obedience, respect, and so forth).

Indeed, qua mechanism, the Utopian machine may be expected to absorb all that unfreedom into itself, to concentrate it where it can best be worked over and controlled: mechanism and the machine always functioning in classical philosophical ideology as somehow the opposite of spirit and freedom, which then equally classically and ideologically becomes characterized in idealistic or spiritualistic terms, so that its rhetoric inevitably tends toward a kind of angelism. Thus the Utopian mechanism by embodying the necessary – labor, constraint, matter – in absolute and concentrated form, by way of its very existence, allows a whole range of freedoms to flourish outside of itself.

It is a process that can be emblematized allegorically by the treatment of the elevator and the city grid in Rem Koolhaas' *Delirious New York*, which poses among other things the problem of Necessity in terms of the component of engineering technology, what has to be included in the building but can neither be made symbolic nor can it be sublimated (as in the sentimentalism of the Hyatt gondola elevators that weightlessly rise and fall in perpetual motion). For Koolhaas, however, that enormous bulk of pipes and wiring that takes up 40 percent of the modern building (and that can only exceptionally be ornamentalized as in the Pompidou Center's exoskeleton) stands as a foreign body unassimilable to praxis or poesis, one that must be dealt with in new ways yet to be invented (what is necessary in the work of art, said Valéry, is what can never be redeemed in value). *Delirious New York* stages one kind of solution on the urban level by designating the invention of the elevator (in mid-nineteenth century) and that of the Manhattan city grid (in the plan of 1811) as mechanisms that concentrate this necessity into a single structure and condense it, like some consolidation of a variety of debts that leaves you only a single bill to pay. These twin vertical and horizontal mechanisms then release all the delirious freedom of New York to develop around themselves: they stand as the price to be paid for matter and materiality (if not mortality itself), the minimum work time, as Marx said, beyond which the "realm of freedom" comes into view. The Utopian text, then, takes such mechanisms as its object of representation, and in that sense counter-texts about terrifying machines – Kafka's infernal machine in *The Penal Colony*, or Platonov's *Foundation Pit* – are structural inversions of Utopia in the strict sense and are formally quite different from the dystopian narrative as such. (The latter may well, however, include the contradiction between its own logic and that of inverted Utopias: as in *1984* where the premise – that no science or real thinking is possible – is contradicted by the sheerly scientific perfection of the anti-Utopian machinery of state surveillance that is then pressed into service as a causal explanation for just that dystopian state of affairs in which no science is possible.)

These mechanisms can reach states of extreme elaboration, as in Fourier's complex series and the astronomical combinations he lays down for them; but they all in one way or another conform to Marx's political program in *Capital*, namely to demonstrate that socialism is not an imagined figment but obeys the laws of nature and is a reality, like mass or energy, like gravity or the table of the elements. What is misleading (and thereby seems anti-Utopian) is Marx's manner of demonstrating this, which involves showing that socialism is already coming into being in the interstices of capitalism itself, as increased cooperative or collective labor, larger and larger impersonal combinations and work or production units, post-individual forms of ownership, and so on (all of which is even truer in our own time than in his); but his objection that the Utopians themselves were not sufficiently concerned with the implementation and realization of their projects is only true politically and not socially or ontologically. Fourier never thought in terms of political revolution, he was indeed profoundly anti-Jacobin in his opinions and could only imagine the intervention of the famous Benefactor in the implementation of the phalanx; yet everything in Fourier is marshaled to demonstrate that Utopianism is in nature, so to speak, and that the various forms of human collectivity from the smallest to the largest imaginable tend by way of their own inner momentum toward an "association" that is somehow the ontological law of the universe. This is therefore at least one sense in which Fourier understood that his representations had to be realistic, had to appeal to Being rather than to imagination, and had to be based on empirically existing phenomena that it only required a new kind of poetic vision to see in the world around us. Marx himself is meanwhile Utopian in precisely the separation of the realms of Necessity and Freedom which has already been referred to, and which sketches out a classic mechanism whereby labor can be reduced drastically and the law of Value (at best, in Marx, an idealistic, fetishistic, spiritualistic principle of "objective appearance or illusion") replaced by more material calculations.

To evoke such Utopian mechanisms, however, where the part of Necessity is invested in whatever ingenious machinery in order to liberate the space that has been emptied and purified of it, is suddenly to recognize another familiar contemporary ideologeme, namely the market itself, the central exhibit in the anti-Utopian arsenal. For the exchange mechanisms of the market very precisely constitute an organization of necessity, a sum of purely mechanical requirements, which, at least according to the theory, is called upon to release freedoms a good deal more delirious than anything Koolhaas's quasi-surrealist manifesto felt able to attribute to New York itself: namely the fulfillment of private life along with the stabilities of representative or parliamentary democracy, law and order, a taming of the human beast, and the lineaments of justice itself. However base the uses of market rhetoric today, and however baleful its effect in places like Eastern Europe, it may be the best policy rather to acknowledge these Utopian dimensions forthrightly, to class market fantasies along with the other glorious Utopian thought-experiments, and thereby in another sense to ensure that all this remains, and is understood to be, merely a not-place and a nowhere. That the celebration of late capitalism is obliged to pass by way of the figuration of its opposite number, Utopian discourse, and to use the weapons of its arch adversary in order to glorify itself and spread its very different message, is a first consequence of the antinomy I had it in mind to outline here.

But that antinomy can also be approached by way of the critique of Utopias; and it is perhaps worthwhile now to take this path on the other side of things, in order to see whether it does not also lead us back to some central place. To be sure, it is difficult to separate the intellectual repudiation of Utopia, which itself knows an exoteric as well as an esoteric form, from a fear of Utopia, which is a thoroughgoing anxiety in the face of everything we stand to lose in the course of so momentous a transformation that – even in imagination – it can be thought to leave little intact of current passions, habits, practices, and values. Indeed, such anxieties, which are based on the difficulties and paradoxes involved in leaping from one system to a radically different one (even in imagination) go some way toward justifying the charge of *ressentiment* that we have seen leveled against Utopians by the counterrevolutionary tradition: for in fact there is little within our system to motivate so absolute a change, and it is inevitable that the motivations that can be thus isolated, and that link the values present in the old system with the changes presented by the new one, are bound to appear as a wilful lust for destruction and change at any price. In this respect, it is revealing to transfer to the collective level Sartre's luminous outline of the structural difficulties faced by an individual in willing a change from one absolute or originary choice of being to another, and to meditate Sartre's conclusion that, in this situation, the concept of willpower is meaningless. Thus the imagination of Utopia is bound to be a stereoptic affair, which places the Utopian fantasist in two distinct worlds at the same time and generates a unique kind of discomfort by the seemingly irreconcilable demands it makes to disengage absolutely from what is at the same time that one cleaves absolutely to the being of the world as some ultimate limit.

There is, I think, no more pressing task for progressive people in the First World than tirelessly to analyze and diagnose the fear and anxiety before Utopia itself: this relatively introspective and self-critical process need not wait on the emergence of new visions of the future, such as are bound to appear when the outlines of the new global order and its postnational class system have become stabilized. There is a collective therapy to be performed on the victims of depoliticization themselves, a rigorous look at everything we fantasize as mutilating, as privative, as oppressive, as mournful and depressing, about all the available visions of a radical transformation in the social order. My sense is that such feelings, which in their ensemble make up that amorphous yet real and active fact that is anti-Utopianism, do not really spring from profound personal happiness and gratification or fulfillment in the present but serve merely to block the experience of present dissatisfaction in such a way that logically "satisfaction" is the only judgment that can be drawn by a puzzled observer from whom the deeper unconscious evidence has been withheld.

Yet, apart from the political fatigue and demoralization of people today around the world, it is not easy to see what positive values are available to fuel an anti-Utopian market rhetoric: the space into which a postpolitical collectivity is supposed to withdraw – nowadays anachronistically celebrated under the rubric of a civil society that has long since ceased to exist in the advanced capitalist countries – is vacuous and utterly colonized by consumption and its codes and languages. It is a negative result of the fulfillment of Marx's prophecy about increasing collectivization that this process has displaced the last remnants of existential experience in what used to be the private sphere, translating formerly private initiatives into so many allusions to corporate products and so many simulated conducts and desires suggested by advertising images. Traditional images of the family (as of other forms of traditional life) scarcely hold any attraction for the subjects of a postmodernity, who are able to fantasize private life only collectively, as new kinds of tribal networks and organized hobbies, which must, however, in order to distinguish them from other, similar social structures, be marked as nonofficial and nonpublic.

But this precisely sets us on the track of the most powerful drive in contemporary ideology, for which anything labeled as public has become irredeemably tainted, everything that smacks of the institution arouses distaste and repels in a subliminal, well-nigh Pavlovian fashion, anything construed as representing the state and the satellite institutions that surround it is at once marked negatively and vigorously repudiated: something state power itself attempts to recuperate by associating it with American frontier cultural traditions and individualism (with which, given the absolute breaks in contemporary historical experience, it cannot possibly have anything to do save by virtue of images and suggestivity) and thereby endowing it with a national ethos that can be mobilized against other national traditions. But this anti-institutionalism can only secondarily be identified as antisocialist or anti-Stalinist, since the more fundamental object at which it is directed is corporate capitalism itself, with its sterile language and made-up structures, its invented hierarchies and simulated psychologies. This is the only experience people in the West have had of omnipotent and impersonal power structures, and it is an experience over which late capitalism works, far more subtly and shrewdly than any left or populist movements, systematically redirecting such energies against fantasies of "big government" and "bureaucracy," as though the corporations were not themselves the fundamental site of everything bureaucratic in First World capitalist countries. Meanwhile, the positive features of older class bureaucracies – the ethics of service in the great feudal bureaucracies; those of enlightenment in the bourgeois era, such as for the teachers of the Third Republic; those of social service in contemporary America – are systematically vilified and obscured in current propaganda, so that anyone happening upon Max Weber's observation that bureaucracy is the most modern form of social organization can only be stunned and puzzled by so bizarre and perverse a reflection (which comes in any case out of a distant and foreign past). But this is the way in which the hatred of genuinely antisocial and alienated structures such as those of the great corporations today – a revulsion that might ordinarily be expected to fuel the production of properly Utopian meditations and fantasies – is redirected against Utopia itself, where it is accompanied by all the properly Utopian fantasies of gratification and consumption that market society is capable of generating (fantasies about which I have tried to show in *Postmodernism, or, The Cultural Logic of Late Capitalism* that they are themselves anything but materialist in the bodily sense, turning essentially and formally, on reified images of capitalist distribution proper).

As for the more esoteric form taken by the resistance to Utopia, and in particular its more highly intellectualized versions, in which what is at stake are misconceptions of "totalization" and reifications of the theme of power and domination, it is important to reintroduce here the dynamics of the various groups, since unlike corporate or hegemonic propaganda, left or radical theory by definition legitimates itself by the claim to "represent" this or that collectivity (or at least to speak in fellow-traveling sympathy as it were alongside it). This fundamentally collective identification and grounding of the anti-Utopian position already suggests deeper contradictions in such arguments where they are not finally mere echoes of liberal, individualist, antipolitical positions.

As essential seriality of small group politics must also be invoked here, and a serial effect whereby each group, wielding all the while its own specific form of influence and prestigeful intimidation, simultaneously imagines itself to be a minority oppressed by another group (which feels the same way). Thus, to take the most grotesquely illustrative example, the white male majority develops its self-consciousness as a group by way of the feeling that it is an embattled minority tyrannized over by marginals who impose their own cultural values on it. Such plays of mirror reflections and projections clearly call out, not for further analyses of power and domination but rather for a psychopathology of the illusions of power and of the ways in which the media entertain and develop such illusions and projections in a kind of infinite regress (it is a phenomenon Sartre began to describe under the term *seriality* used above).

My own sense is that group politics only begin to evolve in a radical direction when the various groups all arrive at the common problem and necessity of their strategic interrelationships, something for which any number of historic terms are available from Gramsci's "historic bloc" through alliance politics to the "popular front" of "marginalities" currently proposed by "queer theory." Only caricatural memories of specific moments of Stalinism encourage the belief that the concept of totalization means repressing all these group differences and reorganizing their former adherents into some ironclad military or party formation for which the time-honored stereotypical adjective always turns out to be "monolithic"; on the contrary, on any meaningful usage – that is to say, one for which totalization is a project rather than the word for an already existent institution – the project necessarily means the complex negotiation of all these individual differences and has perhaps best been described, for our generation, by Laclau and Mouffe in their book, *Hegemony and Socialist Strategy*, which its authors, however, believe to be directed against "totalization" as such. In any case, nowhere have such dilemmas of intergroup relations and of the agonizing adjustments that blocs or popular fronts impose been more insistently represented and reflected upon than in the Utopian tradition, whose high point in Fourier unfolds a panoply of complex intergroup articulations of a mathematical density that leaves Laclau and Mouffe's shorter articulated chains far behind. Fourier's is then totalization at its most inspired, and on a grand scale (but see also Kim Stanley Robinson's Mars trilogy, which will surely be the great political novel of the 1990s and the place in which the interrelations of the various radical or revolutionary groups have been most vividly rehearsed for our own time).

More needs to be said, however, about the structural peculiarities of a politics of difference that is also frequently called the politics of identity: more is at stake here than some mere definition by negation and the inevitable production of difference by way of multiple group identities. Rather, I think it can be affirmed that a politics of difference does not become possible until a considerable degree of social standardization comes into being, that is to say, until universal identity is largely secured. The genuine, radical difference that holds between Columbus and the peoples he encountered can never be articulated into a politics: at best an enslavement, at worst a genocide, and occasionally something like a compassionate attempt at an impossible tolerance (which is itself a form of patronizing condescension). The social revolution of our time, Marx affirmed, is predicated on the universalization of the feeling of equivalence and the irrepressible demands for equality that such juridical equivalence ends up producing; in this he was joined by all the counterrevolutionary thinkers, who saw one thing clearly, namely that "democracy" in this sense – the radical demand for equality – was the most damaging of all threats to social order as it has been able to be maintained in modern societies. It is on the basis of that Identity alone that Difference can be productively transformed into a political program; whether that program can coordinate the demand for equality with the affirmation of a separatist cultural identity (= difference) remains to be seen. But the reversible dynamics of these binary abstractions are surely not a very promising starting point for such a program.

Now we need to take yet another step further back, and look into the Utopian vocation of the individual small group movements themselves, as they attempt to define themselves against the larger hegemonic structures by identifying what is often imperfectly called a group or collective "identity" in a specific tradition of oppression and in a (necessarily constructed) historical past. It is an identity that must be based fully as much on solidarity as on alienation or oppression, and it necessarily feeds on those images of primitive or tribal cohesion which were however always the spiritual property of the Utopian tradition proper: what was once called "primitive communism," what is refracted out culturally in pictures of the horde or the clan, the *gens*, the village, even the manorial family – whatever collective structures seem to resist the anomie of the modern industrial state and to offer some negative and critical power over against the larger and more diffuse demographies in which the group's current oppression is practiced.

But this insistence on the value of the small group itself – which found its first theorist in Rousseau – is the libidinal fountainhead of all Utopian imagination, whatever theoretical problems it raises for a reconceptualization of Utopia under contemporary circumstances (including the critique of Rousseau himself). For it would be illogical to insist on the Utopian component of other kinds of political passions – the appropriation of a rhetoric of collectivity by fascism or the other right-wing movements, the identification of those collective impulses that inform the various mystiques of modern professionalism, from male bonding all the way to English departments – without making an equal place for the conscious or unconscious role of a deeper Utopianism in the dynamics of small group politics.

Nor does it make much sense to redefine this particular anti-Utopianism in terms of the historic opposition of anarchism to either "the desire called Marx" or the Jacobin tradition (as that has known political embodiment from the French all the way down to the Soviet revolution), since this very repudiation of centralism and statism is if anything the purest expression of the Utopianism it imagines itself to be denouncing. At any rate, enough has been said to justify the conclusion that any active or operative political anti-Utopianism (those which are not mere liberalism in disguise) must sooner or later reveal itself as a vibrant form of Utopianism in its own right. This is the final form of the antinomy that it has been the aim of this section to argue.

Bibliography

Jameson's works have been translated into numerous languages and sometimes appear first in a language other than English. This bibliography is restricted primarily to the English-language publications. In addition, it does not indicate many of the reprinted versions of the essays, particularly when the original publication is widely available.

Books

Sartre: The Origins of a Style (New Haven, Conn., Yale University Press, 1961; 2nd edn, New York, Columbia University Press, 1984).

Marxism and Form: Twentieth-century Dialectical Theories of Literature (Princeton, NJ, Princeton University Press, 1971).

The Prison-house of Language: A Critical Account of Structuralism and Russian Formalism (Princeton, NJ, Princeton University Press, 1972).

Fables of Aggression: Wyndham Lewis, the Modernist as Fascist (Berkeley, Calif., University of California Press, 1979).

The Political Unconscious: Narrative as a Socially Symbolic Act (Ithaca, NY, Cornell University Press, 1981).

Postmodernism and Cultural Theories (Houxiandaizhuyi he Wenhualilun), Lectures in China (Xi'an, Shanxi Teacher's University, 1987).

The Ideologies of Theory, Essays 1971–1986, Volume 1: Situations of Theory (Minneapolis, University of Minnesota Press, 1988).

The Ideologies of Theory, Essays 1971–1986, Volume 2: The Syntax of History (Minneapolis, University of Minnesota Press, 1988).

Late Marxism: Adorno, or, The Persistence of the Dialectic (London, Verso, 1990).
Postmodernism, or, The Cultural Logic of Late Capitalism (Durham, Duke University Press, 1991).
Signatures of the Visible (London, Routledge, 1992).
The Geopolitical Aesthetic: Cinema and Space in the World System (Bloomington, Ind., Indiana University Press, 1992).
Theory of Culture: Lectures at Rikkyo (Tokyo, Rikkyo University, 1994).
The Seeds of Time (New York, Columbia University Press, 1994).
Brecht and Method (London, Verso, 1998).
The Cultural Turn: Selected Writings on the Postmodern, 1983–1998 (London, Verso, 1998).

Edited Volumes

Editor, with Masao Miyoshi, *The Cultures of Globalization* (Durham, NC, Duke University Press, 1998).

Articles

"The rhythm of time," in Edith Kern (ed.), *Sartre: A Collection of Critical Essays* (Englewood Cliffs, NJ, Prentice-Hall, 1962), pp. 104–20. [Reprinted from *Sartre: The Origins of a Style*, ch. 3.]
"The problem of acts," in Travis Bogard and William I. Oliver (eds)., *Modern Drama: Essays in Criticism* (New York, Oxford University Press, 1965), pp. 276–89. [Reprinted from *Sartre: The Origins of a Style*, ch. 1.]
"T. W. Adorno, or, historical tropes," *Salmagundi*, 5 (Spring, 1967), pp. 3–43. [Revised version reprinted in *Marxism and Form*, pp. 3–59.]
"On politics and literature," *Salmagundi*, 7 (Spring–Summer, 1968), pp. 17–26.
"Walter Benjamin, or nostalgia," *Salmagundi*, 10–11 (Fall 1969–Winter 1970), pp. 52–68. [Reprinted in *Marxism and Form*, pp. 60–83.]
"Introduction to T. W. Adorno," *Salmagundi*, 10–11 (Fall 1969–Winter 1970), pp. 140–3.
"The case for Georg Lukács," *Salmagundi*, 13 (Summer, 1970), pp. 3–35. [Reprinted in *Marxism and Form*, pp. 160–205.]
"On Raymond Chandler," *Southern Review*, 6 (3) (July, 1970), pp. 624–50.
"Seriality in modern literature," *Bucknell Review*, 18 (1) (Spring, 1970), pp. 63–80.
"Metacommentary," *Publications of the Modern Language Association*, 86 (1) (January, 1971), pp. 9–18. [Reprinted in *The Ideologies of Theory, volume 1*, pp. 3–16.]
"*La Cousine Bette* and allegorical realism," *Publications of the Modern Language Association*, 86 (2) (March, 1971), pp. 241–54.
"The great American hunter, or, ideological content in the novel," *College English*, 34 (2) (November, 1972), pp. 180–97.

"Three methods in Sartre's literary criticism," in John K. Simon (ed.), *Modern French Criticism: From Proust and Valéry to Structuralism* (Chicago, University of Chicago Press, 1972), pp. 193–227.

"Generic Discontinuities in Science Fiction: Brian Aldiss' Starship," *Science Fiction Studies*, 1 (2) (1973), pp. 57–68.

"Wyndham Lewis as futurist," *Hudson Review*, 26 (2) (Summer, 1973), pp. 295–329.

"The vanishing mediator: narrative structure in Max Weber," *New German Critique*, 1 (1) (Winter, 1974), pp. 52–89. [Reprinted as "The vanishing mediator; or, Max Weber as Storyteller," in *The Ideologies of Theory, Volume 2*, pp. 3–34.]

"Benjamin as historian, or how to write a Marxist literary history: a review essay," *Minnesota Review*, 3 (1974), pp. 116–36.

"After Armageddon: character systems in P. K. Dick's *Dr Bloodmoney*," *Science Fiction Studies*, 2 (1) (1975), pp. 31–42.

"Beyond the cave: demystifying the ideology of modernism," *The Bulletin of the Midwest Modern Language Association*, 8 (1) (1975), pp. 1–20. [Reprinted in *Ideologies of Theory, Volume 2*, pp. 115–32.]

"The ideology of the text," *Salmagundi*, 31–2 (Fall, 1975–Winter, 1976), pp. 204–46. [Revised version reprinted in *Ideologies of Theory, Volume 1*, pp. 17–71.]

"Magical narratives: romance as genre,' *New Literary History*, 7 (1975), pp. 135–63. [Revised version reprinted in *The Political Unconscious*, ch. 2.]

"Notes toward a Marxist cultural politics," *Minnesota Review*, 5 (1975), pp. 35–9.

"World-reduction in Le Guin: the emergence of utopian narrative," *Science Fiction Studies*, 2 (3) (1975), pp. 221–30.

"Authentic *ressentiment*: the 'experimental' novels of Gissing," *Nineteenth Century Fiction*, 31 (2) (1976), pp. 127–49. [Revised version reprinted in *The Political Unconscious*, ch. 4.]

"Introduction/prospectus: to reconsider the relationship of Marxism to utopian thought," *Minnesota Review*, 6 (Spring, 1976), pp. 53–8.

"Collective art in the age of cultural imperialism," *alcheringa*, 2 (2) (1976), pp. 108–11.

"On Goffman's *Frame Analysis*," *Theory and Society*, 3 (1) (1976), pp. 119–33.

"Figural relativism, or the poetics of historiography," *Diacritics*, 6 (1) (Spring, 1976), pp. 2–9. [Reprinted in *The Ideologies of Theory, Volume 1*, pp. 153–66.]

"Criticism in history," in Norman Rudich (ed.), *Weapons of Criticism: Marxism in America and the Literary Tradition* (Palo Alto, Calif.: Ramparts Press, 1976), pp. 31–50. [Reprinted in *The Ideologies of Theory, Volume 1*, pp. 119–36.]

"The ideology of form: partial systems in *La Vieille Fille*," *Sub-stance*, 15 (1976), pp. 29–49. [Substantially revised version reprinted in *The Political Unconscious*, ch. 3.]

"Modernism and its repressed: Robbe-Grillet as anti-colonialist," *Diacritics*, 6 (2) (Summer, 1976), pp. 7–14. [Reprinted in *The Ideologies of Theory, Volume 1*, pp. 167–80.]

"Science Fiction as politics: Larry Niven," *New Republic* (October 30, 1976), pp. 34–8.

"Reflections in conclusion," in Ernst Bloch et al., *Aesthetics and Politics* (London, NLB, 1977), pp. 196–213. [Reprinted as "Reflections on the Brecht–Lukács debate," in *The Ideologies of Theory, Volume 2*, pp. 133–47.]

"Class and allegory in contemporary mass culture: *Dog Day Afternoon* as a political film," *College English*, 38 (8) (1977), pp. 843–59. [Reprinted in *Signatures of the Visible*, pp. 35–54.]

"Imaginary and symbolic in *La Rabouilleuse*," *Social Sciences Information*, 16 (1) (1977), pp. 59–81. [Substantially revised version reprinted in *The Political Unconscious*, ch. 3.]

"On jargon," *Minnesota Review*, 9 (Fall, 1977), pp. 30–1.

"Of islands and trenches: neutralization and the production of utopian discourse," *Diacritics*, 7 (2) (Summer, 1977), pp. 2–21. [Reprinted in *The Ideologies of Theory, Volume 2*, pp. 75–101.]

"Imaginary and symbolic in Lacan: Marxism, psychoanalytic criticism, and the problem of the subject," *Yale French Studies*, 55–6 (1977), pp. 338–95. [Reprinted in Shoshana Felman (ed.), *Literature and Psychoanalysis: The Question of Reading Otherwise* (Baltimore, MD, Johns Hopkins University Press, 1982), pp. 338–95. [Reprinted as "Imaginary and symbolic in Lacan," in *The Ideologies of Theory, Volume 1*, pp. 75–115.]

"The symbolic inference; or, Kenneth Burke and ideological analysis," *Critical Inquiry*, 4 (3) (Spring, 1978), pp. 507–23. [Reprinted in *The Ideologies of Theory, Volume 1*, pp. 137–52.]

"Marxism and historicism," *New Literary History*, 11 (1) (Autumn, 1979), pp. 41–73. [Reprinted in *The Ideologies of Theory, Volume 2*, pp. 148–77.]

"Marxism and teaching," *New Political Science*, 2–3 (1979/1980), pp. 31–6.

"Reification and utopia in mass culture," *Social Text*, 1 (1979), pp. 130–48. [Reprinted in *Signatures of the Visible*, pp. 9–34.]

"Towards a libidinal economy of three modern painters," *Social Text*, 1 (1979), pp. 189–99.

"'In the Destructive Element Immerse': Hans Jürgen Syberberg and Cultural Revolution," *October*, 17 (1981), pp. 99–118. [Reprinted in *Signatures of the Visible*, pp. 63–81.]

"Religion and ideology," in Francis Barker et al. (eds), *1642: Literature and Power in the Seventeenth Century* (Colchester, University of Essex, 1981), pp. 315–36. [Reprinted as "Religion and ideology: a political reading of *Paradise Lost*," in Francis Barker et al. (eds), *Literature, Politics and Theory: Papers from the Essex Conference 1976–84* (London, Methuen, 1986), pp. 35–56.]

"*The Shining*," *Social Text*, 4 (1981), pp. 114–25. [Reprinted as "Historicism in *The Shining*," in *Signatures of the Visible*, pp. 82–98.]

"Ulysses in history," in W. J. McCormack and Alistair Stead (eds), *James Joyce and Modern Literature* (London, Routledge and Kegan Paul, 1982), pp. 126–41.

"On Aronson's Sartre," *Minnesota Review*, 18 (Spring, 1982), pp. 116–27.

"Futuristic visions that tell us about right now" (on Phillip K. Dick), *In These Times*, 6 (23) (May 5–11, 1982), p. 17.

"On *Diva*," *Social Text*, 6 (1982), pp. 114–19. [Reprinted as "*Diva* and French socialism," in *Signatures of the Visible*, pp. 55–62.]

"Progress versus utopia; or, can we imagine the future?," *Science Fiction Studies*, 9 (2) (1982), pp. 147–58.

"Reading Hitchcock," *October*, 23 (Winter, 1982), pp. 15–42. [Reprinted as "Allegorizing Hitchcock," in *Signatures of the Visible*, pp. 82–98.]

"Science versus ideology," *Humanities in Society*, 6 (2–3) (Spring/Summer, 1983), pp. 283–302.

"The ideological analysis of space," *Critical Exchange*, 14 (Fall, 1983), pp. 1–15.

"Morality versus ethical substance," *Social Text*, 8 (Fall–Winter, 1983–4), pp. 151–4. [Reprinted as "Morality versus ethical substance; or, Aristotelian Marxism in Alasdair MacIntyre," in *The Ideologies of Theory, Volume 1*, pp. 181–5.]

"Euphorias of substitution: Hubert Aquin and the political novel in Québec," *Yale French Studies*, 65 (1983), pp. 214–23.

"Postmodernism and consumer society," in Hal Foster (ed.), *The Anti-Aesthetic: Essays on Postmodern Culture* (Port Townsend. Bay Press, 1983), pp. 111–25.

"Pleasure: a political issue," in Tony Bennett et al. (eds), *Formations of Pleasure* (London, Routledge and Kegan Paul, 1983), pp. 1–14. [Reprinted in *The Ideologies of Theory, Volume 2*, pp. 61–74.]

"Periodizing the sixties," in Sohnya Sayres, Anders Stephanson, Stanley Aronowitz and Fredric Jameson (eds), *The 60s Without Apology* (Minneapolis, University of Minnesota Press, 1984), pp. 178–209. [The volume corresponds to a special issue of *Social Text*, 3 (3) and 4 (1) (Spring–Summer, 1984). Reprinted in *The Ideologies of Theory, Volume 2*, pp. 178–208.]

"Literary innovation and modes of production: a commentary," *Modern Chinese Literature*, 1 (1) (September, 1984), pp. 67–77.

"Postmodernism, or, the cultural logic of late capitalism," *New Left Review*, 146 (July–August, 1984), pp. 52–92. [Revised version reprinted in *Postmodernism, or, The Cultural Logic of Late Capitalism*, pp. 1–54.]

"The politics of theory: ideological positions in the postmodernism debate," *New German Critique*, 33 (Fall, 1984), pp. 53–65. [Reprinted in *The Ideologies of Theory, Volume 2*, pp. 103–13. Revised version reprinted in *Postmodernism, or, The Cultural Logic of Late Capitalism*, pp. 55–66. Revised version reprinted in *The Cultural Turn*, pp. 21–32.]

"Wallace Stevens," *New Orleans Review*, 11 (1) (1984), pp. 10–19.

"Postmodernism and consumer society," *Amerikastudien–American Studies*, 29 (1) (1984), pp. 55–73.

(With James H. Kavanagh) "The weakest link: Marxism in literary studies," in Bertell Ollman and Edward Vernoff (eds), *The Left Academy: Marxist Scholarship on American Campuses, Volume 2* (New York, Praeger, 1984), pp. 1–23.

"Flaubert's libidinal historicism: *Trois Contes*," in Naomi Schor and Henry F. Majewski (eds), *Flaubert and Postmodernism* (Lincoln, University of Nebraska Press, 1984), pp. 76–83.

"Rimbaud and the spatial text," in Tak-Wai Wong and M. A. Abbas (eds), *Rewriting Literary History* (Hong Kong, Hong Kong University Press, 1984), pp. 66–88.

"Baudelaire as modernist and postmodernist: the dissolution of the referent and the artificial 'sublime'," in Chaviva Hošek and Patricia Parker (eds), *Lyric Poetry: Beyond New Criticism* (Ithaca, Cornell University Press, 1985), pp. 247–63.

"The realist floor plan," in Marshall Blonsky (ed.), *On Signs* (Baltimore, Johns Hopkins University Press, 1985), pp. 373–83.

"Architecture and the critique of ideology," in Joan Ockmam (ed.), *Architecture, Criticism, Ideology* (Princeton, NJ, Princeton Architectural Press, 1985), pp. 51–87. [Reprinted in *The Ideologies of Theory, Volume 2*, pp. 35–60.]

"Four ways of looking at a fairy tale," in *The Fairy Tale: Politics, Desire, and Everyday Life* (October 30–November 26, 1986, New York, Artists Space), pp. 16–24.

"Third-world literature in the era of multinational capitalism," *Social Text*, 15 (Fall, 1986), pp. 65–88. [Revised version published as "World literature in an age of multinational capitalism," in Clayton Koelb and Virgil Lokke (eds), *The Current in Criticism: Essays on the Present and Future of Literary Theory* (West Lafayette, Purdue University Press, 1987), pp. 139–58.]

"On magic realism in film," *Critical Inquiry*, 12 (2) (1986), pp. 301–25. [Reprinted in *Signatures of the Visible*, pp. 128–52.]

"Hans Haacke and the cultural logic of late capitalism," in Brian Wallis (ed.), *Hans Haacke: Unfinished Business* (Cambridge, Mass., MIT Press, 1986), pp. 38–50.

"Science-fiction as a spatial genre: generic discontinuities and the problem of figuration in Vonda McIntyre's *The Exile Waiting*," *Science Fiction Studies*, 14 (1) (1987), pp. 44–59.

"Reading without interpretation: postmodernism and the video-text," in Nigel Fabb, Derek Attridge, Alan Durant and Colin MacCabe (eds), *The Linguistics of Writing: Arguments between Language and Literature* (New York, Methuen, 1987), pp. 199–223. [Reprinted in *Postmodernism, or, The Cultural Logic of Late Capitalism*, pp. 67–96.]

"The state of the subject (III)," *Critical Quarterly*, 29 (4) (Winter, 1987), pp. 16–25.

"Cognitive mapping," in Cary Nelson and Lawrence Grossberg (eds), *Marxism and the Interpretation of Culture* (Urbana, University of Illinois Press, 1988), pp. 347–57.

"*History and Class Consciousness* as an 'unfinished project,'" *Rethinking Marxism*, 1 (1) (Spring, 1988), pp. 49–72.

"Postmodernism and utopia," in The Institute of Contemporary Art, Boston, *Utopia Post Utopia: Configurations of Nature and Culture in Recent Sculpture and Photography* (Cambridge, Mass., MIT Press, 1988), pp. 11–32. [Revised version reprinted in *Postmodernism, or, The Cultural Logic of Late Capitalism*, pp. 154–80.]

"On Negt and Kluge," *October*, 46 (Fall, 1988), pp. 151–77.

"Modernism and imperialism," in *Nationalism, Colonialism and Literature* (Derry, Ireland, Field Day Pamphlet, no. 14, 1988), pp. 5–24. [Reprinted in T. Eagleton, F. Jameson and E. Said, *Nationalism, Colonialism and Literature* (Minneapolis, University of Minnesota Press, 1990), pp. 43–66.]

"Postmodernism and consumer society," in E. Ann Kaplan (ed.), *Postmodernism and its Discontents: Theories, Practices* (London, Verso, 1988), pp. 13–29. [Reprinted in *The Cultural Turn*, pp. 1–20.]

"Nostalgia for the present," *South Atlantic Quarterly*, 88 (2) (Spring, 1989), pp. 517–37. [Reprinted in *Postmodernism, or, The Cultural Logic of Late Capitalism*, pp. 279–96.]

"The space of science fiction: narrative in A. E. Van Vogt," *Polygraph*, 2–3 (1989), pp. 52–65.

"Modernity after postmodernism," *Sociocriticism*, 5 (2), no. 10 (1989), pp. 23–41.

"Afterword – Marxism and postmodernism," in Douglas Kellner (ed.), *Postmodernism/ Jameson/Critique* (Washington, DC, Maisonneuve Press, 1989), pp. 369–87. [Reprinted as "Marxism and postmodernism," in *New Left Review*, 176 (1989), pp. 31–45. Reprinted in part as "A third stage of capitalism," *Frontier*, 22 (26) (February 10, 1990), pp. 8–9. Revised and reprinted in *The Cultural Turn*, pp. 33–49.]

"Spatial equivalents: postmodern architecture and the world system," in David Carroll (ed.), *The States of "Theory": History, Art, and Critical Discourse* (New York, Columbia University Press, 1990), pp. 125–58. [Revised version reprinted in *Postmodernism, or, The Cultural Logic of Late Capitalism*, pp. 97–130.]

"Postmodernism and the market," in Ralph Miliband and Leo Panitch (eds), *The Retreat of the Intellectuals: Socialist Register 1990* (London, Merlin Press, 1990), pp. 95–110. [Revised version reprinted in *Postmodernism, or, The Cultural Logic of Late Capitalism*, pp. 260–78.]

"On literary and cultural import-substitution in the Third World: the case of the Testimonio," *Margins*, 1 (Spring, 1991), pp. 11–34. [Reprinted in George M. Gugelberger (ed.), *The Real Thing: Testimonial Discourse and Latin America* (Durham, Duke University Press, 1996), pp. 172–91.]

"Thoughts on the late war," *Social Text*, 28 (1991), pp. 142–6.

"Demographies of the anonymous," in Cynthia C. Davidson (ed.), *Anyone* (New York, Rizzoli, 1991), pp. 46–61.

"Soseki and western modernism," *boundary 2*, 18 (3) (Fall, 1991), pp. 123–41.

"Allegories of anywhere," in Cynthia C. Davidson (ed.), *Anywhere* (New York, Rizzoli, 1992), pp. 172–7.

"Spatial systems in *North by Northwest*," in Slavoj Žižek (ed.), *Everything You Always Wanted to Know about Lacan (But Were Afraid to Ask Hitchcock)* (London, Verso, 1992), pp. 47–72.

"Benjamin's readings," *Diacritics*, 22 (3–4) (Fall/Winter, 1992), pp. 19–34.

"The synoptic Chandler," in Joan Copjec (ed.), *Shades of Noir: A Reader* (London, Verso, 1993), pp. 33–56.

"Americans abroad: exogamy and letters in late capitalism," in Steven M. Bell, Albert H. Le May and Leonard Orr (eds), *Critical Theory, Cultural Politics, and Latin American Narrative* (Notre Dame, University of Notre Dame Press, 1993), pp. 35–60.

"On 'cultural studies'," *Social Text*, 34 (1993), pp. 17–52.

"Actually existing Marxism," *Polygraph*, 6–7 (1993), pp. 170–95. [Revised and reprinted in Saree Makdisi, Cesare Casarino and Rebecca Karl (eds), *Marxism Beyond Marxism* (New York, Routledge, 1996), pp. 14–54. Edited version reprinted as "Five theses on actually existing Marxism," in *Monthly Review*, 47 (11) (April, 1996), pp. 1–10.]

"Céline and innocence," *South Atlantic Quarterly*, 93 (2) (Spring, 1994), pp. 311–19.

"Tadao Ando and the enclosure of modernism," *ANY*, 1 (6) (May/June, 1994), pp. 28–33.

"Ontology and utopia," *L'Esprit Créateur*, 34 (4) (Winter, 1994), pp. 46–64.

"Marxist literary criticism today: the case of Goethe's *Faust*," *Literary Studies* (Nepal), 5–13 (March, 1994), pp. 7–24.

"The uses of apocalypse," in Cynthia C. Davidson (ed.), *Anyway* (New York, Rizzoli, 1994), pp. 32–41.

"Representations of subjectivity," *Social Discourse*, 6 (1/2) (Winter–Spring, 1994), pp. 47–60.

"Marx's purloined letter," *New Left Review*, 209 (1995), pp. 86–120.

"Is space political?," in Cynthia C. Davidson (ed.), *Anyplace* (Cambridge, Mass. MIT Press, 1995), pp. 192–205.

"The Sartrean origin," *Sartre Studies International*, 1 (1/2) (1995), pp. 1–20.

"City theory in Jacobs and Heidegger," in Cynthia C. Davidson (ed.), *Anywise* (Cambridge, Mass., MIT Press, 1996), pp. 32–9.

"On the sexual production of western subjectivity; or, Saint Augustine as a social democrat," in Renata Salecl and Slavoj Žižek (eds), *Gaze and Voice as Love Objects* (Durham, Duke University Press, 1996), pp. 154–78.

"Longevity as class struggle," in George Slusser, Gary Westfahl and Eric S. Rabkin (eds), *Immortal Engines: Life Extension and Immortality in Science Fiction and Fantasy* (Athens, University of Georgia Press, 1996), pp. 24–42.

"Marxism and dualism in Deleuze," *South Atlantic Quarterly*, 96 (3) (1997), pp. 393–416.

"Absent totality," in Cynthia C. Davidson (ed.), *Anybody* (Cambridge, Mass., MIT Press, 1997), pp. 122–31.

"Culture and finance capital," *Critical Inquiry*, 24 (1) (1997), pp. 246–65. [Revised and reprinted in *The Cultural Turn*, pp. 136–61.]

"Theo Angelopoulos: the past as history, the future as form," in Andrew Horton, (ed.), *The Last Modernist: The Films of Theo Angelopoulos* (Westport, Conn., Greenwood Press, 1997), pp. 78–95.

"The brick and the balloon: architecture, idealism and land speculation," *New Left Review*, 228 (March/April, 1998), pp. 25–46. [Reprinted in *The Cultural Turn*, pp. 162–89.]

"Notes on globalization as a philosophical issue," in Fredric Jameson and Masao Miyoshi (eds), *The Cultures of Globalization* (Durham, NC, Duke University Press, 1998), pp. 54–77.

"Persistencies of the dialectic: three sites," *Science and Society*, 62 (3) (Fall, 1998), pp. 358–72.

"The theoretical hesitation: Benjamin's sociological predecessor," *Critical Inquiry*, 25 (2) (Winter, 1999), pp. 267–88.

"Turbulence in Brenner," *Comparative Studies of South Asia, Africa and the Middle East* (forthcoming).

Interviews

"Interview" with Leonard Green, Jonathan Culler, and Richard Klein, *Diacritics*, 12 (3) (Fall, 1982), pp. 72–91.

"A dialog with Fredric Jameson," by K. Ayyappa Paniker, *Littcrit*, 8 (2) (December 1982), pp. 5–26.

"Interview with Fredric Jameson," by Anders Stephanson, *Flash Art*, 131 (December 1986/January 1987), pp. 69–73. [Longer version reprinted as Anders Stephanson, "Regarding postmodernism – a conversation with Fredric Jameson," *Social Text*, 17 (Fall, 1987), pp. 29–54.]

"Andrea Ward speaks with Fredric Jameson," *Impulse*, 13 (4) (Winter, 1987), pp. 8–9.

"Interview with Fredric Jameson," by Jay Murphy, *Left Curve*, 12 (1987), pp. 4–11.

"On contemporary Marxist theory: an interview with Fredric Jameson," by Sabry Hafez, Abbas Al-Tonsi, Mona Abousenna and Aida Nasr, *Alif: Journal of Comparative Poetics*, 10 (1990), pp. 114–31.

"Clinging to the wreckage: a conversation," with Stuart Hall, *Marxism Today* (September 1990), pp. 28–31.

"Envelopes and enclaves: the space of post-civil society (an architectural conversation)," with Michael Speaks, *Assemblage*, 17 (April 1992), pp. 30–7.

"Culture, technology and politics in the postmodern conditions: an interview with Fredric Jameson," *Iichiko Intercultural*, 6 (1994), pp. 96–107.

"The new forms of capital: *Catholic Agitator* interviews Fredric Jameson on postmodern capitalism and the colonization of the unconscious," *Catholic Agitator*, 25 (3) (May, 1995), pp. 4–6.

"South Korea as social space," Fredric Jameson interviewed by Paik Nak-chung, in Rob Wilson and Wimal Dissanayake (eds), *Global/Local: Cultural Production and the Transnational Imaginary*. (Durham, NC, Duke University Press, 1996), pp. 348–71.

"Marxism and the historicity of theory: an interview with Fredric Jameson," by Xudong Zhang, *New Literary History*, 29 (3) (Summer, 1998), pp. 353–83.

Introductions, Forewords, and Afterwords

"Introduction" to and translation of Wilhelm Dilthey, "The rise of hermeneutics," *New Literary History*, 3 (2) (Winter, 1972), pp. 229–44.

"Introduction" to Henri Avron, *Marxist Esthetics* (Ithaca, Cornell University Press, 1973), pp. vii–xxiv.

"Introduction" to Georg Lukács, *The Historical Novel* (Lincoln, University of Nebraska Press, 1983), pp. 1–8.

"Foreword" to Jean-François Lyotard, *The Postmodern Condition: A Report on Knowledge* (Minneapolis, University of Minnesota Press, 1984), pp. vii–xxi.

"Afterword" to Fredric Jameson, *Sartre: The Origins of a Style* (2nd edn, New York, Columbia University Press, 1984), pp. 205–33.

"Introduction" to Fredric Jameson (ed.), *Sartre After Sartre*, Yale French Studies, 68 (1985), pp. iii–xi.

"Foreword" in Jacques Attali, *Noise: The Political Economy of Music* (Minneapolis, University of Minnesota Press, 1985), pp. vii–xiv.

"Introduction" (to essays on Theories of the Text), *Texte: Revue de Critique et de Théorie Littéraire*, 5–6 (1986/1987), pp. 6–20.

"Foreword" to Algirdas Julien Greimas, *On Meaning: Selected Writings in Semiotic Theory* (Minneapolis, University of Minnesota Press, 1987), pp. vi–xxii.

"Introduction to Borge" and "Interview with Tomás Borge," *New Left Review*, 164 (July–August, 1987), pp. 51–64.

"Foreword" to Roberto Fernández Retamar, *Caliban and Other Essays* (Minneapolis, University of Minnesota Press, 1989), pp. vii–xii.

"Introduction" to Honoré de Balzac, *Eugénie Grandet* (London, Campbell, 1992), pp. v–xxvi.

"In the mirror of alternate modernities: introduction to Karatani Kōjin's *The Origins of Japanese Literature*," *South Atlantic Quarterly*, 92 (2) (Spring, 1993), pp. 295–310. [Reprinted as "Foreword: in the mirror of alternate modernities" to Karatani Kōjin, *Origins of Modern Japanese Literature* (Durham, NC, Duke University Press, 1993), pp. vii–xx.]

"Foreword" to Liu Kang and Xiaobing Tang (eds), *Politics, Ideology, and Literary Discourse in Modern China: Theoretical Interventions and Cultural Critique* (Durham, NC, Duke University Press, 1993), pp. 1–7.

"Introduction" to special issue on "Postmodernism: Center and Periphery," *South Atlantic Quarterly*, 92 (3) (1993), pp. 417–22.

"Afterword" to "Radicalizing radical Shakespeare: the permanent revolution in Shakespeare studies," in Ivo Kamps (ed.), *Materialist Shakespeare: A History* (London, Verso, 1995), pp. 320–8.

Review Essays, Responses, and Occasional Pieces

"Review" (of J. P. Stern, *On Realism*), *Clio*, 3 (3) (June 1974), pp. 346–52.

"Review" (of V. Vološinov, *Marxism and the Philosophy of Language*), *Style*, 8 (3) (Fall, 1974), pp. 535–43.

"Demystifying literary history," *New Literary History*, 5 (3) (Spring, 1974), pp. 605–12.

"Change, science fiction, and Marxism: open or closed universes? In retrospect," *Science Fiction Studies*, 1 (4), (1974), pp. 272–6.

"History and the death wish: *Zardoz* as open form," *Jump Cut*, 3 (September/October, 1974), pp. 5–8.

"The re-invention of Marx," *Times Literary Supplement* (August 22, 1975), pp. 942–3.

"Political painting: new perspectives on the realism controversy," *Praxis*, 1 (2) (Winter, 1976), pp. 225–30.

"Ideology, narrative analysis, and popular culture," *Theory and Society*, 4 (1977), pp. 543–59.

"Ideology and symbolic action: reply to Kenneth Burke," *Critical Inquiry*, 5 (2) (1978), pp. 417–22.

" 'But their cause is just': capitalism, not Zionism, is the problem's real name," *Seven Days*, 3 (11) (September 28, 1979), pp. 19–21.

"SF novel/SF film," *Science Fiction Studies*, 22 (1980), pp. 319–22.

"From criticism to history," *New Literary History*, 12 (2) (1981), pp. 367–76.

"Sartre in search of Flaubert," *New York Times book review* (December 27, 1981), pp. 5, 16, and 18.

"Towards a new awareness of genre," *Science Fiction Studies*, 9 (3) (1982), pp. 322–4.

"On Balzac," *boundary 2*, 12 (1) (Fall, 1983), pp. 227–34.

"An overview" (of papers presented at an international conference of literary theory), in Tak-Wai Wong and M.A. Abbas (eds.), *Rewriting Literary History* (Hong Kong, Hong Kong University Press, 1984), pp. 338–47.

"Science fiction and the German Democratic Republic," *Science Fiction Studies*, 11 (2) (1984), pp. 194–9.

"Reviews" (of Don DeLillo's *The Names* and Sol Yurick's *Richard A.*), *Minnesota Review*, 22 (Spring, 1984), pp. 116–22.

"Shifting contexts of science-fiction theory," *Science Fiction Studies*, 14 (2) (1987), pp. 241–7.

"A brief response" (to Aijaz Ahmad) *Social Text*, 17 (1987), pp. 26–8.

"On habits of the heart," *South Atlantic Quarterly*, 86 (4) (Fall, 1987), pp. 545–65.

"Discussion: contemporary Chinese writing," an interview by Fredric Jameson of Zheng Wanlong, Chen Jiangong, and Li Tuo, *Polygraph*, 1 (Fall, 1987), pp. 3–9.

"Critical agendas," *Science Fiction Studies*, 17 (1) (1990), pp. 93–102.

"Commentary" (on papers on minor/minority discourse in modern Greek culture and modern Greek studies), *Journal of Modern Greek Studies*, 8 (1) (1990), pp. 135–9.

"A conversation with Fredric Jameson," *Semeia*, 59 (1992), pp. 227–37.

"Response" (in "Final panel of respondents"), in Duncan Petrie (ed.), *Screening Europe: Image and Identity in Contemporary European Cinema* (London, British Film Institute, 1992), pp. 86–90.

"Exit Sartre," *London Review of Books*, 16 (13) (July 7, 1994), pp. 12–14.

"An unfinished project," *London Review of Books*, 17 (15) (August 3, 1995), pp. 8–9.

"Space wars," *London Review of Books*, 18 (7) (April 4, 1996), pp. 14–15.

"XXL: Rem Koolhaas's Great Big Buildingsroman," *Voice Literary Supplement*, 145 (May 1996), pp. 17–19.

"Prussian blues," *London Review of Books*, 18 (20) (October 17, 1996), pp. 3, 6–7. [Reprinted as "Ramblings in Old Berlin,'" *South Atlantic Quarterly*, 96 (4) (Fall, 1997), pp. 715–27.]

"Après the avant garde," *London Review of Books*, 18 (24) (December 12, 1996), pp. 5–7.

"Comments" (on a special section on the work of Fredric Jameson) *Utopian Studies*, 9 (2) (1998), pp. 74–7.

Index